Fodor's

CANADIAN ROOKIES

Welcome to the Canadian Rockies

Awe-inspiring doesn't begin to describe Canadian Rockies scenery. It's a landscape filled with snowy summits, turquoise blue lakes, glistening glaciers and thick evergreen forests. The region is brimming with endless recreational opportunities. Amid all the stunning scenery are unforgettable wildlife viewing opportunities. Exploring the parks of the Canadian Rockies gives you a sense of your own smallness in the grandeur of nature. As you plan your travels, please confirm that places are still open and let us know when we need to make updates by writing to us at editors@fodors.com.

TOP REASONS TO GO

★ **Scenery:** Snowcapped peaks, glaciers, forests, waterfalls and turquoise lakes abound in the Rockies.

★ **Wildlife:** From elk and moose to bears, the parks shelter a wide array of species.

★ **Hiking:** Countless scenic trails for all levels inspire and challenge walkers and hikers.

★ **Luxury Lodging:** Grand railway hotels pair luxurious amenities with glorious surroundings.

★ **History:** Museums, Indigenous experiences and national historic sites tell the tales of a fascinating past.

Contents

MAPS

Chapter 1

EXPERIENCE THE CANADIAN ROCKIES

21 ULTIMATE EXPERIENCES

The Canadian Rockies offer terrific experiences that should be on every traveler's list. Here are Fodor's top picks for a memorable trip.

1 Lake Louise and the Victoria Glacier

Banff National Park. The glacier-fed, turquoise water of Lake Louise is a view that draws people from all over the globe. Victoria Glacier, located between the surrounding mountains, creates an extraordinary backdrop. (Ch. 4)

2 Take an easy hike inside Maligne Canyon

Jasper National Park. With a depth of over 50 meters (164 feet) at certain points, this natural wonder was carved out by water erosion about 350 million years ago. (Ch. 9)

3 Summit Sulphur Mountain

Banff National Park. Take the gondola or hike to the top of Sulphur Mountain for views of Banff. Then hike to the Cosmic Ray Station or dine at Sky Bistro. (Ch. 4)

4 Canoe on Moraine Lake

Banff National Park. Just half the size of Lake Louise, Moraine Lake manages to have an equally astonishing view. This glacier-fed lake is the perfect spot to rent a canoe and enjoy a peaceful paddle. (Ch. 4)

5 Upper Hot Springs

Banff National Park. A staple of Banff, these springs surge out of Sulphur Mountain at a temperature of between 32°C (90°F) and 46°C (115°F). (Ch. 4)

6 Ski Jasper and/or Banff

Banff and Jasper National Parks. Jasper's Marmot Basin and Banff's Sunshine Village are popular ski hills to shred some powder, hit the terrain park, or get a ski or snowboard lesson. (Ch. 4, 9)

7 Hike the Lake Agnes Trail

Banff National Park. This 7-km (4.3-mile) hike is worth the challenge to enjoy tea on top of a mountain with glorious views of Lake Agnes or as some like to call it, "The Lake in the Clouds". (Ch. 4)

8 Hike the Bear's Hump Trail

Waterton Lakes National Park. The short but steep trail leads to a clearing resembling a grizzly bear's hump with unparalleled views of the townsite and park. (Ch. 11)

9 Check out the Calgary Stampede

Calgary. Often referred to as "The Greatest Outdoor Show on Earth", visitors attend from all over the world to watch the rodeo, attend live concerts, eat unique food, and so much more. (Ch. 5)

10 Enjoy a soak in Radium Hot Springs

Kootenay National Park. At a temperature of between 37°C (98°F) and 40°C (104°F), the natural mineral water provides a revitalizing soak for guests. (Ch. 8)

11 Paddle a canoe on Emerald Lake

Yoho National Park. Escape the crowds by renting a canoe at this heavenly alpine lake. Enjoy a tranquil paddle over crystal clear, turquoise water with a pristine mountain backdrop. (Ch. 7)

12 Cruise to Spirit Island

Jasper National Park. Knowledgeable guides discuss the history, wildlife, geology, and much more on this interesting and incredibly scenic cruise to the historical Spirit Island. (Ch. 9)

13 Take an international cruise

Waterton Lakes National Park. Waterton Lake is situated on the international border which allows visitors to enter Glacier National Park, Montana by boat on a panoramic and historical cruise. (Ch. 11)

14 Drive Icefields Parkway

Banff and Jasper National Parks. One of the world's most breathtaking drives, the parkway possesses spectacular mountain views, waterfalls, valleys, and glaciers around every turn. (Ch. 4, 9)

15 Hike to Crypt Lake

Waterton Lakes National Park. With four waterfalls and a cave to be crossed before reaching the gorgeous mountain lake, this bucket list hike is just as lovely as the destination. (Ch. 11)

16 Visit Athabasca Glacier

Jasper National Park. Part of the largest icefield in the Canadian Rockies, you can hike to the glacier's edge or hire a guide and walk onto the surface of this remnant of the Ice Age. (Ch. 9)

17 Go whitewater rafting on Kicking Horse River

Yoho National Park. The river is surrounded by gorgeous views while the experience is nothing short of thrilling. Several area companies provide a variety of tour options. (Ch. 7)

18 Tour the Burgess Shale Fossil Beds

Yoho and Kootenay National Parks. Over 500 million years old, these fossils are some of the oldest on earth and a significant UNESCO World Heritage Site. (Ch. 7, 8)

19 See Canada's second-highest waterfall

Yoho National Park. Standing 373 meters (1,223 feet) high, Takakkaw—aptly translated as "wonderful" in Cree—Falls spectacularly appears after a short and easy 1.3-km (0.8-mile) hike. (Ch. 7)

20 Find Big Red Chairs

There are more than 200 Big Red Chairs in Canada's national parks. Each is placed in a spot with amazing views—don't miss the photo-op.

21 Hike to Grassi Lakes

Canmore and Kananaskis Country. The beautiful turquoise-colored lakes can be reached via two hiking routes: an easier route on a wide path or a harder, more scenic route. (Ch. 6)

WHAT'S WHERE

1 **Banff National Park.** Canada's first national park is about a 90-minute drive west of Calgary in the heart of the Canadian Rockies surrounded by rugged mountains, glaciers, and forests. It also has some of the world's best skiing.

2 **Calgary.** A gateway city to the Canadian Rockies, Calgary has great nightlife, a phenomenal trail system, world-class attractions, and fun festivals including the legendary Calgary Stampede.

3 **Canmore and Kananaskis Country.** Canmore is located just 20 minutes east of Banff. This mountain town is quieter than Banff and is often a rendezvous point for travels out to Kananaskis Country. Kananaskis Country is a multi-use recreational area in the foothills and front ranges of the Canadian Rockies near Banff.

4 **Yoho National Park.** Located in the south-east corner of British Columbia and about 66 km (41 miles) northwest of Banff, Yoho is home to picturesque water-falls, glacier-fed lakes, and towering mountain ranges.

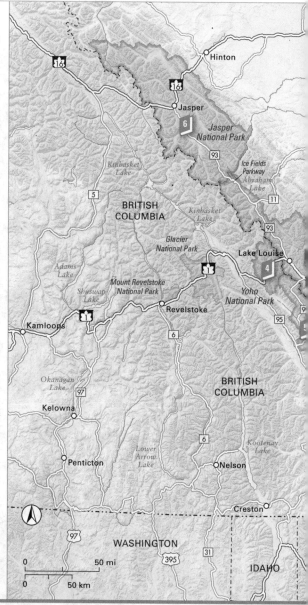

5 Kootenay National Park. The only national park in Canada that contains both cacti and glaciers, Kootenay provides a starting point for a scenic drive through Banff, ending in Yoho National Park.

6 Jasper National Park. One of the largest of the Canadian Rocky Mountain parks, Jasper woos visitors with its lakes, glaciers, waterfalls, and mountains. Jasper is 365 km (227 miles) southwest of Edmonton and 288 km (179 miles) northwest of Banff.

7 Edmonton. Alberta's capital city provides access to Jasper National Park, four hours to the West. Edmonton charms visitors with its restaurants and attractions including one of North America's largest malls.

8 Waterton Lakes National Park. Located in the southwest corner of Alberta, where lush prairies meet towering mountains and a shimmering lake sits below a majestic castle, Waterton is often considered a hidden gem.

Wildlife

COUGAR
Although these enormous carnivores, which can be 2½ meters (8 feet) long and weigh up to 91 kg (200 lbs), live throughout western North America, you won't see them in most parks due to their elusive nature. Also known as mountain lions, they are capable of taking down an elk.

BISON
North America's largest land mammal can be seen at Waterton Lakes National Park. Many efforts have been made to conserve this endangered species from near extinction. In 2017, plains bison were reintroduced into the backcountry of Banff National Park where they are thriving.

BIGHORN SHEEP
Found on rocky ledges throughout the Canadian Rockies, these sheep fascinate with their rutting during autumn mating season and their ability to travel where the rest of us can't. In winter, the docile herd animals descend to lower elevations.

WOLF
These formidable canines communicate with each other through body language, barks, and howls. Wolves are wary of humans and sightings are rare, but you might spot one along Banff National Park's Bow Valley Parkway.

MOOSE
Feeding on fir, willows, and aspens, the moose is the largest member of the deer family: the largest bulls stand 7 feet tall at the shoulders and weigh up to 726 kg (1,600 lbs). Look for them—but keep a safe distance—near marshy areas throughout the Canadian Rockies.

BEAR

Male grizzlies, also known as brown bears, can weigh 318 kg (700 lbs) and reach a height of 2½ meters (8 feet) when standing on their hind legs. Black bears are about half the size. Bear sightings can cause trail closures as a safety measure for the bears and hikers.

MOUNTAIN GOAT

Not really goats at all (they're actually related to antelope), these woolly mountaineers live in high elevations throughout the northwestern United States and Canada. Look for them along the Icefields Parkway in Banff and Jasper.

ELK

These ungulates congregate where forest meets meadows, and are found in large numbers around Banff and Jasper. In September and October, bulls attract mating partners by bugling. Their smaller white-necked cousins, caribou, can be seen in and around Jasper National Park.

DEER

Both whitetail deer and mule deer can be spotted throughout the Canadian Rockies. These mammals graze on plants and tree bark year-round. Watch for them near roads and highways and reduce your speed when needed.

COYOTE

As big as mid-size dogs, coyotes thrive in the Canadian Rockies. Most often alone or in pairs, they occasionally form small packs for hunting. About half the size, their cousin, the red fox, can also be found throughout the Canadian Rockies.

Best Backcountry Lodges in the Canadian Rockies

ASSINIBOINE LODGE

Mount Assiniboine Provincial Park. Built in 1928, Assiniboine Lodge was the first backcountry ski lodge in North America. Nowadays, not much has changed. Visitors spend their days exploring the incredible valley and unwind at night in the comfortable lodge. (Ch. 4)

TALUS BACKCOUNTRY LODGE

Kootenay National Park. Talus gives guests a back-to-the-basics stay where they can disconnect from everyday life and reconnect with nature. In the summer, the lodge can be reached through a guided hike, and in winter, by helicopter or on skis by experienced backcountry skiers. (Ch. 8)

SHADOW LAKE LODGE

Banff National Park. Known for its gourmet meals and luxury feel, this 1920s backcountry lodge is accessed by an easy hike, ski, or snowshoe. Stay in one of their 11 cabins and soak in the beautiful meadows and spectacular mountain ranges that the lodge has to offer. (Ch. 4)

SUNDANCE LODGE

Banff National Park. Conveniently located just 16 km (10 miles) away from Banff and just below Sundance Mountain, this solar-powered log cabin can be reached in any season via an easy 12 km (7½ miles) snowshoe, fat bike, cross country ski, hike, or horseback ride. (Ch. 4)

MOUNT ENGADINE LODGE

Spray Valley Provincial Park. One of the few backcountry lodges you can drive to, Mount Engadine boasts a wide assortment of year-round outdoor activities. Enjoy a nourishing two-course breakfast before kayaking on crystal waters or snowshoeing through sparkling snow-covered trails. After your adventures enjoy a relaxing afternoon tea followed by a gourmet dinner. (Ch. 6)

TONQUIN VALLEY ADVENTURES

Jasper National Park. Visit the Tonquin Valley for some of the best views in Jasper. Hike or take a guided horseback trip into this rustic backcountry lodge and you will be greeted with delicious homestyle meals and a cozy stay while you experience the true beauty of Jasper National Park. (Ch. 9)

Sundance Lodge

TONQUIN VALLEY BACKCOUNTRY LODGE

Jasper National Park. This secluded sanctuary is attainable by hiking or horseback in summer and skiing by proficient skiers in winter. Once there, soak in the views of emerald-colored mountain lakes, wildflower-filled meadows, and soaring peaks. Plan to take a photography workshop in one of the most picturesque places imaginable. (Ch. 9)

MISTAYA LODGE

Yoho National Park. Helicopter into this luxury backcountry lodge and be rewarded with views of spectacular mountain ranges, vibrant wildflowers, and a sapphire-colored lake just steps away from the door. After a day of adventuring, relax in the wood-fired sauna and then enjoy a heavenly three-course dinner (Ch. 7)

LAKE O'HARA LODGE

Yoho National Park. Climb aboard the lodge's shuttle bus to reach this hidden oasis. The sparkling emerald blue waters of Lake O'Hara provide the perfect backdrop for this remote sanctuary. Explore some of the best trails in Yoho or spend your days relaxing and let Lake O'Hara Lodge take care of the rest. (Ch. 7)

SKOKI LODGE

Banff National Park. Canada's first structure built solely for skiers, the lodge now caters to skiers and hikers of all abilities. The lodge, which can be reached by an 11-km (6.8-mile) hike or ski from Lake Louise, has stunning mountain views of the remote backcountry. (Ch. 4)

Family Fun in the Canadian Rockies

Jasper Skytram

Canada's national parks offer a wide range of activities for children of all ages, and kids under 17 get free admission. If there are two or more adults in your family, get the Family Discovery Pass. With one adult and children, an adult pass is your best option.

JASPER SKYTRAM

A seven-minute gondola ride glides you up the mountainside for spectacular panoramic views of the Jasper area. Once at the top, a short but steep hike will lead you to the true summit of Whistlers Mountain. After the hike, grab a bite to eat in the Summit Café and shop in the gift shop before you head back down. (Ch. 9)

LAKE LOUISE SUMMER SIGHTSEEING GONDOLA

Board the Lake Louise enclosed gondola or chairlift up Whitehorn Mountain for an aerial view of Lake Louise. The gondola climbs a total of 2,088 meters (6,850 feet), giving spectacular views for minimal effort.

While aboard, keep your eyes peeled for grizzly bears as they are commonly spotted on these slopes. (Ch. 4)

HIKE JOHNSTON CANYON

This popular 5-km (3.1-mile) round-trip hike gains minimal elevation and is nothing short of spectacular. Maneuver through catwalks suspended over Johnston Creek with towering canyon walls and two waterfalls that are stunning in summer or winter. More experienced hikers often venture onto the ink pots, a series of colorful mountain pools. (Ch. 4)

TAKE AN EASY HIKE TO TROLL FALLS

This 3.4-km (2.1-mile) round-trip hike in Kananaskis leads to a set of majestic waterfalls. The trail itself gains minimal elevation making this hike suitable for any skill level. In the summer, the falls are a gushing stream of sparkling water. Wintertime turns the falls into a magical frozen sculpture, equally as spectacular. (Ch. 6)

TAKE THE BANFF GONDOLA TO THE TOP OF SULPHUR MOUNTAIN

Glide up the mountain in a four-person gondola to get a bird's-eye view of Banff and the surrounding area. Soak in the amazing views, then walk the boardwalk trail to Sanson Peak, or dine at the award-winning Sky Bistro. (Ch. 4)

LAKE MINNEWANKA BOAT CRUISE

Explore Banff's largest lake on a heated, covered boat cruise that can be enjoyed in any weather. Learn about Lake Minnewanka and try to spot some wildlife while you're there. Kids go free on the morning or afternoon summer cruise, which comes with a cold treat. (Ch. 4)

RIDE A SURREY BIKE TO CAMERON FALLS IN WATERTON

For years, Pat's Waterton has been renting surrey bikes out to the public. These bikes can seat up to three people and are an excellent way to explore the area. Pedal down to Cameron Falls for a view of one of Waterton's must-see attractions. (Ch. 11)

Take an easy hike to Troll Falls (Kananaskis)

VISIT THE PARKS CANADA WEBSITE WHEN PLANNING YOUR TRIP

Visit the website to learn about family-friendly programs and activities—guided hikes, nature walks, learning to camp workshops—in the park(s) you plan to visit. It's also a good source for finding Parka, a female beaver who is the official mascot of Parks Canada, at special events; she's worth getting a photo with.

The website also has information about the Club Parka program for children under the age of ten and the Parks Canada Xplorers program for children over 10, which are offered at most parks. Both programs include an educational activity booklet with rewards—collectible cards, stickers, and removable tattoos—for completing a significant portion. If six pages (or more) of the Xplorers program booklet are completed, kids receive a certificate and a dog tag specific to the park after they recite an oath.

PADDLE A CANOE ON EMERALD LAKE

One visit to this BC lake and you'll know how it got its name. Emerald blue water surrounded by towering mountains makes this lake nothing short of breathtaking. Rent a canoe to dodge the shoreline crowds and enjoy a peaceful paddle at this special place. (Ch. 7)

HIKE TO MARBLE CANYON

Glacial blue water and massive canyon walls are what make this spot spectacular. The hike itself is only 1.8 km (1.1 miles) round-trip and suitable for all skill levels. Cross several bridges over the rushing water below and finish off the hike with views of a beautiful waterfall. (Ch. 8)

GO ON A WILDLIFE-WATCHING TOUR

Jasper's diverse ecosystem makes it a great spot to join a wildlife-watching tour. Knowledgeable guides take guests to the best locations for spotting wildlife and provide interesting facts throughout the tour that give young and old an educational and fun experience. (Ch. 9)

Canada's Indigenous Peoples

Two Brothers Totem Pole Jasper

INDIGENOUS HISTORY IN THE ROCKIES

Many years prior to the formation of the Dominion of Canada and the national and provincial parks systems, the Canadian Rockies region was the traditional territory of a variety of Indigenous groups. Most of the natural wonders that we know today were discovered and named by Indigenous nations long before

European settlers arrived and renamed them. The region was considered a spiritual land that was home to holy hot springs and snowcapped peaks that formed "The Backbone of the World." It was a place of spectacular beauty and abundant wildlife. With the arrival of western civilization, treaties were signed with the Indigenous Peoples of Canada that eventually confined them

to reservations, no longer allowed to roam their traditional territories.

The Canadian Constitution recognizes three groups of Indigenous Peoples: First Nations (known as Native Americans in the USA), Inuit (mostly occupying northern regions), and Métis (people of mixed Indigenous and European ancestry). These three groups each have their own

Tunnel Mountain

unique histories, languages, cultural practices, and spiritual beliefs. First Nations is the largest of the three groups. There are more than 630 First Nations communities in Canada that come from more than 50 different Nations and speak 50 different Indigenous languages.

There has been a movement in recent years to recognize and reinsert an Indigenous presence in Canada's national parks. This includes proposals to change the names of some mountains back to their original Indigenous ones. One example is Banff National Park's Tunnel Mountain. Called Sleeping Buffalo by the Stoney people, the mountain resembles a sleeping buffalo when viewed from the north and east. The Stoney people believed the mountain to be a sacred

buffalo guarding the hallowed hot springs. In the 1880s, surveyors with the Canadian Pacific Railway (CPR) considered a plan to blast a tunnel through the mountain for the railway and began calling it Tunnel Mountain. Even though the tunnel was never built, the name stuck. In September 2016, fifteen First Nations signed a resolution calling for the original name of the mountain to be restored. In 2020, a petition supporting the name change was circulated in the Town of Banff. As of 2021, the name has yet to be changed.

LAND ACKNOWLEDGEMENT

In Canada, it has become common practice to acknowledge Indigenous Peoples who have lived on and cared for the land since time immemorial. Indigenous land acknowledgments are a way to show

respect for Indigenous Peoples by recognizing their presence in the past and in the present in a particular territory. It is also an important step towards reconciliation, and as such:

We recognize that the Canadian Rockies in Alberta and British Columbia are the traditional territory of many First Nations, Métis, and Inuit who have lived on and cared for the land since time immemorial. The enduring presence and stewardship of the Indigenous Peoples of Canada have helped to preserve the many natural wonders we enjoy today. The land is tied to them, and they are tied to the land. We make this acknowledgment as an act of gratitude to those who have cared for this land and as a step in the journey of reconciliation.

Indigenous Experiences

While it's difficult to visit Indigenous communities, there are many experiences in the Canadian Rockies that preserve and educate about Indigenous culture and history. Whether it's an Indigenous shop selling authentic beadwork or moccasins, a tour company educating tourists about Indigenous land and culture, or a restaurant serving genuine Indigenous food, these experiences are unique and valuable. Here are a few examples of Indigenous experiences in the Canadian Rockies:

KOOTENAY NATIONAL PARK

■ Ainsworth Hot Springs Resort: This four-season resort is owned by the Lower Kootenay Band of Creston and features hot springs, a resort hotel, dining, and other experiences.

■ Ktunaxa Grill: Enjoy contemporary Indigenous cuisine at this restaurant at Ainsworth Hot Springs Resort.

JASPER NATIONAL PARK

■ Warrior Women: Drumming sessions and guided medicine walks are the focus of this female-run tour company.

■ Jasper Tour Company: Experience the sights of Jasper with a Métis tour guide and learn about the region's Indigenous history.

■ Two Brothers Totem Pole: This Haida Gwaii-designed totem pole sits in downtown Jasper.

■ Our Native Land: This gift shop sells First Nations arts and crafts from throughout North America.

BANFF NATIONAL PARK, CANMORE AND KANANASKIS PROVINCIAL PARK

■ Banff Iiniskim Powwow: People from all nations are welcome to watch and participate in this lively powwow as a unique celebration of culture.

■ Whyte Museum of the Canadian Rockies: Indigenous artifacts and art are displayed in the Heritage Gallery of this Banff Museum.

■ Buffalo Nations Luxton Museum: See Indigenous art and artifacts and explore the heritage of the First Nations People of the Northern Plains and Canadian Rockies at this unique museum.

■ Mahikan Trails: The Métis-owned company offers medicine walks, workshops, and tours in Banff and Canmore.

■ Buffalo Stone Woman Indigescape Tours: Experience the beautiful scenery of Kananaskis from an Indigenous perspective with this tour company.

■ Stoney Nakoda Resort and Casino: This Indigenous-owned resort and casino is located in Kananaskis.

■ Samson Native Gallery: Located in Samson Mall in Lake Louise, this gallery sells paintings, sculptures, and jewelry from First Nations artists.

■ Carter Ryan Gallery: This Canmore-based gallery features the colorful paintings and bold soapstone carvings of renowned Indigenous artist, Jason Carter.

■ Grotto Canyon Pictographs: Ancient pictographs decorate the canyon walls on the Grotto Canyon hike. You may need a guided tour to find them though.

WATERTON LAKES NATIONAL PARK

■ Paahtómahksikimi Cultural Centre: Experience Blackfoot culture through various programs and purchase authentically made artisan crafts at this center.

EDMONTON

■ Royal Alberta Museum: With more than 18,000 Indigenous artifacts, the Human History Hall tells both the historical and contemporary Indigenous stories of Alberta.

■ Fort Edmonton Park: The Indigenous Peoples Experience reveals Indigenous history, art, music, experiences, and perspectives.

■ Bearclaw Gallery: This gallery carries a variety of Canadian First Nations, Métis, and Inuit art in a variety of mediums.

■ Talking Rock Tours: This Métis-owned and -operated tour company provides tours of Edmonton's river valley and Elk Island National Park from an Indigenous perspective.

■ River Cree Resort and Casino: Owned by the Enoch Nation, this resort and casino on the edge of Edmonton features Indigenous art and cuisine.

CALGARY

■ Glenbow Museum: Home to Western Canada's largest public art collection and one of Canada's largest Indigenous collections

■ Moonstone Creation: This family-run gallery and gift shop sells Indigenous artwork, jewelry, clothing, and giftware.

■ Elbow River Camp at the Calgary Stampede: Part of the Calgary Stampede since 1912, this area lets you experience the culture and traditions of the five tribes of Treaty 7: Kainai, Piikani, Siksika, Tsuut'ina, and Stoney Nakoda.

■ Nose Hill Park Medicine Wheel: Built by members of the Blood Confederacy in 2015 on the southeast corner of Nose Hill Park, this medicine wheel is constructed of rocks in the shape of the Siksikaitsitapi logo.

■ Grey Eagle Resort and Casino: Owned by the Tsuut'ina First Nation in southwest Calgary, this resort and casino is decorated with Indigenous art and features Indigenous themes.

Canadian Rockies Today

CREATION OF THE CANADIAN ROCKIES NATIONAL PARKS

The establishment and development of the five national parks of the Canadian Rockies—Banff, Jasper, Kootenay, Yoho, and Waterton Lakes—was an important step in the preservation and protection of Canada's magnificent mountain landscapes. The creation of Parks Canada is all thanks to a chance discovery by three Canadian Pacific Railway construction workers—William McCardell, Thomas McCardell, and Frank McCabe—who, in 1883, discovered hot springs at the base of Sulphur Mountain in what is now Banff National Park. The Canadian government quickly realized that these hot springs needed to be protected before they became overrun with tourists, and in 1885, a 26-square km (10.04 square miles) preserve was created around the springs. Just two years later, the area was increased to 673 square km (260 square miles) and named Rocky Mountains Park; it eventually became Banff National Park, Canada's first national park and the world's third national park.

Yoho National Park was established in 1886 as the Mount Stephen reserve, which made it the second oldest national park in Canada along with Glacier National Park, which was established on the same day. The park has 28 mountain peaks above 3,000 meters (984 feet) and it protects 1,313 square km (507 square miles) of land on the western and central slopes of the Canadian Rockies.

Canadian Rockies tourism really started to take off when the Fairmont Banff Springs, one of Canada's earliest Grand Railway Hotels, opened its doors in 1888. Over the years, "the castle in the Rockies" has hosted everyone from King George VI to Marilyn Monroe. As excitement began to build around the attractions of the Canadian Rockies, the government responded by creating more parks. In 1893, a Pincher Creek rancher, F.W. Godsal, sent a proposal to the Canadian government recommending that Waterton be set aside as a protected area. On May 30, 1895, the government of Canada protected 140 square km (54 square miles) as a Dominion Forest Park. Now known as Waterton Lakes National Park, it was Canada's fourth national park and is the smallest national park in the Canadian Rockies at 505 square km (195 square miles).

Canada's fifth National Park, Jasper, was established in 1907. North of Banff and west of Edmonton, and originally called Jasper Forest Park, it's the largest national park in the Canadian Rockies spanning 11,000 square km (4,200 square miles). Kootenay National Park was established in 1920 as part of an agreement to build a new road across the Rockies.

CANADIAN ROCKY MOUNTAIN PARKS NAMED A UNESCO WORLD HERITAGE SITE

The scenic splendor of these parks and the global significance of the sites and species they protected prompted the establishment of the Canadian Rocky Mountain Parks UNESCO World Heritage Site in 1984 with Banff, Jasper, Kootenay, and Yoho national parks; Mount Robson, Mount Assiniboine, and Hamber provincial parks were added in 1990.

CANADIAN ROCKIES NATIONAL PARKS AND INDIGENOUS PEOPLES

While most will agree that protecting the remarkable landscapes and resources of the Canadian Rockies was a good thing, there was a dark side to it that seldom gets told. The Canadian Rockies had long been the traditional territory of many Indigenous groups. When the parks were created, these groups were forced off their lands and confined to nearby reserves. The Stoney People of the Banff area were only invited back for the annual Banff Indian Days, an event that ran into the 1970s. A 1929 advertisement for the event enticed tourists to come to see "Chiefs and Braves and squaws in full regalia," a phrase that today would be considered offensive.

Excluded for well over a century, Indigenous People are slowly returning to the parks as Parks Canada has made efforts to recognize and include them as valuable partners in the management of national parks. Parks Canada has also included more information about Indigenous People on interpretive signage and on the official websites for the national parks.

THE PARKS TODAY

Today, the Canadian Rockies region attracts millions of visitors annually making it one of Canada's top tourism destinations—Banff alone had more than 4.1 million visitors in 2019/2020. Parks Canada and provincial park staff work tirelessly to manage the parks' wildlife corridors including prescribed burns to prevent the spread of wildfires and the installation of proper tourism infrastructure. There are some threats, however, that cannot be easily addressed such as climate change, fossil fuel dependency, and industrial development. In recent years, the warming climate has caused an increase in the number of forest fires in British Columbia. In 2021, 20 provincial parks in B.C. were closed because of wildfire activity and another three were partially closed, though none were in the Canadian Rockies. You can see evidence of past forest fires in several national and provincial parks within the Canadian Rockies including Waterton Lakes National-al Park, which experienced a massive wildfire in 2017.

Rising temperatures are also causing glaciers in the Rockies to recede farther and faster than ever before. In recent years, there has been pressure to resume surface mining on the eastern slopes of the Rockies near Crowsnest Pass. The region's home to the headwaters of several rivers including the Oldman River and there's a great deal of concern that such an operation would pollute the water system affecting plants, animals, and people for years to come. Then there are the mountain pine beetles, which pose a serious threat to the region's pine forests and have already caused the death of thousands of trees. Park visitors can do their part to protect and preserve the Canadian Rockies by staying on prescribed trails, properly disposing of garbage, and being responsible around wildlife.

BEST BETS

Fodor's writers and editors have chosen our favorites to help you plan. Search individual chapters for details, and see our features on Best Backcountry Lodges, Family Fun, and Indigenous Experiences.

BEST VIEW HIKES
Berg Lake Trail (Mount Robson Provincial Park)
Crypt Lake (Waterton Lakes National Park)
Parker Ridge (Banff National Park)
Smutwood Peak (Kananaskis)
Wilcox Pass (Jasper National Park)

BEST ICEWALKS
Athabasca Glacier (Jasper National Park)
Grotto Canyon (Canmore)
Johnston Canyon (Banff National Park)
Maligne Canyon (Jasper National Park)
Star Creek Falls (Crowsnest Pass)

BEST WATERFALLS
Athabasca Falls (Jasper National Park)
Bow Falls (Banff National Park)
Cameron Falls (Waterton Lakes National Park)
Takakkaw Falls (Yoho National Park)
Troll Falls (Kananaskis)

BEST STARGAZING
Medicine Lake (Jasper National Park)
Pyramid Lake (Jasper National Park)
Lake Minnewanka (Banff National Park)

Vermillion Lakes (Banff National Park)
Lake O'Hara (Yoho National Park)

BEST HOT SPRINGS
Banff Upper Hot Springs (Banff National Park)
Miette Hot Springs (Jasper National Park)
Radium Hot Springs (Kootenay National Park)

BEST FAMILY-FRIENDLY HIKES
Lake Louise Lakeshore Hike (Banff National Park)
Marble Canyon (Kootenay National Park)
Bears Hump (Waterton Lakes National Park)
Old Fort Point Trail (Jasper National Park)
Emerald Lake Loop (Yoho National Park)

BEST CAMPGROUNDS
Two Jacks Main and Lakeside Campgrounds (Banff National Park)
Whistlers Campground (Jasper National Park)
Townsite Campground (Waterton Lakes National Park)
Boulton Creek Creek Campground (Peter Lougheed Provincial Park, Kananaskis)
Redstreak Campground (Kootenay National Park)

BEST WILDFLOWERS HIKES
Healy Pass (Banff National Park)
Horseshoe Basin (Waterton Lakes National Park)
Many Springs Trail (Kananaskis)
Sunshine Meadows (Banff National Park)
Cavell Meadows (Jasper National Park)

BEST FOR FISHING
Bow River (Calgary)
Fortress Lake (Hamber Provincial Park)
Amethyst Lake (Jasper National Park)
Spray Lakes (Kananaskis)
Kinbasket Reservoir (Golden, BC)

BEST LARCH HIKES
Larch Valley and Sentinel Pass (Banff National Park)
Arethusa Cirque (Kananaskis)
Pocaterra Ridge (Kananaskis)
Buller Pass (Kananaskis)
Chester Lake (Kananaskis)

BEST MOUNTAIN LAKES

Lake Louise (Banff National Park)

Lake O'Hara (Yoho National Park)

Moraine Lake (Banff National Park)

Berg Lake (Mount Robson Provincial Park)

Peyto Lake (Banff National Park)

BEST SCENIC DRIVES

Icefields Parkway (Banff National Park/Jasper National Park)

Maligne Lake Road (Jasper National Park)

Highwood Pass (Kananaskis)

Yoho Valley Road (Yoho National Park)

Bow Valley Parkway (Banff National Park)

BEST SKI AREAS

Lake Louise Ski Resort (Banff National Park)

Sunshine Village Ski Resort (Banff National Park)

Kicking Horse Mountain Resort (Golden, BC)

Marmot Basin Ski Resort (Jasper National Park)

Nakiska Ski Area (Kananaskis)

BEST BACKPACKING TRAILS

Skyline Trail (Jasper National Park)

Berg Lake Trail (Mount Robson Provincial Park)

Tonquin Valley (Jasper National Park)

Sunshine Village to Mount Assiniboine (Banff National Park/Mount Assiniboine Provincial Park)

Skoki Loop (Banff National Park)

BEST BIRD-WATCHING

Vermilion Lakes (Banff National Park)

Talbot Lake (Jasper National Park)

Emerald Lake (Yoho National Park)

The Cave and Basin Marsh (Banff National Park)

Banff Townsite Area (Banff National Park)

BEST NORTHERN LIGHTS VIEWING

Pyramid Lake (Jasper National Park)

Lake Minnewanka (Banff National Park)

Peyto Lake Lookout (Banff National Park)

Abraham Lake (off Highway 11 near Nordegg)

Mt. Yamnuska (Bow Valley Provincial Park)

Spray Lakes (Kananaskis)

BEST SUNSETS

Vermillion Lakes (Banff National Park)

Lake Louise (Banff National Park)

Mount Norquay (Banff National Park)

Medicine Lake (Jasper National Park)

Upper and Lower Kananaskis Lakes (Kananaskis)

BEST SUNRISES

Moraine Lake (Banff National Park)

Emerald Lake (Yoho National Park)

Two Jack Lake (Banff National Park)

Pyramid Lake (Jasper National Park)

Wedge Pond (Kananaskis)

BEST HIKES FOR ALL ABILITIES

Tunnel Mountain (Banff National Park)

Johnston Canyon Lower/ Upper Falls (Banff National Park)

Maligne Canyon Trail (Jasper National Park)

Emerald Lake Trail (Yoho National Park)

Troll Falls (Kananaskis)

BEST NIGHTTIME EXPERIENCES

Night Skiing and Tubing at Mount Norquay (Banff National Park)

Jasper Dark Sky Festival in October (Jasper National Park)

Moonlight Skating on Lake Louise (Banff National Park)

Evening Guided Icewalk at Johnston Canyon (Banff National Park)

Ride up the Jasper Skytram for a "Star Session" (Jasper National Park)

What to Read and Watch

THE REVENANT

Leonardo DiCaprio received his first Oscar for this 2015 film about an adventurer that gets attacked by a bear and becomes stranded alone in the wilderness. This story of survival accurately portrays the Canadian Rockies as it was filmed in Kananaskis Country and areas of Bow Valley.

JUMANJI: THE NEXT LEVEL

In the third continuation of the Jumanji Series, the stars traveled to Fortress Mountain in Kananaskis Country to film a portion of the movie. The recognizable snow-covered mountaintops are a striking contrast to the jungle and desert locations that were also filming locations.

INCEPTION

A climactic scene in this sci-fi action movie was filmed at Fortress Mountain in Kananaskis. Just look for the towering snowcapped peaks that almost look like a green screen due to their spectacular beauty.

MOUNTAIN NATURE AND CULTURE PODCAST

This podcast by Ward Cameron covers everything from Canadian Rockies' wildlife and vegetation to history and current events happening around the area. It provides a thought-provoking look into all things Canadian Rockies.

BROKEBACK MOUNTAIN

With filming locations throughout Kananaskis, Canmore, and Calgary, this western romance paints a vivid picture of the landscape of the Rockies and the prairies. Upper Kananaskis Lakes, Goat Creek, and Elbow Falls are all featured in the film as well as Fortress Mountain, Moose Mountain, and Mount Lougheed near Canmore.

THE SKOKI COOKBOOK BY KATIE MITZEL

This unique cookbook is filled with favorite Canadian rustic recipes, as well as historical information about the area. Mitzel also incorporates humorous anecdotes, fascinating facts, and lovely photographs from Skoki Lodge travelers.

THE CANADIAN ROCKIES: REDISCOVERED BY PAUL ZIZKA

Paul Zizka captures the beauty of the Canadian Rockies in a way that only an expert photographer can. Highlighting 200 images, Zizka traveled off the beaten path and utilized innovative photography techniques to curate a finished product worthy of admiration.

RAVEN'S END: A TALE FROM THE CANADIAN ROCKIES BY BEN GADD

This fictional young adult novel tells the story of a young raven that joins a flock near Banff, Alberta. The beautifully written book eloquently explains the landscape and animal life of the Canadian Rockies.

WAR FOR THE PLANET OF THE APES

Portions of the third installment in the Planet of the Apes franchise were filmed in Kananaskis, Alberta. Though it was filmed primarily in British Columbia and Alberta, several scenes occured at Fortress Mountain.

THE MAGIC OF THE WILD: BANFF NATIONAL PARK IN THE CANADIAN ROCKIES

In this docuseries episode, the geography, wildlife, and history of Canada's first national park is portrayed with beautifully crisp videography. The narrative consists of information from a variety of Banff's experts and provides a captivating look into the charming national park.

Chapter 2

TRAVEL SMART

By
Debbie Olsen

★ **CAPITAL:**
Edmonton, Alberta. Victoria, British Columbia.

 POPULATION:
4.4 million (Alberta); 5.2 million (British Columbia)

 LANGUAGE:
English

$ **CURRENCY:**
CAD (Canadian Dollar)

 AREA CODE:
Alberta: 403, 780, 587, 825; Kootenay and Yoho: 250

⚠ **EMERGENCIES:**
911

 DRIVING:
On the right

✈ **AIRPORTS:**
Edmonton International Airport (YEG); Calgary International Airport (YYC)

ϟ **ELECTRICITY:**
120–220 v/60 cycles; plugs have two or three rectangular prongs

 TIME:
2 hours behind New York

 WEB RESOURCES:
www.pc.gc.ca; albertaparks.ca; bcparks.ca

Know Before You Go

Planning can ensure you get the most out of your visit to the Canadian Rockies. Do some research so you know in advance which locations are open, what to expect, how to prepare, and what services are available. Here are a few tips to help you make the most of your trip.

PETS IN THE PARKS
Generally, pets are allowed in the national parks, including drive-in campgrounds and picnic areas, but they must be kept on a leash at all times. However, pets, with the exception of guide dogs, are not allowed inside most buildings, concessions, on some trails, or in the backcountry, so be sure to check before you travel. There are many accommodations in the national parks that provide pet-friendly rooms, but those should be booked well in advance.

RECOGNIZE AND RESPECT THE INDIGENOUS HISTORY
The Canadian Rockies in Alberta and British Columbia are the traditional territory of many First Nations, Métis, and Inuit who have lived on and cared for the land since time immemorial. It is crucial that visitors treat these areas with respect as many of the top tourist attractions are considered sacred lands. For some of the best insight into Canadian Indigenous History, plan a visit to Paahtómahksikimi Cultural Centre, Buffalo Nations Museum, or book a tour with Buffalo Stone Woman Indigescape Tours, or *Warrior Women*.

CANADA'S NATIONAL PARKS PASS
Parks Canada (877/737–3783; *www.pc.gc.ca*), the Canadian equivalent of the US's NPS, issues an annual Discovery Pass (*www.commandesparcs-parksorders.ca*) that allows free entry to 80 parks and other sites. Prices range from about C$70 for a single adult to C$140 for a family/group pass.

DON'T SKIP THE VISITOR CENTER
A national parks visitor center is more than just a place to get information on the best hiking trails. Centers often have museum-quality displays on the park's ecology, geology, and biology; some even have archaeological artifacts on view. You'll also find helpful maps, brochures, and great local advice and tips.

FIRES ARE A HUGE CONCERN
Wildfires have always been an issue, but in recent years, dry conditions, overgrown forests, and unhealthy trees have turned the Canadian Rockies into a tinderbox, and wildfires have ravaged the landscape. It's critical that visitors are mindful of fire alerts and follow fire prevention protocols. Outside of the park's designated campfire areas, fires are both illegal and incredibly dangerous. If you plan to camp in the backcountry and need fire for cooking, bring a small camp stove or propane burner.

HIKING IS NO JOKE
Before heading out on a hike it's important to check the trail reports on the Parks Canada website (*www.pc.gc.ca*) for trail conditions, closures, and restrictions as well as what hiking gear is recommended for each specified trail. When you're hiking, stay on marked trails to avoid damaging fragile vegetation. And, if you plan to hike in the backcountry, invest in detailed maps and a compass. Maps are sold in well-equipped outdoor stores (Atmosphere and Cabela's, for example) or can be downloaded directly on your smartphone via several downloadable apps.

FIND BEAUTY AND SOLITUDE AWAY FROM THE FAMOUS SITES
It's kind of a catch-22: you go to a national park to experience the beauty and solitude of the natural world only to discover that everyone else had the same plan. Rather than visiting

the most popular sites, hit the trails (or water), particularly routes that are longer than 3 miles and can't be traversed by baby carriages and large tour groups. They may not be listed as the park's must-see locations, but they're almost guaranteed to be just as spectacular, yet apart from the crowds.

FOLLOW WILDLIFE SAFETY PROTOCOLS

A visit to the Canadian Rockies comes with a high probability of seeing wildlife, and there are certain steps you should be aware of in order to keep yourself and the wildlife safe. If you're driving and you see wildlife on or near the road, always stay in your vehicle with the windows up, slow down, and don't stop on the road unless there's a safe place to pull over. If you plan on hiking, especially in the backcountry, bring bear spray in case you encounter a territorial or aggressive bear.

LEAVE NO TRACE

Anything you bring into the park must be carried back out or put in the appropriate garbage or recycling receptacle. Don't pick up any rocks or artifacts or fossils; don't collect flowers or firewood; never touch or interact with a wild animal.

TAKE WARNING SIGNS AND RANGER ADVICE SERIOUSLY

National parks are among the few remaining places in Canada that have not been entirely engineered for your safety; in some cases the only thing that stands between you and certain death is a sign. Visitors die every year in climbing, hiking, and swimming accidents and animal encounters in Canada's national parks. Always take precautionary signs and ranger advice seriously.

BE PREPARED

The weather is highly unpredictable in the Canadian Rockies. Always carry extra layers when you're out and about, especially if you're hiking, and pack water and snacks.

SOME CAMPSITES ARE RESERVED FOR WALK-UPS

Most parks keep some campsites for first-come, first-served walk-ups. As long as you get there as early in the morning as possible, you're likely to get a spot, even on weekends. They aren't always the most desirable campgrounds in the park, but it's still much better than staying home.

EATING AND DRINKING

Tap water is drinkable. In fact, some of the water in the Rockies is particularly pure as it comes from glaciers or high-altitude rivers.

6 pm is the most common dinner time in Canada. And, if you're eating out, servers at most sit-down restaurants expect a tip of approximately 15 percent.

YOU MUST MAKE RESERVATIONS TO HIKE

The most popular hikes—Lake O'Hara in Yoho National Park or Skyline Trail in Jasper National Park—must be booked months in advance. Parks Canada limits the number of people it allows into these areas in order to protect fragile terrain. There is a reservation system, but all of the reservations typically are fully booked within a few hours on the day that reservations open.

THE ALPINE CLUB OF CANADA

Established in 1906, the Alpine Club of Canada (ACC) operates four frontcountry hostels in the Canadian Rockies and more than two dozen backcountry huts and cabins, which you must hike, climb, ski or helicopter in to reach. While some huts are open year-round, most are seasonal, and range from rustic huts such as Banff's Castle Mountain to luxurious properties like the Kokanee Glacier Cabin, or those like the Shadow Lake Lodge that include gourmet meals. In most cases, ACC accommodations must be booked well in advance; some are so popular that there's a lottery system. There are member (you don't have to live in Canada to join) and nonmember rates starting at C$37 per night for a hostel dorm bed to C$1,000 per night for the Elizabeth Parker Hut in Yoho National Park.

The ACC also offers ice climbing, backcountry skiing, and avalanche safety courses in winter, and mountaineering, trekking, rock climbing, trail running, and other activities in summer.

Getting Here and Around

Air

Most visitors access the Canadian Rockies by flying into Calgary International Airport (YYC) or Edmonton International Airport (YEG). Some visitors who are visiting both Banff and Jasper as part of their planned itinerary choose to fly into Calgary and fly out of Edmonton or vice-versa to avoid backtracking. Calgary is the busiest airport of the two with the most flights and the most direct flights. Direct flights are available from certain cities to either airport. There tend to be more flights during the peak seasons.

AIRPORTS
The two closest airports to the Canadian Rockies are Calgary International Airport (YYC) and Edmonton International Airport (YEG). Calgary is the closest airport to Kananaskis, Canmore, Banff, Kootenay, and Yoho National Parks. Edmonton is the closest airport to Jasper and Mount Robson National Parks.

AIRPORT TRANSFERS
There are several companies that offer bus shuttle transfers from Calgary and Edmonton airports. Information about bus shuttle service is listed in the chapters.

Car

Car travel is the easiest and most convenient way to get around the Canadian Rockies.

CAR RENTALS
Vehicle rentals can be conveniently arranged at the international airports or in major cities. There are many different rental companies available and prices will vary with the dates of travel. Prices will be higher during peak travel seasons such as July and August or Christmas. Booking in advance typically saves money. Be sure to compare prices between rental companies before making a reservation. Check to see if your credit card or your personal insurance policy provides rental car insurance. If it does, be prepared to provide proof of insurance to the rental company. If you do not have rental insurance, the car rental company can provide rental insurance, though the cost of rental insurance can be almost as much as the cost of the rental. Nonetheless, you should make sure you have insurance. You usually need to be at least 21 years of age and have at least 12 months of driving experience to rent a vehicle. Renters under the age of 21 will have to pay an additional fee. You may pay extra for an additional driver or for picking up the vehicle at one location and dropping it off at another location. Make sure your driver's license is valid for at least six months after your trip. If your license is in a foreign language, you may need to get an International driver's permit. It's very difficult to rent a vehicle in Canada without a credit card. The name on the credit card should match the driver's name. Car seats or booster seats are required by law for children under 18 kg (40 lbs). Many airlines allow you to check a car seat without an additional fee or you can rent car seats from the car rental agency.

DRIVING
The Trans-Canada Highway (Hwy. 1) is the main route from Calgary to Canmore, Banff, and Yoho National Park. Highway 16 is the main route from Edmonton to Jasper National Park and Mount Robson Provincial Park.

GASOLINE

Gas is sold by the liter in Canada and there are about 3.8 liters in one U.S. gallon. Gas prices fluctuate, but gas is more expensive in Canada than it is in the US, but less expensive than it is in Europe. You'll usually find better prices in towns and cities.

PARKING

Parking can be challenging in some parts of the Canadian Rockies. In Banff, there is very little parking in the downtown area. It's usually best to park in one of the free parking lots and walk from there.

ROAD CONDITIONS

Roads can get slippery during the late fall and winter months. It's best to drive slowly when roads are icy. Real-time Alberta road reports can be found on the website: 511.alberta.ca.

RULES OF THE ROAD

Vehicles drive on the right side of the road in Canada. Unless a sign indicates otherwise, you are allowed to turn right when you are stopped at a red light. Seat belts are mandatory in Canada and talking on a mobile phone while driving can result in a distracted driving violation. It's illegal to drink alcohol and drive. Speeds and distances are measured in kilometers. Wildlife sightings are common in the Canadian Rockies, so you should stay alert and travel at reasonable speeds to avoid a collision with an animal—especially at dawn or dusk. If you wish to stop to view wildlife, carefully pull over to the side of the road and put on your hazard lights.

Public Transport

There is public transport in most major centers like Edmonton, Calgary, Banff, and Canmore (Roam Bus). If you need bus transportation from the airports to cities in the Canadian Rockies, there are several companies that offer bus shuttle services. Brewster Express has service from Calgary to Canmore or Banff as well as from Banff to Jasper. Sundog Tours offers a shuttle bus service from Edmonton to Jasper and from Jasper to Banff.

Ride-Sharing

Uber is available in Edmonton and Calgary, but there are no ride-sharing options in the national parks.

Taxi

While ride-sharing services are limited outside of Calgary and Edmonton, taxis are readily available in larger towns and cities.

Train

VIA Rail offers train service from downtown Edmonton to the Jasper townsite, but service is not offered daily. There is no train service from Calgary.

The Rocky Mountaineer operates luxury scenic train trips with destinations in Banff and Jasper.

Essentials

Dining

There are some amazing restaurants in the Canadian Rockies and you can find many different kinds of food including the unique-to-the-region Rocky Mountain cuisine, which is made with high-quality, locally sourced ingredients. Look for game meats like elk, bison, and venison, as well as trout, Arctic char, and Pacific halibut, and Alberta beef and lamb. Seasonal vegetables, prairie-grown grains, and local fruits such as Saskatoon berries, rhubarb, apples, and haskap berries are also commonly seen on menus.

DISCOUNTS AND DEALS

If you eat early or late you may be able to take advantage of prix fixe deals or happy hour drink specials not offered at peak hours. Many upscale restaurants offer great lunch deals with special menus at cut-rate prices designed to give customers a true taste of the place. At high-end restaurants ask for tap water to avoid paying high rates for bottled water—you'll most probably be drinking glacier water!

PAYING

Most restaurants take credit cards, but some smaller places do not; it's worth asking before you arrive. Waiters expect a 15–20% tip at high-end restaurants; some add an automatic gratuity for groups of six or more.

RESERVATIONS AND DRESS

Always make a reservation at an upscale restaurant when you can as some are booked weeks in advance; there are a few popular restaurants that don't accept them. Business casual attire is acceptable at most restaurants, but a few pricier restaurants require jackets, and some insist on ties. In reviews, we mention dress only where men are required to wear a jacket or a jacket and tie. If you have doubts, call the restaurant and ask.

Restaurant reviews have been shortened. For full information, visit Fodors.com.

MEALS AND MEALTIMES

The busiest dinner times in the Canadian Rockies are between 6 and 7 pm and in smaller parks, restaurants tend to close early. In the busiest parks, restaurants will stay open until 9 pm or later. It's a good idea to confirm the hours of the local dining establishments so you are not disappointed.

SMOKING

Smoking is banned in all restaurants and bars.

● Electricity

If you're traveling from the U.S. you do not need a converter for small appliances (hairdryers, irons, razors, etc.) as both countries use the same standard voltage (120 V) and frequency (60 Hz).

● Health & Safety

Maintaining your health and safety is an important consideration when traveling in the Canadian Rockies. Always bring some hand sanitizer to use as some remote outhouses may not have any. Bring layers, water, snacks, and bear spray on hikes. Be conscious of road conditions and avalanche zones, especially in winter. Keep your distance from wildlife for the safety of the animals and for your own safety. If you're traveling in the backcountry, you may wish to bring a satellite phone or other emergency communication device as cell phones will not work in most backcountry locations. Call 911 if there is a serious emergency.

COVID-19

Although COVID-19 brought travel to a virtual standstill for most of 2020 and into 2021, vaccinations have made travel possible and safe again. Remaining requirements and restrictions—including those for non-vaccinated travelers—can, however, vary from one place (or even business) to the next. Check out the the websites of the Government of Canada, the CDC, and the U.S. Department of State, all of which have destination-specific, COVID-19 guidance. Also, in case travel is curtailed abruptly again, consider buying trip insurance. Just be sure to read the fine print: not all travel-insurance policies cover pandemic-related cancellations.

🛏 Lodging

The Canadian Rockies is one of Canada's top tourism destinations and there are a wide variety of accommodations ranging from basic hostels to luxurious accommodations that are ranked as some of the best in the world.

In parks with nearby ski resorts, there are two peak seasons: June to September and December through February. The Christmas season is the busiest time in the winter peak season and July and August are the busiest months in summer. Book well in advance if you're traveling then. Prices will be lower during the shoulder season or if you choose accommodations outside the park.

FACILITIES

You can assume that all rooms have private baths, phones, TVs, and air-conditioning unless otherwise indicated. Breakfast is noted when it's included in the rate, but it's not a typical perk at many Canadian Rockies hotels. There are some hotels with pools and hot tubs, though some are indoors.

PARKING

Parking can be limited at some properties, particularly in Banff. In some cases, there is an extra fee for parking, but street parking is often free.

PRICES

Most hotels accept credit cards.

RESERVATIONS

It's a good idea to make reservations in advance, especially during peak travel times when hotels fill up. The summer months and the Christmas holidays are particularly busy.

Hotel reviews have been shortened. For full information, visit Fodors.com.

📶 Internet and Mobile Phones

If you need to download maps, do so before you head out to explore the parks. Luckily, the main roads are clearly marked and easy to follow.

If you're in Edmonton or Calgary, you should have no problems with mobile or internet service, though you should check with your service provider to see if your plan includes service in Canada.

📦 Mail

Canada Post (*www.canadapost-postes-canada.ca*) is the official postal service of Canada. If you're planning to send a letter or postcard home to the US, a stamp will cost you C$1.30.

💲 Money

Canada's official currency is the Canadian dollar (C$); a C$1 is divided into 100 cents. At the time of press, C$1 equaled

Essentials

US$0.78. The coin and bill denominations are the same as in the U.S., i.e. 25 cents, C$5, C$10, etc., but Canada has eliminated the penny. There is also a dollar coin that has a loon on its back, which has given it the nickname "the loonie", as well as a two-dollar coin that is known locally as a "toonie." If you pay with a credit card, the exact amount of your purchase will be charged. If you pay with cash, the amount will be rounded to the nearest 5 cents.

All major credit and debit cards are accepted in Canada, and ATMs dispense local currency. US currency is accepted in some hotels and shops, but the exchange rate is not as good as you'd get from a bank. It's best to pay in Canadian dollars, whether you're paying in cash or by credit card.

Passport

All visitors to Canada require a passport that is valid for six months beyond their expected period of stay. If you think you might cross the border, particularly if you're visiting Waterton Lakes National Park, be sure to have your passport with you.

Time

The Canadian Rockies are in the Mountain Time Zone (UTC/GMT-7 hours), which is 2 hours behind New York.

Tipping

When it comes to tipping, Canadians follow pretty much the same rules as Americans, giving 15-20% for a meal at a sit-down restaurant. Plan to also tip at your hotel or bar, if you take a taxi, or get your nails or hair done.

When to Go

Due to high elevations, weather can be unpredictable in the Canadian Rockies, and winters can be harsh. Snow typically arrives by early November and begins melting by late April, though it can start earlier and last longer in any given year.

Wildflowers start blossoming as early as late March and can be seen until mid-September, but the peak season at all elevations is from mid-July to mid-August. Larch trees usually start to turn golden in mid-September and the larch hiking season runs from mid-September to early October.

Elk rutting season runs from late August until mid-October. This is the elk breeding season, and the male elk, or bull elk, can become very aggressive during this time. Female elk become aggressive in the spring when elk calves are born. Caution should be taken around this species during both seasons.

Bears generally hibernate from mid-November through early April, though they can come out of hibernation even in winter and you should be bear aware and carry bear spray whenever you hike in the Canadian Rockies.

It's always wise to dress in layers and bring a backpack to carry outerwear even on a sunny summer day.

Low Season: October to November and April to May

Shoulder Season: June and September

High Season: July through August; Christmas holidays, spring break (typically in March)

Contacts

✈ Air

AIRPORTS

Calgary International Airport. ✉ *2000 Airport Rd. NE, McCall North* ☎ *403/735–1234* ⊕ *www. yyc.com.* **Edmonton International Airport.** (*YEG*). ✉ *1000 Airport Rd., Edmonton* ☎ *780/890–8382* ⊕ *flyeia.com.*

AIRPORT SHUTTLES

Banff Airporter. ✉ *141 Eagle Crescent, Banff* ☎ *888/449–2901* ⊕ *banff-fairporter.com.* **Brewster Express.** ✉ *100 Gopher St., Banff* ☎ *403/762–6700, 866/606–6700 toll-free* ⊕ *www.banffjasper-collection.com/brewster-express.* **Discover Banff Tours Airport Shuttle.** ✉ *215 Banff Ave., Banff* ☎ *877/565–9372 toll-free, 403/760–5007* ⊕ *www. banfftours.com.* **SunDog Tours.** ☎ *888/786–3641* ⊕ *www.sundogtours.com.*

🚍 Public Transit

CONTACTS Roam. ✉ *Canmore* ⊕ *roamtransit.com.*

📍 Park Websites

Banff National Park. ✉ *Banff* ☎ *403/762–1550* ⊕ *www.pc.gc.ca/banff.* **Jasper National Park.** ☎ *780/852–6176* ⊕ *www. pc.gc.ca/jasper.* **Kananaskis Country.** ✉ *Kananaskis Village* ⊕ *www.alberta-parks.ca/parks/kananaskis/kananaskis-country.* **Waterton Lakes National Park.** ✉ *Waterton Townsite* ☎ *403/859–5133, 403/859–2224 year-round* ⊕ *www.pc.gc.ca/waterton.* **Yoho National Park.** ✉ *5764 Trans-Canada Hwy., Field* ☎ *250/343–6783* ⊕ *www.pc.gc.ca/en/pn-np/bc/yoho.*

🚆 Train

Rocky Mountaineer. ☎ *877/460–3200* ⊕ *www. rockymountaineer. com.* **VIA Rail Canada.** ☎ *888/842–7245* ⊕ *www. viarail.ca.*

📍 Visitor Information

Alpine of Canada. ✉ *Canmore* ☎ *403/678–3200 Ext. 0* ⊕ *www.alpine-clubofcanada.ca.* **Explore Edmonton.** ✉ *Edmonton* ☎ *780/401–7696* ⊕ *exploreedmonton.com.* **Tourism Calgary.** ✉ *238 11th Ave. SE, Suite 200, Calgary* ☎ *800/661–1678* ⊕ *www. visitcalgary.com.* **Tourism Golden.** ✉ *521 9th Ave. N, Golden* ☎ *250/439–1111* ⊕ *www.tourismgolden. com.* **Tourism Jasper.** ✉ *414 Patricia St., Jasper* ☎ *780/852–6236* ⊕ *www. jasper.travel.* **Waterton Lakes Chamber of Commerce.** ✉ *Waterton Lakes National Park* ⊕ *www. mywaterton.ca.*

On the Calendar

January

Banff SnowDays. This winter festival features snow and ice sculptures and winter activities. *www.banfflakelouise.com/snowdays.*

Ice on Whyte. Sculptors from all over the world descend on Edmonton's McIntyre Park to transform 93,000 pounds of ice into a frozen art gallery at western Canada's premier winter carnival. *www.iceonwhyte.ca.*

Jasper in January. The biggest winter festival in Jasper features live music, activities, and ski and accommodation discounts. *www.jasperinjanuary.com.*

February

Jasper Beer & Spirits Festival. Enjoy exceptional craft beer, seminars, food, and activities at the Fairmont Jasper Park Lodge. *albertabeerfestivals.com/festivals/jasper-beer-spirits-festival.*

March

Marmot's Revenge Ski Mountaineering. This annual mountaineering ski race is held at Marmot Basin in Jasper. *www.skimarmot.com.*

April

Jasper Pride Festival. This is the third-largest pride celebration in Alberta and the only winter pride festival in the Canadian Rockies. *jasperpride.ca.*

May

Slush Cup. This event at Banff Sunshine Village is the longest-running end-of-winter celebration in North America. *www.skibanff.com.*

Wings Over The Rockies Festival. This festival held in Invermere on the Lake educates about birds, wildlife, and habitat. *www.wingsovertherockies.org.*

June

National Indigenous Peoples Day. Held on June 21, there are events across Canada to celebrate Indigenous Peoples. *www.canada.ca.*

Waterton Wildflower Festival. This multiday festival is all about wildflowers. *mywaterton.ca.*

July

Calgary Stampede. Called the "Greatest Outdoor Show on Earth," this 10-day festival has been entertaining folks since 1912 with a series of events that include a parade, a midway, an exhibition, and a rodeo. *www.calgarystampede.com.*

Calgary Folk Music Festival. A four-day genre-bending, family-friendly affair that takes over Prince's Island Park. Past artists have included k.d. lang, David Byrne, and Elvis Costello. *www.calgaryfolkfest.com.*

Canada Day. July 1 is a national holiday with events happening across the nation.

Parks Day. The third Saturday in July is Parks Day at all national parks in Canada. Each national park will have events and may also offer free entrance. *www.albertaparks.ca.*

August

Canmore Folk Music Festival. This is the longest-running folk music festival in Alberta and features more than 30 acts. *canmorefolkfestival.com.*

Edmonton Folk Music Festival. Dozens of musicians—from pop superstars to obscure folkies—perform on six stages on the banks of the North Saskatchewan River in what is perhaps one of Canada's best music festivals. *www.edmontonfolkfest.org.*

Edmonton International Fringe Festival. This is North America's oldest and largest fringe theatre festival. *www.fringetheatre.ca.*

September

Canmore Highland Games. Celtic culture and tradition in all its forms—dance, music, and sports are celebrated at this annual festival. *canmorehighlandgames.ca.*

CSIO Spruce Meadows Masters Tournament. More than a half-million visitors descend upon Spruce Meadows, one of the world's most prestigious equestrian facilities, to watch the best horses and riders in the world compete for $4 million in prizes. *www.sprucemeadows.com.*

Waterton Wildlife Weekend. Learn all about wildlife in the Rocky Mountains at this annual event. *mywaterton.ca.*

October

Banff Pride. This multiday event features parties, celebrations, and activities. *www.banffpride.ca.*

Jasper Dark Sky Festival. This annual festival features events, speakers, and celebrations in an incredible Dark Sky Preserve. *jasperdarksky.travel.*

November

Christmas in November. For more than 30 years this multiday event at the Fairmont Jasper Park Lodge has hosted presenters, activities, and culinary events. It sells out months in advance. *www.fairmont. com/jasper/offers/christmas-in-november.*

Santa Claus Parade of Lights. This special parade kicks off six weeks of Christmas celebrations. *www.banfflakelouise.com/Christmas.*

December

Lake Louise Audi FIS Ski World Cup. This event hosts the first downhill and Super-G races of the season. *lakelouiseworldcup.com.*

Chapter 3

GREAT ITINERARIES

By
Kelsey Olsen

Jasper and Banff National Parks, 8 Days

Jasper and Banff offer spectacular scenery like glaciers, hot springs, snow-capped peaks, and the incomparable blue waters of Lake Louise. For this itinerary, we recommend flying into Edmonton International Airport and flying out of Calgary International Airport; you can also do the itinerary in reverse and fly into Calgary and out of Edmonton to save backtracking.

Day 1: Arrival

Most visitors arrive at Edmonton International Airport (EIA). Spend your first night in a hotel close to the airport or make the drive to Jasper right away; it's a four-hour drive from the airport.

If you decide to fly into Calgary International Airport (YYC), the drive to the town of Jasper will take about 5 hours.

Days 2 and 3: Jasper National Park

396 km (246 miles) or a 4-hour drive from Edmonton International

Keep an eye out for wildlife on your drive to Jasper. Along the way, consider taking a detour off Highway 16 and driving Miette Hot Springs Road where you can enjoy a soak in the hot mineral pools. If it's a sunny day, you might also stop at the roadside pullout by Jasper Lake and wade in the shallow water. Visit the Jasper Information Centre to get trail maps and information about free park interpretive programs before exploring the historic Jasper Townsite. Book a room in Jasper (Alpine Village is a cozy favorite) for the next two nights.

Spend the next morning exploring Mount Edith Cavell, located off Highway 93 (the Icefields Parkway) and Cavell Road about 28 km (17 miles) south of Jasper. The 1-km (0.5-mile) trail from the parking lot leads to the base of an imposing cliff, where you can see the stunning Angel Glacier. A steep 3-km (2-mile) trail climbs up the valley to Cavell Meadows, which are carpeted with wildflowers from mid-July to mid-August. There are many options for the afternoon: hiking in nearby Maligne Canyon, kayaking at Pyramid Lake, horseback riding, or mountain biking (the park has 300 km [186 miles] of trails with options for riders of all levels). An evening drive along Maligne Lake Road is a great way to see wildlife.

Day 4: Icefields Parkway to Lake Louise

230 km (140 miles) or a 3-hour drive to Lake Louise

From Jasper, head south 31 km (19 miles) on Highway 93, otherwise known as the Icefields Parkway, to Athabasca Falls. The 75-foot falls are some of the most powerful in the Canadian national parks. Continue along the Parkway until you reach Sunwapta Falls and view the upper falls. If you have the time and inclination, you can do the short hike to the lower falls. Make the Athabasca Glacier, one of the eight major glaciers making up the Columbia Icefield, your next stop. This incredible icefield covers an area of approximately 325 square km (125 square miles) and is one of the largest accumulations of ice and snow south of the Arctic Circle. Enjoy lunch at the Columbia Icefield Glacier Discovery Centre, and then experience an ice explorer bus tour or a guided hike of the Athabasca Glacier. For safety reasons, do not venture onto the glacier without a guide. Continue driving along the Icefields Parkway and into Banff National Park, passing the Weeping Wall and stopping to stretch your legs at Peyto Lake, the Saskatchewan River Crossing, and scenic Bow Lake, before stopping for the night at Lake Louise.

Day 5: Lake Louise

Spend the morning enjoying the scenery at beautiful Lake Louise, snapping a few pictures of the impressive Victoria Glacier flowing off the mountain at the lake's end. You can enjoy afternoon tea at the classy Fairmont Chateau Lake Louise adjacent to the lake, then ride the Lake Louise Sightseeing Gondola to the Wildlife Interpretive Centre at the top, where you can participate in a guided hike or presentation (or just have a picnic lunch) on an alpine plateau with a view of a dozen-plus glaciers. If time permits, take a drive 40 km (24 miles) west to Yoho National Park and Emerald Lake, where you can rent a canoe, have dinner, or just take a stroll. Afterward, head back to Lake Louise for the night.

Days 6 and 7: Banff National Park

57 km (36 miles) or an hour drive from Lake Louise

Spend the morning of Day 6 exploring the quaint shops and restaurants crammed together on Banff Avenue in the town of Banff. Stop at the Fairmont Banff Springs, a National Historic Site, and stroll the grounds or take a guided horseback ride from the on-site stables. Stop at Bow Falls for a photo-op then finish your day with a late-night dip in the Banff Upper Hot Springs. Spend the next two nights at the gorgeous Fairmont Banff Springs; there are many more affordable lodging options in the park as well.

On your second day in Banff, hike around Vermillion Lakes, off Highway 1. Common wildlife sightings in this wetlands setting include elk, bighorn sheep, muskrats, and the occasional moose. Then hop on the Banff Gondola to enjoy the view from the 7,500-foot summit of Sulphur Mountain. Later on, you can hike the 3-km (1-mile)

trail around Johnson Lake or hit the water in a canoe or kayak.

Day 8: Heading Home

145 km (90 miles), about 1½ hours of driving, from Banff to the Calgary International Airport

The highway is well maintained, but you should give yourself a little extra time if you're traveling in winter. Morning rush-hour traffic in Calgary is typically between 7:30 am and 9:30 am; evening rush-hour traffic is generally between 3:30 pm and 5:30 pm. If you end up with extra time in Calgary, you could visit Heritage Park, TELUS Spark, the Calgary Zoo, or the Glenbow Museum; the city has many excellent attractions. If you want to stick close to the airport, the Hangar Flight Museum and Cross Iron Mills shopping center are both located within a 15-minute drive of the Calgary International Airport.

Winter Fun in Kananaskis, Canmore and Banff, 10 Days

The Canadian Rockies has much to offer not only in summer, but also in winter. Spectacular canyon icewalks, snowshoeing on top of waist-deep snow, stunning frozen waterfalls, and some of the world's best downhill and cross-country skiing can be enjoyed on a winter trip to Kananaskis, Canmore, and Banff. For this itinerary, it's recommended that you fly into and out of Calgary International Airport (YYC). You can rent a car in Calgary or if you're uncomfortable driving on winter roads, use a bus shuttle service to get from the airport to Kananaskis, Canmore, Banff, and Lake Louise.

Day 1: Arrival

117 km (73 miles) or 90-minute drive from Calgary International Airport (YYC)

After you arrive at the Calgary International Airport, head straight to Kananaskis–your base for the next two nights. Book a stay for 2 nights in Kananaskis at the Pomeroy Kananaskis Mountain Lodge near Kananaskis Village.

Day 2: Nakiska Ski Area

There are many ways to experience the beauty of Kananaskis in winter. If you're a downhill skier, you'll want to rise early to take the free shuttle from the Pomeroy Kananaskis Mountain Lodge to nearby Nakiska Ski Area where you can spend the day on the slopes. Built for the 1988 Winter Olympics, the resort has world-class terrain for experienced skiers and snowboarders as well as a wide array of runs and lessons for beginners.

Another option is to head to nearby Boundary Ranch and spend an afternoon

or a full day dogsledding. Or, if you're traveling with children, you could visit the resort's Children's Creative Centre, play at the indoor waterpark, or participate in one of the regularly scheduled family activities. In the evening, you can rent skates and go ice skating on the resort's outdoor skating rink. Make sure you plan time to enjoy a soak in the Pomeroy Kananaskis Mountain Lodge's outdoor hot tub before bed.

Day 3: Explore Kananaskis

121 km (75 miles) or a 75-minute drive from Kananaskis

Make sure you pack up before you head out, as you'll be driving to Canmore after your activities to spend the next two nights. But before you head out, there are a variety of recreational options for your third day. The least strenuous, and some might say most relaxing, option is spending the morning or evening soaking and relaxing in the outdoor pools, saunas, and steam rooms at the Kananaskis Nordic Spa at the Pomeroy Kananaskis Mountain Lodge.

If you're looking for more adventure, head to Kananaskis Village where you can rent cross-country skis, snowshoes, or fat bikes to explore the nearby winter trails. You can also go snow tubing at Nakiska Ski Area or enjoy a winter sleigh ride at Boundary Ranch. After exploring the Kananaskis area, make the drive out to Canmore and spend the night at one of the many accommodations in town.

Day 4 and 5: Canmore

26 km (16 miles) or 25-minute drive from Canmore

Spend your fourth day exploring 60 km (37 miles) of cross-country ski trails at Canmore Nordic Centre Provincial Park, another excellent facility built for the 1988 Winter Olympics. There's a day lodge with equipment rentals, lessons,

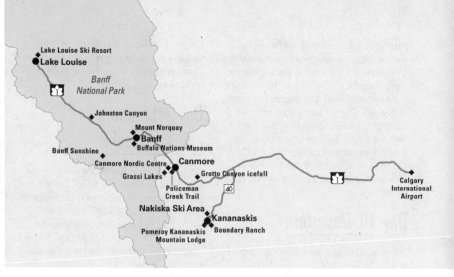

and a cafeteria. If cross-country skiing doesn't appeal to you, spend the day exploring the art galleries and boutique shops that Canmore has to offer and take a winter walk along the scenic Policeman's Creek Boardwalk. You can experience the unique history of this region at the Canmore Museum and Geoscience Centre and the North-West Mounted Police Barracks. In the evening, if you're feeling adventurous, consider trying the chef's surprise three-course tasting menu at The Sensory restaurant for a unique fine dining experience.

On the fifth day, consider a Grotto Canyon icewalk tour with Mahikan Trails or Kananaskis Outfitters. You could also hike to Grassi Lakes (ice cleats and hiking poles recommended in winter) or go dogsledding with Snowy Owl Sled Dog Tours. After your activities, head to Banff to spend the next 4 nights.

Days 6, 7, and 8: Banff

25 km (16 miles) or 25-minute drive from Canmore

Purchase a Ski Big 3 (*www.skibig3. com*) 3-day pass and spend three days experiencing amazing Canadian Rockies skiing at Banff Sunshine, Lake Louise, and Norquay Ski Resorts. Free ski shuttles pick up at most accommodations in Banff.

If you're not into skiing, or just need a break from the slopes, downtown Banff is full of boutique shops, restaurants, and some great après-ski nightlife. You can also enjoy winter hiking, snowshoeing, or a stop at the Buffalo Nations Museum to learn about the local Indigenous Canadians and their history.

Another option is to visit Cave and Basin National Historic Site, the birthplace of Banff National Park. End your day with a rejuvenating soak in the Banff Upper Hot Springs. ■TIP→ **Reservations are not required for the hot springs as they operate on a first-come, first-served basis.**

Day 9: Lake Louise

57 km (35 miles) or a 40-minute drive from Banff

On the drive from Banff to Lake Louise, consider a stop at the Johnston Canyon Trailhead. A short 2.7-km (1.7-mile) hike will take you up catwalks through a towering canyon to see the frozen waterfalls. Ice cleats are recommended in winter. Allow 2-3 hours for this adventure.

After your hike, continue to Lake Louise via the Trans-Canada Highway. Spend the afternoon at Lake Louise skating on the picturesque ice rink. Take some photos of the spectacular life-size frozen ice castle built every year for Ice Magic, an International Ice Carving Competition held in January. Enjoy a sleigh ride around the frozen lake and grab a bite to eat at one of the several delicious restaurants in Chateau Lake Louise before driving back to Banff.

Day 10: Departure

145 km (90 miles) from Banff to Calgary International Airport.

The highway is well maintained, but you should give yourself a little extra time if you're traveling in winter.

■TIP→ **See Day 8 of the Jasper and Banff National Parks itinerary for information about the drive to Calgary or for ideas about what to do in Calgary if you have extra time.**

Calgary–Kananaskis–Banff–Lake Louise–Yoho–Kootenay–Calgary, 8 days

The national parks and protected areas of the Canadian Rockies are vast and full of extraordinary experiences. In this itinerary, you will spend the week exploring the wonderful areas around Kananaskis, Banff, Lake Louise, Yoho National Park, and Kootenay National Park. This itinerary begins and ends in Calgary.

Day 1: Arrival

Arrive in Calgary at the Calgary International Airport (YYC). From the airport, make the 120-km (75-mile) drive to Canmore, Alberta. The drive will take you about one hour and twenty minutes. There are plenty of accommodation options located in the area.

Day 2: Canmore and Kananaskis

Begin your day in Canmore with a stop at the Rocky Mountain Bagel Co. for some delicious house-made bagels and local coffee located just off the Bow Valley Trail. After you are fueled up for the day, drive 40 minutes to the Troll Falls Trailhead by following the Trans-Canada Highway until you reach Kananaskis Trail which will take you to the trail located beside Nakiska Ski Area. The 3.4-km (2.1-mile) round-trip hike gives an excellent glimpse of what Kananaskis Country has to offer. Gaining minimal elevation, you are led through a mystical mountain forest before reaching a spectacular waterfall. After the hike, continue south on Kananaskis Trail for 5 minutes until you reach the Kananaskis Nordic Spa. Stop for a lunch at one of the restaurants at the Pomeroy Kananaskis Mountain Lodge followed by a relaxing afternoon hydrotherapy session at the spa. From here you can either stay at the lovely Kananaskis Mountain lodge for the night or make your way back to Canmore.

Day 3: Banff National Park

From Canmore: 25 km (15 miles) or a 20-minute drive to Banff

From Kananaskis Mountain Lodge: 81 km (50 miles) or an hour drive to Banff.

Start Day 3 by stopping at Lake Minnewanka for a scenic boat cruise. To get here from Banff, head north on Banff Avenue until you reach Lake Minnewanka Scenic Drive. Enjoy the beautiful surroundings before joining the morning cruise. Bonus: kids go free

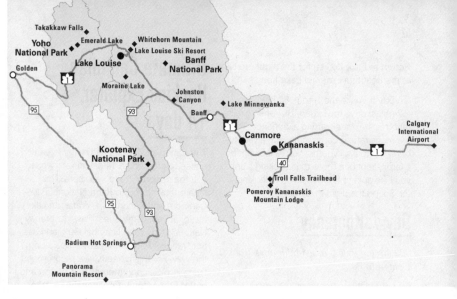

on the morning cruise so this option is great for families. In the afternoon, make your way toward Johnston Canyon via the Bow Valley Parkway. This 5-km (3.1-mile) hike will take you through catwalks below towering canyon walls before reaching two stunning waterfalls. Budget about an hour and a half to get to the Upper Falls or venture 5-km (3.1-miles) farther to the Ink Pots (small vibrant colored ponds), which will take you closer to four hours to return. After your hike, spend the rest of the day exploring the townsite of Banff. Grab dinner at one of the many top-notch restaurants that Banff has to offer.

Day 4: Lake Louise

57 km (35 miles) or a 40-minute drive from Banff

To start off day 4, savor the spectacular view of Lake Louise and the Victoria Glacier and enjoy a coffee or tea with one of the best views in the world. When you're done soaking in the view, hop on the Lake Louise Sightseeing Gondola. The gondola climbs up Whitehorn Mountain and is one of the best (and safest) places to spot wildlife—especially grizzly bears. At the

top, check out the Wildlife Interpretive Centre. Grab a coffee or lunch at one of the restaurants after you return to the base. Later on, take a short drive out to Moraine Lake, another breathtaking spot with equally stunning views. Enjoy a delicious dinner at the Moraine Lake Lodge and watch the sunset before making your way back to Lake Louise for the night.

Days 5 and 6: Yoho National Park

38 km (24 miles) or a 30-minute drive

Leave bright and early on Day 5 as the Emerald Lake parking lot fills up fast. If you are planning to stay at the Emerald Lake Lodge for the night, there is a specific parking lot for hotel guests so parking won't be an issue. Once you arrive at the lake, take a nice walk along the shoreline and enjoy a delicious upscale breakfast at the Mount Burgess Dining Room. Snap some photos before renting a canoe and paddling on the crystal blue waters. Afterward, drive a half-hour to the Takakkaw Falls Trailhead. The 1.3-km (0.8-mile) easy hike has a spectacular reward—views of the second highest waterfall in Canada.

Return to Lake Louise for the night or stay at the beautiful Emerald Lake Lodge.

On Day 6, make the 1-hour, 84-km (52-miles) drive to Golden, BC for an exhilarating white water rafting experience. There are many rafting companies with a variety of rafting tours. Whether you're looking for a family tour or a more thrill-seeking jaunt you'll be able to find what you're looking for. Spend the night in Golden.

Day 7: Kootenay

103 km (64 miles) or a 1-hour drive from Golden to Radium

On your last day, make the drive out to Radium Hot Springs. Soak in the mineral waters of the hot springs in the morning, a must-do experience in Radium. After your relaxing morning, take a 30-minute drive towards Panorama Mountain Resort to do some downhill mountain biking. With many different trails, Panorama provides mountain biking for bikers of all abilities. Return to Radium for the night.

Day 8: Heading Home

277 km (172 miles) or a 3-hour drive to Calgary International Airport from Radium

Remember to give yourself a little extra time if you're traveling in winter and keep in mind rush hour traffic in Calgary (morning between 7:30 and 9:30 am; evening between 3:30 and 5:30 pm).

■ TIP→ **If you have extra time in Calgary, check out Day 8 of the Jasper and Banff National Parks itinerary for some ideas.**

Ultimate Canadian Rockies Explorer, 14 days

The Canadian Rockies has many experiences to offer and a 14-day itinerary gives you the opportunity to see more. This itinerary takes you to Banff National Park, Canmore and Kananaskis, Waterton Lakes National Park, Crowsnest Pass, Kootenay National Park, Yoho National Park, and Jasper National Park with many stops along the way. For this itinerary, we recommend flying into Calgary International Airport and out of Edmonton International Airport to save having to backtrack.

Day 1 and 2: Banff

129 km (80 miles) or about an hour-and-a-half from the Calgary International Airport

Arrive at the Calgary International Airport then head straight to Banff National Park. Watch for wildlife and enjoy the mountain views along the way. Take an evening dip in Banff Upper Hot Springs before settling into your accommodation for the night.

Spend your first morning in Banff exploring Banff Avenue. Pick up a famous Beavertail pastry while perusing the fun shops on Banff's main drag. In the afternoon, play a round of golf at the renowned Banff Springs Golf Course or catch the Banff Gondola up Sulphur Mountain to enjoy an incredible view of the town.

Day 3: Canmore, AB

25 km (15 miles) from Banff or a 20-min-ute drive

Pick up a picnic lunch in Banff and then drive to the Grassi Lakes Trailhead near Canmore. This 4.3-km (2.7-mile) return hike leads to two beautiful lakes. Watch rock climbers above the lakes while you enjoy lunch. Afterward, head to Canmore Nordic Centre Provincial Park where you can rent mountain bikes and enjoy a leisurely ride or some single-track excite-ment, depending on your riding level. After dinner in town, take a walk along the Policeman's Creek Boardwalk. Spend the night in Canmore, Alberta.

Days 4-6: Waterton Lakes National Park, AB

349 km (217 miles) or a 4-hour drive from Canmore

A long drive takes you from Canmore to Waterton along the Cowboy Trail. If you have time, make a stop at Bar U Ranch National Historic Site of Canada near Longview to learn about Alberta's ranching history. If you're a *Heartland* fan, you may want to take a short detour into High River to visit Maggie's Diner and the local museum. You'll be spending the next three nights in Waterton Lakes National Park. After arriving, rent a surrey bike or an e-bike from Pat's and explore the townsite. Be sure to stop at Cameron Falls, the park's most accessible waterfall.

The next day, pick up a picnic lunch and catch the boat to the Crypt Lake Trailhead. One of Canada's most spectacular hikes, this 17-km (10.6-mile) hike is an experi-ence like no other. With four waterfalls, a cave to be crossed, and a stunning moun-tain lake, your day will be well spent.

On your final day in Waterton, take a morning scenic boat cruise into the USA.

Upper Waterton Lake is situated on the international border and this unique expe-rience allows you to cross the border without a passport. In the afternoon, take a hike up the popular Bear's Hump trail. The short and steep 2.4-km (1.5-mile) trail leads to one of the best views in the Canadian Rockies.

Day 7: Radium, B.C.

392 km (244 miles) or a 4 1/2-hour drive

The longest drive on your trip takes you from Waterton to Radium through the Crowsnest Pass. There are many great stops along this route including Lundbreck Falls, the Burmis Tree, and Frank Slide Interpretive Centre. Stretch your legs on the Star Creek Falls trail. When you arrive in Radium, take a dip in the soothing mineral waters of Radi-um Hot Springs. Be sure to take in the view of the Kootenay River meeting the

Columbia River at the Kootenay Valley Viewpoint. Overnight in Radium.

Day 8: Golden, B.C.

103 km (64 miles) or a 1-hour drive from Radium

Spend a morning whitewater rafting the Kicking Horse River near Golden, BC. There are many tour operators in the area with varying options for all rafting abilities from beginner to advanced. You can spend the afternoon at Kicking Horse Mountain Resort. Ride the Gondola up and enjoy the views, check out the Via Ferrata, go mountain biking, or visit Boo the Bear at the Grizzly Bear Refuge. Enjoy dinner at the top of the mountain at Eagle's Eye Restaurant, Canada's highest restaurant. Overnight in Golden.

Day 9: Lake O'Hara, B.C.

82 km (51 miles) or a 1 1/2-hour drive from Golden

Plan ahead, and book the morning day shuttle to Lake O'Hara. Note that the shuttle fills up fast and is a random draw reservation system, so significant planning (and sometimes luck) is required to secure this reservation. If you're able to get a reservation on the day bus, bring your hiking gear as there's an excellent trail system surrounding the lake. Whether you prefer an easy hike along the shoreline of Lake O'Hara or a more technical hike up to a viewpoint such as the Opabin Plateau Circuit, Lake O'Hara has something to offer all abilities and the view speaks for itself. If you can't secure a spot on the day shuttle, consider splurging on an overnight stay at Lake O'Hara Lodge, which has its own shuttle. Alternatively, spend the night at an accommodation along the Bow Valley Parkway.

Day 10: Moraine Lake and Lake Louise

38 km (28 miles) or 1 hour and 15 minutes from Lake O'Hara

Head to Moraine Lake in the early morning to get a spot as the parking lot fills up fast; you can also book a spot on the Parks Canada shuttle bus. Grab a coffee or tea and snap some photos of this vibrantly colored lake. Walk along the Rockpile Trail to reach a phenomenal viewpoint. After spending the morning taking in the views at Moraine Lake, head northwest on Moraine Lake Road to Lake Louise. At Lake Louise, walk along the lakeshore trail until you see the trailhead for Lake Agnes Teahouse. The 7.4-km (4.6-mi) moderately steep return hike will take you to a secluded teahouse on a beautiful mountain lake. Spend your afternoon sipping tea and appreciating the wonderful view. Afterward, spend some time taking photos and admiring the view at Lake Louise before spending the night at the Fairmont Chateau Lake Louise or another accommodation in the area.

Day 11: Icefields Parkway to Jasper

231 km (143 miles) or a 3-hour drive from Lake Louise

This scenic drive is one of the best in the world and has many spectacular stops along the way. From Lake Louise, head north along Highway 93 for 45 km (28 miles) or a half-hour until you reach Peyto Lake. Stop and stretch your legs with a short walk down to a terrific view of the impossibly blue lake. Continue north for another 90 km (56 miles) until you reach the Glacier Skywalk. Take a walk along the spectacular glass-floored walkway before continuing on the parkway. Stop at Tangle Falls before continuing on to Jasper where you will spend the next three nights. If time permits, consider stopping for a hike along the Icefields Parkway. Top picks include Beauty Creek to Stanley Falls, Parker Ridge, or Wilcox Pass trails.

Days 12 and 13: Jasper

Spend your first morning in Jasper exploring the townsite. Stop at the Jasper Information Centre for trail maps and take a walk down the historic main street. In the afternoon, take a boat cruise on Maligne Lake out to the famous Spirit Island and learn about the history, geology, wildlife, and ecology of the area. Spend the evening relaxing in the nearby Miette Hot Springs and grabbing a bite to eat at one of the many renowned Jasper restaurants.

On the morning of your last day, take a ride up the Jasper Skytram. The seven-minute ride will zip you up the mountainside to enjoy spectacular views of the Jasper area. After a short, but steep, hike to the true summit, enjoy a bite to eat at Summit Restaurant or bring your own picnic and enjoy it with a view. Visit Pyramid Lake in the afternoon and enjoy the short hike to Pyramid Island or rent a canoe and paddle the lake. In the evening, go on a wildlife-watching tour where knowledgeable guides will take you to the best areas for spotting wildlife.

Day 14: Heading Home

391 km (243 miles) or a four-hour drive to the Edmonton International Airport (YEG) from Jasper

The highway is well maintained, but you should allow yourself extra time and drive slower if you are traveling in winter. Morning rush-hour traffic in Edmonton is typically between 7:30 am and 9:30 am; evening rush-hour traffic is usually between 3:30 pm and 5:30 pm on weekdays. If you end up with time to kill at Edmonton International Airport, there's a huge outlet mall called Premium Outlet Collection Edmonton International Airport a short 5-minute drive from the airport. Free on-airport transit shuttles provide hop-on/hop-off service from the airport to the shopping center every half-hour between 5:30 am and 10:30 pm daily; the free shuttle picks up at door 8 on the Arrivals level. At the mall, the shuttle leaves from Entrance 2.

Chapter 4

BANFF
NATIONAL PARK

4

By
Debbie Olsen

🏕 Camping
★★★★★

🏨 Hotels
★★★★★

🏃 Activities
★★★★★

👁 Scenery
★★★★★

👥 Crowds
★★★★★

WELCOME TO BANFF NATIONAL PARK

TOP REASONS TO GO

★ **Scenery:** Visitors are often unprepared for the sheer scale of the Canadian Rockies. Scattered between the peaks are glaciers, forests, valleys, meadows, rivers, and the bluest lakes on the planet.

★ **Spectacular ski slopes:** The light, dry, airy powder in the Canadian Rockies is legendary and more than 8,000 acres of skiing and riding terrain at three ski resorts can be accessed with a single SkiBig3 lift ticket.

★ **Trails galore:** More than 1,600 km (1,000 miles) of defined hiking trails lead to scenic lakes, alpine meadows, glaciers, forests, and deep canyons.

★ **Banff Upper Hot Springs:** Relax in naturally hot mineral springs as you watch snowflakes swirl around you, or gaze at the stars as you "take the waters" on a cool summer's evening.

★ **Icefields Parkway:** One of the most scenic drives on the continent, this 230-km (143-mile) roadway links Banff and Jasper.

1 Banff Townsite. The hub of the park is the place to find shops, restaurants, hotels, and other facilities. Highlights include the Banff Visitor Centre, Whyte Museum, Banff Centre, Upper Hot Springs Pool, Banff Gondola, and the fingerlike rock formations known as hoodoos.

2 Lake Louise, Moraine Lake, and the Bow Valley Parkway. Backed by snowcapped mountains and fantastically ice-blue, Lake Louise is one of the most photographed bodies of water in the world. It along with Moraine Lake, the Valley of the Ten Peaks, and stunning Johnston Canyon are highlights of this region.

3 Icefields Parkway. Some of the most striking scenery in Banff National Park, if not the entire continent, is along the Icefields Parkway (Highway 93), which runs 230 km (143 miles) north from the village of Lake Louise, connecting Banff and Jasper national parks. There are scenic stops and attractions in both parks, but noteworthy Banff-section diversions include Bow Lake, Bow Glacier Falls, Crowfoot Glacier, Bow Summit and Peyto Lake.

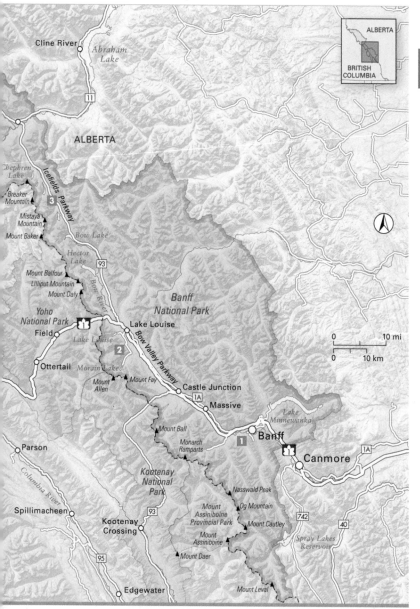

Comparing mountains is a subjective business, yet few would deny that the Canadian Rockies are among the most extravagantly beautiful ranges on Earth. The vast Rocky Mountain expanse in this, Canada's first national park, not only has snowcapped peaks, but also glaciers, lakes, valleys, hot springs, and wildlife—including an abundance of deer and elk.

There's a human side to Banff's story, too. Indigenous peoples lived and hunted in the foothills and forests of the Rocky Mountains since ancient times; the park is located on Treaty 7 lands and is in the traditional territory of the Blackfoot, Stoney, Tsuut'ina, Ktunaxa, Maskwacis, Mountain Cree clan of Peechee, the Dene, and the Métis. Most of the mountains and lakes had Indigenous names long before they were "discovered" by European explorers, and the Bow River, which flows through the park and was used for travel, hunting, and fishing, is called Makhabn in the Blackfoot language, which means "river where the bow reeds grow." The land was considered a sacred place because of the region's natural, healing hot springs and many medicinal plants.

In 1883, after three Canadian Pacific Railway workers came upon the springs, a dispute over their ownership ensued, prompting the Canadian government to protect the springs by establishing Canada's first national park (and the third such park in the world) in 1885. The park reserve was enlarged and renamed the Rocky Mountain Parks of Canada in 1887. Its name was changed to Banff—after a Canadian Pacific Railway station, which was itself named after the Banffshire region of Scotland—when the National Parks Act came into effect in 1930.

Unlike some other national parks, Banff was developed as a tourism destination first and foremost. The government and others recognized that visitors would be eager to visit Cave and Basin hot springs and take in the surrounding beauty of the park. The town of Banff was settled soon after the park was established, and the Canadian Pacific Railway quickly began construction on the Banff Springs Hotel, which opened in 1888. It wasn't long before the area was being promoted as an international resort and spa.

Over the years, Banff National Park has continued to attract people for many of the same reasons that drew the first visitors. Rugged mountains, stunning blue lakes, icefields, massive glaciers, wildlife, and natural hot springs make the park unique in the world. This was confirmed in 1984 when Banff National Park was

AVG. HIGH/LOW TEMPS. IN CELSIUS					
Jan.	Feb.	Mar.	Apr.	May	June
-4/-15	0/-11	4/-8	9/-1	14/2	19/6
July	Aug.	Sept.	Oct.	Nov.	Dec.
22/7	22/7	16/3	10/-1	1/-8	-6/-14

AVG. HIGH/LOW TEMPS. IN FAHRENHEIT					
Jan.	Feb.	Mar.	Apr.	May	June
22/5	32/12	39/18	48/30	58/35	66/42
July	Aug.	Sept.	Oct.	Nov.	Dec.
71/45	71/44	61/37	50/30	33/17	22/7

4

included in the Canadian Rocky Mountain Parks UNESCO World Heritage Site, a recognition of its "striking mountain landscape" and "exceptional natural beauty."

Planning

When to Go

Banff National Park is an all-seasons destination. Visit in summer to hike the mountain trails, or go in winter to enjoy some of the world's best skiing. Millions of people visit Banff every year, with the vast majority traveling during July and August, the warmest and driest months.

■ TIP→ **If you can, visit in late spring or early fall when prices are lower, the crowds smaller, and the temperatures usually still comfortable.**

The downside to an off-season visit is the fact that you miss the summer interpretive programs and the wildflowers that reach their peak from early July to mid-August. Nevertheless, both of the park's information centers are open all year, with extended hours during the summer months.

FESTIVALS AND EVENTS

Canada Day. Admission to the national park is free on this July 1 holiday, and big celebrations take place in Canmore and Banff that include parades, fireworks, and live music. *www.banff.com.*

Lake Louise WonderFall. Part of the magic of the Canadian Rockies is seeing magnificent stands of larch trees glistening golden on a crisp autumn afternoon. WonderFall celebrates this season with special discount packages, larch hikes, photography workshops, and other special activities. *www.bannfflakelouise.com.*

Santa Claus Parade of Lights & Festive Fun. Banff welcomes the holiday season in early December with a day of events that include photo ops with Santa in Central Park, craft shows, children's ice-carving stations, and an evening parade of lights. On Christmas Day, Santa shows off his downhill skills at the three area ski resorts. *www.bannfflakelouise.com.*

SnowDays. A highlight of this month-long winter celebration is the Ice Magic International Ice Carving Competition, which features world-class ice-carving and outdoor events. The festivities begin in early January and also include a snow sculpture competition, exclusive culinary offerings, a skijoring exhibition, and a play zone for kids. *www.bannfflakelouise.com/snowdays.*

Banff National Park in One Day

Start with a visit to the **Banff Visitor Centre** to pick up maps and information about the major sites. Buy lunch provisions, and drive to beautiful **Lake Louise.** Walk the flat shoreline trail, and venture upward along the **Lake Agnes Trail** to the teahouse (or turn back once you get a lofty view of Lake Louise). On the drive back to Banff Townsite, stop at Johnston Canyon, and allow an hour for the easy round-trip hike to the dramatic lower waterfall. Have dinner at one of Banff's many amazing restaurants. Afterward, explore the shops downtown, and then end the day with a dip in the **Banff Upper Hot Springs.**

Summer Events at the Banff Centre. The center's summer cultural-events lineup, a Banff staple for more than four decades, includes film screenings, visual-arts displays, theater, opera, dance, literary readings, lectures, and musical productions. There's a charge for some events, but many are free or "pay what you can." *www.banffcentre.ca.*

Getting Here and Around

Banff National Park, in west-central Alberta, is 128 km (80 miles) west of Calgary, 401 km (249 miles) southwest of Edmonton, and 850 km (528 miles) east of Vancouver.

AIR

The closest international airports are in Calgary (YYC) and Edmonton (YEG).

Major airlines serve both airports.

The quickest, but not cheapest, way to get from Edmonton Airport to Banff National Park is to fly, which costs C$400–C$800 and takes about 3 hours.

BUS

The towns of Banff and Lake Louise have transit systems. Public buses run between Canmore, Banff, and Lake Louise, and a wintertime ski shuttle transports guests at most Banff area hotels to the park's three ski resorts. The Brewster Express, the Banff Airporter, and Discover Banff Tours offer bus transportation that connects Calgary's airport with Kananaskis, Banff, Lake Louise, and Jasper.

BUS CONTACT INFORMATION Banff Airporter. ✉ *141 Eagle Crescent, Banff* ☎ *888/449–2901* ⊕ *banffairporter.com.* **Brewster Express.** ✉ *100 Gopher St., Banff* ☎ *403/762–6700, 866/606–6700 toll-free* ⊕ *www.banffjaspercollection.com/brewster-express.* **Discover Banff Tours Airport Shuttle.** ✉ *215 Banff Ave., Banff* ☎ *877/565–9372 toll-free, 403/760–5007* ⊕ *www.bannftours.com.*

CAR

The easiest way to get from Calgary to Banff is by car on Trans-Canada Highway 1; the drive is less than two hours. Use Icefields Parkway (Highway 93) to get from Jasper to Banff. Car-rental agencies operate at Edmonton and Calgary airports and in Canmore, Banff, Lake Louise, and Jasper. Banff Townsite and Lake Louise have local taxi companies.

If you're driving from Edmonton airport, expect to be in the car for about 4 hours.

Inspiration

River of No Return: Banff's Bow Falls is featured in this classic 1954 film starring Marilyn Monroe and Robert Mitchum. Directed by Otto Preminger, this Western movie is about a widower, his son, and a saloon singer on a journey down a raging river.

Canadian Rockies: Rediscovered and *Summits and Starlight: The Canadian Rockies* will inspire you with Rocky Mountain scenery; both books are by Paul Zizka, an award-winning mountain landscape and adventure photographer who is based in Banff.

The End of the Line, by Stephen Legault, weaves Canadian history into a murder mystery that is set in the winter of 1884, when the Canadian Pacific Railway Company was working to complete its transcontinental railway through the Canadian Rockies.

A Jazz Guide to Banff and the Universe, by Mike Lauchlan and Jerry Auld, is a fun thriller that is set in the town of Banff and combines strong visuals, fascinating history, jazz, and cosmology.

*Legends of the Fall:*The funeral and cemetery scenes in this 1993 academy award-winning film were shot along the Bow River near Banff. The film was directed by Edward Zwick and starred Brad Pitt, Anthony Hopkins, Aidan Quinn, Julia Ormond, and Henry Thomas.

These Mountains are Our Sacred Places: The Story of the Stoney People, by Chief John Snow, is a fascinating account of the Stoney People before and after the signing of Treaty 7 in 1877; it's a great way to learn more about Indigenous history, tradition, and culture in the Canadian Rockies.

Park Essentials

ACCESSIBILITY
Both visitor information centers are fully accessible. Many campgrounds are wheelchair accessible, as are several trails, and Banff Transit operates one fully accessible shuttle. For the specifics on accessible campgrounds and trails, call the information center at *403/762–1550.*

PARK FEES AND PERMITS
■ TIP→ **All prices in this chapter are in Canadian dollars, unless stated otherwise.**

A park entrance pass costs C$10 per person or C$20 per vehicle per day for up to seven people. Children and youths age 17 and under get into Canada's national parks for free. An annual pass costs C$69.19 per adult or C$139.40 per family or group. Larger buses and vans pay a group commercial rate. If you're staying a week or more, your best bet is an annual pass.

Permits are required for backcountry camping and some other activities. Back-country camping permits (C$10.02 per person per night) can be booked online (*reserve.albertaparks.ca*) or by phone (*877/537–2757*). There is a reservation fee (C$11.96). Fishing permits (C$9.80 per day) are available at the park visitor information center and at some campgrounds. In most cases, a fire permit is included in your camping fees, but check with campground staff.

PARK HOURS
The park, open 24/7 year-round, is in the Mountain Time Zone.

CELL PHONE RECEPTION
Although sometimes unpredictable, cell service is fairly good near Banff Townsite. Public telephones can be found at the information centers, at most hotels and bars, and at several key spots around both Banff Lake Louise.

Hotels

The eclectic accommodations lineup in Banff includes historic mountain resorts, supremely luxurious hotels, quaint inns, roadside motels, and even some backcountry lodges without electricity or running water. Most lodgings do not have meal plans, though some offer breakfast.

With just a few exceptions, room rates are highest from mid-June to late

September and between Christmas and New Year's. In many cases, the best rates can be found from October to mid-November and from May to mid-June.

More accommodations can be found just outside the park in Canmore and in Kananaskis Country, a large, multiuse, provincial recreation area.

Hotel reviews have been shortened. For full information, visit Fodors.com.

Restaurants

More than 100 restaurants operate in Banff National Park, and they range from fast-food outlets to award-winning fine-dining establishments. Trout, venison, elk, moose, and bison appear on the menus of even the most modest eateries. It's best to make reservations at popular places, especially during the peak summer and ski seasons. As at most national parks, prices are slightly inflated. Except for the fanciest spots, casual dress is the norm. Many restaurants offer takeout service.

Restaurant reviews have been shortened. For full information, visit Fodors.com.

What It Costs in Canadian Dollars			
$	$$	$$$	$$$$
RESTAURANTS			
under C$25	C$25–C$30	C$31–C$35	over C$35
HOTELS			
under C$250	C$250–C$300	C$301–C$350	over C$350

Tours

Alpine Helicopters
Helicopter sightseeing, heli-hiking, and even heli-weddings in and around Canmore and Banff are this company's specialty. Note: You must provide your own transportation to the heliport in Canmore. ⊠ *91 Bow Valley Tr., Canmore* ☎ *403/678–4802* ⊕ *www.alpinehelicopter.com* ⊠ *From C$200.*

Banff Adventures
Book almost any type of tour with this Banff-based tour company. They offer a wide variety of tours in summer and winter and they can arrange tour packages for multiple activities including cycling, canoeing and skiing. ⊠ *211 Bear St., Banff* ☎ *800/664–8888 toll-free, 403/762–4554* ⊕ *www.banffadventures.com* ⊠ *from C$37.*

CMH
This company offers multiday heli-skiing, heli-hiking, glacier-climbing, and other adventures with accommodations in remote mountain lodges. ⊠ *217 Bear St., Banff* ☎ *403/762–7100, 800/661–0252* ⊕ *www.canadianmountainholidays.com* ⊠ *From C$2,900.*

Discover Banff Tours
A wide variety of group and private tours can be booked in summer and winter through this Banff-based company. They offer everything from wildlife and scenery viewing to ghost tours, caving and icewalks. ⊠ *215 Banff Ave., Banff* ☎ *403/760–5007, 877/565–9372 toll-free* ⊕ *www.banfftours.com* ⊠ *from C$42.*

Kingmik Dog Sled Tours
Minutes from the village of Lake Louise, this is the only company that offers dog sled tours inside Banff National Park. Tours vary in length from 30 minutes to a full-day. Some include transportation from Banff hotels. ⊠ *16430 Hwy. 1A, Lake Louise* ☎ *855/482–4592* ⊕ *kingmikdogsledtours.com* ☞ *from C$250.*

Pursuit Adventure Centres
The Banff Gondola, Lake Minnewanka cruise and open top bus tours operate in Banff National Park and are run by this company. They also have adventures in Jasper and Golden. The company also owns several Banff area hotels. You can book tours on their website, over the

phone, or at one of the Pursuit Adventure Centres in Banff. There are several locations. ✉ *333 Banff Ave., Banff* ☎ *403/760–3291, 866/606–6700 toll-free* ⊕ *www.banffjaspercollection.com* 🚋 *from C$52.*

Rockies Heli Canada
Helicopter tours in Banff, Lake Louise, and Jasper, including the Columbia Icefield, are conducted by this company, which also arranges heli-camping, hiking, yoga, and horseback-riding trips. ✉ *20 Cline River Heliport Hwy. #11, Banff* ☎ *403/721–2100, 888/844–3514* ⊕ *www.rockiesheli.com* 🚋 *From C$199.*

SkiBig3
SkiBig3 works in conjunction with all three ski resorts within Banff National Park, so its lift tickets (C$354 for three days) are valid at Banff Sunshine, Lake Louise Ski Resort, and Mt. Norquay. SkiBig3 also provides vacation-planning services, including discounted ski-and-stay packages with accommodation partners in Banff and Lake Louise. In addition, its guided adventures pair you with a certified snow pro who provides inside knowledge of the ski resorts as well as ski tips and advice. ✉ *215 Banff Ave., Suite 207, Banff* ☎ *403/762–4561* ⊕ *www.skibig3.com.*

White Mountain Adventures
Daily guided hikes, ATV-assisted hiking, heli-hiking and guided e-bike tours can be arranged through this outfitter. In winter, you can try snowshoeing or a guided ice walk. ✉ *202 Bear St., Banff* ☎ *403/760–4403, 800/408–0005* ⊕ *www.whitemountainadventures.com* 🚋 *From C$89.*

Visitor Information

The visitor information centers in Banff Townsite and the village of Lake Louise are jointly operated by Parks Canada and Banff and Lake Louise Tourism, though each organization has its own website with useful pretrip planning information.

On the ground, Parks Canada staff can assist with park information, maps, brochures, permits, and backcountry reservations, as well as updates on weather, trail, and road conditions. Be sure to check out the interpretive exhibits and inquire about current park programs. Tourism-board staff can provide information not only on accommodations, restaurants, tour operators, and other businesses in and around the park, but also on community festivals and events.

Visitors receive a copy of the *Banff Visitor Guide* upon entering the park. The guide contains several maps, along with information about points of interest, safety, programs and events, camping, and fees. To view it ahead of your trip, visit the Parks Canada website.

PARK CONTACT INFORMATION Banff and Lake Louise Tourism. ✉ *Banff* ☎ *877/762–8421 toll free* ⊕ *www.banfflakelouise.com.* **Banff National Park - Parks Canada.** ✉ *Banff* ☎ *403/762–1550* ⊕ *www.pc.gc.ca/banff.*

Banff Townsite

126 km (78 miles) west of Calgary, 25 km (15.5 miles) west of Canmore, 288 km (179 miles) southeast of town of Jasper.

The hub of the park, Banff Townsite, not only has plenty of outfitters, tour operators, and other amenities to help you explore the park, but it also has a performing arts center, museums, shops, and some of the best restaurants and hotels in Canada. Get your bearings at the Banff Visitor Centre; get oriented with a bird's-eye view of the area aboard a gondola or chairlift; and then get out into the park, perhaps hiking past a waterfall to meadows and woods or taking advantage of world-class downhill skiing at nearby Mt. Norquay or Banff Sunshine Village. Time relaxing in the waters of the historic Banff Upper Hot Springs is a great way to cap off an active day or two—or three.

◉ Sights

HISTORIC SITES

Banff Park Museum National Historic Site

HISTORIC SIGHT | A remarkable 1903 building made chiefly of Douglas-fir log houses one of western Canada's oldest natural history museums. From bees to bears, the collection, whose origins date to Chicago's fabled World's Columbian Exposition of 1893, encompasses more than 5,000 historical botanical and zoological specimens, many of them quite striking. In addition to providing the opportunity to get up close and personal with some of Banff's largest mammals—a grizzly bear, bison, mountain goats, and bighorn sheep among them—this unique museum offers a window into past generations' priorities regarding the natural world. ⊠ *91 Banff Ave., at Bow River Bridge, Banff National Park* ☎ *403/762–1558* ⊕ *pc.gc.ca/banffparkmuseum* ⊡ *C$4.25.*

Banff Upper Hot Springs

HOT SPRING | **FAMILY** | Discovered in 1884, Banff's hot, natural mineral springs were the impetus for the development of Canada's first national park. Early Banff visitors came primarily to experience the "healing waters"—something you can still do today at the popular Banff Upper Hot Springs pools. The waters at the facility, which is child-friendly during the day (think family swimming pool rather than couples' hot-tub vibe), are especially inviting on a dull, cold day or when it's snowing, and the views of the mountains are spectacular. You can rent lockers, bathing suits (circa 1920s or modern), and towels. Although the recommended limit for a soak is 20 minutes, you'll likely want to stay an hour or two. It's a short uphill walk from the parking lot to the springs. ⊠ *1 Mountain Ave., Banff National Park* ⊹ *3 km (2 miles) south of downtown* ☎ *800/767–1611* ⊕ *www.pc.gc.ca/en/voyage-travel/promotion/sources-springs/banff* ⊡ *C$8.48.*

Buffalo Nations Luxton Museum

MUSEUM VILLAGE | Founded in 1953, this museum is one of Alberta's oldest. Its goal is to educate visitors on First Nations' cultures. The museum displays Indigenous artifacts, hunting equipment, ornamental regalia, and arts and crafts. There's also a decorated teepee to explore. ⊠ *1 Birch Ave, Banff* ☎ *403/762 2388* ⊕ *www.buffalonationsmuseum.com* ⊡ *C$10.*

★ Cave and Basin National Historic Site

NOTABLE BUILDING | **FAMILY** | This site commemorates the birthplace of Canada's national parks system, which began with the protection of the Banff hot springs in 1885. You'll find restored historic buildings, a plaza, and splendid interpretive displays about Banff and the country's other national parks. An interpretive trail explains the area's geology, plant life, wildlife, and history. While walking past the cave's pools, keep an eye out for the park's most endangered species: the Banff Springs snail, which makes its home in the warm mineral waters, cannot be found anywhere else in the world. Children under age 17 enter the site for free, and combo tickets that include admission to Banff Upper Hot Springs are available. ⊠ *311 Cave Ave., 2 km (1 mile) west of downtown, Banff National Park* ☎ *403/762–1566* ⊕ *www.pc.gc.ca/cave* ⊡ *C$7.90.*

Fairmont Banff Springs

HOTEL | Banff's architectural showpiece and a National Historic Site, this hotel south of downtown is easily recognized by its castlelike exterior. Heritage Hall, a small museum above the Grand Lobby, has exhibits describing the hotel's history. On guided tours you can learn additional details about the local area, the hotel's grand opening in 1888, the 1920s fire that destroyed the original structure, subsequent construction, and the many illustrious guests who have stayed here. ⊠ *405 Spray Ave., 2 km (1 mile) south of downtown, Banff National Park*

The "healing waters" of Banff Upper Hot Springs pools are worth a visit, especially after a day spent outdoors.

☎ 403/762–2211, 800/441–1414 ⊕ www. fairmont.com/banff-springs 🖾 Hotel and museum free; tours free for hotel guests, C$15 for nonguests.

Sulphur Mountain Weather Station & Cosmic Ray Station

HISTORIC SIGHT | The small, stone weather station, a recognized heritage building, sits on top of an exposed ridge at the peak of Sulphur Mountain. It was built in 1902 and Norman Sanson was in charge of the weather station from 1902–1945. He summited the peak more than a thousand times in all seasons and his weather reports were published in the Banff newspaper under the pseudonym "Seer Altitudinous." He was 84 years old when he retired from the job and the peak was renamed Sanson's Peak in his honor in 1948. Nearby is a concrete foundation and a bronze plaque recognizing Sulphur Mountain Cosmic Ray Station National Historic Site. Between 1957 and 1978, geophysicists studied cosmic rays and space particles entering the atmosphere from the station on top of Sulphur Mountain. Today you can hike up as Sanson did, or ride the gondola. 🖾 Sulphur Mountain Weather Station, Banff National Park.

Whyte Museum of the Canadian Rockies

OTHER MUSEUM | Founded by the late Peter and Catharine Whyte, two Banff artists, this museum exhibits artworks, artifacts, and other items relating to the cultural heritage of the Canadian Rockies. Many of the earliest photos of Banff National Park can be found here, either on the walls or in the archives. 🖾 111 Bear St., Banff ☎ 403/762–2291 ⊕ www. whyte.org 🖾 C$10.

PICNIC AREAS
Banff Central Park

OTHER ATTRACTION | Located along the Bow River inside the town of Banff, this scenic park has picnic tables, a gazebo, restrooms, and a natural playground for children. A paved footpath winds alongside the river. 🖾 110 Bear St., Banff.

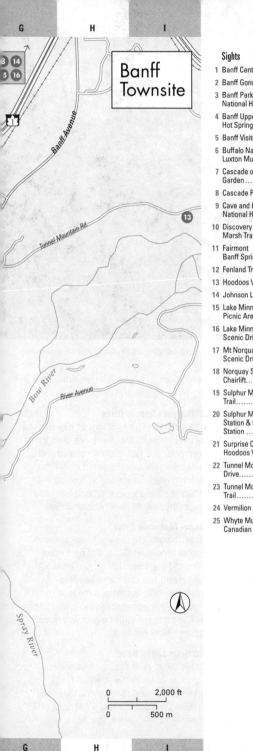

Banff Townsite

0   2,000 ft

0   500 m

The eight-minute ride to the top of Sulphur Mountain in the Banff Gondola is a fun family-friendly experience.

Cascade Ponds

OTHER ATTRACTION | This spot has picnic tables, a kitchen shelter, and flush toilets, and it's one of the only picnic areas with fire pits. There's also access to trails, swimming in the summer, and plenty of room for kids to run around. ⊠ *Banff National Park* ✛ *Off Lake Minnewanka Rd.*

Lake Minnewanka Picnic Area

OTHER ATTRACTION | **FAMILY** | A popular spot, this area has picnic shelters, tables, flush toilets, fire rings, and fireplaces. Hike, rent a boat, or try your luck at fishing. ⊠ *Banff National Park* ✛ *10 km (6 miles) from Banff on Minnewanka Loop.*

SCENIC DRIVES

Lake Minnewanka Scenic Drive

SCENIC DRIVE | It's easy to spend the day along this 25-km (15-mile) loop. Traveling clockwise, you can explore Lower Bankhead and Upper Bankhead, an abandoned coal mine and mining community. Just 3 km (2 miles) farther you come to Lake Minnewanka, the park's largest lake. Boat and fishing rentals are available. Still farther along are more lakes and picnic areas. ⊠ *Lake Minnewanka Scenic Dr., Banff National Park.*

Mt Norquay Scenic Drive

SCENIC DRIVE | The highlight of this 6½-km (4-mile) route is the viewpoint over Banff from near the top. Bighorn sheep and mule deer are often sighted along the twisting road. Trailheads at the top lead to Stoney Squaw Summit and Cascade Amphitheatre. ⊠ *Banff National Park.*

Tunnel Mountain Drive

SCENIC DRIVE | On the east side of Banff, Tunnel Mountain Drive makes a scenic 5-km (3-mile) loop. It's closed in winter, but just off the drive, the **hoodoos**—fingerlike rock formations created by erosion—are accessible year-round (signs on Banff's main street direct you there). ⊠ *Banff National Park.*

Vermilion Lakes Road

SCENIC DRIVE | Off the Trans-Canada Highway close to the town of Banff, this 4.3 km (2.7 mile) roadway passes the tranquil Vermilion Lakes, a network of marshlands and lakes. The lakes have wonderful views of Mount Rundle and Sulphur Mountain and they are a popular spot for picnicking, paddling, relaxing, and reflection photography. It's also common to spot birds and other wildlife in this area. The road is quiet and it's a good place to ride a bike. The 2-km (1.2-mile) Fenland Trail is a lovely walk through the marshlands near the Vermilion Lakes. In some seasons, insect repellant is a must. ⊠ *Banff National Park* ⊹ *Take Mt. Norquay Rd. northeast of Banff and turn east onto Vermillion Lakes Rd. just prior to exit for Trans-Canada Hwy. (Hwy. 1).*

SCENIC STOPS

Banff Gondola

VIEWPOINT | FAMILY | Views during the steep eight-minute ride to and from the 7,500-foot summit of Sulphur Mountain are spectacular in the enclosed four-person gondolas. From the upper terminal, you can hike the short distance to the mountain's true summit on the South East Ridge Trail, perhaps catching sight of grazing bighorn sheep. You can also visit the gift shop, enjoy a quick bite at the cafe, or indulge in a gourmet lunch or dinner at the Sky Bistro. Be sure to walk the easy 1-km (0.6-mile) boardwalk to the Sulphur Mountain Weather Observatory on Sanson's Peak for excellent views and to break away from the crowds. The gondola is south of the center of Banff; you can catch a Roam public transit bus to get here. Riding the gondola is a very popular activity—go early or late to avoid crowds. ⊠ *1 Mountain Ave., 3 km (2 miles) south of downtown, Banff* ☎ *403/762–2523, 866/756–1904* ⊕ *www.banffjaspercollection.com/attractions/banff-gondola* ⊡ *C$56 round-trip.*

Cascade of Time Garden

GARDEN | This four-acre park was built in the 1930s and showcases gardens terraced into a hillside, water features, pavilions, gazebos, and more. The park is behind the administration building, a short walk from downtown Banff. It blooms from late June to early September and is a great place for a picnic or a short escape from the busy downtown area. ⊠ *101 Mountain Ave., Banff* ⊡ *Free.*

Hoodoos Viewpoint

VIEWPOINT | A scenic view of the rocky spires known as hoodoos can be seen from this viewpoint 3.2 km (2 miles) up Tunnel Mountain Road. If you want to get closer to the hoodoos, you can hike along the trail that leaves from the viewpoint. ⊠ *Hoodoos Viewpoint, Improvement District No. 9, Banff* ⊹ *3.2 km (2 miles) up Tunnel Mountain Rd.*

Johnson Lake

BODY OF WATER | A family-friendly 3.1 km (1.9 mile) loop trail circles this lake passing some of the oldest Douglas fir trees in Alberta. The lake is in the montane zone of the park and is a good place to spot wildlife. There are lovely views of Mount Rundle and Cascade Mountain and picnic tables if you want to linger. Because the lake is smaller and somewhat sheltered, it tends to have smoother water for paddling. ⊠ *Johnson Lake, Banff National Park* ⊹ *11 km (6.8 mi) from Banff townsite. Follow Lake Minnewanka Scenic Drive and turn onto Johnson Lake Road.*

Norquay Sightseeing Chairlift

OTHER ATTRACTION | Great views of the Bow Valley, Banff Townsite, and surrounding mountain peaks can be enjoyed from the top of the Norquay chairlift. The ride up takes 10 minutes. An interpretive path, a viewpoint, and the historic Cliffhouse Bistro, where you can have lunch, dinner, or drinks, are at the top. ⊠ *2 Mt. Norquay Rd., Banff* ☎ *844/667–7829* ⊕ *banffnorquay.com/summer* ⊡ *C$39.*

TRAILS

Discovery Trail and Marsh Trail

TRAIL | FAMILY | On a hillside above the Cave and Basin National Historic Site, this 0.8-km (½-mile) boardwalk takes you past the vent of the cave to a spring flowing out of the hillside. Interpretive

Plants and Wildlife in Banff

Awesome forces of nature combined to thrust wildly folded sedimentary and metamorphic rock up into ragged peaks and high cliffs. Add glaciers and snowfields to the lofty peaks, carpet the valleys with forests, mix in a generous helping of small and large mammals, wildflowers, rivers, and crystal-clear lakes, and you've got the recipe for Banff National Park.

Complex Life Zones

This diverse topography has resulted in three complex life zones in Banff: montane, subalpine, and alpine. Each zone has characteristic physical environments along with its own species of plants and animals. The montane zone features valleys and grasslands as well as alders, willows, birches, and cottonwoods. The Douglas firs and lodgepole pines that cover the lower slopes of the mountains are also in the montane zone. Subalpine forest extends from the montane to about 6,500 feet and is made up of mostly spruce and pine trees. The fragile alpine zone is found at the highest elevations. The rocky terrain and cold, howling winds mean far fewer plants and animals can survive there.

Where the Wild Things Are

Most of the wildlife is found in the montane zone, where bighorn sheep, deer, elk, and caribou abound. Moose and mountain goats can also be seen, as well as the occasional black bear. Other park animals include grizzly bears, wolves, coyotes, and cougars, as well as smaller mammals such as squirrels, marmots, muskrats, porcupines, and beavers. Birds commonly spotted are grouse, larks, finches, ptarmigans, bald eagles, golden eagles, loons, and Canada geese.

signage explains the geology and history of the cave and basin. Follow the Marsh Trail to observe the birdlife and the lush vegetation fed by the mineral water. Along the boardwalk are telescopes, benches, and interpretive signage as well as a bird blind on the marsh itself. Wheelchairs have limited access to the boardwalk. *Easy.* ⊠ *Banff* ✢ *Trailhead: at parking lot of Cave and Basin National Historic Site.*

Fenland Trail

TRAIL | FAMILY | It will take about an hour round-trip to walk the 2-km (1-mile) trail that slowly changes from marsh to dense forest. Watch for beavers, muskrat, and waterfowl. The trail is popular with joggers and cyclists. *Easy.* ⊠ *Banff* ✢ *Trailhead: at Forty Mile Picnic Area.*

Sulphur Mountain Trail

TRAIL | This well-maintained trail crisscrosses underneath the gondola on Sulphur Mountain and climbs from the parking lot to the summit. You can hike up and take the gondola down, but you should check schedules first. A restaurant and cafeteria are located at the summit along with a viewing platform and interpretive signage. Allow four hours to hike the trail round trip. *Difficult.* ⊠ *Banff National Park* ✢ *Trailhead: at corner of Upper Hot Springs parking lot closest to pool.*

Surprise Corner to Hoodoos Viewpoint

TRAIL | This 4.8-km (3-mile) trail begins with a view of a waterfall on Bow River, leads through meadows and forests and past sheer cliffs, and ends at the hoodoos (spirelike rock formations formed by erosion) in the eastern part of Banff Townsite.

Easy. ✉ *Banff* ✣ *Trailhead: at Bow Falls Overlook on Tunnel Mountain Dr.*

Tunnel Mountain Trail

TRAIL | If you want to summit a mountain in the Canadian Rockies, this 4.8-km (3-mile) round-trip hike is a good bet. The trailhead is a short walk from downtown Banff and the hike leads to a low summit with incredible views of the town, the Bow Valley, and surrounding mountains. *Moderate.* ✉ *Banff* ✣ *Lower parking area and trailhead off St. Julien Road.*

VISITOR CENTERS

Banff Visitor Centre

VISITOR CENTER | Parks Canada and Banff Lake Louise Tourism (BLLT) run this center jointly. On one side of the building, Parks Canada staffers dispense excellent advice about camping, hiking, interpretive programs, and sightseeing. On the other side, BLLT counselors (*www.banfflakelouise.com*) provide information about restaurants, tour operators, and accommodations. In spring, stop by to find out which hiking trails are open—many remain closed into May due to avalanche risk. ✉ *224 Banff Ave., Banff* ☎ *403/762–8421* 🌐 *www.pc.gc.ca/banff.*

🍴 Restaurants

The Bison

$$$$ | CANADIAN | Not only is the "Rocky Mountain comfort food" served here made with organic local ingredients, but there's also an emphasis on slow cooking, with everything—down to the ketchup and mustard for the bison burgers—prepared from scratch. The contemporary decor, with hardwood floors and vaulted ceilings, focuses attention on the open kitchen, where the chefs prepare signature dishes such as bison onion soup and braised bison short ribs with roasted potatoes. **Known for:** popular à la carte Sunday brunch; locally sourced Rocky Mountain cuisine; bison specialties. [$] *Average main: C$42* ✉ *211 Bear St., Suite 213, Banff* ☎ *403/762–5550* 🌐 *www.thebison.ca* 🕓 *No lunch weekdays.*

Block Kitchen & Bar

$$ | ECLECTIC | Offering everything from curry ramen and poke bowls to mushroom risotto and smoked bison flatbread, this small eclectic downtown tapas bar mixes Asian influences with local flavors. Both large and small plates are served in an intimate space with rough-hewn wooden tables, colorful artwork, and bare-bulb lighting. **Known for:** great drinks menu; trendy vibe; gluten-free and vegetarian options available. [$] *Average main: C$25* ✉ *201-5 Banff Ave., Banff* ☎ *403/985–2887* 🌐 *www.banffblock.com.*

Chuck's Steakhouse

$$$$ | STEAKHOUSE | This second-floor restaurant has great views of Banff Avenue and incredible steaks, namely grass-fed, Wagyu, prime beef that's sourced from ranches along the Cowboy Trail—the heart of Alberta's ranch country—dry aged in house, started on a mesquite-wood grill, and finished in a copper pan with herbs and butter. Servers are well-versed in the various cuts of beef, but if steak isn't your thing, alternatives include slow-cooked barbecue chicken, vegan cauliflower cross-cut, and wild British Columbia salmon. **Known for:** signature mud pie for dessert; prime steaks and family-style side dishes; excellent wine list. [$] *Average main: C$36* ✉ *101 Banff Ave., Banff* ☎ *403/762–4825* 🌐 *www.chuckssteakhouse.ca.*

Cliffhouse Bistro

$ | AMERICAN | Breakfast or lunch at this mountainside restaurant involves a ride up the sightseeing chairlift to a cool retro-style chalet. The food is delicious and unpretentious; brunch is served all day, the salads are meal-sized, and the nachos and the charcuterie board are great for sharing. **Known for:** fantastic nachos and charcuterie board for sharing; amazing views; unique atmosphere in a retro chalet. [$] *Average main: C$20* ✉ *2 Mount Norquay Rd., Banff* ☎ *403/762–4421* 🌐 *banffnorquay.com/*

dining/cliffhouse-bistro/ ⊘ Closed mid-Sept.–mid-June; no dinner.

Coyotes Southwestern Grill

$$ | SOUTHWESTERN | A small restaurant decorated with log beams and bathed in warm Santa Fe colors, Coyotes serves healthful Southwestern-style dishes for breakfast, lunch, and dinner. Scrambled eggs and salmon, stuffed French toast, and warm seven-grain cereal topped with fresh berries, pecans, and yogurt stand out among the breakfast offerings. **Known for:** in-house deli for picnic fixings; wholesome food; extensive breakfast menu. $ Average main: C$26 ⊠ 206 Caribou St., Banff ☎ 403/762–3963 ⊕ coyotesbanff.com.

★ Eden

$$$$ | FRENCH | Ultraluxe decor and magnificent mountain views provide the interior and exterior backdrops for prix fixe, three- to eight-course dinners of regionally influenced French cuisine. The presentation is awe-inspiring, and the food is prepared à-la-minute, so entrées change frequently but have included British Columbia sablefish with tomato, watermelon, and onion; rabbit with nuts, wild berries, and foraged mushrooms; and cinnamon-smoked short ribs. **Known for:** a place to linger with a meal; perfect wine pairings; exquisitely crafted French cuisine. $ Average main: C$79 ⊠ Rimrock Resort Hotel, 300 Mountain Ave., Banff ☎ 403/762–1865 ⊕ www.banffeden.com ⊘ Closed Mon. and Tues. No lunch.

1888 Chop House at the Fairmont Banff Springs

$$$$ | STEAKHOUSE | Alberta is world-famous for its beef, and this restaurant is a great place to sample it, along with pork, lamb, and sustainable wild game and seafood. All steaks are hand-cut on-site and grilled on cherrywood, and everything, from the butter to the garnishes, is made in-house. **Known for:** not many vegetarian options; delicious hand-cut steaks; carefully sourced fish and game. $ Average main: C$65 ⊠ 405 Spray Ave., Banff ☎ 403/762–2211 ⊕ www.1888chophouse.com.

Farm & Fire

$ | CANADIAN | Canadian flair is the hallmark of this modern, airy restaurant—a recent addition to the Elk + Avenue Hotel—where ingredients sourced from small, local, organic farmers are used in appetizers such as barbecue "pig wings" (made from pork shanks and served with celery and buttermilk-blue-cheese dressing) and entrees like slow-roasted rotisserie chicken, mushroom orecchiette pasta, and flatbread pizza. The drinks menu features Canadian wines, local craft beers, and unique cocktails made using the best Canadian spirits. **Known for:** children's and extensive brunch menus; farm-fresh ingredients prepared in a wood-fired craft kitchen; patio dining area with propane heaters. $ Average main: C$23 ⊠ Elk + Avenue Hotel, 333 Banff Ave., Banff ☎ 403/760–3298 ⊕ www.farmandfirebanff.com.

Juniper Bistro

$ | CANADIAN | Ask for a table on the engaging patio or inside near one of the dining room's walls of windows to enjoy some of Banff's best views while dining on dishes made from fresh local ingredients. The brunch menu features stuffed French toast, huevos rancheros, and several kinds of eggs Benedict; lunch options include burgers, sandwiches, and pulled-pork poutine. **Known for:** gluten-free and vegetarian options; popular brunch spot; great views, indoors and out. $ Average main: C$17 ⊠ Juniper Hotel, 1 Juniper Way, Banff ☎ 866/551–2281, 403/762–2281 ⊕ thejuniper.com/dining ⊘ No dinner Mon.-Tues.

Nourish Bistro

$ | VEGETARIAN | Vegan-friendly Nourish lives up to its name with intricate and diverse plant-based cuisine. Twenty different ingredients power the explosion of flavors in each bite of Banff's most intriguing nachos: strawberries, toasted quinoa, smoked blackberry sauce, garlic gherkins, six kinds of beans, Monterey Jack, and nine more items. **Known for:**

dishes that even die-hard carnivores can love; exceptional vegan food; truly unique nachos. $ *Average main: C$23* ✉ *211 Bear St., Suite 110, Banff* ☎ *403/760–3933* ⊕ *www.nourishbistro.com.*

Park Distillery

$$$ | CANADIAN | With water from six Canadian Rockies glaciers and grain sourced from high-altitude family farms, Park Distillery produces spirits with aromas and flavors like no others. Its restaurant features a fun campfire-cuisine theme with classic coleslaw, warm potato salad, or mac and cheese served alongside rotisserie chicken, salmon, ribs, burgers, or steaks. **Known for:** distillery tours and tastings daily at 3:30; Banff's first and only distillery restaurant; dining room has a playful, summer-camp vibe. $ *Average main: C$31* ✉ *219 Banff Ave., Banff* ☎ *403/762–5114* ⊕ *www.parkdistillery.com.*

Shoku Izakaya

$$ | ASIAN | Opened in 2021 by Chef Stephane Provost, Shoku Izakaya is Banff's first Japanese pub. This friendly and fun izakaya-inspired restaurant serves small plates and snacks with an extensive selection of saki, Japanese-inspired cocktails, and beers. **Known for:** Japanese Izakaya ambience; great variety of small plates; nice selection of saki, wine, and mixed drinks. $ *Average main: C$30* ✉ *304 Caribou St., Banff* ☎ *403/985–1112* ⊕ *shokubanff.com.*

Sky Bistro

$$$ | CANADIAN | You can't beat the panoramic mountain views from this restaurant on the third floor of the Banff Gondola at 2281 meters (7,486 feet) above sea level. There are floor-to-ceiling windows on all sides and the cuisine is just as elevated as the scenery with a regularly changing menu that features local ingredients like Alberta beef, British Columbia salmon, and prairie-grown vegetables complimented by local craft beers, craft spirits, and Canadian wines. **Known for:** craft beers, craft cocktails, and

Canadian wines; floor-to-ceiling windows on a mountaintop; locally sourced ingredients. $ *Average main: C$33* ✉ *Banff Gondola, Banff* ☎ *403/762–7475* ⊕ *www.banffjaspercollection.com/dining/sky-bistro/.*

Three Bears Brewery and Restaurant

$$ | BISTRO | This brewery restaurant is designed to feel like you're in the middle of a forest—complete with a 25-foot pine tree, wood features, plants, leaves, and a retractable rooftop patio. The menu is casual and includes a variety of appetizers, sandwiches, and mains that all pair nicely with a flight of craft beer made on site. **Known for:** nice rooftop patio; great pizza; good beer made at onsite brewery. $ *Average main: C$25* ✉ *205 Bear St., Banff* ☎ *403/985–8038* ⊕ *threebears-banff.com.*

Three Ravens

$$$$ | ECLECTIC | A corner location and floor-to-ceiling windows make this a great spot to catch spectacular mountain sunsets while enjoying carefully crafted dishes. The menu changes twice yearly but might include Alberta bison strip loin with crispy kale and a charred shallot and Merlot glaze, Spanish paprika–crusted British Columbia halibut, or grilled Alberta beef tenderloin with truffle mac and cheese *rissolé* (small croquette). **Known for:** stellar selection of Canadian wines; hidden gem with wonderful views and fine dining; in-house preparation of everything, from bread to spiced butters and fruit sorbets. $ *Average main: C$42* ✉ *Banff Centre, Sally Borden Bldg., 107 Tunnel Mountain Dr., Banff* ☎ *403/762–6300* ⊕ *banffcentre.ca/three-ravens-restaurant-wine-bar.*

☕ Coffee and Quick Bites

Wild Flour Bakery

$ | BAKERY | At breakfast, enjoy a regular coffee or espresso, hot chocolate, or tea from the local Banff Tea Company with your breakfast panini, toast, or house-made granola. Lunchtime soups, sandwiches and salads are often innovative; consider trying the buddha bowls with fresh veggies, falafel, quinoa and tangy tahini lemon dressing. **Known for:** often busy (but lines move quickly); breakfasts and lunches that don't break the bank; local favorite artisanal bakery. [$] *Average main: C$12* ✉ *211 Bear St., Suite 101, Banff* ☎ *403/760–5074* 🌐 *www.wildflourbakery.ca* 🕓 *No dinner.*

Hotels

Banff Centre

$$ | **HOTEL** | Two properties—the Lloyd Hall Hotel and the Hotel at the Professional Development Centre—with standard rooms and a variety of suites comprise the lodgings at the Banff Centre, which is perched on the side of Tunnel Mountain and has superb dining, arts, and recreational facilities. **Pros:** reasonably priced; free access to superb fitness center; excellent dining. **Cons:** located on the campus of an arts institute; away from town; Professional Development Centre hotel needs an update. [$] *Rooms from: C$279* ✉ *107 Tunnel Mountain Dr., Banff* ☎ *403/762–6100, 800/884–7574* 🌐 *www.banffcentre.ca/hotels* 🍴 *No Meals* 🛏 *422 units.*

Elk + Avenue

$$$$ | **HOTEL** | Some rooms at this hotel, a short walk from busy downtown Banff, have mountain views, while others overlook a courtyard; all have contemporary minimalist decor, flat-screen TVs, mini-refrigerators, coffee stations, and free Wi-Fi. **Pros:** great on-site restaurant and lounge; within walking distance of shops and restaurants; handy amenities like ski lockers and laundry facilities. **Cons:** no swimming pool; no fitness center; free underground parking lot is often full. [$] *Rooms from: C$359* ✉ *333 Banff Ave., Banff* ☎ *877/442–2623 toll-free* 🌐 *www.elkandavenue.com* 🍴 *No Meals* 🛏 *162 rooms.*

★ **Fairmont Banff Springs**

$$$$ | **RESORT** | Affectionately known as "The Castle in the Rockies," this massive property—originally developed by the Canadian Pacific Railway, debuting in 1888 and ushering in Banff's tourism boom—is a destination in itself thanks to magnificent views of the Bow River and the surrounding mountains and an abundance of modern amenities. **Pros:** historical property; many amenities, including a spa; ultraluxurious. **Cons:** hotel charges a resort fee; parking is in an outdoor lot and is expensive; costly rooms and dining. [$] *Rooms from: C$719* ✉ *405 Spray Ave., Banff National Park* ☎ *403/762–2211, 800/441–1414* 🌐 *www.fairmont.com/banffsprings* 🍴 *No Meals* 🛏 *757 rooms.*

Fox Hotel & Suites

$$$ | **HOTEL** | The Fox is close enough to downtown that you can walk to most of the shopping and nightlife, but far enough away that you won't be bothered by noise while staying in its comfortable standard rooms or suites with kitchenettes and separate living areas. **Pros:** heated underground parking; artificial hot-springs pool; free local calls, Wi-Fi, and transit passes. **Cons:** hotel parking is limited; small fitness facility; some rooms do not have a/c. [$] *Rooms from: C$329* ✉ *461 Banff Ave., Banff* ☎ *403/760–8500, 800/563–8764* 🌐 *www.foxhotelandsuites.com* 🛏 *182 rooms* 🍴 *No Meals.*

Juniper Hotel

$$ | **HOTEL** | A little oasis only a short drive from downtown, this independently owned hotel sits at the base of Mt. Norquay, surrounded by the woodlands of Banff National Park. **Pros:** close to Discovery Trail and Mt. Norquay skiing; great restaurant; small, intimate, and away from crowds. **Cons:** no lunch on-site; away from downtown; some rooms are on the smaller side. [$] *Rooms from: C$289* ✉ *1 Juniper Way, Banff* ☎ *403/762–2281, 866/551–2281* 🌐 *thejuniper.com* 🍴 *No Meals* 🛏 *52 units.*

Moose Hotel and Suites

$$$$ | **HOTEL** | Done in neutral tones and decorated with works by local artists, rooms at this hotel, which opened in 2017 not far from downtown, surround a lovely interior courtyard that is itself anchored by one of Banff's most unique lodgings: a heritage house that was moved here from its original location and restored. **Pros:** within walking distance of downtown; unique heritage-home lodging option; large swimming pool, sauna, spa, and rooftop hot tubs. **Cons:** on-site restaurant is adequate but not outstanding; rooms facing courtyard lack privacy when blinds are open; pricey. $ *Rooms from: C$449 ✉ 345 Banff Ave., Banff* ☎ 866/379–0021 toll-free, 403/760–8570 ⊕ *moosehotelandsuites. com* ❑ *No Meals* ⇔ *174 rooms.*

Mount Royal Hotel

$$$$ | **HOTEL** | Close to the action, with prime shops and restaurants right outside the door, this classic hotel combines the old with the new: it was built in 1908 and rebuilt in 2018 after having suffered damage in a devastating 2016 fire, and while the original facade wasn't changed, everything on the inside is up to modern standards. **Pros:** newly rebuilt; fantastic location in downtown Banff; two rooftop hot tubs. **Cons:** no fitness facilities; no swimming pool; free on-site parking is limited. $ *Rooms from: C$389 ✉ 138 Banff Ave., Banff* ☎ 877/862–2623 toll free ⊕ *www.mountroyalhotel.com* ❑ *No Meals* ⇔ *133 rooms.*

Peaks Hotel & Suites

$$$$ | **HOTEL** | The lobby of this newly constructed hotel is open and airy and when you walk down the hallways, it feels like you're walking in a forest with leaf motifs in the carpet and etched interior glass. **Pros:** modern style and architecture; located right in downtown Banff; new hotel. **Cons:** parking fee; no on-site pool or hot tub; restaurant facilities across the street in sister hotel. $ *Rooms from: C$449 ✉ 218 Linx St., Banff* ☎ 403/762–4471, 800/661–1021

toll free ⊕ *www.peaksbanff.com* ❑ *No Meals* ⇔ *71 rooms.*

The Rimrock Resort Hotel

$$$$ | **RESORT** | Luxurious appointments and natural splendor coexist harmoniously at this nine-story hotel on the steep slope of Sulphur Mountain: the Grand Lobby has a 25-foot ceiling, giant windows, a massive marble fireplace, and a balcony facing the Rockies. **Pros:** world-class dining; spectacular views; close to hot springs and gondola. **Cons:** self parking costs C$22 per day; farther from townsite than other options; long walk from the parking garage to some rooms. $ *Rooms from: C$457 ✉ 300 Mountain Ave., Banff National Park* ☎ 403/762–3356, 888/746–7625 ⊕ *www.rimrockresort.com* ⇔ *333 rooms* ❑ *No Meals.*

Royal Canadian Lodge

$$$$ | **HOTEL** | An indoor, grotto-style, mineral pool intended to mimic natural hot springs is a highlight of this recently renovated, stone-and-wood lodge set among the evergreens. **Pros:** mineral pool, steam room, and on-site spa; intimate property; 10-minute walk to downtown. **Cons:** small gym; parking fee; on-site restaurant not open for lunch. $ *Rooms from: C$429 ✉ 459 Banff Ave., Banff National Park* ☎ 403/762–3307, 800/661–1379 ⊕ *www. royalcanadianlodge.com* ⇔ *99 rooms* ❑ *No Meals.*

Rundlestone Lodge

$$$$ | **HOTEL** | A wood-burning fireplace and rough-hewn front desk make the lobby of this Swiss-style alpine lodge warm and inviting. **Pros:** comfortable lobby; large swimming pool; free underground parking. **Cons:** some rooms have interior views of the pool; no lunch service at on-site restaurant; 15-minute walk to town. $ *Rooms from: C$369 ✉ 537 Banff Ave., Banff National Park* ☎ 403/762–2201, 800/661–8630 in North America ⊕ *www.rundlestone.com* ⇔ *96 units* ❑ *No Meals.*

Sunshine Mountain Lodge

$$$ | RESORT | The only ski-in, ski-out accommodation in Banff, the lodge has two onsite restaurants, a coffee shop, a massive outdoor hot tub, and a fitness center. **Pros:** Banff's only ski-in, ski-out hotel; amazing hiking on the doorstep; huge outdoor hot tub. **Cons:** no complimentary breakfast; no pool; farther away from amenities in Banff townsite. $ *Rooms from: C$325 ⊠ Sunshine Village Ski Resort, 1 Sunshine Access Rd., Banff National Park* ☎ *403/762–6500, 877/542–2633 toll-free* ⊕ *www.sunshinemountain-lodge.com* ❍ *No Meals* ⇆ *87 rooms.*

⦿ Performing Arts

Banff Centre for Arts and Creativity

ARTS CENTERS | Most of the cultural activities in the Canadian Rockies take place in and around Banff, and these 16 buildings spread across 43 acres are the hub of that activity. The center presents pop and classical music, theater, and dance throughout the year. The season peaks in summer with concerts, performances, films, and other events, many in an outdoor amphitheater. The Walter Phillips Gallery showcases contemporary artworks by Canadian and international artists. ⊠ *107 Tunnel Mountain Dr., Banff National Park* ☎ *403/762–6100, 800/413–8368 in Alberta and British Columbia* ⊕ *www.banffcentre.ca* ◿ *Gallery free.*

Lake Louise, Moraine Lake, and the Bow Valley Parkway

Hamlet of Lake Louise is 58 km (36 miles) northwest of town of Banff, 233 km (145 miles) southeast of town of Jasper.

The province of Alberta and beautiful Lake Louise were both named after Princess Louise Caroline Alberta (1848–1939), the fourth daughter of Queen Victoria. She was also the wife of the Marquess of Lorne, who served as the fourth governor general of Canada from 1878 to 1883, the period when Alberta was first established as a provisional district of the North West Territories (1882). Lake Louise, one of the most beautiful lakes in the Canadian Rockies, got its name in 1884. Six years later, the hamlet that today shares its name was founded as Laggan Station— an outpost at the end of the Canadian Pacific Railway. It's now home to hotels, restaurants, shops, and gas stations, and the area of the park in which it's set has world-class hiking trails, one of the nation's top ski resorts, and two of the most beautiful lakes you will ever see: Lake Louise itself and Moraine Lake.

The Bow Valley Parkway is a 48-kilometer (30-mile) scenic secondary highway that connects Banff Townsite with the hamlet of Lake Louise. Wildlife is abundant along this roadway, and there are scenic hikes and lookouts, too. The eastern portion of the Bow Valley Parkway passes through the montane of Banff National Park, a region that provides critical habitat for large carnivores like wolves, cougars, and bears.

⦿ Sights

PICNIC AREAS

Fireside

OTHER ATTRACTION | This area has picnic tables and toilets nearby. ⊠ *Banff National Park* ✛ *Off Bow Valley Pkwy.*

Moraine Lake

OTHER ATTRACTION | One of the most beautiful lakes in the Canadian Rockies is the setting for this picnic area near the village of Lake Louise. The site has two kitchen shelters, a few tables, and toilets. ✛ *Off Moraine Lake Rd., 5 km (3 miles) from village of Lake Louise.*

SCENIC DRIVES

Bow Valley Parkway

SCENIC DRIVE | Formerly known as Highway 1A, this scenic drive between Banff and Lake Louise leads to Hillsdale

The snow capped peaks of the 2,766-meter (9,075-foot) Castle Mountain tower above the Bow River Valley.

Meadows, Johnston Canyon, Castle Mountain, and Baker Creek. There are plenty of viewpoints and picnic sites along the way. In 2020 and 2021, Parks Canada closed portions of the road to most motor vehicles to improve the route for cyclists. Visitors should consult the Parks Canada website for the latest information on road closures. ⊠ *Banff National Park* ⊕ *www.pc.gc.ca/en/pn-np/ ab/banff/visit/les10-top10/promenade-de- la-vallee-de-la-bow-bow-valley-parkway.*

SCENIC STOPS
Castle Mountain
MOUNTAIN | Castle Mountain, one of the most striking peaks between Banff and Jasper, got its name from Scottish geologist James Hector who thought the 11-kilometer (6.8-mile) long mountain resembled an ancient fortress with steep walls. When U.S. General Dwight D. Eisenhower, Supreme Commander of the Allied Forces in Europe, visited Canada in 1949, Prime Minister Mackenzie King ordered the Geographical Board of Canada to officially change Castle Mountain

to "Mount Eisenhower." Eisenhower had been given a castle in Scotland and Canada would not be outdone. However, the Alberta government was not consulted or informed of the name change until afterward, causing such a controversy that in 1979, the name was changed back to Castle Mountain; a pinnacle on the southeastern side of the mountain was named Eisenhower Tower. ⊠ *Castle Mountain, Banff National Park* ⊕ *21 km (13 miles) southeast of Lake Louise off the Bow Valley Parkway.*

Lake Louise
SCENIC DRIVE | This is one of the most photographed spots in the park. In summer, you can walk beside the lake and enjoy the nearby hiking trails. Winter offers skating on the ice and sleigh rides. The lakeside Fairmont Château Lake Louise hotel is a departure point for several short, moderately strenuous, well-traveled hiking routes, including the popular 3-km (2-mile) trail to Lake Agnes. The tiny lake hangs on a mountain-surrounded shelf that opens to the east

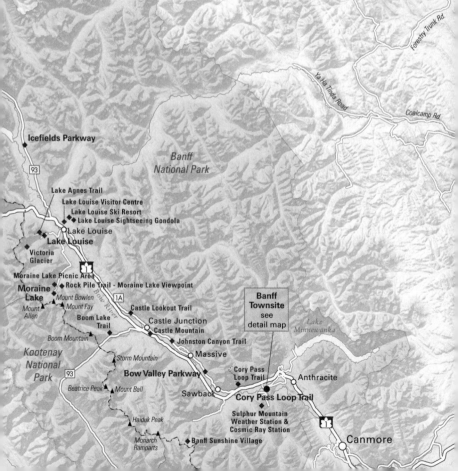

Lake Louise, Moraine Lake, Bow Valley Parkway, and the Icefields Parkway

Icefields Parkway

Banff
National Park

Lake Agnes Trail
Lake Louise Visitor Centre
Lake Louise Ski Resort
Lake Louise Sightseeing Gondola
Lake Louise
Lake Louise
Victoria
Glacier

Moraine Lake Picnic Area
Rock Pile Trail - Moraine Lake Viewpoint
**Moraine
Lake**
Mount Bowlen
Mount Fay
Mount
Allen
Boom Lake
Trail
Castle Lookout Trail
Bow River
Castle Junction
Castle Mountain
Boom Mountain
Johnston Canyon Trail
Massive
Storm Mountain
**Banff
Townsite**
see
detail map
Lake
Minnewanka
Kootenay
National
Park
93
Beatrice Peak
Mount Ball
Bow Valley Parkway
Cory Pass
Loop Trail
Anthracite
Sawback
Cory Pass Loop Trail
Haiduk Peak
Sulphur Mountain
Weather Station &
Cosmic Ray Station
Monarch
Ramparts
Banff Sunshine Village
Canmore

Forestry Trunk Rd.
Ya Ha Tinda Road
Coalcamp Rd.

with a bird's-eye view of the Beehives and Mount Whitehorn. The teahouse (cash only) by Lake Agnes serves soups, sandwiches, and snacks. In 2021, Parks Canada implemented a mandatory parking fee for the Lake Louise parking lot mid-May to mid-October. Parks Canada also operates a shuttle bus service during peak season. Bus tickets must be booked in advance. ✉ *Fairmont Château Lake Louise, 111 Lake Louise Dr., Lake Louise* ☎ *403/522–3511* 🚌 *parking C$11.70, shuttle C$8.*

Lake Louise Sightseeing Gondola

TRANSPORTATION | FAMILY | Hop on the gondola to an alpine plateau for a stunning view that includes more than a dozen glaciers. The deck of the viewing platform is a good place to enjoy an ice-cream cone, a cold drink, or a picnic lunch, or you can buy a ticket that includes breakfast or lunch at the lodge near the gondola's base. Several easy hikes are accessible from the top of the lift and guided interpretive walks (45 minutes) take place several times daily. The Wildlife Interpretive Centre is a 5–10 minute walk from the top of the gondola and it has programming, life-size animal displays, and information about local wildlife. It's common to see grizzly bears from the safety of the gondola. ✉ *1 Whitehorn Rd., off Hwy. 1 (Lake Louise exit), Banff National Park* ☎ *403/522–3555* ⊕ *www.skilouise. com* 🚌 *C$49.99 ride only, C$54.99 with breakfast, C$59.99 with lunch, C$74.99 with gourmet dinner, C$16.95 for guided hiking tour.*

Moraine Lake

SCENIC DRIVE | Set in the Valley of the Ten Peaks, 11 km (7 miles) south of Lake Louise, this beauty is a photographic highlight of the park thanks to reflections of the snow-clad mountaintops that rise abruptly around it. It's also a major stop for tour buses and is popular with hikers and canoeists, too, so visit early or late in the day to avoid crowds. Moderate

hiking trails lead from the lodge at Moraine Lake into some spectacular alpine country. During peak times (larch season), Parks Canada operates a shuttle service from the hamlet of Lake Louise to Moraine Lake. ✉ *Banff National Park.*

Victoria Glacier

NATURE SIGHT | Victoria Mountain and Victoria Glacier were named after Queen Victoria; Lake Louise was named after the queen's fourth daughter, Princess Louise Caroline Alberta. The lake is fed by Victoria Glacier which sits near the top of Mount Victoria at the western end of the lake. Glacial rock flour (a.k.a dust) gives the lake its remarkable turquoise color. From the shores of the lake you can see the mountain and glacier. ✉ *111 Lake Louise Dr., Banff National Park.*

TRAILS

Boom Lake Trail

TRAIL | This 5-km (3.2-mile) hike climbs through a forest of pine, fir, and spruce amid mountains and glaciers. The waters of the lake itself are crystal clear. Allow half a day for this hike round-trip. *Moderate.* ✉ *Banff National Park* ⊹ *Trailhead: off Hwy. 93 S, 7 km (4½ miles) west of Castle Junction.*

Castle Lookout Trail

TRAIL | Outstanding views of the mountains above the Bow River Valley are the highlight of this 3.7-km (2.3-mile) one-way trail that is somewhat steep. *Moderate.* ✉ *Banff National Park* ⊹ *Trailhead: off Hwy. 1A at parking lot on north side of Bow Valley Pkwy., 5 km (3.1 miles) west of Castle Junction.*

Cory Pass Loop Trail

TRAIL | Although those who hike this 13-km (8-mile) trail are rewarded with awesome views, it's one of the park's most strenuous treks, requiring about six hours to complete, and so it's recommended only for experienced hikers who can trace a difficult route. The return trip loops around Mount Edith Clavell and descends the Edith Pass Trail. *Difficult.*

✉ *Banff National Park* ✥ *Trailhead: at Fireside picnic area, eastern end of Bow Valley Pkwy.*

★ Johnston Canyon Trail

TRAIL | Rushing water has carved a path through this must-see limestone canyon. The first 1.1 km (0.7 mile) is a paved walkway that leads to the 10-meter (33-foot) Lower Falls. From here, a slightly more rugged 2.7-km (1¾-mile) trail leads to the nearly 30-meter (100-foot) Upper Falls and a 5-km (3-mile) trail runs to the Ink Pots—six green pools filled with springwater. It takes four to five hours round-trip to complete. *Moderate.* ✉ *Banff National Park* ✥ *Trailhead: off Hwy. 1A at Johnston Canyon parking lot.*

Lake Agnes Trail

TRAIL | Winding north of Lake Louise, this 7-km (4½-mile) trail has stunning views of Lake Agnes and Mirror Lake. The trail passes through an old-growth forest and comes up the right side of a waterfall before ending at a teahouse where you can stop for dessert. It will take at least four hours to complete this trail. *Moderate.* ✉ *Lake Louise* ✥ *Trailhead: accessed from Lake Louise Shoreline Trail, which begins in front of Fairmont Château Lake Louise.*

Rockpile Trail - Moraine Lake Viewpoint

TRAIL | This short 0.8 km (0.5 mile) trail leads up stairs that have been built into rocks and takes you to the top of a rock pile to enjoy an incredible view of Moraine Lake. There are a variety of lookout points from the top of the rock pile, but it's important to stay on the trail, as walking over rocks and logs off-trail can be dangerous. *Easy.* ✉ *Moraine Lake, Banff National Park* ✥ *Trailhead: Moraine Lake Parking lot.*

VISITOR CENTER

Lake Louise Visitor Centre

VISITOR CENTER | Stop here to get maps and information about area attractions and trails. Parks Canada staff can assist with up-to-date park information. Banff and Lake Louise Tourism staff can provide information on area accommodations and amenities, and you can purchase educational books and other materials. ✉ *202 Village Rd., Lake Louise* ☎ *403/522–3833* 🌐 *www.banfflakelouise.com.*

🍴 Restaurants

★ Post Hotel

$$$$ | **CANADIAN** | One of the true epicurean experiences in the Canadian Rockies, the Post delivers daring, regionally inspired cuisine accompanied by excellent wines (it's one of only four restaurants in Canada to receive the *Wine Spectator*'s Grand Award). A low, exposed-beam ceiling and a stone fireplace aglow in winter create an in-from-the-cold aura; white napery provides a touch of elegance; and a changing menu keeps things interesting, with dishes that might include Alaskan king crab drizzled with lemongrass-ginger butter, sautéed wild British Columbia halibut in lemongrass-thyme sauce, or Alberta beef tenderloin in bordelaise. **Known for:** innovative, regularly changing menu; outstanding wine selection (more than 26,000 bottles); artful blend of rusticity and elegance. [$] *Average main: C$50* ✉ *200 Pipestone Rd., Lake Louise* ☎ *403/522–3989, 800/661–1586* 🌐 *www.posthotel.com.*

The Station Restaurant

$$$ | **CANADIAN** | Dine on the patio or inside at this restaurant serving classic Canadian food in a unique setting: the original Lake Louise Railway Station. Daily lunch specials round out the menu of salads, burgers, steaks, and salmon. **Known for:** fantastic rhubarb-strawberry pie; casual atmosphere; set in the oldest building in town. [$] *Average main: C$33* ✉ *200 Sentinel Rd., Lake Louise* ☎ *403/522–2600* 🌐 *www.lakelouisestation.com* 🕓 *Closed mid-Oct.–late-Nov.*

Walliser Stube

$$$$ | **SWISS** | For something fun and a little different, try this restaurant's three-course Château Experience, consisting of a mushroom-and-shallot cheese fondue to start, an eight-ounce beef tenderloin with farm vegetables and whipped potatoes for the main course, and chocolate fondue with banana bread and fresh fruit for dessert. If fondue isn't for you, other classic Swiss, German, and Alpine dishes are served à la carte. **Known for:** robust wine list favoring Canadian and California vintages; a taste of the Alps in the Rockies; excellent fondue options. $ *Average main: C$45* ✉ *Fairmont Château Lake Louise, 111 Lake Louise Dr., Lake Louise* ☎ *403/522–1818* ⊕ *www. fairmont.com/lakelouise* ⊘ *Closed Sun.*

☕ Coffee and Quick Bites

Trailhead Cafe

$ | **CAFÉ** | Local work crews, mountain guides, and park wardens love this small café for a hot breakfast, lunch, or early dinner (until 6). Baked goods, made-to-order sandwiches, wraps, and salads are the specialties, and the coffee is excellent. **Known for:** limited seating; loved by locals; quick stop for picnic fixings. $ *Average main: C$10* ✉ *Samson Mall, Hwy. 1, Lake Louise* ☎ *403/522–2006.*

🛏 Hotels

Baker Creek Mountain Resort

$$$$ | **B&B/INN** | Tucked away off the scenic Bow Valley Parkway, this intimate, amenities-loaded, log-cabin resort has main-lodge rooms as well as private cabins with kitchens and fireplaces. **Pros:** many outdoor activities and amenities; beautiful location beside Baker Creek; log cabins with fireplaces. **Cons:** 15-minute drive to village of Lake Louise; no TV, phone, or high-speed Wi-Fi; no scheduled transportation to resort. $ *Rooms from: C$595* ✉ *Bow Valley Pkwy., Banff National Park* ✛ *12 km (7.5 miles) northwest of Lake Louise* ☎ *403/522–3761* ⊕ *bakercreek. com* ⤳ *35 units* ⦿ *No Meals.*

Fairmont Château Lake Louise

$$$$ | **RESORT** | The view out the Fairmont's back door is dramatic and then some, with terraces and lawns that reach to the famous aquamarine lake, itself backed by the Victoria Glacier. **Pros:** luxurious accommodations; stunning setting; abundant amenities. **Cons:** a bit away from the townsite; costly rooms and dining; trails around the lake can be crowded in summer. $ *Rooms from: C$687* ✉ *Lake Louise Dr., Lake Louise* ☎ *403/522–3511, 800/441–1414* ⊕ *www.fairmont.com/ lakelouise* ⦿ *No Meals* ⤳ *487 rooms.*

Paradise Lodge & Bungalows

$$$$ | **HOTEL** | Secluded in a forest near beautiful Lake Louise and owned by the same family for more than 50 years, this property offers comfortable, upgraded, 1930s suites and cute cabins—each with a unique name and country-style furnishings, most with kitchenettes, some with jetted or claw-foot tubs. **Pros:** picturesque setting; very clean; comfortable, well-appointed cabins. **Cons:** no a/c; need to drive to get to lake or townsite; frontage road is busy during the day. $ *Rooms from: C$360* ✉ *105 Lake Louise Dr., Lake Louise* ☎ *403/522–3595* ⊕ *www. paradiselodge.com* ⊘ *Closed Oct.–Apr.* ⤳ *45 units* ⦿ *No Meals.*

Post Hotel

$$$$ | **HOTEL** | A bright red roof and post-and-beam construction have made this Swiss chalet–style, Relais & Châteaux property—one of the finest retreats in the Rocky Mountains—something of a Lake Louise landmark; understated elegance, stellar dining, and lots of amenities have made it internationally renowned. **Pros:** gourmet dining with famous wine menu; understated elegance and personalized service; full-service spa. **Cons:** fewer services in Lake Louise than in Banff; costly rooms and dining; train nearby. $ *Rooms from: C$445* ✉ *200 Pipestone Rd., Lake Louise*

☎ *403/522–3989, 800/661–1586* ⊕ *www. posthotel.com* ❄ *No Meals* ⊷ *98 units.*

Shadow Lake Lodge

$$$$ | ALL-INCLUSIVE | Established in 1928, this backcountry retreat is located near gorgeous Shadow Lake surrounded by stunning mountain peaks. **Pros:** great location to access other hiking trails; beautiful views of the lake and mountains; delicious hot meals and tea included. **Cons:** no cell signal or Wi-Fi; shared bathroom facilities; must be reached by hiking, snow shoeing, or skiing. $ *Rooms from: C$730* ⊠ *Shadow Lake Lodge, Banff National Park* ☎ *403/678–3200* ⊕ *www.shadowlakelodge.com* ⊘ *Closed mid-Mar.–mid-June and mid Sept.–mid-Jan.* ❄ *All-Inclusive* ⊷ *11 cabins.*

Skoki

$ | ALL-INCLUSIVE | Situated in a stunning high alpine area of Banff National Park, this historic lodge built in 1931 is a wonderful accommodation for hikers and skiers. **Pros:** delicious house-made meals and afternoon tea included; historic backcountry lodge; beautiful alpine setting. **Cons:** 50 percent non-refundable deposit required; no electricity and no running water; only accessible on foot, skis, or snowshoes. $ *Rooms from: C$240* ⊠ *Skoki Lodge, Banff National Park* ☎ *888/997–5654, 403/522–1347* ⊕ *www.skoki.com* ⊘ *Closed mid-Apr.–mid-June and early Oct.–late Dec.* ❄ *All-Inclusive* ⊷ *5 lodge rooms, 3 cabins.*

Sundance Lodge

$$$$ | ALL-INCLUSIVE | Built in 1991, this 10-room log lodge is surrounded by trees and sits on the ends of a river with stunning views of the Sundance Mountain Range. **Pros:** daily horseback rides included; beautiful mountain views; delicious meals included. **Cons:** secluded location; shared bathrooms; must be reached by horseback, skis, fat bike, or snowshoes. $ *Rooms from: C$729* ⊠ *Sundance Lodge, Banff National Park* ☎ *800/661–8352, 403/762–4551* ⊕ *horseback.com/sundance-lodge/* ⊘ *Closed mid-Oct.–early Jan. and mid-Mar.–mid-May* ❄ *All-Inclusive* ⊷ *10 rooms.*

Icefields Parkway

230 km (140 miles) north from village of Lake Louise to Jasper Townsite.

An absolute highlight of the Canadian Rockies, the 230-km (143-mile) Icefields Parkway (Highway 93) snakes north from the village of Lake Louise, connecting Banff National Park with Jasper National Park. You could drive it in three or four hours, but why rush? Make a full day of it so you can enjoy some of the many scenic overlooks and/or signposted hiking trails.

Sightings of elk, deer, and bighorn sheep are fairly common; occasionally, you might also spot bears, moose, or mountain goats. In summer, alpine wildflowers carpet mountain passes like Bow and Sunwapta. The scenery is especially dramatic in the northern reaches of Banff and the southern portion of Jasper, where there are both icefields (massive reservoirs of ice) and glaciers (slow-moving rivers of ice that originate in icefields).

The road rises to near the tree line at several points, and the weather can be chilly and unsettled at these high elevations, so check conditions in advance, and bring warm clothing along, even in midsummer. Also, the gas station at Saskatchewan River Crossing, 80 km (50 miles) north of Lake Louise, is the only one on the parkway and is only open seasonally, so check your gas gauge before setting out.

◉ Sights

PICNIC AREAS

Bow Lake Day Use Area

OTHER ATTRACTION | This gorgeous lake is surrounded by incredible scenery, including Wapta Icefield, Bow Peak, Bow Glacier, Mt. Thompson, Crowfoot Mountain, and Crowfoot Glacier. Its picnic area is just off the highway with ample parking, restrooms, and tables along the

What's There to See?

Many of the most striking scenic stops in Banff National Park are along the Icefields Parkway, also signed as Highway 93, which continues north into Jasper National Park. Other noteworthy diversions include the Banff Gondola ride up Sulphur Mountain, another gondola ride that reveals the beauty of Lake Louise, and a trip to Moraine Lake. You can visit Moraine Lake and many of the stops along the parkway for free, but to get out on a glacier (Athabasca), walk above one on a glass-floored walkway (Glacier Skywalk), or ride the gondolas, you'll need to purchase tickets online or in person from Pursuit, located inside the Columbia Icefield Glacier Discovery Centre and at several other locations. You can purchase tickets to individual attractions or save money by getting a package discount to visit multiple sights.

shore. ⊠ *Icefields Pkwy. (Hwy. 93), Banff National Park* ⚓ *37 km (23 miles) north of Lake Louise, 194 km (120 miles) south of Jasper Townsite.*

SCENIC STOPS

Bow Lake

BODY OF WATER | Fed by meltwater from the Bow Glacier, one of the largest lakes in Banff National Park is surrounded by mountains and has views of Crowfoot Glacier. This spot is a beautiful place to snap some photos or enjoy a picnic at one of the lakeside tables. There are also public dry toilets here. ⊠ *Icefields Pkwy. (Hwy. 93), Banff National Park* ⚓ *40 km (25 miles) north of Lake Louise, 190 km (118 miles) south of Jasper.*

Bow Summit Lookout

NATURE SIGHT | At 2,070 meters (6,791 feet), Bow Pass is the highest drivable pass in the Canadian Rockies national parks and the highest point of the Icefields Parkway. Bow Summit Lookout is on the same trail as the better-known Peyto Lake Lookout. Stop and take in the view of Peyto Lake and then head up the upper self-guided nature trail and follow an old fire road to the lookout. The hike is 2.9 km (1.8 miles) one-way. Watch for pikas, marmots, and ptarmigan on the trail and at the lookout. From the lookout, you can see Bow Lake to the south Peyto to the Waterfowl Lakes to the north. ⊠ *Peyto Lake Upper Viewpoint, Banff National Park* ⚓ *46 km (29 miles) northwest of Lake Louise on the Icefields Parkway.*

Crowfoot Glacier and Crowfoot Mountain

NATURE SIGHT | About 34 km (21 miles) northwest of Lake Louise, the Crowfoot Glacier is one of the first glaciers you see on the Icefields Parkway. Situated on the northeastern side of Crowfoot Mountain, the glacier overlooks Bow Lake—if you stop at the Bow Lake pullout, you can see the glacier and mountain on the other side of the lake. Runoff from the glacier flows into the Bow River, which runs from Banff National Park to the City of Calgary and beyond to the prairies. ⊠ *Crowfoot Glacier, Banff National Park.*

★ Peyto Lake Lookout

VIEWPOINT | Named after Bill Peyto, a mountain guide, and early park warden of Banff National Park, Peyto Lake is one of the most beautiful lakes in the Canadian Rockies. The viewpoint for this brilliant turquoise glacier-fed lake is a short 20-minute stroll from the parking area just off the Icefields Parkway. At the lookout, you'll get a view of Peyto Lake, Peyto Glacier, and the Mistaya Valley. Interpretive signage along the trail explains its history and provides information about

The 230-km (143-mile) Icefields Parkway connects Banff and Jasper National Parks, passing some incredible scenery along the way.

flora and fauna in the area. The lookout is accessed at Bow Pass, the highest point on the Icefields Parkway; it's wheelchair accessible from the upper parking lot that tour buses use. ⊠ *Icefields Pkwy. (Hwy. 93), Banff National Park* ✛ *40 km (25 miles) north of Lake Louise, 190 km (118 miles) south of Jasper Townsite.*

Saskatchewan River Crossing

OTHER ATTRACTION | Located at the junction of the Icefields Parkway (Highway 93) and Highway 11, this is the only place that offers basic services (gas, convenience store, restaurant, and lodgings) between the hamlet of Lake Louise and the town of Jasper. ⊠ *At junction of Hwy. 11, Icefields Pkwy. (Hwy. 93), Banff National Park* ✛ *80 km (50 miles) north of Lake Louise, 153 km (95 miles) south of Jasper Townsite.*

Sunwapta Pass

SCENIC DRIVE | Marking the border between Banff and Jasper national parks, Sunwapta is the second-highest drivable pass—2,034 meters (6,675 feet)—in the national parks. Wildlife is most visible in spring and autumn after a snowfall, when herds of bighorn sheep come to the road to lick up the salt used to melt snow and ice. Be prepared for hairpin turns as you switchback up to the pass summit. ⊠ *Icefields Pkwy. (Hwy. 93), Banff National Park* ✛ *122 km (76 miles) north of Lake Louise, 108 km (67 miles) south of Jasper Townsite.*

TRAILS

Bow Glacier Falls Trail

TRAIL | A trail from the bottom of the parking lot at Bow Lake leads to this stunning cascade, which can't be seen from the road. At the base of the falls, you'll not only feel the spray and hear the roar, you'll also witness the birth of the Bow River—part of western Canada's largest watershed. The hike is about 4 km (2½ miles) one-way and takes from 1½ to 3 hours to complete, depending on how many photos you stop to take. ⊠ *Icefields Pkwy. (Hwy. 93), Banff National Park* ✛ *Trailhead: 40 km (25 miles) north of Lake Louise, 190 km (118 miles) south of Jasper Townsite.*

Mistaya Canyon

TRAIL | A 1.8-km (1.1-mile) loop trail leads from a well marked highway pullout to a footbridge over a deep winding slot canyon where you can view the Mistaya River swirling far below. The highway pullout is 74 km (46 miles) northwest of Lake Louise. ✉ *Icefields Pkwy. (Hwy. 93), Banff National Park ✛ Trailhead: 74 km (46 mi) northwest of Lake Louise.*

Activities

BIKING

Biking season in Banff typically runs from May through October, and several world-class cycling events take place in the area. The park contains more than 189 km (118 miles) of mountain-bike trails—some suitable for beginners, others for advanced bikers. It also has plenty of scenic roads that are perfect for rides ranging from just a few hours to several days. Note that bikers and hikers often share the trails, with hikers having the right of way.

Shorter rides include the Bow Lake Trail, Vermilion Lakes Drive, and the loop around Tunnel Mountain. For free riding or down-hilling, head to nearby areas like Calgary's Canada Olympic Park, Fernie, or Golden. The popular Legacy Trail (aka the Rocky Mountain Legacy Trail) is a paved, 24-km (15-mile) route that allows users to avoid the Trans-Canada Highway and travel more safely between Banff and Canmore. Many riders follow this route southward, as it's slightly more downhill than in the reverse direction, and return in the Roam Transit Bus (*403/762-0606, www. roamtransit.com*). All transit buses have bike racks. Many of the area's multisport outfitters have bike rentals or even tours in their mix of offerings.

Banff Adventures Unlimited

BIKING | Rent bikes here, or come by to sign up for almost any area activity. ✉ *211 Bear St., Banff* ☎ *403/762-4554, 800/644-8888* ⊕ *www.banffadventures.com.*

Banff Cycle

BIKING | This outfit offers e-bike, hybrid, and road-bike rentals and tours in Banff. Pick-up and delivery service is also an option. The company operates in conjunction with its partner shop, Banff Soul, Ski + Bike, which offers cycling equipment sales and service. ✉ *203 Bear St, Banff* ☎ *403/985-4848* ⊕ *www.banffcycle.com.*

BIRD-WATCHING

Birdlife is abundant in the montane and wetland habitats of the lower Bow Valley, and more than 260 species of birds have been recorded in the park. Come in the spring to observe the annual migration of waterfowl, including common species of ducks and Canada geese as well as occasional tundra swans, cinnamon teal, Northern shovelers, white-winged and surf scoters, and hooded and common mergansers. Bald eagles are also seen regularly. Come in mid-October if you want to observe the annual migration of golden eagles along the "super flyway" of the Canadian Rockies.

BOATING

Lake Minnewanka, near town, is the only place in Banff National Park that allows private motorboats. Aluminum fishing boats with 8-horsepower motors and kayaks can be rented at the dock; contact **Lake Minnewanka Cruise**. Canoe rentals are available at Lake Louise, Moraine Lake, and in Banff, where you launch along the Bow River and explore the waterways of the Bow Valley. Rafting options range from scenic float trips to family-friendly white-water excursions on the Kananaskis River to the intense white water of the Kicking Horse River, with its Class IV rapids.

Banff Canoe Club

BOATING | This operator near downtown rents canoes, kayaks, stand-up paddleboards, and bicycles and offers guided canoe and kayak excursions. From the docks, you can enjoy a gentle leg of the Bow River or follow Forty Mile Creek into the Vermillion Lakes. ✉ *Banff ✛ Banff* *docks on the corner of Wolf St. and Bow Ave. ☎ 403/762–5005 ⊕ banffcanoeclub. com.*

Canadian Rockies Rafting

RAFTING | This company offers half-day and full-day rafting trips on three area rivers. Experiences range from scenic nature floats, to intense whitewater experiences including guided river boarding for those who want to get right into the water. *✉ 909A Railway Ave., Canmore ☎ 877/226–7625 toll-free, 403/678–6535 ⊕ rafting.ca ☒ From C$40 ⊘ Closed Oct.-Apr.*

Chinook Rafting

BOATING | Chinook offers half- or full-day rafting trips—suitable for either families or for more adventurous adults—along three different rivers. Packages that combine rafting with other activities qualify for discounts. *✉ 215 Banff Ave., Banff ☎ 403/763–2007, 866/330–7238 ⊕ www. chinookrafting.com ☒ From C$110 ⊘ Closed Oct.-Apr.*

Fairmont Château Lake Louise Voyageur Canoe Experience

BOATING | Paddle the tranquil waters of Lake Louise in a 26-foot, cedar-strip-and-canvas canoe as part of this 90-minute experience. The accompanying guide shares stories about canoes in Canada from the perspectives of First Nations people, voyagers, explorers, and fur traders. Trips depart from the Fairmont's boathouse, which also rents regular canoes. *✉ 111 Lake Louise Dr., Lake Louise ☎ 403/522–3511, 800/441–1414 ⊕ www.fairmont.com/lake-louise/activities/canoeing-on-lake-louise ☒ C$65.*

Hydra River Guides

BOATING | The guides here lead rides through thrilling Class IV rapids on the Kicking Horse River. *✉ 211 Bear St., Banff ☎ 403/762–4554, 800/644–8888 ⊕ www. raftbanff.com ☒ From C$109.*

Lake Minnewanka Cruise

BOATING | FAMILY | From mid-May to mid-October, Minnewanka conducts 1½-hour lake tours. *✉ Minnewanka Lake, Banff National Park ☎ 403/762–3473, 800/760–6934 ⊕ www.minnewanka.com ☒ From C$53.*

★ Moraine Lake Lodge

BOATING | From June through September, you can paddle on beautiful Moraine Lake, one of the most photographed bodies of water in the Canada Rockies, in a canoe rented at the lodge's dock. If you want to combine canoeing and walking, trails for several scenic hikes also begin near the lodge. *✉ End of Moraine Lake Rd., Lake Louise ☎ 403/522–3733, 877/522–2777 ⊕ www.morainelake.com ☒ From C$95.*

Rocky Mountain Raft Tours

BOATING | FAMILY | This Banff-based outfit specializes in one- and two-hour float trips on the Bow River. *✉ Golf Course Loop Rd., Banff ☎ 403/762–3632 ⊕ www. banffrafttours.com ☒ From C$70.*

Wild Water Adventures

BOATING | Based 60 km (37 miles) north of Lake Louise, this outfitter has trips ranging from "mild to wild" whitewater rafting experiences. Half-day and full-day trips are available. *☎ 403/522–2211, 888/647–6444 ⊕ www.wildwater.com ☒ From C$79.*

CAMPING

Excluding backcountry sites for hikers and climbers, Parks Canada operates 13 campgrounds in Banff National Park, and prices for a one-night stay at a tent site range from C$17.99 to C$28. The camping season generally runs from mid-May through October, although the Tunnel Mountain and Lake Louise campgrounds remain open year-round. Hookups are available at most of the park campgrounds and at four of the 31 Kananaskis Country campgrounds. Parks Canada also offers two types of equipped sites: one version has a tent, sleeping pads, and a stove (C$71.54 a night + C$8.80 fire permit); the other features an oTENTik unit (a cross between a cabin and a tent that's heated and sleeps up to six people on foam mattresses), a fire pit, a bear-proof food locker, a picnic table, and a barbecue (C$122.64 a night).

Starting from C$55 per day, you can rent camping equipment for up to six people from **BacTrax** (*www.snowtips-bactrax.com*), which also offers a setup and pack-down service, so you can arrive at your campsite to find everything ready for you, and have it all taken away when your stay is over.

Castle Mountain Campground. This campground is in a beautiful wooded area close to a small store, a gas station, and a restaurant. *34 km (21 miles) from Banff on Bow Valley Pkwy.*

Johnston Canyon Campground. The scenery is spectacular and the wildlife abundant in and around this campground across from Johnston Canyon. A small creek flows right by the camping area. *25 km (15½ miles) from Banff on Bow Valley Pkwy. 403/762–1550 or 877/737–3783.*

Lake Louise Campground. This forested area next to the Bow River is open year-round, but in early spring and late fall tents and soft-sided trailers are not permitted in order to protect both people and bears. *1 km (½ mile) from Lake Louise Village and 4 km (2½ miles) from the lake 877/737–3783.*

Tunnel Mountain Campground. Close to the townsite, this campground has a great view of the valley, hoodoo formations, and the Fairmont Banff Springs Golf Course. *2½ km (1½ miles) from Banff Townsite on Tunnel Mountain 403/762–1550 or 877/737–3783.*

Two Jack Lakeside Campground. This secluded campground is on the shores of beautiful Two Jack Lake—one of the park's most scenic areas. There are interpretive programs, and Parks Canada has 10 lakefront oTENTiks that visitors can rent. *12 km (7½ miles) from Banff on the Minnewanka Loop 403/762–1550 or 877/737–3783.*

EDUCATIONAL OFFERINGS
★ Xplorer Program
COLLEGE | FAMILY | Year-round, the park offers the Xplorer Program for kids age 6 to 11. Pick up an Xplorer Booklet at one of the park's visitor centers. Kids who complete at least six of the booklet's 22 activities receive a souvenir. ⊠ *Banff* ⊕ *www.pc.gc.ca/en/serapprocher-connect/xplorateurs-xplorers* ⊠ *Free.*

FISHING
There's world-class trout fishing on the Bow River, Lake Minnewanka, and several other mountain lakes. You will need a national park fishing permit to fish within the park and must follow strict regulations, including no use of live bait. Some waterways are permanently closed to anglers, while others are open only at certain times of the year. Before heading out, read the regulations or speak to the park staff.

Alpine Anglers
FISHING | This company gives fly-fishing lessons and conducts fly-fishing excursions of a full day or longer. ⊠ *Banff* ☎ *403/760–1133* ⊕ *www.alpineanglers.com* ⊠ *Call for pricing.*

Banff Fishing Unlimited
FISHING | The experiences this company arranges include fishing for trophy lake trout on Lake Minnewanka and fly-fishing for brown trout on the Bow River. In winter, the company also conducts ice-fishing excursions. ⊠ *Banff* ☎ *403/762–4936, 866/678–2486* ⊕ *www.banff-fishing.com* ⊠ *From C$560 (price per person varies depending on group size).*

Hawgwild Fly Fishing Guides
FISHING | Learn how to fly-fish from local guide Big Jim Dykstra by signing up with this outfit, which also offers ice fishing in winter. ⊠ *Banff* ☎ *403/760–2446* ⊕ *www.*

banffflyfishingguides.com ✉ *From C$395.*

Tightline Adventures

FISHING | Daylong and multiday fly-fishing trips can be arranged through Tightline. ✉ *129 Banff Ave., Banff* ☎ *403/763–9669* ⊕ *www.tightlineadventures.com* ✉ *From C$600.*

GOLF
Fairmont Banff Springs Golf Course

GOLF | Breathtaking views are the norm on this championship course, whose challenging 27 holes wind along the Bow River beneath snowcapped peaks. Stanley Thompson, a major Canadian course architect of his day, designed the original 18-hole course, which opened in 1928. The 9-hole Tunnel Course, designed by Cornish and Robinson (the former a Thompson protégé), opened in the late 1980s. ✉ *Fairmont Banff Springs, 405 Spray Ave., Banff* ☎ *403/762–6801, 877/591–2525* ⊕ *www.fairmont.com/banff-springs/golf* ✉ *Stanley Thompson Course, C$220; Tunnel Course, C$98* ⊘ *Closed Nov.–Apr.* 🏌 *Stanley Thompson Course: 18 holes, 6938 yards, par 71; Tunnel course: 9 holes, 3287 yards, par 36.*

HIKING

The trail system in Banff National Park allows you to access the heart of the Canadian Rockies. The scenery is spectacular, and you can see wildlife such as birds, squirrels, deer, and sheep along many of the trails. Make noise as you travel the trails so you don't surprise a bear or other large animal. Also, prepare for any and all weather conditions by dressing in layers and bringing at least a half gallon of drinking water along per person on all full-day hikes. Get a trail map at the information center. Some of the more popular trails have bathrooms or outhouses at the trailhead. Dogs should be leashed at all times, and hikers should carry bear spray. You can purchase bear spray for about C$40 at most sporting goods shops in Banff or it can

be rented for C$10 per day from **Bactrax** (*snowtips-bactrax.com*).

Great Divide Nature Interpretation

HIKING & WALKING | Fun, guided, interpretive full-day summer hikes and half-day winter snowshoeing treks are this company's specialty. ✉ *Banff* ☎ *403/522–2735* ⊕ *www.greatdivide.ca* ✉ *From C$74 (snowshoeing trips) and C$80 (hikes).*

White Mountain Adventures

ADVENTURE TOURS | Daily guided hikes, ATV-assisted hiking, heli-hiking and guided e-bike tours can be arranged through this outfitter. In winter, you can try snowshoeing or a guided ice walk. ✉ *202 Bear St., Banff* ☎ *403/760–4403, 800/408–0005* ⊕ *www.whitemountainadventures.com* ✉ *From C$89.*

HORSEBACK RIDING

Experiencing the Canadian Rockies on horseback takes you back to the era of Banff's early explorers. Several outfitters conduct guided trips lasting from an hour to a few days. Make your reservations well ahead, though, especially in summer and for multiday journeys. Short-term boarding is available in Canmore and a few other communities outside Banff.

Banff Trail Riders

HORSEBACK RIDING | **FAMILY** | In addition to riding lessons, hour- or daylong horseback rides, and multiday backcountry trips, this company offers summertime carriage rides and cowboy cookouts, as well as wintertime sleigh rides. ✉ *138 Banff Ave., Banff* ☎ *403/762–4551, 800/661–8352* ⊕ *www.horseback.com* ✉ *From C$42.*

Brewster Adventures

HORSEBACK RIDING | This Lake Louise-based outfit conducts daily summer trail rides to the Plain of Six Glaciers, Lake Agnes Tea House, and Paradise Valley. Barbecues and barn dances are other summer offerings, or you can experience the "cowboy way of life" on overnight to multiday pack adventures featuring accommodations in rustic cabins. In the winter, sleigh rides depart from the lakefront at the Fairmont Château Lake Louise. Ask about the company's country Christmas dinner that includes a sleigh ride. ⊠ *Lake Louise* ☎ *403/762–5454, 800/691–5085* ⊕ *www.brewsteradventures.com* ⊠ *From C$45.*

Timberline Tours

HORSEBACK RIDING | Trail rides ranging from 10 minutes to 10 days can be arranged with Timberline Tours. ⊠ *St Piran Dr., Lake Louise* ☎ *403/522–3743, 888/858–3388* ⊕ *www.timberlinetours.ca* ⊠ *From C$15.*

MULTISPORT OUTFITTERS
Abominable Ski & Sportswear

SKIING & SNOWBOARDING | Here you can rent or buy snowshoes or ski and snowboarding equipment ⊠ *229 Banff Ave., Banff* ☎ *403/762–2905* ⊕ *www.abominablesports.com.*

★ Snowtips Bactrax

SKIING & SNOWBOARDING | In summer, this is the place to rent backcountry gear as well as road, trail, tandem, or e-bikes. In winter, look for Banff's largest selection of snow-sport equipment rentals, including snowboards, downhill and Nordic skis, snowshoes, fat bikes, and hockey skates. ⊠ *225 Bear St., Banff* ☎ *403/762–8177* ⊕ *www.snowtips-bactrax.com.*

Soul Ski + Bike

LOCAL SPORTS | This great spot sells, rents, and services bicycles, skis, and snowboards. Soul Ski is also well known for its custom ski boot–fitting service, and the company rents and sells standard, deluxe, and premium equipment. ⊠ *203A Bear St., Banff* ☎ *403/760–1650* ⊕ *www.soulskiandbike.com.*

Ultimate Sports

SKIING & SNOWBOARDING | You can rent ski and snowboard equipment and bikes here and take advantage of the shop's free hotel delivery. ⊠ *206 Banff Ave., Banff* ☎ *403/762–0547, 866/754–7433* ⊕ *www.ultimatebanff.com* ⊠ *From C$45.*

ROCK CLIMBING
★ Via Ferrata

ROCK CLIMBING | Even a novice can climb a mountain safely using Norquay's awesome Via Ferrata. The term "Via Ferrata" is Italian for "iron road," and this protected climbing route uses metal cable fixed to the rock along with iron rungs, pegs, carved footholds, ladders, and bridges. After gearing up, you take a chairlift up the mountain and then follow a certified guide along a route that takes two, four, or six hours to complete. This activity requires good hiking shoes, but shoes are available for loan if you don't have your own. ⊠ *2 Mt. Norquay Rd., Banff* ☎ *844/667—7829* ⊕ *banffnorquay.com* ⊠ *From C$175.*

★ Yamnuska

ROCK CLIMBING | Canada's largest mountain-guide company conducts guided mountaineering, rock climbing, backcountry skiing, and ice-climbing trips and lessons. ⊠ *50 Lincoln Park, Canmore* ☎ *403/678–4164, 866/678–4164* ⊕ *www.yamnuska.com* ⊠ *From C$280.*

SKIING

Not only does Banff have three outstanding downhill ski areas, but Banff, Lake Louise, and Castle Junction also have a vast network of classic and skate-skiing cross-country trails. You can rent equipment out on slopes or at in-town shops, many of which are concentrated along Bear Street and Banff Avenue.

For downhill ski or boarding instruction, consider booking the program called Guided Adventures (*www.skibig3.com*). For C$440, participants receive one day of instruction at each of the three resorts with the same instructor, guided tours of each resort, lift-line priority, and a souvenir photo. Lift tickets are not included.

■ TIP→ **A good bargain is a three-day pass (C$354) that allows you to ski at the Sunshine Village, Mt. Norquay, and Lake Louise ski areas. The pass, available at the ski areas and the Banff Ski Hub store or online** at www.skibig3.com, includes free shuttle service to the slopes.

Banff Sunshine Village
SKIING & SNOWBOARDING | About a 15-minute drive from Banff Townsite, this high-altitude resort with skiable terrain on three mountains has the longest non-glacial ski season in Canada and some of the prettiest views. Sunshine gets as many as 9 meters (30 feet) of dry, powdery snow in a season. Canada's first heated chairlift was installed here for the 2015–2016 season. Sunshine Mountain Lodge is Banff's only ski-in ski-out mountain lodge. The resort's free ride zones including Delirium Dive and the Wild West are some of the most extreme resort-accessed terrain in North America requiring skiers and riders in these zones to come equipped with avalanche gear. **Facilities:** 139 trails; 3,358 acres; 3,514-foot vertical drop; 12 lifts. ⊠ 1 Sunshine Access Rd., off Hwy. 1, Banff ☎ 403/762–6500, 877/542–2633 ⊕ www.skibanff.com ⊠ Lift ticket: C$127 ☉ Closed mid-May–mid-Nov.

Lake Louise Ski Resort
SKIING & SNOWBOARDING | FAMILY | Lake Louise is one of the largest ski resorts in North America, and it keeps getting larger, with the addition of a quad chair and 480 more acres of terrain in 2020. With beginner, intermediate, and expert runs from every chair, this is a great place for families—the downhill terrain on four mountain faces and north-facing back bowls are expansive and varied. Also here are an excellent ski school, a terrain park, a tube park and a beginner's fun zone. **Facilities:** 163 trails; 4,200 acres; 3,250-foot vertical drop; 12 lifts. ⊠ 1 Whitehorn Rd., off Lake Louise Dr., Lake Louise ☎ 403/522–3555, 877/956–8473 ⊕ www.skilouise.com ⊠ Lift ticket: C$124.

Mt. Norquay
SKIING & SNOWBOARDING | The oldest ski resort in the Canadian Rockies is only a five-minute drive from Banff. Locals like this six-lift, 60-run mountain, and so do Olympic and World Cup trainees. Night skiing and tubing take place here, too. **Facilities:** 38 trails; 190 acres; 1,650-foot vertical drop; 6 lifts. ☎ 403/762–4421 ⊕ www.banffnorquay.com ⊠ Lift ticket: C$93.

SWIMMING
Banff Centre Sally Borden Fitness Centre
SWIMMING | FAMILY | Amenities here include a 25-meter (82-foot) swimming pool, a wading pool, an outdoor sundeck, a climbing wall, a fitness center, a gymnasium, and a squash center. You can also attend a fitness class. ⊠ 107 Tunnel Mountain Rd., Banff ☎ 403/762–6100 ⊕ www.banffcentre.ca ⊠ C$5.50 public swim (free last Sun. of month).

What's Nearby

Mount Assiniboine Provincial Park and the Bighorn Backcountry near Banff offer incredible scenery, spectacular hiking, wildlife viewing, camping, skiing and fishing.

Mount Assiniboine Provincial Park

Mount Assiniboine Provincial Park is a place of remarkable beauty with glistening lakes, ancient glaciers, rugged peaks, and high alpine meadows. The 39,050-hectare (96,500-acre) triangle-shaped provincial park lies between Kootenay Provincial Park and Banff National Park and though the park is in British Columbia, it's most often accessed from Alberta. The park is also home to remarkable ski terrain and North America's oldest backcountry ski lodge, Assiniboine Lodge.

At 3,618 meters (11,870 feet), Mount Assiniboine is the highest peak in the Southern Continental Ranges of the Canadian Rockies and is the undisputed

Did You Know?

A staggering 30 feet of powder fall on Banff's Sunshine Village each year, creating a winter-sports paradise. Snowboarders and skiers can hit more than 3,300 acres of terrain on three mountains.

highlight of Mount Assiniboine Provincial Park. The pyramidal peak at the continental divide has been dubbed the "Matterhorn of the Canadian Rockies." The stunning peak towers over glacier-fed Lake Magog and is surrounded by alpine meadows.

Mount Assiniboine was named by George M. Dawson, a Canadian geologist and surveyor, in 1885. He saw the peak from another mountain and its shape and the cloud formations above it reminded him of smoke escaping from the top of an Assiniboine teepee. The name "Assiniboine" means "stone boilers," which references the preferred cooking method of this Indigenous group. The first summit of Mount Assiniboine was achieved in 1901 by James Outrum and two Swiss guides, Christian Bohren and Christian Hasler.

This unique provincial park is also one of the premier backpacking destinations in the Canadian Rockies offering truly unspoiled wilderness. There are no roads and few amenities. You can reach the park on foot, by helicopter, or on horseback on certain trails with a special park permit. Hiking, mountain climbing, fishing, horseback riding, camping, and backcountry skiing are the main activities. Mount Assiniboine Provincial Park is part of the Canadian Rocky Mountain UNESCO World Heritage Site.

GETTING HERE AND AROUND
The easiest way to access Mount Assiniboine Provincial Park is by helicopter from the Mount Shark Heliport in Spray Valley Provincial Park, about 40 km (25 miles) southwest of Canmore. Alpine Helicopters (*alpinehelicopters.com*) operates the flights, but they are booked through Assiniboine Lodge (*403/678-2883, assiniboinelodge.com*). The flight costs C$190 per person one-way and each person is allowed 40 lbs of luggage plus one set of skis. If you're hiking into the lodge, you can make the hike easier

by arranging to have most of your gear flown in at a cost of C$4 per pound.

Hiking is the other main way to access this park. The two main trails both begin in Alberta.

The Bryant Creek route in Spray Valley Provincial Park is 26.7 km (16.6 miles) one-way with a 460 meters (1509 feet) elevation gain. This strenuous hike will take 8-10 hours one-way and you'll find the trailhead near the Mount Shark Heliport.

The Sunshine Village approach is 29 km (18 miles) one-way and has 400 meters (1312 feet) elevation gain. The route is slightly longer than the Bryant Creek approach, but the terrain is less steep and the alpine scenery is stunning on this hike.

◉ Sights

SCENIC STOPS
Lake Magog
BODY OF WATER | Beautiful glacier-fed Lake Magog sits in front of Mt. Assiniboine and it is the site of most of the park's facilities and trailheads. The two main hiking routes into the park lead to this lake. An easy 3.2-km (2-mile) trail around the west shore of the lake offers wonderful views of Mt. Assiniboine reflecting off the lake surface. ✉ *Mt. Assiniboine Provincial Park ✛ 26.7 km (16.6 miles) from the Bryant Creek Trailhead.*

TRAILS
Niblet and Nublet
TRAIL | This moderately difficult 3-km (1.9-mile) hike offers stunning views of Sunburst, Elizabeth, Cerulean, Magog, and Wedgewood Lakes as well as Sunburst Peak and Mount Assiniboine. The hike begins at the lodge and climbs up to a ridge known as the Niblet and then continues on to the summit of the Nublet. The total elevation gain is 350 meters (1,148 feet). *Moderate.* ✉ *Assiniboine Lodge, Mt. Assiniboine Provincial Park ✛ Trailhead: located at the Assiniboine Lodge.*

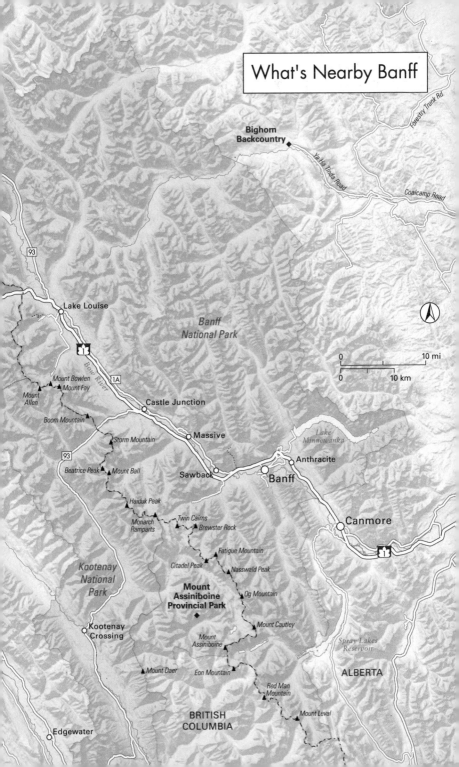

What's Nearby Banff

Sunburst, Cerulean and Elizabeth Lakes
TRAIL | It's a beautiful and relatively easy hike along the Sunburst Trail from Assiniboine Lodge to Elizabeth Lake. The Sunburst Trail branches off the Lake Magog Trail just before the campground. The trail goes along the shore of Sunburst Lake past Lizzie Rummel's log cabin to Cerulean Lake and then climbs a ridge where you have the option of turning east to hike 1 km (0.6 mile) up to the Niblet or continuing straight to Elizabeth Lake. The hike is 4.4 km (2.7 miles) one-way to Elizabeth Lake without adding the Niblet and Nublet. You can do it in a loop by continuing on from Elizabeth Lake and turning east along the shore of Cerulean Lake. *Easy.* ✉ *Assiniboine Lodge, Mt. Assiniboine Provincial Park* ✥ *Trailheads: begins at Assiniboine Lodge.*

Wonder Pass
TRAIL | This 3.1-km (2-mile) trail leads to Wonder Pass and the spectacular views that inspired the name. The trail begins at Assiniboine Lodge and goes past the Naiset Huts to Gog Lake. From there it climbs past a lovely waterfall to reach Wonder Pass, which lies between Wonder Peak and the Towers. *Moderate.* ✉ *Assiniboine Lodge, Mt. Assiniboine Provincial Park* ✥ *Trailhead: begins at Assiniboine Lodge.*

Hotels

Assiniboine Lodge
$$$$ | **ALL-INCLUSIVE** | The only lodge in Mount Assiniboine Provincial Park is also the oldest backcountry ski lodge in the Canadian Rockies. **Pros:** historic lodge; incredible views; delicious meals included. **Cons:** costly; only accessible on foot or by helicopter; limited electricity, no Wi-Fi, no cell signal. [$] *Rooms from: C$760* ✉ *Lake Magog, Mt. Assiniboine Provincial Park* ☎ *403/678–2883, 403/678–4877* 🌐 *assiniboinelodge.com* 🕘 *Closed mid-Oct.–mid-Feb. and April–late June* 🍴 *All-Inclusive* 🛏 *6 rooms, 7 cabins.*

Activities

CAMPING

Lake Magog Campground. This 40-site campground sits on the west shore of Lake Magog, 1.6 km (1 mile) from the lodge and the helipad. Reserve a campsite up to four months in advance through the BC Parks reservations system. *discovercamping.ca 800/689–9025.*

Og Lake Campground. This 10-site campground sits on the shores of a beautiful alpine lake. A 5.6-km (3½-mile) trail connects the campground to the lodge and the helipad. Sites can be reserved up to four months in advance through the BC Parks reservation system. *discovercamping.ca 800/689–9025.*

Bighorn Backcountry

Bighorn Backcountry is a collection of 12 Public Land Use Zones that protect more than 5,000 square kilometers (1,930 square miles) of land just east of Banff and Jasper National Parks. This region on the eastern slopes of the Rocky Mountains has wonderful mountain scenery, excellent hiking trails, comfortable campgrounds, sparkling lakes, rivers, and waterfalls. There aren't many hotels, shops, or restaurants, but each zone has its own rules and there are areas for hikers, snowmobilers, equestrians, and even off-highway vehicles.

This part of Alberta is also known as David Thompson Country because it stretches along the highway of the same name. David Thompson was a British Canadian fur trader, surveyor, and explorer who mapped about one-fifth of the North American continent—including the Bighorn Backcountry.

Indigenous people have deep connections to this land and you may find the remains of sweat lodges and prayer sites in some areas. Please be respectful and do not touch or remove artifacts. The

Kootenay Plains area was an important overwintering area for Indigenous people for thousands of years. When you hike the trails, view the wildlife, and see the stunning scenery, you'll understand why Indigenous people still consider this place to be sacred.

GETTING HERE AND AROUND

Both Calgary and Edmonton International Airports are about a three-hour drive from Bighorn Backcountry. Red Deer Regional Airport is a little more than a two-hour drive.

A vehicle is essential for getting around Bighorn Backcountry. There are very few facilities and no public transportation. This region is far less developed than the nearby national parks.

Pursuit Adventures

Half-day and full-day guided hiking tours, snowshoeing, ice bubble tours, and heli-hiking excursions can be booked with pick up in Nordegg. ⊠ *4 Stuart St., Nordegg* ☎ *403/986–6190, 877/907–6071 toll-free* ⊕ *pursuitadventures.ca* ⊠ *from C$60.*

⊙ Sights

HISTORIC SITES
Brazeau Collieries Historic Mine Site

HISTORIC SIGHT | Guided tours of Brazeau Collieries Historic Mine Site offer a glimpse into an industrial coal mine operation and the lives of miners who worked and lived in this area. Two-hour guided tours are given of the mine, a Provincial and National Historic Resource, three times daily during the summer. ⊠ *Nordegg, Bighorn Backcountry* ✛ *600 meters (0.4 miles) southwest from downtown Nordegg* ☎ *403/845–4444 administrator Clearwater County, 403/721–2625 Nordegg Heritage Centre* ⊕ *www.clearwatercounty.ca* ⊠ *C$10 adults, C$30 family pass* ☉ *Closed Wed. and early Sept.–mid-May.*

SCENIC STOPS
Abraham Lake

BODY OF WATER | Alberta's largest reservoir is beautiful in every season, but it has become Instagram famous in winter when bubbles freeze in the ice—pockets of methane gas freeze in layers that coat the lake. Methane gas bubbles are formed when bacteria breaks down organic matter at the bottom of the lake. It's a phenomenon that's found in other Rocky Mountain lakes, but it's more visible in Abraham Lake because high winds tend to keep the ice clear of snow; January and February are peak months to view the bubbles. The manmade lake was created in 1972 with the construction of the Bighorn Dam. The lake has a surface area of 53.7 square km (20.7 square miles). Although the lake is manmade, it still has the turquoise blue color of other Rocky Mountain Lakes. Watch for bighorn sheep, black bears, and other wildlife nearby. ⊠ *Abraham Lake, Bighorn Backcountry* ✛ *43 km (27 miles) southwest of Nordegg.*

Crescent Falls

WATERFALL | Crescent Falls is a 27-meter (89-foot) two-tiered waterfall that is beautiful in every season. The turnoff for Crescent Falls Provincial Recreation Area is 22 km (13.7 miles) west of Nordegg on Highway 11. The gravel access road is 6 km (3.7 miles) long and there's a lookout point partway along the road where you get great views of the Bighorn Gorge. There's also a 29-site campground near the falls. ⊠ *Crescent Falls, Bighorn Backcountry* ✛ *27 km (16.8 miles) southwest of Nordegg.*

TRAILS
Allstones Lake

TRAIL | This moderately strenuous 13-km (8.1-mile) round-trip hike leads to a lovely alpine lake with beautiful views along the way. If you climb to the top of the peak near the lake you'll have a stunning view of Abraham Lake and the surrounding mountains. *Moderate.* ⊠ *Abraham Lake,*

Bighorn Backcountry ⊕ Trailhead: across from Abraham Lake, 33 km (20 miles) southwest of Nordegg on Hwy. 11.

Siffleur Falls

TRAIL | Siffleur Falls is one of the most popular trails in Bighorn Country. The relatively easy 8-km (5-mile) round-trip hike will take you across a suspension bridge, a boardwalk, and along a deep gorge with several viewing points before you reach beautiful Siffleur Falls. The trail is wide and relatively easy with only about 100 meters (328 feet) of elevation gain. It's a good hike for families, but it cannot accommodate strollers or wheelchairs. Ambitious hikers can continue on past the first falls to see two more waterfalls at 6.2 km (3.9 miles) and 6.9 km (4.3 miles) one-way. This trail can be busy in summer. *Easy.* ✉ *Siffleur Falls, Bighorn Backcountry ⊕ Trailhead: Approximately 62 km (38 miles) west of Nordegg and 21 km (13 miles) east of the Banff National Park boundary.*

Coffee and Quick Bites

The Nordegg Cantine

$ | **CANADIAN** | This casual little restaurant serves all-day breakfast, sandwiches, snacks, baked goods, house-made donuts, salads and picnic lunches to go. It's a great place to stop for a hot dog, French fries, poutine, ice cream, house-made ice pops or house-made marshmallows for ultra special camping s'mores. **Known for:** good stop for a quick bite; house-made donuts; craft beers and pop. [$] *Average main: C$10* ✉ *4 Stuart St., Nordegg* ☎ *403/986–6190* 🌐 *orders.nordeggcanteen.ca.*

Hotels

Aurum Lodge

$ | **B&B/INN** | Surrounded by trees and mountains, this rustic ecolodge overlooking Abraham Lake has six lodge rooms, one apartment with a full kitchen, and two duplex cabin units with kitchens. **Pros:** great location overlooking Abraham Lake; secluded and romantic; delicious breakfast included. **Cons:** limited cellphone coverage; no TVs; no phones. [$] *Rooms from: C$199* ✉ *18032 David Thompson Hwy. #17562, Abraham Lake, Bighorn Backcountry ⊕ 46.3 km (28.8 miles) southwest of Nordegg at the Cline River* ☎ *403/721–2117* 🌐 *www.aurum-lodge.ca* 🍴 *Free Breakfast* ☞ *Minimum 3-night stay* ⇨ *7 units.*

Activities

CAMPING

Two O'Clock Creek Campground. Located in Kootenay Plains Provincial Recreation Area, this campground has 20 unserviced sites and six tent sites. Each site has a firepit and a picnic table and there's a water pump and pit toilets in the campground. There are a few sites near the creek and more in the grassy plains area. *C$28 per night, 67 km (41.6 miles) west of Nordegg on Hwy. 11 403/721–3975 www.albertaparks.ca/parks/central/kootenay-plains-pra.*

CANYONING

Western Canyoning Adventures

ROCK CLIMBING | This company offers canyoning tours with certified guides in several canyons near Abraham Lake. Canyoning, also known as canyoneering, involves traversing a canyon or gorge by hiking, climbing, swimming, and rappelling. It's a high adrenaline activity and guests need to be somewhat physically fit in order to hike, swim, and climb through a canyon. Certified guides provide all of the safety equipment needed. ✉ *Windy Point, Abraham Lake, Bighorn Backcountry ⊕ guests are met at Windy Point near Abraham Lake* ☎ *587/838–5336* 🌐 *www.westcanyon.ca* 🎫 *From C$179* ⏲ *Closed mid-Sept.–early June.*

HELICOPTER TOURS
Rockies Heli Canada
AIR EXCURSIONS | A wide variety of helicopter tours are on offer with this company based in Bighorn Backcountry near Abraham Lake. Sightseeing, heli-hiking, heli-glamping, heli-fishing, heli-snowshoeing, and heli-ice bubble tours are some of the unique experiences available. ✉ *Abraham Lake* ✛ *49.2 km (30 miles) southwest of Nordegg near the Cline River* ☎ *403/721–2100, 888/844–3514 toll-free* ⊕ *www.rockiesheli.com* 🎫 *from C$199 per person.*

HORSEBACK RIDING
McKenzie's Trails West
HORSEBACK RIDING | This family-run outfitter has a 50-year history of guiding horseback riding vacations near the Cline River area. They offer rides ranging from 10 minutes to day rides to multiday pack trips. They also host a variety of special events including cowboy barbecues and women's retreats. ✉ *Whitegoat Lakes* ✛ *48.2 km (30 miles) southwest of Nordegg on Hwy. 11* ☎ *403/721–7433* ⊕ *mctrails.com* 🎫 *From C$12* ⊘ *Closed mid-Sept.–mid-May.*

ROCK CLIMBING
Girth Hitch Guiding
ROCK CLIMBING | Guided climbing tours with this company are ideal for those who have always wanted to learn to rock climb as well as experienced climbers who want to challenge themselves. Tim Taylor, a proud Métis climber and company owner, feels that his connection with the mountains is deeply rooted in his cultural background. Girth Hitch Guiding offers personalized and customized climbing adventures—everything from Via Ferrata climbs to rappelling, skills courses, and multi-pitch climbing. ✉ *25 Page Ave., Red Deer* ☎ *403/318–1364* ⊕ *www.girthhitchguiding.ca* 🎫 *from C$499 for up to four people* ⊘ *Closed mid-Oct.–mid-June.*

Chapter 5

CALGARY

By
Jeff Gailus

Sights ⭐⭐⭐⭐⭐   Restaurants ⭐⭐⭐⭐⭐   Hotels ⭐⭐⭐⭐⭐   Shopping ⭐⭐⭐⭐⭐   Nightlife ⭐⭐⭐⭐⭐

WELCOME TO CALGARY

TOP REASONS TO GO

★ **Calgary Stampede:** Four million people a year can't be wrong about this 10-day party billed as the Greatest Outdoor Show On Earth.

★ **Gastronomy:** Calgary is home to many of Canada's best restaurants and an almost infinite number of cocktail lounges, wine bars, pubs, and microbreweries.

★ **Friendly vibes:** In 2019, Calgary beat out Zurich as the world's cleanest city, and it's one of the friendliest, most welcoming destinations you'll ever visit.

★ **Gateway to the Rockies:** Most visitors enjoy Calgary before (or after) heading to the mountains to ski, hike, and relax.

★ **Winter Wonderland:** There are five major ski hills, hundreds of kilometers of cross-country trails, and limitless backcountry terrain in the mountains and foothills west of Calgary.

★ **Cycle City:** Calgary boasts more kilometers of bike lanes, pathways, and trails than any other North American city.

1 **Downtown.** All shiny and mostly new, this is Stampede City's heart and soul, where you can enjoy museums and galleries and dine in some of Canada's best restaurants.

2 **Kensington.** Full of cool shops, cafés, and bars, this cozy neighborhood across the river is famous for its patios and walkability.

3 **The Beltline and 17th Avenue.** Sandwiched between Downtown and 17th Avenue, the Beltline is Calgary's most urban and eclectic district and Downtown's alter ego. Known as the "Red Mile," 17th Avenue is a lively 13-block retail and entertainment district that boasts more than a hundred boutique shops, fine-dining restaurants, and lively lounges close to Downtown and Stampede Park.

4 **The Mission.** This old Francophone settlement turned hip hotspot hosts the annual Lilac Festival each June.

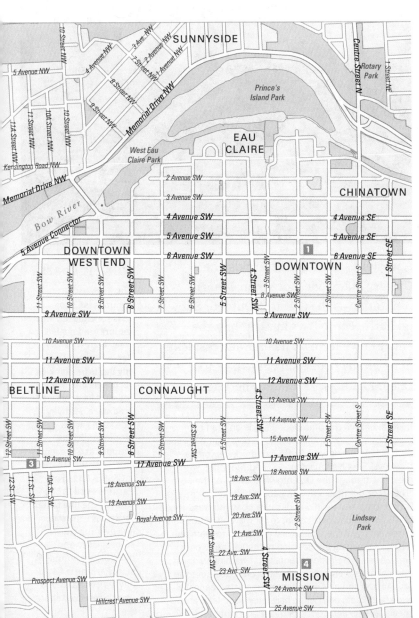

CALGARY STAMPEDE

A panoramic view of the Calgary Stampede at sunset.

A western state fair on steroids, the Calgary Stampede more than earns its reputation as the Greatest Outdoor Show on Earth. For 10 days in early July, the entire city lets down its hair, and residents don cowboy boots and white hats to celebrate Calgary's western heritage.

It kicks off with the Stampede Parade on the first morning, a Friday, when 350,000 people watch dozens of marching bands, 150 floats, hundreds of horses, cowboys, First Nations dancers, and Mounties wend their way through the Downtown core. Over the next 10 days, more than a million people head to Stampede Park to drop and whirl on rides, watch world-class rodeo cowboys and cowgirls compete for millions of dollars in prizes, and visit the agricultural exhibition to learn about Alberta's ranching and farming heritage. The Evening Show sees more rodeo events and awarding-winning musical guests entertain until fireworks close out the day. All over the city, volunteers put on free pancake breakfasts, bars and dance halls stay open late, and special events and concerts take place night and day.

WHAT IT COSTS

Entrance to the Grounds is C$20, C$12 for children and seniors (under 7 is free). ■TIP→ Family Day is free, and Community Day is free for kids, but tickets are limited and must be purchased in advance. Midway rides and games require multiple coupons at C$1 each; an all-day wristband is C$58. A C$25 Fast Pass gets you to the front of the line faster. Tickets for the rodeo and evening shows start at C$50 and include gate admission. Parking is C$25/day, twice that if you want a reserved spot.

Midway has rides for all ages and levels of thrill-seekers.

s a full-blown country bar that has hosted greats like Johnny Cash, Eric Church, and the Nitty Gritty Dirt Band. The Saddledome also hosts superstar musicians for a concert or two; in 2019, it was Sugarland.

TIPS FOR FIRST-TIMERS

Buy Tickets in Advance: Rodeo, evening show, and value day tickets sell out fast.

Getting There: There is parking on the Grounds, but it fills up fast. Better to park outside Downtown at a C-train station and take the train to the Erlton or Victoria Park stations.

Keep Cool: July is Calgary's hottest month. Remember to wear sunscreen and a hat, stay hydrated, and get out of the sun in the indoor exhibits and other air-conditioned spaces.

Stay Close: If the Stampede is your primary reason to visit Calgary, stay Downtown or in the Beltline district as it's an easy walk or a short cab ride to the Grounds. It also puts you in the heart of the city's entertainment and shopping districts, where restaurants, bars, and shops abound.

Pace Yourself: This is not your average state fair. There's lots to see and do; if you want to experience all that Stampede City has to offer, plan to spend at least two days (preferably three).

HISTORY OF THE STAMPEDE

2022 marks the Stampede's 110th anniversary. It all began in 191_ American Wild West performer_ Weadick was invited to produce _ "Frontier Days and Cowboy Champ_ ship Contest," the first iteration of the Stampede. Despite the fact that the Calgary population was only 60,000, 80,000 people lined the streets to watch the first parade. Weadick was the brainchild of many of the most popular events, including the chuckwagon races, and it grew ever bigger after WWII; by the 1950s it had become the Greatest Outdoor Show on Earth, and stars and celebrities, including Bing Crosby and Queen Elizabeth, made regular appearances. Today, more than a million visitors attend annually, making it a cultural and economic lodestone for the City of Calgary.

WHAT'S HERE

The Calgary Stampede has grown by leaps and bounds over the years, and there are a few different aspects to the Big Show these days.

Midway: This giant amusement park—rides and rows of booths offering all kinds of food and games of skill and chance—is the first thing you see when you enter the gates. The age-old Zipper is still around, as is the Mega

More than 350,000 people pass through the Calgary Stampede entrance every July.

Experience_
Elbow River _

Drop and the _
FUNtier offers a_
and other kids' act_
items include pickle _
flaming hot Cheetos c_
food ramen poutine, an_
bombs.

Rodeo: Every afternoon, more of North America's best cowboy_ cowgirls compete to make Stamp_ history in nine events, from bull ridin_ to barrel racing. Contestants compete all week to see who makes the Sunday finals. Tickets must be purchased in advance, and they often sell out.

Evening Show: A combination of grit, glamour, and live music, horsemanship is showcased with the bareback relay races and bronc riding, followed by the Rangeland Derby, the world's premier chuckwagon races. As darkness falls, a variety show for the ages takes place, with magicians, stunt artists, familiar musical guests, and a fabulous pyrotechnic display.

Live Music: The Stampede Summer Stage offers free rock, pop, and hip-hop music daily. The Big Four Roadhouse offers the opportunity to get out of the sun, grab a cold drink, watch the live feed of the rodeo in the afternoon, or listen to live tunes in the evening. Nashville North, on the other hand,

With the eastern face of the Rockies as its backdrop, the bright steel-and-glass skyline makes Calgary Alberta's shiny city on the hill, rising from the plains as if by sheer force of will. Indeed, all the elements in the great saga of the Canadian West—Mounties, Indigenous people, railroads, cowboys, cattle, oil—have converged to create a city with a modern face and a surprisingly traditional soul.

The city supports professional football and hockey teams, and in July the rodeo events, midway, and nonstop parties of the Calgary Stampede attract visitors from around the world. Calgary garnered global attention when it hosted the 1988 Winter Olympics, and the legacy is everywhere: a speed-skating track and bobsled run in town, and downhill slopes and miles of cross-country ski trails in Kananaskis, less than 90 minutes west of town. The city is also the perfect starting point for one of the preeminent dinosaur exploration sites in the world, a world-class dinosaur exploration tour at Dinosaur Provincial Park near Brooks and the Royal Tyrell Museum in Drumheller. The Glenbow Museum is one of Canada's top museums, and the EPCOR Centre for the Performing Arts showcases theater and musical performances.

The soul of Calgary is the bustling, cosmopolitan Stephen Avenue Walk, which was declared a National Historic District in 2002. Shops and restaurants in restored, turn-of-the-20th-century sandstone buildings line the promenade, while shoppers, businesspeople, and street performers pack the street. In warm weather, outdoor patios spill onto the sidewalks and are perfect for people-watching. The residential Eau Claire district, with its high-rise apartments and condominium developments, begins north of 8th Avenue and stretches toward the Bow River, bordering walking, cycling, and running paths. The large and vibrant Chinatown covers several square blocks adjacent to the city core; look for the bright blue cone on top of the spectacular Chinese Cultural Centre, which has its own restaurant. The Kensington district, just north of the city center, has boutique stores and cafés in restored, Victorian-style houses. Beyond the Downtown core but still in the heart of the city are the Beltline and Mission districts, scenic southwest neighborhoods with thriving shopping and nightlife scenes. The Beltline lies south of the railway tracks through Downtown and extends to 17th Avenue; Mission runs north along 4th Street SW from the Elbow River to 17th Avenue.

Calgary's history as a city began in 1875 when a detachment of Northwest Mounted Police arrived and established Fort Calgary. It wasn't until the Canadian Pacific Railway arrived in 1883 that the population began to climb, and with the establishment of a station in what is now the Downtown core, businesses began to gravitate to the area. The city is divided into four quadrants: northwest, north-east, southwest, and southeast. In the Calgary grid pattern, numbered streets run north–south in both directions from Centre Street and numbered avenues run east–west in both directions from Centre Avenue.

As the railway grew in importance in Calgary, it also established subdivisions aimed at specific income groups. Calgary's emerging elite built palatial homes on large lots in the Mount Royal district while the Ogden subdivision was developed for railway workers. To the east of Downtown is Inglewood, the heart of Calgary's first business district. Many of Calgary's first citizens lived here before the Canadian Pacific Railway arrived, forcing business to move to the Downtown core. Ninth Avenue South-east is now lined with antique stores and home furnishings stores, eateries, and cappuccino bars. As the city grew during the 1950s to the 1970s, sub-urban neighborhoods were established across sprawling ranch lands following the Northeast, Northwest, Southeast, and Southwest quadrants as they flow out from the Downtown core. Most commuters use major arteries such as Crowchild Trail, Bow Trail, Deerfoot Trail, Glenmore Trail, and Memorial Drive to enter and exit the Downtown core for their workday, so expect traffic on these major routes during morning (7–8:30 am) and afternoon (4:30–6 pm) rush hours.

Planning

When to Go

With the most comfortable weather overall in Canada, Alberta is a four-season destination. Calgary in particular gets more than its fair share of sun, and the summer rarely sees anything but minor showers. Summer high temperatures are generally in the low 70s F, though temps can reach into the high 90s in July and August. Winters generally hover in the 23 to 5 F range, and can plunge down to -20 F or lower for short periods of time. On average, April is the windiest month, June is the wettest, July the hottest, and January the coldest.

From June through September you're likely to encounter more festivals and the greatest number of open lodgings (some close seasonally). The Calgary Stampede, billed as the Greatest Outdoor Show on Earth, takes place in the middle of July. Spring and fall months offer a more tranquil experience for travelers, and September can be particularly rewarding, with a combination of warm weather and some autumn foliage. Summer and fall also offer perfect weather for hiking cycling and other outdoor activities.

Although winter can be cold, it's also a magical time to visit, with plenty of fluffy white snow and clear starry night skies that provide good views of the northern lights—visible from mid-August to early April. Winter is ideal for the many winter activities available, including easy access to downhill, backcountry, and cross-country skiing, as well as pond skating and dogsledding.

FESTIVALS AND EVENTS

Calgary Folk Music Festival. In late July, Prince's Island Park gets turned into a concert venue for the four-day Calgary Folk Music Festival. It's always a genre-bending affair, with past artists including k.d. lang, Emmylou Harris, David Byrne, and Elvis Costello. It's also a very family-friendly affair. *www.calgary-folkfest.com.*

Calgary Stampede. For 10 days in early July, rodeo events and chuck-wagon races draw the world's top cowboys and plenty of greenhorns to one of Canada's most popular events, the Calgary Stampede. In addition to rodeo events, there are livestock shows, concerts, a midway, and high-spirited Western-style entertainment. You should make room and ticket reservations well in advance (at least three months) if you plan to attend. *www.calgarystampede.com.*

CSIO Spruce Meadows Masters Tournament. Spruce Meadows, on the southern outskirts of Calgary, is one of the most prestigious equestrian facilities in the world, and the Masters is its biggest event of the year. In early September, a half-million visitors arrive to watch the best horses and riders in the world compete for $4 million in prizes. *www.sprucemeadows.com.*

Getting Here and Around

AIR

Calgary International Airport (YYC) is a modern, international airport 20 minutes northeast of the city center. Taxis make the trip between the airport and Downtown for C$40 to C$45, and airport sedans will cost C$50. Most major hotels offer shuttle service to and from the airport. You can also pick up a rental car at the airport, from which eight major car rental companies operate.

Major airlines serving Calgary include Air Canada, Airtransat, Alaska Airlines, American, British Airways, Delta, KLM, United, and WestJet.

AIRPORT Calgary International Airport. ✉ *2000 Airport Rd. NE, McCall North* ☎ *403/735–1234* ⊕ *www.yyc.com.*

BICYCLE

One of the best ways to get around town is to rent a shared e-scooter (*downtowncalgary.com/getting-around*), which you can find and rent via the Neuron or Bird smartphone apps. They are especially handy for zipping around Downtown, where you'll find hundreds of them lining the sidewalks.

CAR

The Trans-Canada Highway (Highway 1) runs southeast to west across southern Alberta through Calgary, and will take you to Canmore and Banff (1 ½-hour drive) and the Rocky Mountains. Highway 2 passes through Calgary on its way from the U.S. border to Edmonton and points north. Calgary is 690 km (428 miles) northwest of Helena, Montana; it's 670 km (415 miles) northeast of Seattle, via the Trans-Canada Highway. Within Calgary, although many sights are in the Downtown area and can be reached on foot, a car is useful for visiting outlying attractions.

PUBLIC TRANSPORTATION

Calgary Transit (CT) operates a comprehensive bus and light rail transit system throughout the city. Fares are C$3.50 and you can ask for a free transfer from the driver. Ten-ticket books are C$35. A Calgary Transit Day Pass good for unlimited rides costs C$11.

The C-Train has lines running northwest (Tuscay), northeast (Saddletowne), and south (Somerset-Bridlewood) from Downtown. The C-Train is free within the Downtown core. Download the Calgary Transit app to simplify your transit experience.

CONTACTS Calgary Transit. *(CT)* ✉ *125 7th Ave. SE, Calgary* ☎ *403/262–1000* ⊕ *www.calgarytransit.com.*

TAXI

Taxis start at C$3 and charge about C$2.50 for each additional 2 km (1 mile). Uber and TappCar, Canada's third-largest ride-sharing service, are also options for getting yourself around town.

CONTACTS Associated Cabs. ✉ *Calgary* ☎ *403/299–1111.***Checker.** ✉ *316 Meridian Rd. SE, Calgary* ☎ *403/299–9999* ⊕ *www.thecheckergroup.com.***TappCar.** ✉ *Calgary* ⊕ *www.tappcar.ca.*

Activities

BIKING

With approximately 850 km (528 miles) of regional pathways and 95 km (59 miles) of trails, Calgary has North America's most extensive urban pathway and cycle path network. Many of Calgary's major streets have dedicated bike lanes, including 12 Avenue SW, 8 Avenue SW, and 5 Street SW in the city center. If you want to get your kicks on dirt trails, head to Fish Creek Provincial Park (south Calgary) for flats and rolling hills or the Paskapoo Slopes (NW Calgary, east of Canada Olympic Park) for steeper terrain. If you can't bring your bike with you, Bow Cycle (*406/265–5422*; *www.bowcycle.com*) rents both bikes and bike racks.

CANOEING

There's nothing more quintessentially Canadian than paddling a canoe. You can get your chance at the Calgary Canoe Club (*403/246–5757*; *www.calgarycanoeclub.com*), which rents canoes (and paddles and life jackets) for use on the Glenmore Reservoir, where you can follow 14 km (8.7 miles) of shoreline and admire the beauty of the Weasel Flats natural area.

FISHING

The Bow River is one of the best trout streams in North America and it runs right through Calgary. The lower stretch below the city is renowned for abundant trophy-sized rainbow and brown trout. Although the Bow can be fished year-round, the best times of the year are the spring (particularly late June during the golden stonefly hatch) and September, when the fish are strong and feeding heavily to get ready for winter. Even experienced anglers are surprised by the ferocity of the fight. There are numerous guides in the Calgary area that will be happy to take you out for a float on their favorite stretches of the river.

GOLF

Calgarians are crazy about golf. The city even hosts the Shaw Charity Classic at the Canyon Meadows Golf and Country Club in mid-August, one of the top events on the PGA Tour Champions. The City of Calgary manages seven municipal golf courses, and there are another 12 public courses in or near the city. Try Bearspaw just north of the city limits or, if you want a real challenge, drive a few miles farther west to tackle the Mickelson National course near Springbank.

SKATING

Calgary offers some exceptional skating opportunities–even in the summer. The Olympic Oval at the University of Calgary (*www.oval.ucalgary.ca*) hosts public skating sessions year round, one of the few places in the world where you can rent a pair of speed skates and see how you do on some of the fastest ice in the world. In the winter, venture out to the Bowness Lagoon or Downtown's Olympic Plaza, where you can skate under the sun or stars. Both places rent skates, helmets, and pads; you can also try an ice bike at the Bowness Lagoon.

Restaurants

Restaurants reflect the region's ethnic makeup and offer a wide variety of cuisines—Ukrainian, Italian, Greek, Chinese, Scandinavian, French, Japanese—to fit every price range, though many of the newer eateries focus on "contemporary Canadian" cuisine. Places specializing in generous helpings of Canadian beef still dominate the scene in Calgary, owing to the city's cowboy heritage. Dress in the prairie cities tends toward formality in expensive restaurants but is casual in moderately priced and inexpensive restaurants.

Restaurant reviews have been shortened. For full information, visit Fodors.com.

Hotels

Relatively generic chain hotels in every price range dominate the lodging landscape in Calgary, especially Downtown and out by the airport. Notable exceptions include a few boutique hotels in some of the hipper districts around the city center. Motel Village, 5 km (3 miles) northwest of Downtown and close to the university, offers a handful of cheaper options. There is also a comfortable hostel that offers private rooms right Downtown.

If you visit Calgary during the annual Global Energy Show Conference and Exhibition in late September or during the Calgary Stampede in early July, you should book your accommodations well in advance and expect to pay premium rates.

Hotel reviews have been shortened. For full information, visit Fodors.com.

What It Costs in Canadian Dollars			
$	$$	$$$	$$$$
RESTAURANTS			
under C$16	C$16-C$22	C$22-C$30	over C$30
HOTELS			
under C$125	C$125-C$175	C$176-C$225	over C$225

Nightlife

Calgary has a work-hard, play-hard attitude, and that translates to a varied and vibrant nightlife. The scene ranges from cocktail bars and late-night pubs to house-music clubs and country dance halls. Most of these spots are located Downtown and in the Beltline district just to the south. The best way to experience Calgary's dark side is to don your cowboy boots and go for a long evening stroll to nosh, drink, and dance the night away.

Performing Arts

Although Calgary is known for cowboys, oil, and the Canadian Rockies, it also boasts a thriving theater and ballet scene and has in recent years made major investments in its music offerings. Most of the venues are located in Calgary's Cultural District in the downtown core. At the heart of it is the Arts Commons (formerly EPCOR Centre for the Performing Arts), which occupies a full city block and is home to five theaters and the world-class Jack Singer Concert Hall. Resident companies include Alberta Theatre Projects, Arts Commons Presents, the Calgary Philharmonic Orchestra, Downstage, One Yellow Rabbit, and Theatre Calgary. The Southern Alberta Jubilee Auditorium also hosts performances by Alberta Ballet, CPO, and a variety of other, mostly musical performances. Tickets can be purchased through Ticketmaster or from the individual companies.

MAJOR EVENTS

High Performance Rodeo: For three wild weeks in January, One Yellow Rabbit takes over performance spaces in Downtown Calgary to put on its High Performance Rodeo, Calgary's international festival of the arts. It always includes touring performances from across Canada, acclaimed international shows, and new and experimental work from artists here in Calgary. The programming is bold, cutting-edge, funny, frank, and full of heart. Tickets can be purchased from the Arts Commons box office (*403/294–9494*; *www.hprodeo.ca*).

Calgary Fringe Festival: Inglewood hosts this celebration of edgy, no-holds-barred music, art, and theatre for 10 days in early August. Be forewarned: Like all fringe events, what you'll experience here is uncensored, unexpected, and unforgettable. You'll find comedy, drama, improv, dance, magic, and more from a mix of young emerging artists and seasoned pros. You'll need to buy a fringe button (C$5) and the cost of the affordable tickets for each event (about C$15) goes into the pockets of the artists themselves. (403/451–9726; www. calgaryfringe.ca).

Shopping

Calgary's major shopping districts include Kensington, 17th Avenue, 4th Street Southwest, Inglewood, the Eau Claire Market, and Downtown on 8th. Various shopping malls include Chinook Center, Bankers Hall, WestHills Towne Center, and Market Mall.

Tours

Various tour companies run guided city-sightseeing excursions that cover historic and modern Calgary in either vans or buses. A typical three- to four-hour tour includes Fort Calgary and Canada Olympic Park; some include the Stampede Grounds, the Calgary Tower, and the Olympic Speedskating Oval at the University of Calgary. Prices range between C$29 for 1½ hours (without stops) and C$45 for 4 hours, which includes guided tours of Fort Calgary and Canada Olympic Park, as well as an elevation pass for the Calgary Tower. There are also walking tours, culinary tours, craft beer tours, and motorcycle-sidecar tours. Some companies operate seasonally; reservations are required for all companies.

Day trips to Banff, Lake Louise, and the Columbia Icefields are offered in buses or 15-passenger touring vans. The C$175 Icefields tour is 15 hours round-trip and includes a SnoCoach ride onto the glacier. Banff and Lake Louise tours (C$94–C$107) generally run nine hours and include a driver–guide who explains the history, geology, and ecology of the mountains.

Some tours include shopping stops in Banff, a drive around Lake Minnewanka, Moraine Lake, Johnson's Canyon, and the Banff Gondola. A few tours go north to Drumheller and the Royal Tyrrell Museum or south to Head-Smashed-In Buffalo Jump, a UNESCO World Heritage Site.

CONTACTS Hammerhead Scenic Tours. ⊠ 44 Riverview Gardens SE, Calgary ☎ 403/590–6930 ⊕ www.calgary-tourcompany.com.

Visitor Information

The main visitor information center for Tourism Calgary is located on 11th Avenue, but there are also walk-in visitor centers on the arrival and departure floors at the airport.

CONTACTS Tourism Calgary. ⊠ 238 11th Ave. SE, Suite 200, Calgary ☎ 800/661–1678 ⊕ www.visitcalgary.com.

Downtown

Downtown is the heart and soul of Calgary. As the headquarters of Canada's prominent oil industry, and the home of the second most corporate headquarters in Canada, the skyline is a marvel, its steel-and-glass skyscrapers towering over Downtown. Despite its corporate roots, it's also the city's cultural and culinary hotspot. You'll find some of the finest restaurants and bars here, particularly along Stephen Avenue Walk. Most of Calgary's prominent performing arts venues are here, including Arts Commons, as well as the Glenbow Museum, western Canada's largest museum. (The Glenbow is closed for renovations until late 2024.) It's also the location of the Calgary New Central Library, which won several architectural and design awards when it was built in 2018. With a range of accommodations, you could spend a week here and never need to leave Downtown.

The 191-meter (626-foot) Calgary Tower was completed in 1968.

GETTING AROUND

Parking: Calgarians love their cars, and Downtown is full of them. There's also plenty of parking, though weekdays can be tough. Limited street parking is available almost everywhere, and there are parking lots scattered around, too. Pay by card at the kiosks.

C-train: The C-train runs through Downtown along 7th Avenue, and it's free.

E-scooters: One of the best ways to get around Downtown is to rent an e-scooter, which are on almost every street corner. You can find and rent one via the Neuron or Bird smartphone apps. Visit downtowncalgary.com/getting-around for more information.

Cycling: With its plentiful bike lanes and pathways, Downtown Calgary is easily navigated on your two-wheel stallion.

TIMING

If you can, plan to avoid the commuters into Downtown. Rush hour traffic into Downtown is heavy between 7:30 and 9:30 am; outbound traffic peaks between 3:30 and 5:30 pm.

◉ Sights

Arts Commons

ARTS CENTER | The complex of four theater spaces and a state-of-the-art concert hall was pieced together in the 1980s by incorporating the historic **Calgary Public Building** (1930) and the **Burns Building** (1913). It's one of the largest arts complexes in Canada. ⊠ *205 8th Ave. SE, Downtown* ☎ *403/294–7455* ⊕ *www. artscommons.ca.*

Calgary Chinese Cultural Centre

NOTABLE BUILDING | The focal point of this ornate building in the heart of Chinatown is the Dr. Henry Fok Cultural Hall; the column details and paintings include 561 dragons and 40 phoenixes. It's modeled after the Temple of Heaven in Beijing. The center houses a cultural museum, an art gallery, a crafts store, an herbal-medicine store, and a 330-seat Chinese restaurant. ⊠ *197 1st St. SW, Chinatown*

Calgary

☎ *403/262–5071* ⊕ *www.culturalcentre. ca* ✉ *Free.*

Calgary Municipal Building
GOVERNMENT BUILDING | Reflected in the angular, mirrored walls of this building are several city landmarks, including the stunning City Hall, a stately 1911 sandstone building that houses the mayor's office and other city offices. ✉ *800 Macleod Trail SE, East Village* ☎ *403/268–2489* ⊕ *www.calgary.ca* ⊘ *Closed weekends.*

Calgary Tower
OBSERVATORY | **FAMILY** | The views from this 191-meter (626-foot) scepter-shaped edifice take in the city's layout, the surrounding plains, and the face of the Rockies rising 80 km (50 miles) to the west. A "torch" that crowns the tower is lighted for special events and occasions. The tower top also holds the revolving Sky 360 Restaurant and Lounge, which serves dinner nightly and weekend brunch; Ruth's Chris Steakhouse; and a gift shop. ✉ *101 9th Ave. SW, Downtown* ☎ *403/266–7171* ⊕ *www.calgarytower. com* ✉ *C$18.*

Calgary Zoo
ZOO | **FAMILY** | The zoo, on St. George's Island in the middle of Bow River, is one of Canada's largest, with more than 1000 creatures from 119 species in natural settings. The Canadian Wilds section replicates endangered Canadian ecosystems, and the Exploration Asia exhibit allows you to (safely) get up close to Amur tigers. Prehistoric Park, a Mesozoic landscape, displays 22 life-size dinosaur replicas. Destination Africa showcases two African ecosystems, the TransAlta Rainforest and the African Savannah, and has mixed-species exhibits of more than 100 animals, the largest indoor hippo immersion habitat in North America, and 84 plant species indigenous to the African continent. ✉ *1300 Zoo Rd. NE, East Village* ☎ *403/232–9300* ⊕ *www. calgaryzoo.com* ✉ *C$34.95.*

Plus 15 Skywalk 👁

Calgary winters can be harsh. To help people get around Downtown no matter the weather, the Skywalk was built in 1969. A network of 86 elevated and enclosed bridges, the skywalk covers more than 16 km (10 miles) including major sights like the Calgary Central Library, Calgary City Hall, and Calgary Tower. The skywalk is free, and while most of the bridges are open 365 days a year, some are not, and most do close in the evening. Visit Calgary's website (*www.calgary.ca/ transportation*) for a downloadable map and up-to-date closures.

Central Library
LIBRARY | Architecture buffs should plan a visit to Calgary's newish central library. When it opened in 2018, it was one of Architectural Digest's most anticipated buildings of the year. The building's curved surface is composed of hexagonal panels that give way to an expansive archway at the entrance, created entirely of western red cedar planks from British Columbia. Inside, six floors provide all the trappings of a modern, tech-enriched library, from a children's library on the main floor to the Great Reading Room on the top floor, designed so Calgarians and visitors can ruminate over their books and computers in the glow of natural light. ✉ *800 3rd St. SE, Downtown* ☎ *403/260–2600* ⊕ *www.calgarylibrary. ca.*

Devonian Gardens
GARDEN | **FAMILY** | Above the CORE Shopping Centre, this balmy 2½-acre enclosed tropical roof garden provides a welcome escape from the business of Downtown. It holds 20,000 trees and plants, nearly 2 km (1 mile) of lush walkways, a sculpture

The 2½-acre roof-top Devonian Gardens has 20,000 trees and plants and nearly 2 km (1 mile) of walkways.

court, and a playground. Alberta's largest indoor gardens, which are reached by two glass-enclosed elevators just inside the 7th Avenue light-rail transit (LRT) entrance, have a living wall and numerous ponds with rainbow trout, koi, goldfish, and turtles. Art exhibitions are held here, and there's a stage for performances. ⊠ *CORE Shopping Centre, 333 7th Ave. SW, 4th floor, Downtown* 🕾 *403/268–2489* ⊕ *www.calgary.ca* 🖾 *Free.*

Fort Calgary

HISTORY MUSEUM | The fort was established in 1875 at the confluence of the Bow and Elbow rivers by the North West Mounted Police. Designed to stop Montana whiskey traders from selling alcohol to the locals, it remained in operation until 1914. The **Interpretive Centre** here traces the history of the First Nations people, Mounties, and European settlers with the aid of artifacts, audiovisual displays, and interpretive walks. **Deane House Restaurant,** next to Fort Calgary, is one of Calgary's best restaurants and

a nice place to stop for lunch or dinner. It's the restored 1906 fort superintendent's house. The **Hunt House,** directly behind the restaurant, was built in 1876 and is believed to be Calgary's oldest building. ⊠ *750 9th Ave. SE, East Village* 🕾 *403/290–1875* ⊕ *www.fortcalgary.com* 🖾 *C$12.*

Olympic Plaza

PLAZA/SQUARE | **FAMILY** | The site of the 1988 Olympic Games medals presentation, the plaza is a popular venue for festivals and entertainment. The wading pool is turned into a skating rink in winter. ⊠ *228 8th Ave. SE, Downtown* 🕾 *403/268–2489* ⊕ *www.calgary.ca.*

Peace Bridge

BRIDGE | With it's bright red hue, webbed walls and glass roof, the once-controversial Peace Bridge has become a cultural icon of Downtown; because of its tubular shape, some have compared it to a Chinese finger puzzle. The bridge crosses the Bow River just west of Prince's Island Park, allowing pedestrians and cyclists to move back and forth between

Downtown and the communities on the north side of the river. It provides ready access to Kensington. ✉ *Memorial Dr. NW, Downtown.*

Prince's Island Park

NATURE SIGHT | Prince's Island Park is a beautiful festival park that hosts the Calgary Folk Festival and the city's Canada Day celebration. It's easily accessible by foot or bicycle from either side of the river and offers a pleasant natural getaway from the city. Grab a picnic lunch at River Cafe and make a day of it. ✉ *Downtown* 🌐 *www.calgary.ca/csps/parks.*

Stampede Park

FAIRGROUND | Home of the world-famous Calgary Stampede, the park hosts a number of other events throughout the year. Part of the grounds, the BMO Centre, Big Four Building, and Agriculture Building host trade shows, and Boyce Theatre hosts theatre and small concerts. ✉ *1410 Olympic Way SE, Victoria Park* ☎ *403/261–0101* 🌐 *www.calgarystampede.com.*

Stephen Avenue Walk

STORE/MALL | This vibrant pedestrians-only shopping area is a National Historic District, and boasts dozens of stores, nightclubs, and restaurants on the ground floors of Calgary's oldest structures. The mostly sandstone buildings were erected after an 1886 fire destroyed almost all of the older buildings. ✉ *340 8th Ave. SW, Downtown.*

★ **Studio Bell National Music Centre**

OTHER ATTRACTION | FAMILY | This 160,000-square-foot building resonates with the sounds of music and activity, drawing visitors up through five floors of acoustically and visually distinct exhibition, performance, and gallery spaces. You can unleash your inner rock star by jamming out on the tools of the trade, and build and test instruments made from everyday objects. It's also home to a number of attractions, including the Canadian Music Hall of Fame, the Canadian Songwriters Hall of Fame, and the Canadian Country Music Hall of Fame Collection. ✉ *850 4 St. SE, East Village* ☎ *403/543–5129* 🌐 *www.studiobell.ca.*

🍴 Restaurants

Deane House Restaurant

$$$$ | CANADIAN | Located in the turn-of-the-century home of RCMP Superintendent Captain Richard Burton Deane, this award-winning restaurant is an easy and delightful walk from Downtown. The restaurant specializes in contemporary Canadian fine dining, with some of the dishes based on archival recipes and photographs from Calgary's Wild West past. **Known for:** a garden of colorful flowers and native plants; situated on the site of historic Fort Calgary; house-made preserves. [$] *Average main: C$45* ✉ *806 9th Ave. SE, Downtown* 🌐 *www.deanehouse.com* ⏲ *Closed Mon. No lunch.*

Joey Eau Claire

$$$ | MODERN CANADIAN | Enjoy good food and drinks in a fun, casual atmosphere at this Eau Claire Market staple that has a loyal following among the locals. While they serve the usual Calgary fare—steaks, burgers, ribs, salmon—much of the menu is Asian-inspired: lettuce wraps, sushi, and a variety of rice bowls. **Known for:** plenty of parking evenings and weekends; lively happy hour with good deals on food and drinks; friendly service. [$] *Average main: C$25* ✉ *200 Eau Claire Market, Downtown* ☎ *403/263–6336* 🌐 *www.joeyrestaurants.com.*

Modern Steak

$$$$ | MODERN CANADIAN | When in Calgary, do as the Calgarians do and enjoy the bounty of the land. Alberta is famous for its beef, and this restaurant has perfected the fine art of steak and they only serve fresh, ranch-specific Alberta beef, and they grill it at 1800F to make the outside crispy and the inside juicy. **Known for:** casual fine-dining with top-notch service; ranch-specific Alberta beef,

Opened in 2012, the Peace Bridge is fondly known as the "Finger Trap Bridge" for its striking similarity to the children's toy.

to compare steaks from three different ranches. $ *Average main: C$40 ⊠ 100 8th Ave. SE, Downtown* ☎ *403/244–3600* ⊕ *www.modernsteak.ca.*

OEB Breakfast Company

$$ | **MODERN CANADIAN** | This is not your average diner as this place offers creative riffs on brunch classics—try the Hog & Scallops (breakfast poutine with scallops, bacon, duck-fat-fried potatoes, and brown butter hollandaise) or the cold-smoked salmon benny—in a hyper-modern setting. Locals know to use the Yelp app to check wait times and have your name put on the waitlist. **Known for:** creative riffs on breakfast; funky ambience; slow service when busy. $ *Average main: C$20 ⊠ 222 5th Ave. SW, #110, Downtown* ☎ *587/352–3447* ⊕ *www. eatoeb.com* ☺ *No dinner.*

★ River Cafe

$$$$ | **MODERN CANADIAN** | An annual recipient of Calgary's best restaurant award, River Cafe focuses on creating top-tier Canadian food, even going so far as to shun imported kitchen staples like

pepper and olive oil. The stroll through Prince's Island Park will whet your appetite and the beautifully woodsy dining room will get you in the mood for dining. **Known for:** the chef's tasting menu; taking environmental responsibility seriously; locally sourced seasonal ingredients. $ *Average main: C$40 ⊠ 25 Prince's Island, Downtown* ☎ *403/261–7670* ⊕ *www.river-cafe.com.*

Teatro

$$$$ | **MEDITERRANEAN** | A local favorite for high dining, the elegant Teatro is in an old bank building on Olympic Plaza, where classical features blend with contemporary decor to create an exquisite setting for fine Mediterranean-inspired cuisine. Specialties include numerous antipasti, pizzas from a wood-burning oven, pastas, and risottos—try the lobster and scallop lasagna. **Known for:** excellent service; impressive wine list; proximity to performing arts venues. $ *Average main: C$45 ⊠ 200 8th Ave. SE, Downtown* ☎ *403/290–1012* ⊕ *www.teatro.ca.*

Coffee and Quick Bites

Deville Coffee
$ | **CANADIAN** | Deville brews direct-trade, small-batch coffee beans and serves fresh baked goods and other tasty breakfast and lunch items as well. There are four locations Downtown but only the Fashion Central Location, near Stephen Avenue Mall, is open on weekends. **Known for:** hip décor; Nutella lattes; tasty sandwiches and pastries. [$] *Average main: C$5* ✉ *807 1st St. SW, Downtown* ☎ *587/664–9338* 🌐 *www.devillecoffee.ca* 🕑 *No dinner.*

Hotels

Delta Hotels Calgary Downtown
$$$ | **HOTEL** | This recently renovated first-class high-rise is within easy walking distance of the main business district as well as major attractions. **Pros:** Plus 15 Skyway access to Downtown keeps you warm in the winter; free parking on weekends; Shoe and Canoe serves good food and beverages. **Cons:** room service is pricey; busy Downtown location; underground parking fits larger vehicles. [$] *Rooms from: C$200* ✉ *209 4th Ave. SE, Downtown* ☎ *403/266–1980* 🌐 *www.marriott.com/hotels/travel/yycbv-delta-hotels-calgary-downtown* 🛏 *394 rooms* 🍴 *No Meals.*

Fairmont Palliser Hotel
$$$$ | **HOTEL** | Built in 1914 as Calgary's grand railroad hotel, the Palliser remains the city's most elegant accommodation. **Pros:** adjacent to Calgary Tower; great Sunday brunch; close to Stephen Avenue Mall. **Cons:** back rooms are right above the noisy train tracks; parking can be a hassle; located in the busiest part of Downtown. [$] *Rooms from: C$350* ✉ *133 9th Ave. SW, Downtown* ☎ *403/262–1234* 🌐 *www.fairmont.com* 🛏 *407 rooms* 🍴 *No Meals.*

Hyatt Regency Calgary
$$$$ | **HOTEL** | Turn-of-the-19th-century buildings combine with a state-of-the-art tower at this 21-story luxury hotel. **Pros:** rooms have large windows with scenic views; located in the heart of Downtown; easy access to the C-train. **Cons:** one of the more expensive options; busy Downtown location; paid parking available, but it fills up quickly. [$] *Rooms from: C$450* ✉ *700 Centre St. SE, Downtown* ☎ *403/717–1234* 🌐 *www.hyatt.com* 🛏 *355 rooms* 🍴 *No Meals.*

Sheraton Suites Calgary Eau Claire
$$$$ | **HOTEL** | Excellent views from this all-suites hotel take in Downtown, the river, and the park. **Pros:** convenient access to river trails and Prince's Island Park; the Plus 15 Skywalk is convenient in the winter; stylish rooms. **Cons:** larger vehicles won't fit in underground parking; only offers valet parking, which is pricey; busy Downtown location. [$] *Rooms from: C$300* ✉ *255 Barclay Parade SW, Downtown* ☎ *403/266–7200* 🌐 *www.mariott.com* 🍴 *No Meals* 🛏 *323 rooms.*

Nightlife

BARS AND CLUBS

James Joyce Irish Pub and Restaurant
LIVE MUSIC | The James Joyce Pub is a classic Irish pub where you can have Guinness stout served at three different temperatures at the long antique bar, along with some traditional Irish fare. ✉ *114 8th Ave. SW, Downtown* ☎ *403/262–0708* 🌐 *www.jamesjoycepub.com.*

Melrose Cafe and Bar
LIVE MUSIC | With more than 40 TVs, this popular bar is a great place to watch the Calgary Flames and the Calgary Stampeders. It also shows Buzztime, the national trivia network, on its many screens. ✉ *421 12th Ave. SE, Downtown* ☎ *403/984–3577* 🌐 *www.melrosecalgary.com.*

MUSIC CLUBS
The Blues Can
LIVE MUSIC | Calgary's home of the blues, the Can features nightly live performances, cocktails, and homestyle Southern cooking. ✉ *1429 9th Ave. SE, Inglewood* ☎ *403/262–2666* ⊕ *www.thebluescan.com.*

Ironwood Stage & Grill
LIVE MUSIC | The Ironwood is a 140-seat restaurant and lounge that has been the heart of Calgary's live music scene for decades, and hosts live music every night of the year. Located just east of Downtown in the Inglewood district, it's an easy walk or a short drive, and there's plenty of public parking nearby. ✉ *1229 9th Ave. SE, Inglewood* ☎ *403/269–5581* ⊕ *ironwoodstage.ca.*

🛍 Shopping

CLOTHING
Hudson's Bay
DEPARTMENT STORE | FAMILY | The Bay, formerly known as the Hudson's Bay Company, was incorporated in 1670. It is Calgary's—and Canada's—oldest retailer and a good source for extra-warm clothing. ✉ *200 8th Ave. SW, Downtown* ☎ *403/262–0345* ⊕ *www.thebay.com.*

Lammle's Western Wear
OTHER SPECIALTY STORE | The official western wear of the Calgary Stampede, Lammle's is the perfect place to grab yourself a white cowboy (or girl) hat and a pair of boots. It's located on Stephen Avenue Walk right beside The Unicorn Superpub. ✉ *211 8th Ave., Downtown* ☎ *403/266–5226* ⊕ *www.lammles.com* ⊘ *Closed Sun.*

SHOPPING CENTERS AND MALLS
Bankers Hall
MALL | Bankers Hall has upscale clothing stores such as La Chic and Blu's. ✉ *315 8th Ave. SW, Downtown* ☎ *403/770–7145* ⊕ *www.bankershall.ca* ⊘ *Closed Sun.*

The CORE Shopping Centre
MALL | You'll find many large chain clothing stores, such as the Gap, as well as more upscale spots like Harry Rosen and Holt Renfrew at the Scotia Centre and TD Square. There are also a mixture of jewelry and imported goods stores, a variety of restaurants, and the beautiful Devonian Gardens. ✉ *324 8th Ave. SW, Downtown* ☎ *403/441–4940* ⊕ *www.coreshopping.ca.*

Stephen Avenue Walk
MALL | FAMILY | The Stephen Avenue Walk, a national historic site, is a pedestrian-only stretch of 8th Avenue (between Macleod Trail and 4th Street Southwest), where some of the city's oldest buildings house dozens of exciting shops, bars and restaurants. It's a great place to people watch on one of the many patios. ✉ *304 8th Ave. SW, Downtown.*

🏃 Activities

BIKING
Many Downtown streets have dedicated bike lanes, including 12th Avenue SW, 8th Avenue SW, and 5th Street SW. Pathways along the Bow River and on Prince's Island Park are worth exploring by bike or foot.

Bow Cycle
BIKING | With approximately 850 km (528 miles) of regional pathways and 95 km (59 miles) of trails, Calgary has the most extensive urban pathway and cycle path network in North America. Pathways along the Bow River and on Prince's Island Park are worth exploring by bike or foot. If you can't bring your bike with you, Bow Cycle rents both bikes and bike racks. ✉ *632 Confluence Way SE, Calgary* ☎ *406/265–5422* ⊕ *www.bowcycle.com.*

HOCKEY
Calgary Flames
HOCKEY | Calgarians are passionate about their Calgary Flames National Hockey League team, which plays matches October through April at the Scotiabank

The Cowboy Trail

Stretching 584 km (363 miles) from the town of Mayerthorpe (90 minutes northwest of Edmonton), south to Lundbreck (200 km [124 miles] south of Calgary), the Cowboy Trail (*www.travelalberta.com*) follows Highway 22 through the Rocky Mountain foothills, one of Alberta's most beautiful and iconic landscapes. With majestic peaks rising to the west and the plains falling away to the east, the route got its name from the historic ranching lands that it passes through.

Most visitors to Calgary drive west along Highway 1A to Cochrane, where you can stroll along Main Street and visit shops and cafes with old-fashioned storefronts or wander along the banks of the Bow River. Bragg Creek, 20 miles to the south, is a

hamlet in the woods offering antiques and trails for hiking, mountain biking, and horseback riding. The next stop is bucolic Millarville, famous for its summer farmers' market. Further south is Turner Valley, the locus of Alberta's first oil well and the birth of Alberta's oil industry, and Black Diamond, both of which boast a lively arts scene and traditional western arts and crafts. Longview, a favorite setting for Hollywood filmmakers (think *Interstellar* and *Unforgiven*) is also home to the world-famous Longview Jerky Shop (*www.longviewjerkyshop.com*). The last stop is the Bar U National Historic Site (*www.pc.gc.ca/en/lhn-nhs/ab/baru*), where you can hang out with ranch hands and learn to saddle a horse or rope a steer.

Saddledome in Stampede Park. Tickets start at C$130, but plan to buy them well in advance. ⊠ *Stampede Park, 555 Saddledome Rise SE, Calgary* ☎ *403/777–4746* ⊕ *www.nhl.com.*

Kensington

With more than 200 shops, restaurants, and bars in a quaint suburban neighborhood, Kensington is a popular destination for visitors and locals alike. It's been a part of Calgary for over a century, so it has an eclectic mix of historic buildings and modern architecture. In the summer, Kensington is renowned for its patios, people-watching, and all-around walkability, and it's only a short jaunt across the river from Downtown.

◉ Sights

Riley Park

CITY PARK | A couple of blocks to the north of Kensington's major concentration of shops, bars, and restaurants is this large green space with big trees and a wading pool and playground for the kiddos. Grab a picnic lunch from one of the many great cafés in Kensington, plop down a blanket and have yourself a picnic. In the evening, you can watch the lads play cricket or listen to live music on the small stage here. ⊠ *800 12th St.* ✢ *Located between 10th and 12th sts.*

🍴 Restaurants

Dairy Lane

$$ | CAFÉ | Calgary's oldest restaurant started as a milk bar in the 1950s serving organic food before it was trendy; today it's best known for breakfast, which is served until 3 pm, but it's a fine place for lunch and supper too. While this gem is not technically in Kensington, it's certainly worth the short walk. **Known for:** there's always a line; large portions of excellent food; friendly staff and good service. $ *Average main: C$20* ⊠ *319 19th St. NW* ☎ *403/283–2497* ⊕ *www. dairylanecafe.ca* ⊘ *Closed Mon.*

Modern Ocean

$$$$ | SEAFOOD | Although Calgary is 500 miles from the nearest salt water, Modern Ocean manages to serve up mighty fine seafood—Hawaiian ahi tuna is a local favorite, as is the BC halibut. The sister restaurant to Modern Steak, Modern Ocean provides diners with the same upscale experience in a sublime dining environment. **Known for:** at the higher end of the price spectrum; half-price oysters from 5-6 pm; humanely raised sea bass. $ *Average main: C$35* ⊠ *107 10a St. NW* ☎ *403/670–6873* ⊕ *www.modernocean. ca* ⊘ *Closed Mon.–Tues. No lunch.*

Pulcinella

$$$ | ITALIAN | If you're looking for authentic Neapolitan pizza, look no further than Pulcinella, one of only a few Associazione Pizzaiuoli Napoletani-certified pizzerias in North America. Chef Domenic Tudda, whose parents owned an Italian restaurant in the same location for decades, trained in Naples, and locals rave about the pizza, as well as the fabulous wine list, calamari fritti, and caprese salad. **Known for:** authentic Neapolitan food; warm and friendly service; dining on the outdoor patio. $ *Average main: C$25* ⊠ *1147 Kensington Crescent* ☎ *403/283– 1166* ⊕ *www.pulcinella.ca.*

Vendome Cafe

$$$ | EUROPEAN | Fine artwork adorns the brick walls of this bright and charming French-style café perfectly blending old and new; there's a great Euro-vibed patio for summer dining. Menu items range from the Vendome Caprese to delicious shared plates like truffle puffs or sauteed pea shoots to steamed mussels. **Known for:** perfect lattes; a vintage panoramic

image of Calgary from the early 1900s; Sunday brunch. $ *Average main: C$25* ⊠ *940 2nd Ave. NW* ☎ *403/453–1140* ⊕ *vendomecafe.com.*

☕ Coffee and Quick Bites

Higher Ground Cafe

$ | CAFÉ | Always cozy and full of sunshine, Higher Ground has been the go-to coffee shop in Kensington for decades. They serve 100% organic coffee and tea, so you can feel good about quaffing a hot beverage while sampling one of their fresh-baked goods or all-day breakfast items (particularly the Tuscan Sunrise—a panini with egg, sausage, tomato, onion, Swiss cheese, and basil pesto). **Known for:** local art adorns the walls; open-mic night on Tuesdays; quiet, cozy atmosphere. $ *Average main: C$6* ⊠ *1126 Kensington Rd. NW, Second Flr.* ☎ *403/270–3780* ⊕ *www.higherground-cafe.ca* ⊘ *No dinner.*

🛏 Hotels

Hotel Arts Kensington

$$$ | HOTEL | A short walk from Calgary's business center, Hotel Arts Kensington (formerly the Kensington Riverside Inn) is a stylish boutique hotel with views of the Bow River and the Downtown skyline. **Pros:** underground parking; best location in town; great customer service. **Cons:** a bit of a hike to the Stampede Grounds; books up quickly; some road noise from Memorial Drive. $ *Rooms from: C$225* ⊠ *1126 Memorial Dr. NW, Kensington* ☎ *403/228–4422* ⊕ *www.hotelartskens-ington.com* ❑ *No Meals* ⇆ *19 rooms.*

▼ Nightlife

Free House Beer and Food Hall

PUBS | Not your average pub, Free House provides a warm inviting vibe, delicious food, and a great selection of Calgary microbrews. Happy hour runs from 9 pm to midnight when small plates are half-price and cocktails and draft beer are cheap. Sit under twinkling string lights on the rooftop patio and watch the stars materialize in the night sky. ⊠ *1153 Kensington Crescent N.W., Kensington* ☎ *403/452–1339* ⊕ *www.freehouseyyc. com.*

Hayden Block Smoke & Whiskey

BARS | This popular restaurant-bar serves Texas-style BBQ and 100+ brands of whiskey, as well as a fine selection of microbrews. The chic-rustic decor and private Whiskey Garden patio out back makes it easy to while away a few hours here. Their signature smoked meats–brisket, pulled pork, spare ribs–are sold by weight and half-price after 10 pm. Wash it all down with their signature cocktail, a smoked Old Fashioned. ⊠ *1136 Kensington Rd. NW, Kensington* ☎ *403/283–3021* ⊕ *www.haydenblockyyc.com.*

Hexagon Board Game Cafe

CAFÉS | **FAMILY** | With more than 700 board and card games in the library, this unique and popular cafe is the perfect place to spend a rainy afternoon or cold winter evening. The menu is average, but it's fully licensed, and, anyway, you come for the games, which are $3 an hour per person with a purchase of food or beverage. ⊠ *#200 1140 Kensington Rd. NW, Kensington* ☎ *403/209-2881* ⊕ *thehexcafe.com/.*

🛍 Shopping

Hot Wax Records

RECORDS | This boutique record store has been curating and collecting popular and underground records for more than four decades. While they specialize in high-quality used vinyl, they also carry CDs and cassettes. Ask to peruse the treasure trove in the basement. ⊠ *114 10th St. NW, Kensington* ☎ *403/283–0055* ⊕ *www.hotwaxrecords.ca* ☽ *Closed Sun.*

Manjana Imports

CRAFTS | Browse an eclectic collection of handmade folk art, jewelry, and clothing from all over the world. A family business focused on fair-trade, the owners travel the globe buying directly from local artisans in more than 30 countries. ⊠ *1132 Kensington Rd. NW, Kensington* ☎ *403/283–6537* ⊕ *www.mananaimports.ca.*

Pages on Kensington

BOOKS | Pages is Calgary's finest local bookstore, where you'll find a vast selection of new and used fiction, non-fiction, and poetry. If you're looking for the work of local Alberta or Canadian Indigenous writers, this is the place. There's always a rack of bargain books just outside the front door, and the knowledgeable staff inside can help you find some literary gems. ⊠ *1135 Kensington Rd. NW, Kensington* ☎ *403/283–6655* ⊕ *www. pageskensington.com.*

Beltline and 17th Avenue

Named for an old tram line through Downtown, the Beltline district has become one of Calgary's more vibrant neighborhoods that's a fun-filled destination for locals and visitors alike. South of Downtown and bordered by 17th Avenue, this "Design District" is home to the Stampede Grounds. It's also Calgary's most urban area, where high-rise apartments and office buildings provide ground-level spaces for an eclectic cornucopia of restaurants, shops, and nightlife unlike any other neighborhood in the city. Keep your eyes out for all the building art installed each year as part of the Beltline Urban Art Project.

17th Avenue, also known as the "Red Mile," is a retail and entertainment district that spans 13 blocks. Close to Downtown and Stampede Park, the

Central Memorial Park is Calgary's oldest surviving public park.

area is home to more than a hundred boutique shops, fine-dining restaurants, and lively lounges.

[👁] Sights

Central Memorial Park

HISTORIC SIGHT | This is Calgary's oldest surviving public park and a shady respite from the frenetic energy of the Beltline. A cenotaph and two statues memorialize Canadian soldiers who fell in various 19th and 20th century wars. At the east end is Central Memorial Library, a national historic site, which was constructed in 1910 with financial support from the Carnegie Foundation. ✉ *1221 2 St. SW, Beltline* ☎ *403/260–2600.*

Lougheed House

HISTORIC HOME | One of the few surviving examples of a grand sandstone prairie mansion, Lougheed House is the former residence of some of Calgary's most influential citizens, including Peter Lougheed, premier of Alberta from 1971 to 1985. Both a national and provincial historic site, Lougheed House hosts history and art exhibits and is surrounded by large and wonderful gardens that are worth exploring in the summer months. ✉ *707 13th Ave. SW, Beltline* ☎ *403/244–6333* 🌐 *www.lougheedhouse.com.*

🍴 Restaurants

Bottlescrew Bills Pub

$ | **BURGER** | Another Calgary icon, Bottlescrew Bills is a second-generation family establishment that has been serving high-quality versions of classic pub food and an enormous selection of beer for more than 40 years. Daily specials and a generous happy hour only add to the fun; if you're feeling adventurous, try their unique riff on the traditional Caesar (a Canadian cocktail invented in Calgary) that includes a "prairie oyster". **Known for:** best-ever wings; prairie oyster Caesar (it's like a Bloody Mary); best beer selection in town. [$] *Average main: C$15* ✉ *140 10th Ave. SW, Beltline* ☎ *403/263–7900* 🌐 *www.bottlescrewbill.com.*

★ Foreign Concept

$$$ | ASIAN FUSION | Well known among local foodies as one of Calgary's best chefs, it's unsurprising that Chef Duncan Ly has created one of the city's best restaurants, which serves up some of the best pan-Asian food you will ever eat. Try the Mama Ly's Pork & Shrimp Imperial Rolls and the Steelhead Trout Cha Ca La Vong (Steelhead trout with scallion rice noodles, dill, turmeric, and chili shrimp paste), though it's hard to go wrong with anything on the menu. **Known for:** reservations a must; outstanding service; excellent cocktails. $ *Average main: C$30* ✉ *1011 1st St. SW, Beltline* ☎ *403/719–7288* ⊕ *www.foreignconcept.ca* ⊗ *Closed Mon. No lunch.*

Galaxie Diner

$ | DINER | A small all-day breakfast place that has been around for more than 25 years, the Galaxie Diner is a great option for a fair-priced breakfast (especially if you slept past noon). The decor is vintage diner, the staff is friendly and helpful, and you can have as many hash browns as you like. **Known for:** old-school diner vibe; all-day breakfast; almost always a line. $ *Average main: C$15* ✉ *1413 11th St. SW, Beltline* ☎ *403/228–0001* ⊕ *www.galaxiediner.ca* ⊗ *No dinner.*

Model Milk

$$$$ | MODERN CANADIAN | Named for the former dairy it now inhabits, Model Milk serves upscale comfort food (think burgers, fried chicken, and roasted cauliflower) beneath chandeliers made of glass milk bottles and brick walls, concrete floors, and steel beams that recall the building's industrial heritage. This trendy restaurant has been on every best restaurant list since it opened in 2011; don't miss the small plates to share like the roasted Alberta carrots or the house pickles or cabbage chips. **Known for:** centrally located on 17th Ave.; the "Big Milk" burger with special sauce and handcut fries; hip and energetic vibe. $ *Average main: C$35* ✉ *308 17th Ave. SW, Beltline* ☎ *403/265–7343* ⊕ *www.modelmilk.ca* ⊗ *Closed Mon. No lunch.*

Ten Foot Henry

$$$ | MODERN CANADIAN | Named after a ten-foot replica of the 1930s comic character, which you'll meet on the way to the washroom, this fresh veggie-centric eatery offers family-style dining in an airy space enhanced by lush green plants. This is not your average salad shop as Chef Steve Smee's talents in the kitchen have earned Ten Foot Henry's a spot as one of the top 50 restaurants in Canada. **Known for:** delicious plant-based menu items; cozy atmosphere; top-notch service. $ *Average main: C$25* ✉ *1209 1st St. SW, Beltline* ☎ *403/475–5537* ⊕ *www.tenfoothenry.com/.*

☕ Coffee and Quick Bites

Good Earth Coffeehouse

$ | CAFÉ | Spacious and bright with large tables, Beltline's Good Earth is a great spot to grab fresh-baked goods and as ethical and responsible a coffee you will ever find. This feel-good coffee house also serves fresh and nutritious sandwiches, soups, and salads. **Known for:** ethically sourced coffee; delicious baked goods; friendly service. $ *Average main: C$10* ✉ *1502 11th St. SW, Beltline* ☎ *403/264–3445* ⊕ *www.goodearthcoffeehouse.com* ⊗ *No dinner.*

🛏 Hotels

Hotel Arts

$$$ | HOTEL | In the heart of the Beltline district, Hotel Arts is a hipper alternative to the business-oriented chains found Downtown. **Pros:** perfect location to explore Calgary's best entertainment district; parking is plentiful and included; easy access to Downtown and the Stampede Grounds. **Cons:** street-facing rooms can be a bit noisy; no views to speak of; not as fancy as some of the upscale Downtown skyrises. $ *Rooms from: C$200* ✉ *119 12th Ave. SW, Beltline* ☎ *403/266–4611* ⊕ *www.hotelarts.ca* ❍ *No Meals* ⇥ *185 rooms.*

☻ Nightlife

BARS AND PUBS

Last Best Brewing and Distilling

BREWPUBS | Last Best Brewing and Distilling is widely recognized as one of Calgary's best brewpubs. They have a dozen of their own craft beers on tap—try the Tokyo Drift IPA—and make delicious cocktails with the three kinds of gin they distill in-house. On top of that, they serve the best pub food in the greater Downtown area in an upscale but casual atmosphere anchored by a beautiful rectangular bar in the center of it all. ✉ 607 11th Ave. SW, Beltline ☎ 587/353–7387 ⊕ www.lastbestbrewing.com.

National on 10th

PUBS | Hankering for some quality pub food, an extensive selection of Canadian microbrews, and a few games of bowling and/or ping pong? The National on 10th is the place for you. The menu is dominated by wings and nachos and the like, but there are a few hefty salads and rice bowls for those looking for something more nutritious. All in all, this spacious pub is just a fun place to hang out for an evening. ✉ 341 10th Ave. SW, Beltline ☎ 403/474–2739 ⊕ www.ntnl. ca/10th-avenue.

MUSIC CLUBS

Commonwealth Bar and Stage

LIVE MUSIC | Built on the foundation of an old warehouse, this rustic-chic club hosts DJ sets and live music gigs on Friday and Saturday nights. Check the website for special events other days of the week. ✉ 731 10th Ave. SW, Beltline ☎ 403/247–4633 ⊕ www.commonwealthbar.ca ⊘ Closed Sun.–Thurs.

Cowboys Dancehall and Casino

DANCE CLUBS | This bar and a dance hall combo plays Top 40 country, dance, and rock tunes, with live entertainment on occasion. It's open Wednesday through Saturday and holds 1,200 people, but during the Calgary Stampede, it's a popular destination as it's open every day and night. ✉ 421 12th Ave. SE, Beltline ☎ 403/265–0699 ⊕ www.cowboysnightclub.com ⊘ Closed Sun.–Tues.

⌂ Shopping

Mountain Equipment Company

SPORTING GOODS | Recently rebranded as MEC, this is the Canadian version of REI and it has been the go-to place to get quality outdoor gear since 1971. Whether you need a backpack or a water bottle, or just want to get your bike or skis tuned up, this is the place to go. ✉ 830 10th Ave. SW, Beltline ☎ 403/269–2420 ⊕ www.mec.ca.

Mission

Mission was originally a Francophone community and one of the earliest non-Indigenous settlements. Only a 20-minute walk from Downtown and the Beltline district, it's now a trendy neighborhood full of hip bars, great restaurants, and a whole lot of specialty shops. There's plenty of paid parking, but if you prefer to take public transportation, get off the C-train at Erlton Station and stroll west along the Elbow River.

♨ Restaurants

Earls Calgary Tin Palace

$$$ | **MODERN CANADIAN** | The Tin Palace has been the signature location of this upscale chain for years and with a large and varied menu that ranges from sushi to BBQ ribs, almost anyone can find something they prefer. Portions are large, but the food is quite good, and a generous happy hour inspires the locals to head to the bar or patio, depending on the season, for drinks. **Known for:** great happy hour; neighborhood institution; menu has a lot of options. ⓢ Average main: C$25 ✉ 2401 4th St. SW, Mission ☎ 403/228-4141 ⊕ www.earls.ca.

★ Mercato Market Restaurant

$$$$ | **MODERN ITALIAN** | Victor and Cathy Caracciolo opened Mercato 15 years ago and it has been a local favorite ever since. Mamma Cathy is still in the kitchen every day, whipping up delicious contemporary Italian fare for a constant stream of regular customers; try the family-style mixed grill or Mamma's handmade gnocchi using the same recipe she learned from her own mama. **Known for:** large portions; excellent pasta dishes; books up fast. $ *Average main: C$40* ⊠ *2224 4th St. SW, Mission* ☎ *403/263-5535* ⊕ *www. mercatogourmet.com* ⊙ *Closed Mon.*

Shokunin Izakaya

$$$ | **JAPANESE** | An izakaya is the Japanese version of a British pub or a Spanish tapas bar, and this one is extraordinary. The vibe is Tokyo underground and though it's authentic Japanese fare, the specialty here is grilled meats and vegetables, particularly yakitori (skewered chicken). **Known for:** owner and chef Darren MacLean was a finalist on Netflix's The Final Table; award-winning cooking; make reservations well ahead. $ *Average main: C$25* ⊠ *2016 4th St. SW, Mission* ☎ *403/229-3444* ⊕ *www.shokuninyyc.ca* ⊙ *Closed Mon.–Tues. No lunch.*

☕ Coffee and Quick Bites

La Boulangerie Bakery Cafe

$ | **BAKERY** | The smell of Illy coffee and French baked goods makes La Boulangerie feel like a little slice of Paris in Cowtown. The cappuccinos and lattes are works of art, and the fresh-baked baguettes, pastries, and house-made crepes make this a perfect stop for breakfast, an afternoon snack, or to take a break from shopping. **Known for:** friendly service; lovely covered patio; to die for creme brûlée. $ *Average main: C$10* ⊠ *2435 4th St. SW, Mission* ☎ *403/984–9294* ⊕ *www.facebook.com/ laboulangerieyyc/* ⊙ *No dinner.*

☾ Nightlife

Anejo Restaurant

GATHERING PLACES | Although Anejo is only open until 11 pm, it's worth making an evening visit for what they call HalfyHour. After 9 pm, tacos (some of the best in the city) and tequila (of which they have more than 100 kinds) are half off, and beer and margaritas are only $6. ⊠ *2116 4th St. SW, Mission* ☎ *587/353–2656* ⊕ *www.anejo.ca.*

Joyce on 4th Irish Pub

PUBS | Good food, great patio, friendly staff, and 72 draught beers on tap— what more could you ask from a pub? There are food and drink specials every day, including cheap wings on Mondays. ⊠ *506 24th Ave. SW, Mission* ☎ *403/541–9168* ⊕ *www.calgarysbest-pubs.com.*

Vin Room

WINE BARS | The Vin Room has one of the best wine lists in Calgary, and its two patios (one out front that allows dogs, the other on the roof) make it the perfect spot for a glass or two of wine or a cocktail in the evening. It's also a great place for a date or an outing with a small group of your human and/or canine best friends. ⊠ *2310 4th St. SW, Mission* ☎ *403/457–5522* ⊕ *www.vinroom.com.*

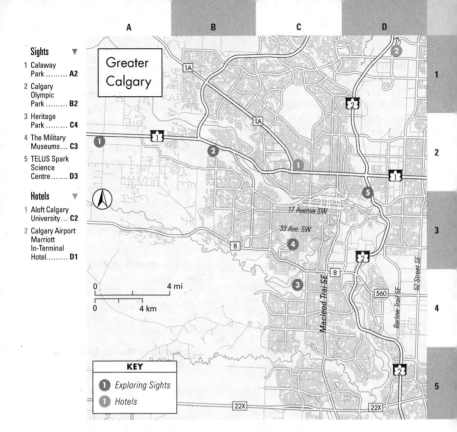

Greater
Calgary

12 Avenue SW

33 Ave. SW

KEY

1 Exploring Sights

1 Hotels

Greater Calgary

◉ Sights

Calaway Park

AMUSEMENT PARK/CARNIVAL | FAMILY | In the foothills, 10 km (6 miles) west of Calgary, is western Canada's largest outdoor family amusement park. It includes live entertainment, miniature golf, a fishing pond, shops, and an RV park. ✉ 245033 Range Rd. 33, Springbank South ☎ 403/240–3822 ⊕ www.calawaypark. com ☞ C$50.

Calgary Olympic Park

SPORTS VENUE | FAMILY | One of the sites of the 1988 Winter Olympics, Winsport operates this year-round attraction. Summer activities include bob-sleighing, mountain biking, and downhill karting. In winter the slopes are open to the public for skiing and snowboarding; lessons are available. There's also a day lodge with a cafeteria and the **Olympic Hall of Fame** on the premises. ✉ 88 Olympic Rd. SW, Aspen Village ☎ 403/247–5452 ⊕ www. winsport.ca.

Heritage Park

HISTORY MUSEUM | FAMILY | On 127 acres of parkland beside the Glenmore Reservoir, Heritage Park is Canada's largest living-history village. More than 200 exhibits, hundreds of costumed staff and volunteers, and 45,000 artifacts re-create western Canadian life prior to 1914. You can visit an 1850s fur-trading post, a ranch, and an old town; ride on a steam locomotive or horse-drawn wagon; cruise the reservoir on a stern-wheeler; and partake of a free pancake breakfast daily at 9 am. ⊠ *1900 Heritage Dr. SW, Eagle Ridge* ☎ *403/268–8500* ⊕ *www.heritagepark.ca* ☏ *Summer C$29.95.*

The Military Museums

MILITARY SIGHT | Western Canada's largest military museum has a collection of memorabilia that depicts the history of Calgary-based regiments dating back to 1900. ⊠ *4520 Crowchild Trail SW* ☎ *403/410–2340* ⊕ *www.themilitarymuseums.ca* ☏ *C$15.*

TELUS Spark Science Centre

SCIENCE MUSEUM | The first science center built in Canada in 25 years and is now a city jewel. It houses the largest dome theater in western Canada and a 6500-square-foot digital immersion gallery that allows visitors to follow a storyline as they walk through a digital dream world. There's also a sensory-rich area for younger children, where they can make music on a bubble piano (among other things). ⊠ *220 St. George's Dr. NE, Calgary* ☎ *403/817–6800* ⊕ *www.sparkscience.ca* ☏ *C$26* ⊗ *Closed Mon.–Tues.*

🛏 Hotels

Aloft Calgary University

$$$ | HOTEL | This recently renovated Marriott boutique hotel is one of several cheaper offerings in what Calgarians know as Motel Village. **Pros:** good value; buffet breakfast included; free parking. **Cons:**; adjacent to busy roads; pool is tiny. 🅢 *Rooms from: C$200* ⊠ *2359 Banff Trail NW, Greater Calgary* ☎ *403/289–1973* ⊕ *www.marriott.com* ⦿ *Free Breakfast* ⇱ *140 rooms.*

Calgary Airport Marriott In-Terminal Hotel

$$ | HOTEL | Located right inside Calgary International Airport, this hotel offers convenience and comfort for those flying in or out of Calgary at night or early in the morning. **Pros:** views over the airport; well-appointed; no need to get a shuttle to the airport. **Cons:** parking is pricey; noise from planes is noticeable; far from everything but the airport. 🅢 *Rooms from: C$195* ⊠ *2008 Airport Rd. NE, Greater Calgary* ☎ *403/717–0522* ⊕ *www.marriott.com* ⦿ *No Meals* ⇱ *318 rooms.*

🎭 Performing Arts

Southern Alberta Jubilee Auditorium

CONCERTS | The Southern Alberta Jubilee Auditorium hosts the Alberta Ballet Company as well as classical music, opera, dance, pop, and rock concerts. ⊠ *1415 14th Ave. NW, Greater Calgary* ☎ *403/297–8000* ⊕ *www.jubileeauditorium.com.*

Tim Hortons 🍴

Like hockey, Tim Hortons (*www.timhortons.ca*) has become a Canadian institution, and you're never far from one of their coffee shops. They aren't fancy, and that's part of their charm, but they are all the same and they all provide good hot coffee, a variety of baked goods (try the Boston cream), and soup and sandwiches for a reasonable price.

University Theatre
THEATER | Concerts and classic and contemporary theater works are staged at the 550-seat University of Calgary Theatre. ✉ *Craigie Hall, CHD 100, 2500 University Dr. NW, Greater Calgary* ☎ *403/220–4901* ⊕ *www.arts.ucalgary.ca/ creative-performing-arts/theatre-services/ rental-facilities/university-theatre.*

🛍 Shopping

SHOPPING CENTERS AND MALLS
CF Chinook Centre
MALL | Calgary's largest shopping mall has 250 shops, including department stores, restaurants, and a five-pin bowling alley. ✉ *6455 Macleod Trail SW, Greater Calgary* ☎ *403/259–2022* ⊕ *www.cfshops. com.*

CF Market Mall
MALL | Located northwest of Downtown, this mall is a great place to stop and pick up what you need on your way to Banff. There's a Safeway and a Sport Check, as well as various specialty stores. ✉ *3625 Shaganappi Trail NW, Greater Calgary* ☎ *403/288-5466* ⊕ *www.shops.cadillac-fairview.com.*

🏃 Activities

FOOTBALL
Calgary Stampeders
FOOTBALL | Coached by Montana native Dave Dickenson, the Calgary Stampeders are perennially competitive in the Canadian Football League, last winning the Grey Cup in 2018. Games take place at McMahon Stadium Friday and Saturday night, September through November. ✉ *McMahon Stadium, 1817 Crowchild Tr. NW, Greater Calgary* ☎ *403/289-0258* ⊕ *www.stampeders.com* 🎟 *From C$47.*

HORSE RACING
Century Downs Racetrack and Casino
HORSE RACING | Located just north of the city limits, Century Downs is southern Alberta's one-stop-shop for gambling. Horse racing, slots, VLTs, and roulette are available. The casino is open until 3 am seven days a week. ✉ *260 Century Downs Drive, Greater Calgary* ☎ *587/349-7777* ⊕ *www.cnty.com/ centurydowns.*

SKIING
Nakiska
SKIING & SNOWBOARDING | **FAMILY** | Nakiska is less than an hour's drive west of Calgary. The resort has skiing and snowboarding with a sophisticated snowmaking system. There are four lifts, three of which are high-speed quads. ✉ *1505 17th Ave. SW, Greater Calgary* ☎ *403/581-7777* ⊕ *www.skinakiska.com* 🎟 *Day ticket C$127.*

WinSport
SKIING & SNOWBOARDING | **FAMILY** | Canada Olympic Park has downhill skiing, a luge track, and snowboarding, on-site rentals, and first-class instruction. The ski hill has a racing section, a casual ski area, and an exceptionally good terrain park. A total of six lifts service the hill, including a high-speed chair lift. ✉ *88 Canada Olympic Rd. SW, Greater Calgary* ☎ *403/247-5452* ⊕ *www.winsport.ca* 🎟 *Day ticket C$45.99.*

Chapter 6

CANMORE AND KANANASKIS COUNTRY

By
Debbie Olsen

◉ Sights	🍴 Restaurants	🛏 Hotels	🛍 Shopping	🍸 Nightlife
★★★★☆	★★★★☆	★★★★★	★★★★★	★★★★☆

WELCOME TO CANMORE AND KANANASKIS COUNTRY

TOP REASONS TO GO

★ **Magnificent mountain scenery:** Canmore and Kananaskis are in the heart of the Rockies and the Three Sisters mountains sit majestically above the Town of Canmore.

★ **An outdoor adventure wonderland:** This region offers hiking and cycling trails, ski resorts, cross-country ski trails, golf courses, and more.

★ **Canmore:** This gateway city to the mountain parks has a laidback vibe and can be less busy than the Town of Banff – just 20 minutes away.

★ **Only Nordic Spa in the Canadian Rockies:** Kananaskis Nordic Spa is an adults-only alpine sanctuary with hot and cold pools, saunas, steam rooms, and relaxation areas.

★ **Elevation Place:** One of the biggest recreation centers in the Canadian Rockies, it has an aquatic center, a fitness center, and an incredible climbing gym.

Kananaskis Country sits on the east side of the Continental Divide, south of Banff National Park, and about an hour's drive from Calgary. This more than 4,200-square-km (1,600-square-mile) area is an outdoor recreation paradise that includes several provincial parks and provincial recreation areas, and an ecological reserve. At the northern edge of Kananaskis Country, just outside Banff National Park, the Town of Canmore is the region's hub.

1 Canmore. This laidback mountain town, just outside Banff, is the region's epicenter with shops, services, and most hotels.

2 Bow Valley Provincial Park. At the north end of Kananaskis Country, the park protects the Bow Valley region. Main facilities, including a visitor's center, are located between the Trans-Canada Highway and the Bow River.

3 Kananaskis Valley. The most developed region of Kananaskis Country contains Kananaskis Village, with a number of shops and services. It sits between the Trans-Canada Highway and Peter Lougheed Provincial Park along Highway 40.

4 Peter Lougheed Provincial Park. At the southern end of the Kananaskis Valley, Upper and Lower Kananaskis Lakes are two undisputed highlights of this park.

5 Spray Valley Provincial Park. Created in 2001, the park protects 358 square km (138 square miles) of spectacular mountain terrain north of Peter Lougheed Provincial Park.

6 Sibbald Lake Provincial Recreation Area. A small recreation area in the northern region of Kananaskis Country that protects rolling foothills west of Calgary.

7 Elbow and Sheep River Valleys and Vicinity. East of Peter Lougheed Provincial Park, Elbow Lake in Elbow-Sheep Wildland Provincial Park is the source of the Elbow River Valley; the Sheep River Valley lies just south between ranchlands and mountains.

8 Highwood/Cataract Creek. In the southern region of Kananaskis Country, these areas are the region's least developed areas with a wide variety of wildlife.

9 Bragg Creek Area. The Gateway to Kananaskis offers a variety of outdoor activities as well as shops and restaurants despite its tiny size.

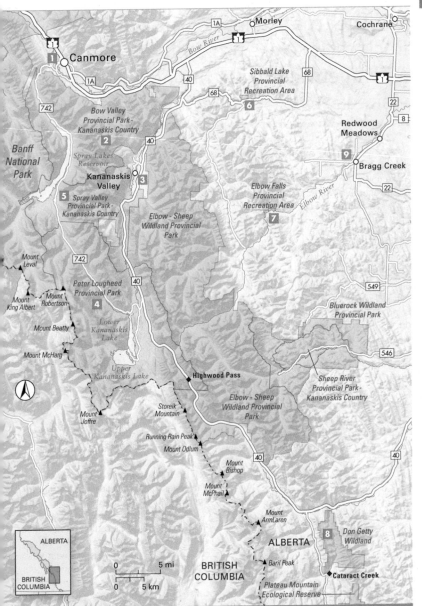

Kanananskis includes 51 parks of various classifications as well as public land use zones east of Calgary in the foothills and the front ranges of the Canadian Rockies. Its close proximity to Banff, size, and amenities makes it one of the most visited areas in the Rockies.

Nine provincial parks and over 50 recreation, wilderness, and natural areas make up the more than 4,200-square-km (1,600-square-mile) recreational region known as **Kananaskis Country,** whose northern entrance is 26 km (16 miles) southeast of Canmore. Although the mountain scenery here doesn't quite match that in the adjacent national parks, it's still grand, and the area allows some activities that are prohibited within the national park system, such as snowmobiling, motorized boating, and off-road driving. It's also home to some spectacular cross-country and mountain biking trails. The hiking is good here, too, with more than 175 established trails ranging in difficulty from beginner to advanced. For a few weeks in late September and early October, you can enjoy a number of wonderful larch hikes in Kananaskis, just be sure to start early as parking lots at the most popular trailheads fill up quickly during this season.

The main route through Kananaskis Country is Highway 40, also known as the Kananaskis Trail. It runs north–south through the front ranges of the Rockies. Only the northern 40 km (25 miles) of the road remain open from December to mid-June, in part because of the extreme conditions of Highwood Pass (at 7,280 feet, the highest drivable pass in Canada), and in part to protect winter wildlife habitats in Peter Lougheed Provincial Park. Highway 40 continues south to join Highway 541 west of Longview. Access to East Kananaskis Country, a popular area for horseback trips, is on Highway 66, which heads west from the town of Priddis. You'll find equipment rentals and other services in Kananaskis Village, which is 57 km (35 miles) southeast of Canmore.

Kananaskis has excellent facilities including more than 30 campgrounds and some good barrier-free facilities for people with physical disabilities like the William Watson Lodge and campground, a number of paved trails, and TrailRider and Park Explorer vehicles that allow people with disabilities to access more rugged terrain.

There is a wide variety of terrain in Kananaskis Country and the area's home to many species of plants and animals including black bears and grizzly bears. ■TIP→ It's important to be bear aware and carry bear spray when camping, hiking, or cycling in Kananaskis Country. Dawn and dusk are the best times to go for a wildlife watching drive as you might see deer, elk, moose, bears, coyotes, or bighorn sheep along the roadways and near trails. Sometimes you can spot mountain goats on high mountain peaks with the assistance of binoculars. Other elusive small and large carnivores like wolves, cougars, lynx, weasels, and wolverines live in the park, but sightings are rare. ■TIP→ **To protect wildlife and yourself, drive slowly and attentively, pull over and engage your four-way flashers if you stop, stay inside the car and never feed wildlife.**

Planning

Getting Here and Around

Kananaskis Village, in the heart of Kananaskis Country is located 117 km (73 miles) southwest of Calgary International Airport. The Town of Canmore is located 120 km (75 miles) west of Calgary International Airport.

AIR
The closest international airport is Calgary International Airport (YYC) located 117 km (73 miles) northeast of Kananaskis Village and 120 km (75 miles) east of Canmore.

BUS
Brewster Express offers shuttle service from Calgary International Airport and downtown Calgary to Kananaskis Village and Canmore. Banff Airporter has shuttles from Calgary International Airport to Canmore. There is no local transit bus in Kananaskis Country, but the town of Canmore has a public transit system and there are local taxi companies. Roam public transit buses run between Canmore, Banff, and Lake Louise and are fully accessible with room for up to three bicycles. Canmore Local (Route 5) is free to ride and service extends from Three Sisters to Cougar Creek.

CONTACTS Roam. ✉ *Canmore* ⊕ *roamtransit.com.*

CAR
The easiest way to get from Calgary to Kananaskis and Canmore is by car on Trans-Canada Highway 1 (AB-1 W).

Kananaskis is vast and a car is the most convenient and effective way to explore it. If you're staying in Canmore, and don't have access to a vehicle, you could use Roam (*see Bus Travel*), the local transit bus, or a taxi to get around.

As of June 1, 2021, a Kananaskis Conservation Pass is required to park your vehicle at provincial park and public land sites in Kananaskis and the Bow Valley. The cost is C$15 for a day pass or C$90 for an annual pass. The pass can be purchased at any of the visitor information centers or online (*conservationpass. alberta.ca/kcp*).

Hotels

There are a wide variety of accommodations in Canmore and Kananaskis ranging from luxurious resorts with many amenities to standard hotels, quaint inns, condos, and B&Bs. There's also one all-inclusive backcountry lodge (Mount Engadine Lodge). Most lodgings do not have a meal plan, but some offer a free breakfast. Room rates are typically highest in July and August and between Christmas and New Year's. The best rates can often be found in the shoulder seasons that run from October to mid-November and from May to early June. There may be fewer activities to enjoy during the shoulder seasons though and the weather may not be as good for outdoor adventures.

Hotel reviews have been shortened. For full information, visit Fodors.com.

Restaurants

Most of the restaurants in this region are found in the Town of Canmore, but there are a few in Kananaskis. In Canmore, you'll find everything from fast-food chains to fine dining. It's a very laidback town and you can wear business casual style clothes in even the nicest restaurants. It's common to see bison, elk, and trout—traditional Rocky Mountain ingredients—on the menu at upscale establishments. There are a lot of places serving pizza and pub food too, but you'll also find ethnic cuisine including Brazilian, Asian, Spanish, Indian, and Mexican. It's a good idea to make reservations at the most popular dining establishments, especially if you're there in the peak summer season.

Restaurant reviews have been shortened. For full information, visit Fodors.com.

HOTEL AND RESTAURANT PRICES

Hotel prices in the reviews are the lowest cost of a standard double room in high season. Restaurant prices in the reviews are the average cost of a main course at dinner, or if dinner is not served, at lunch.

What It Costs In Canadian Dollars			
$	$$	$$$	$$$$
RESTAURANTS			
under C$25	C$25–C$30	C$31–C$35	over C$35
HOTELS			
under C$250	C$250–C$300	C$301–C$350	over C$350

Tours

Kananaskis Outfitters

A variety of different guided tours are offered year-round and mountain biking and cross country ski lessons can also be arranged through this family-run outfitter in Kananaskis Village. You can also rent the gear you need to go exploring on your own. Bike rentals, canoes, stand-up paddleboards, kayaks, hiking gear, tennis, and basketball equipment are available

to rent in summer. In winter, you can rent skis, snowshoes, winter boots, fat bikes, ice skates, and hockey sticks. ⊠ *1 Mt Sparrowhawk Crescent, Kananaskis Village* ☎ *403/591–7000* ⊕ *kananaskisoutfitters.com* 🚲 *from C$5.*

Visitor Information

There are four visitor information centers in this region: the Travel Alberta Visitor Information Centre in Canmore and three information centers in Kananaskis Country located in Bow Valley Provincial Park, Peter Lougheed Provincial Park, and the Gooseberry Provincial Recreation Area. Pre-trip planning can be accomplished by visiting the Alberta Tourism, Parks and Recreation website for Kananaskis or by phoning the Kananaskis information line.

The Friends of Kananaskis Country website (*www.kananaskis.org*) can also be a valuable resource when planning a trip. This nonprofit organization engages volunteers in trail care, stewardship, education, and research. There are trail maps, reports and information on their website and the organization holds various events throughout the year including a summer speaker and discovery series.

The Peter Lougheed Park Discovery & Information has trained staff who can provide information about Kananaskis Country.

The wheelchair-accessible Kananaskis Visitor Information Centre can supply maps, brochures, and information about Kananaskis Country. There are also public toilets, sewage disposal, and free Wi-Fi.

CONTACTS Friends of Kananaskis Country. ⊠ *Kananaskis Village* ⊕ *www.kananaskis.org* .**Kananaskis Visitor Information Centre.** ⊠ *Kananaskis Visitor Information Centre* ☎ *403/678–0760* ⊕ *www.albertaparks.ca.*

In the morning light, Ha Ling Peak is beautifully reflected in the calm waters of Rundle Forebay Reservoir.

Canmore

25 km (15 miles) southeast of Banff and 105 km (65 miles) west of Calgary

Canmore used to be considered simply a gateway community to Banff National Park, but today it has morphed into a destination in itself. The town has wonderful facilities, attractions, trails, accommodations, and restaurants and the surrounding mountains provide for countless recreational opportunities. But, it also has a fascinating history. When the Canadian Pacific Railway (CPR) chose the Bow Valley as its route through the mountains in 1884, a CPR employee named Donald A. Smith chose the name Canmore for the first divisional point west of Calgary. It's believed the name originated in Scotland, possibly in honor of King Malcolm III. It's the anglicized version of the Gaelic *Ceann Mór*, which translates roughly to "big head" or "chief."

The Canmore valley is rich in coal and in 1887 the first coal mine was opened to mine the lower slopes of the Three Sisters and Mount Rundle. Before long, there were numerous mines in the area and Canmore became a full-fledged mining town. In 1890, the North-West Mounted Police built their first barracks in Canmore. Before long, the town had hotels and businesses, a hospital, and an opera house. Many immigrants moved to Canmore to either work in the mines or work in the businesses the miners frequented and those people left their mark forever on the area. The Grassi Lakes were named after Lawrence Grassi, an Italian immigrant miner who built many trails in the area, including the one that bears his name. Ha Ling Peak was named for a Chinese cook named Ha Ling who was bet $50 that he couldn't climb the peak and return to Canmore in under six hours. When he accomplished the feat, townsfolk began calling it Chinaman's Peak. In 1997, the name was officially revised to the more appropriate name of Ha Ling.

In 1965, Canmore was officially incorporated as a town with 2,000 residents. The last mine closed down in 1979 and the nearby towns of Anthracite, Georgetown, and Bankhead closed down and residents relocated. For a while, the fate of Canmore also seemed to be in question. The announcement in the early 1980s that the Nordic events for the 1988 Olympic Winter Games would be hosted in Canmore was welcome news for the small community that at the time was struggling.

Today, Canmore is a vibrant mountain community with a population of almost 15,000 people. Tourism is a major industry, and many of the companies that offer tours in nearby Banff National Park are based in town.

GETTING HERE AND AROUND

The Town of Canmore is located 120 km (75 miles) west of Calgary International Airport. Renting a car to get to Canmore is the most convenient option, but shuttle buses that stop in Banff also stop in Canmore (see the planner section of the Banff National Park chapter for contact information). There is no public transportation.

TOURS

Many tour operators that operate in Banff have their base in Canmore and offer a variety of adventures in Kananaskis, Canmore, and Banff.

Alpine Helicopters

Helicopter sightseeing, heli-hiking, and even heli-weddings in and around Canmore and Banff are this company's specialty. Note: You must provide your own transportation to the heliport in Canmore. ⊠ *91 Bow Valley Tr., Canmore* ☎ *403/678–4802* ⊕ *www.alpinehelicopter.com* ➱ *From C$200.*

Bow Valley SUP & Surf

This company offers stand-up paddleboard lessons and tours in Banff and in Canmore. The Canmore tours let you experience the sport on a flowing river. ⊠ *327 Railway Ave., Banff* ⊹ *in*

the Mount Norquay Heritage Train Station ☎ *403/707–7202* ⊕ *bowvalleysup.ca* ➱ *from C$85* ⊙ *Closed mid-Sept.–mid-May.*

Canadian Rockies Experience

All-inclusive luxury private guided sightseeing and hiking tours are offered by this Canmore-based tour company. Local guides take you to the top sights in Kananaskis and Banff. Tours can be customized to fit the needs of the guests. ⊠ *Armstrong Place, Canmore* ☎ *403/708–2164* ⊕ *canadianrockiesexperience.com* ➱ *from C$485.*

Canmore Trails and Tales

Explore the most scenic trails in and around Canmore and learn about wildlife, culture, and history with a knowledgeable local guide from Canmore Trails and Tails. ⊠ *1001 6th Ave., Canmore* ☎ *403/679–1572* ⊕ *www.canmoretrailsandtales.com* ➱ *from C$30.*

Get Outside

Guided hiking, backpacking, and snowshoeing adventures are offered through this local company in all seasons. Day tours and multiday tours are also available, and you can arrange private guided trips. ⊠ *Canmore* ☎ *403/478–1331* ⊕ *www.getoutsideadventures.ca* ➱ *from C$75.*

Mahikan Trails

This Canmore-based company offers unique Indigenous tours, workshops, and courses. You can discover the medicinal uses of the plants in the Canadian Rockies on a medicine walk, see ancient Indigenous pictographs on a winter icewalk, or gain more in-depth knowledge in a workshop or a course. ⊠ *82 Grotto Way, Canmore* ☎ *403/679–8379* ⊕ *mahikan.ca* ➱ *from C$60.*

VISITOR INFORMATION

Gather information about Canmore, Banff, and the rest of Alberta at this visitor center which is open from mid-May through September. There's an RV Sani-Dump station, free Wi-Fi lounge, bathrooms, and an off-leash area.

CONTACTS Travel Alberta Canmore Visitor Information Center. ⊠ *2801 Bow Valley Trail, Canmore.* ☎ *403/678–5277; 855/678–1295* ⊕ *www.explorecanmore.ca.*

⊙ Sights

HISTORIC SIGHTS

Canmore Museum and Geoscience Centre
HISTORY MUSEUM | Browse through the displays at this museum and learn about the history of Canmore and the region from millions of years ago to the present day. Enjoy a fun virtual tour of a coal mine and learn about the geology of the region too. ⊠ *902B 7th Ave., Canmore* ☎ *403/678–2462* ⊕ *canmoremuseum. com* ☐ *C$5* ☉ *Closed Tues.–Wed.*

North-West Mounted Police Barracks
HISTORY MUSEUM | Built in 1893, this building is the oldest North-West Mounted Police detachment still standing in its original location. The building served as a home, lodging, and jail for police officers stationed in Canmore until 1929. It's also Canmore's third-oldest remaining building. ⊠ *609 8th St., Canmore* ☎ *403/678–1955* ☐ *donations accepted.*

Ralph Connor United Church
HISTORIC SIGHT | Built between 1890 and 1891, this historic structure is the little white church on Canmore's Main Street. The church was named in 1942 for its founder and first minister, Charles W. Gordon, who wrote popular stories and novels under the pen name Ralph Connor. ⊠ *617 Main St., Canmore* ☎ *403/678–5354* ⊕ *ralphconnor.ca.*

SCENIC SIGHTS

Elevation Place
OTHER ATTRACTION | Elevation Place is a great place to spend a rainy day in Canmore. There's an aquatics center, a fitness center, a huge climbing gym, and a library. ⊠ *#100, 700 Railway Ave, Canmore* ☎ *403/678-8920* ⊕ *www. elevationplace.ca* ☐ *C$8 Swim C$15 Full Facility Pass.*

Quarry Lake Park
CITY PARK | Reclaimed from an old mining area, Quarry Lake is a popular local recreation area. There's a beach area where the water is shallow with a sandy bottom and the swimming and wading are best on hot days in July and August. The lake is fed by an underground spring and is over 100 meters (328 feet) deep in some places. There's also a grassy area with picnic tables and toilets and about 5 km (3 miles) of trails are nearby. The picnic area is adjacent to an off-leash dog park. ⊠ *Quarry Park, Canmore* ⊕ *www. quarrylakecanmore.ca.*

TRAILS

Grassi Lakes
TRAIL | A 4.3-km (2.7-mile) round-trip trek leads to these two small blue-green lakes, above which is a popular rock-climbing area. You can choose between an easy route through the forest or a more difficult route, which passes a waterfall and has nice views of Canmore and the Bow Valley. The trailhead is about 9 km (5.6 miles) southwest of Canmore. ⊠ *Grassi Lakes Trailhead, Canmore* ✛ *Drive 4.6 km (2.9 miles) on the Three Sisters Pkwy. (AB-742) and turn left on Ken Richie Way.*

Grotto Canyon
TRAIL | Situated southeast of downtown Canmore, Grotto Canyon is accessible only on foot. A waterfall and ancient pictographs are among the highlights of the popular 4.2-km (2.6-mile) round-trip hike to reach the steep canyon. Wear microspikes if you do the hike in winter. ⊠ *Grotto Canyon Trailhead, Canmore* ✛ *12.8 km (9 miles) southeast of Canmore off Bow Valley Trail (Hwy. 1A).*

Ha Ling Peak
TRAIL | This peak was named in honor of a Chinese cook who won a bet that he couldn't hike to the top and make it back to town in under six hours. To this day, some people still run the steep 7.4-km (4.6-mile) trail with 748 meter (2,454-foot) elevation gain. Whether you walk or

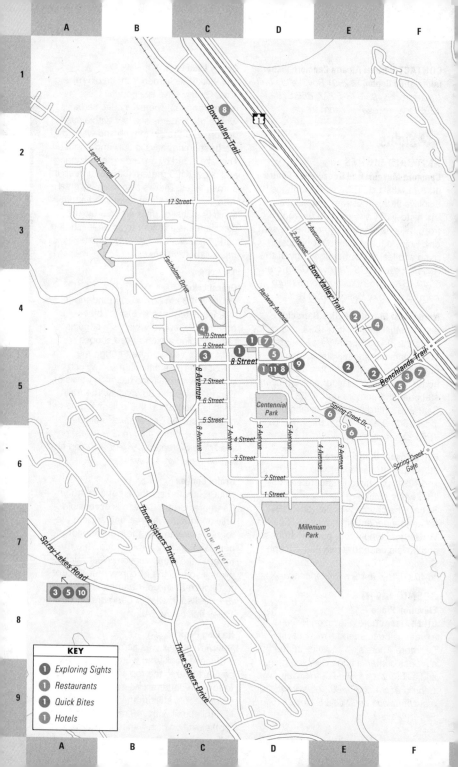

Canmore

0   1,000 ft

0   200 m

There is great hiking to and from Grassi Lakes.

run, the views from the top are outstanding. ✉ *Ha Ling Trailhead, Canmore.*

Heart Creek

TRAIL | This easy 4-km (2.5-mile) round-trip hike is a nice walk through a gorgeous canyon along a creek with a waterfall at the end. ✉ *Heart Creek Trailhead, Canmore.*

Heart Mountain Horseshoe Hike

TRAIL | Summit three mountains on this hike that takes you to the summit of Heart Mountain and then along a ridge walk to summit two more Canadian Rockies peaks. It's a challenging hike with a total hiking distance of 10.3 km (6.4 miles) and an elevation gain of 940 meters (3,084 feet). ✉ *Heart Creek Trailhead, Canmore.*

Policeman's Creek Boardwalk

TRAIL | This 3.9-km (2.4 mile) boardwalk runs alongside Policeman's Creek and passes ponds and forested areas with views of the mountains. It's a good place to see ducks, birds, and other wildlife and there are plenty of spots with pretty views. ✉ *Policeman's Creek Boardwalk, Canmore* ✣ *Trailhead is near the big head sculpture in downtown Canmore.*

🍴 Restaurants

Gaucho Brazilian Barbecue Canmore

$$$$ | **BRAZILIAN** | Bring a healthy appetite and a love for delicious slow-roasted meat when you visit this authentic Brazilian house of barbecue. With rodizio-style dining, you pay one price and skewers of perfectly roasted steaming meat are carried to your table and sliced onto your plate until you tell them to stop. **Known for:** authentic Brazilian barbecue; endless meat and side dishes; delightful ambience. [$] *Average main: C$57* ✉ *629 8th St., Canmore* ☎ *403/678–9886* 🌐 *www.brazilianbbq.ca* 🕒 *Closed Mon.–Tues. No lunch.*

Georgetown Pub

$ | **BRITISH** | This spot resembles an old English pub in every way, including having a red phone booth and the best fish-and-chips in town. Other British pub classics like Scotch eggs, bangers and mash, stuffed Yorkshire pudding, shepherd's pie, and beef Wellington are on the menu alongside Canadian favorites like salads, burgers, poutine, and steak sandwiches. **Known for:** best fish-and-chips in town; beers on tap; Old English pub atmosphere. $ *Average main: C$22* ⊠ *1101 Bow Valley Trail, Canmore* ☎ *403/678–3439* ⊕ *www.georgetowninn. ca.*

Rocket Pie

$ | PIZZA | Neapolitan-style pizza baked in a stone-fired oven is the specialty of this local pizza place that serves their pizzas with their own secret finishing oil. The menu also features calzones, lasagna, salads, and tiramisu for dessert. **Known for:** Neapolitan-style pizza; stone-fired oven; secret dipping sauce. $ *Average main: C$21* ⊠ *304 Old Canmore Rd. #101, Canmore* ☎ *403/675–2865* ⊕ *www. rocketpie.ca* ☾ *No lunch.*

Rocky Mountain Flatbread Co.

$ | PIZZA | This award-winning family pizza chain began in Canmore and now has locations in Vancouver and Calgary as well. The secret to their success is local organic produce, free-range organic meats, and Ocean Wise seafood on the flatbread pizzas, pastas, and salads. **Known for:** wood-fired pizza oven; farm-to-pizza philosophy; organic ingredients. $ *Average main: C$19* ⊠ *838 10th St., Canmore* ☎ *403/609–5508* ⊕ *www.rocky-mountainflatbread.ca.*

★ The Sensory

$$$$ | CANADIAN | The cozy main-floor lounge serves casual comfort food. The top-level restaurant serves more elaborate dishes—perhaps, maple-rosemary braised short rib with Saskatoon berry sauce or grilled Arctic char with beetroot risotto—in a modern dining room with floor-to-ceiling windows, wood-plank walls, and dark-wood tables. **Known for:** nice selection of reasonably priced wines; fine dining with wonderful views; creative use of local ingredients, some of them hand-foraged. $ *Average*

main: C$38 ⊠ *101-300 Old Canmore Rd., Canmore* ☎ *403/812–0837* ⊕ *www.the-sensory.ca* ☾ *Closed Wed. No lunch.*

The Stirling Lounge

$ | BRITISH | This Scottish-inspired restaurant is decorated in dark wood and has a long granite bar and cozy private booths with a wall of TVs playing various sports games. There are a wide array of nibbles on the lounge menu and a great bar menu—burgers, fish and chips, stuffed Yorkshire pudding—with 10 beers on tap, local canned craft beers, and ciders, cocktails, spirits, and wine by the glass or bottle. **Known for:** lively atmosphere; 10 beers on tap; delicious pub food. $ *Average main: C$24* ⊠ *Malcolm Hotel, 321 Spring Creek Dr., Canmore* ☎ *403/812–0690* ⊕ *www.malcolmhotel.ca.*

Tank 310 at the Grizzly Paw Brewery

$ | AMERICAN | Located on the third floor of Grizzly Paw Brewery, this restaurant embraces craft beer culture with a seasonally inspired menu that pairs well with the beers made at the brewery. Each dish has a suggested pairing and the menu includes salads, a wide array of pub-style starters, oven-fired flatbreads, burgers, steaks, pasta, and other dishes. **Known for:** craft beer and sodas; pub food; mountain views. $ *Average main: C$24* ⊠ *310 Old Canmore Rd., Canmore* ☎ *403/678–2487* ⊕ *www.thegrizzlypaw. com* ☾ *Closed Tues.*

☕ Coffee and Quick Bites

Communitea Cafe

$ | CAFÉ | More than 80 varieties of loose leaf teas, craft beverages, and artisan coffees are served alongside fresh, healthy, and local food at this downtown café. Look for pad Thai noodle bowls, rice bowls, salads, sandwiches, and delicious wraps. **Known for:** healthy, local fare; more than 80 loose leaf teas; vegan and vegetarian food. $ *Average main: C$15* ⊠ *1001 6th Ave., Canmore* ☎ *403/688–2233* ⊕ *www.thecommunitea.com.*

Eclipse Coffee Roasters

$ | **CAFÉ** | On any day, this specialty coffee roaster carries 15–20 different environmentally grown and socially responsible coffees which they roast on-site—they've won numerous roasting competitions. Each aromatic blend is perfectly brewed and can be enjoyed with baked goods, snacks, wraps, and other light fare. **Known for:** delicious baked goods; amazing coffee; award-winning roasters. $ *Average main: C$10* ⊠ *113-702 Bow Valley Trail, Canmore* ⊕ *eclipsecoffeeroasters.com.*

Rocky Mountain Bagel Co.

$ | **BAKERY** | Every night bakers at this establishment make between 60 and 120 dozen artisan "Mountain Style" (cooked in a steam-injected oven and then baked) bagels in nine different flavors as well as muffins, cinnamon buns, and scones. Flavored cream cheeses, soups, cookies, and squares are also on the menu and everything is served with a nice selection of coffees, teas, and juices. **Known for:** good coffee; delicious bagels; inexpensive and quick breakfast or lunch. $ *Average main: C$10* ⊠ *102 830 8th St., Canmore* ☎ *403/678–9968* ⊕ *thebagel.ca.*

Valbella Gourmet Foods

$ | **CAFÉ** | First established in 1978, this company produces gourmet cured meats and artisan sausages. In the on-site deli, you can buy locally grown and made foods and enjoy a variety of freshly made sandwiches, chicken pot pies, sausage rolls, paninis, snacks, and treats served alongside coffee or tea. **Known for:** good coffee; exceptional gourmet smoked meats; delicious sandwiches. $ *Average main: C$7* ⊠ *104 Elk Run Blvd., Canmore* ☎ *403/678–9989* ⊕ *valbellagourmet-foods.ca* ⊙ *Closed Sun.*

 # Hotels

A Bear & Bison Inn

$$$$ | **B&B/INN** | Built and run by a chef who has worked at top restaurants in Canada and abroad, this charming country inn has mountain views from every room and patios or balconies from which to enjoy those views. **Pros:** romantic ambience; delicious gourmet breakfast; mountain views from every room. **Cons:** 20-minute walk from downtown; no on-site restaurant; no in-room fridges. $ *Rooms from: C$359* ⊠ *705 Benchlands Trail, Canmore* ☎ *403/678–2058* ⊕ *abearandbisoninn.com* ⊙| *Free Breakfast* ⇄ *10 rooms.*

Copperstone Resort

$$ | **RESORT** | **FAMILY** | Located five minutes east of Canmore in Dead Man's Flats, this condo-style property backs onto a forest with hiking and cycling trails, a creek, and the Bow River nearby. **Pros:** all units have patios or balconies; home away from home; great trails right outside the door. **Cons:** poor cell service; not very wheelchair accessible; no daily maid service. $ *Rooms from: C$280* ⊠ *250 2nd Ave., Dead Man's Flats* ☎ *866/571–0303 toll-free* ⊕ *www.copperstoneresort.com* ⊙| *No Meals* ⇄ *35 units.*

Falcon Crest Lodge

$$$$ | **HOTEL** | These modern condos have all the comforts of home—fully equipped kitchens, marble bathrooms, gas fireplaces, and balconies with individual gas barbecues. **Pros:** kitchens with granite countertops and barbecues; feels like a home away from home; great views. **Cons:** small gym; no pool; 20-minute drive to Banff. $ *Rooms from: C$384* ⊠ *190 Kananaskis Way, Canmore* ☎ *403/678–6150, 866/609–3222 in North America* ⊕ *www.falconcrestlodge.ca* ⇄ *54 condos, 18 suites* ⊙| *No Meals.*

Georgetown Inn

$$ | **B&B/INN** | From its Tudor-style exterior and English gardens to its interior decor, this charming Canmore inn makes you feel like you are in England—there's even a really good on-site pub and restaurant that carries on the theme, right down to an outdoor red phone booth. **Pros:** fireplaces in all rooms; great on-site restaurant; romantic Old English-style inn. **Cons:** slow elevator; older property;

no swimming pool or hot tub. $ Rooms from: C$290 ✉ 1101 Bow Valley Trail, Canmore ☎ 403/678–3439, 866/695–5955 toll-free reservations ⊕ www.georgetowninn.ca ⦵ No Meals ⤵ 21 rooms.

Lamphouse Hotel

$$$$ | MOTEL | This boutique motel on Canmore's Main Street is within easy walking distance to restaurants, shops, and sights. **Pros:** outdoor hot tub; downtown location with free parking; keyless entry. **Cons:** loud air-conditioning; no in-room phones; no elevator. $ Rooms from: C$369 ✉ 610 8th St., Canmore ☎ 855/219–4707 toll-free ⊕ www. basecampresorts.com/lamphouse ⦵ No Meals ⤵ 25 rooms, 1 apartment.

★ The Malcolm Hotel

$$$$ | HOTEL | Taking its name from a town on Scotland's northwest shores that was itself named after Scottish King Malcom III (1058–93), this luxury hotel blends modernity with touches of bygone royal decadence: the lobby has a massive stone fireplace and a large portrait of his majesty, but guest rooms are more contemporary, done in neutral tones and equipped with flat-screen TVs, Nespresso machines, and bathrooms that have walk-in showers. **Pros:** many resort-style amenities; new, modern hotel; 5-minute walk to downtown Canmore. **Cons:** some rooms are smaller than others; underground parking is limited, and the alternate lot is outdoors; outdoor pool is heated but walk to it is chilly in winter. $ Rooms from: C$375 ✉ 321 Spring Creek Dr., Canmore ☎ 403/812–0680, 888/570–0603 toll-free ⊕ www.malcolmhotel.ca ⤵ 124 rooms ⦵ No Meals.

Paintbox Lodge

$$ | B&B/INN | Olympic cross-country skiing medalist Sara Renner and World Cup alpine skiing champion Thomas Grandi own this intimate boutique hotel, where individually decorated, country-style rooms have wood furnishings, and amenities include a comfortable lounge with an open-beam ceiling, a fireplace, a breakfast area with a professional kitchen, and a cappuccino bar. **Pros:** free bikes and Wi-Fi; downtown Canmore location; breakfast included. **Cons:** no a/c; not staffed 24 hours; small property. $ Rooms from: C$275 ✉ 629 10th St., Canmore ☎ 403/609–0482, 888/678–6100 ⊕ paintboxlodge.com ⤵ 5 rooms ⦵ Free Breakfast.

Pocaterra Inn & Waterslide

$$ | HOTEL | FAMILY | A free hot buffet breakfast, an indoor pool, a waterslide, and a sauna are highlights of this family-friendly property. **Pros:** indoor pool and waterslide; fridge, microwaves, coffee makers in rooms; free hot breakfast included. **Cons:** no on-site restaurant; near the busy Trans-Canada Highway; older property. $ Rooms from: C$299 ✉ 1725 Bow Valley Trail, Canmore ☎ 403/678–4334 ⊕ pocaterrainn.com ⦵ Free Breakfast ⤵ 86 rooms.

Stoneridge Mountain Resort

$$$$ | APARTMENT | FAMILY | With mountain views on all sides, this condo-style resort has one-, two-, and three-bedroom condos that sleep two to eight people depending on the size of the unit. **Pros:** outdoor pool and hot tub; home away from home; all rooms have mountain views. **Cons:** small gym; 15-minute walk from downtown; no on-site restaurant. $ Rooms from: C$450 ✉ 30 Lincoln Park, Canmore ☎ 877/675–5001 toll-free reservations, 403/675–5000 ⊕ www. stoneridgeresort.ca ⦵ No Meals ⤵ 73 rooms.

🏃 Activities

Many of the outfitters and operators who run tours in Banff National Park are based in Canmore, so if you're staying here, you can often join the tour from Canmore rather than having to drive to the park. Equipment for a variety of activities can be rented at most sports shops in Canmore.

Built for the 1988 Olympic Nordic skiing events, the Canmore Nordic Centre Provincial Park has cross-country trails and ice skating in the winter.

BOATING

Canadian Rockies Rafting

RAFTING | Scenic floats and thrilling white-water rafting tours on the Bow, Kananaskis, and Kicking Horse rivers are conducted by these local experts. The rates include pickup in Banff or Canmore. ⊠ *909 Railway Ave., Canmore* ☎ *403/678–6535, 877/226–7625* ⊕ *www.rafting.ca* ⊠ *From C$40* ⊘ *Closed Oct.–Apr.*

Canmore Raft Tours

RAFTING | A variety of scenic river floats is available through this Canmore-based company. They also offer multiday whitewater rafting trips. ⊠ *829 8th St., Canmore* ☎ *888/748–3770 toll-free, 403/688–1775* ⊕ *www.canmorerafttours.com* ⊠ *from C$40* ⊘ *Closed Oct.–Apr.*

Canmore River Adventures

RAFTING | Scenic float trips with this company depart from the Canmore public boat launch. ⊠ *Canmore Boat Launch, Canmore* ☎ *403/542–4396* ⊕ *www.canmoreriveradventures.com* ⊠ *from C$50* ⊘ *Closed Oct.–Apr.*

White Wolf Rafting

RAFTING | This company offers raft tours on the Bow River, the Kananaskis River, and in Horseshoe Canyon on rapids that are grade 2-4. They also have packages that combine rafting with dog carting. ⊠ *829 10th St., #109, Canmore* ☎ *403/675–0632, 888/655–7238 toll-free* ⊕ *www.whitewolfrafting.com* ⊠ *from C$70* ⊘ *Closed Oct.–Apr.*

GOLF

Canmore Golf and Curling Club

GOLF | This 18-hole course is set along the Bow River with views of the Three Sisters Mountains. It's a generally forgiving course and one of the better priced courses in this area. There's an on-site pro shop and a restaurant. ⊠ *2000 8th Ave., Canmore* ☎ *877/678–5959, 403/678–5959* ⊕ *canmoregolf.net* ⊠ *C$95* ⊘ *Closed Oct.–Apr.* ⅄ *18 holes, 6460 yards, par 71.*

Silvertip Golf Course

GOLF | Dramatic elevation changes and views of the valley and mountains from most holes make an outing at this course memorable. Designed by Canmore-based Les Furber, responsible for dozens of Canadian courses and many worldwide, Silvertip is the area's only south-oriented one—the resulting extra sun can be a boon when temperatures dip. This 18-hole par-72 course has 600 feet of elevation change and multiple tees for both scratch golfers and recreational players. ⊠ *2000 Silvertip Trail, Canmore* ☎ *403/678–1600, 877/877–5444* ⊕ *www. silvertipresort.com* ⊠ *C$150* 🎿 *18 holes, 6534 yards, par 72* ⊙ *Closed Oct.–Apr.*

Stewart Creek Golf Course

GOLF | Designed by renowned golf architect Gary Browning, this 18-hole, par 71 course has layered fairways, gently sloping greens, and stunning mountain scenery. It's received a number of awards and accolades. ⊠ *4100 Stewart Creek Dr., Canmore* ☎ *877/993–4653 toll free, 403/609–6099* ⊕ *stewartcreekgolf. com* ⊠ *Mon.–Thurs. C$200; Fri.–Sun. (June 1–Sept. 6) C$220; discounted rates for early- and late-season golf* ⊙ *Closed Oct.–Apr.* 🎿 *18 holes, par 71, 7009 yards.*

HORSEBACK RIDING

Cross Zee Ranch

HORSEBACK RIDING | Experience the beauty of the Rockies on horseback. One- and two-hour trail rides are offered in the morning and the afternoon. The ranch also hosts private barbecues for groups of 45 to 140 guests. ⊠ *2500 Palliser Trail, Canmore* ☎ *403/678-4171* ⊕ *crosszeeranch.ca* ⊠ *from C$67.*

SKIING

Canmore Nordic Centre Provincial Park

SKIING & SNOWBOARDING | **FAMILY** | Built for the 1988 Olympic Nordic skiing events, the center has 70 km (43 miles) of groomed cross-country trails in winter that become hiking and mountain-biking trails in summer. Some trails are lighted for night skiing, and a 1½-km (1-mile) paved trail is open in summer for roller skiing and rollerblading. Other winter sports include ice-skating, winter disc golf, and fat biking; in summer you can

also play disc golf and participate in a roller biathlon. The state-of-the-art facility is south of Canmore in the northwestern corner of Kananaskis Country. In late January, an international biathlon and dogsled races take place here as part of the Canmore Winter Carnival. ⊠ *1988 Olympic Way, Canmore* ☎ *403/678–2400* ⊕ *www.albertaparks.ca/parks/kananaskis/ canmore-nordic-centre-pp* ⊠ *Trails free Apr.–Oct., C$15 per day Nov.–Mar.*

SLEDDING

Howling Dog Tours

SNOW SPORTS | Experience the sport of dog sledding in Spray Lakes Provincial Park with a team of five to seven huskies. Tours run December through April and include round-trip transportation from all major hotels in Banff and Canmore, snacks, and a hot beverage. ⊠ *712 Bow Valley Trail, #105, Canmore* ☎ *877/364–7533 toll free, 403/678–9588* ⊕ *howlingdogtours.com* ⊙ *Closed May– Nov.* ⊠ *from C$225.*

Snowy Owl Sled Dog Tours

SNOW SPORTS | This company offers dog sled tours in winter and kennel visits, dog carting and rafting in summer. All tours include a campfire with hot beverages and baked goods; some tours also let you embrace your inner musher and drive the sled yourself. ⊠ *109-829 10th St., Canmore* ☎ *888/311–6874 toll-free, 587/807–0896* ⊕ *snowyowltours.com* ⊠ *from C$125 summer dog cart; from C$262.50.*

SPELUNKING

Bow Valley Canyon Tours

ADVENTURE TOURS | Canyoning trips with this company include descents, jumps, slides, waterfalls, pools, and rappels into several area canyons in both summer and winter. Half-day and full-day trips are available and trained guides teach and assist guests in learning to maneuver and descend safely. ⊠ *42 Des Arcs Dr. Lac Des Arcs, Canmore* ☎ *877/554-0116* ⊕ *www.bowvalleycanyoning.ca* ⊠ *from C$185.*

With 9 provincial parks and over 50 recreation, wilderness, and natural areas, there are wonderful trails and sites to discover throughout Kananaskis.

Canmore Cave Tours

SPELUNKING | FAMILY | If you have ever wanted to don a headlamp and explore an undeveloped cave, you can arrange a guided tour of the Rat's Nest Cave with Canmore Caverns. The outfitter supplies the knowledge and equipment, and you bring the enthusiasm. Although there are offerings for all levels, children must be at least nine years of age to participate. The most adventurous tour involves an 18-meter (59-foot) rappel and a squeeze through the laundry shoot. ✉ *202-129 Bow Meadows Crescent, Canmore* ☎ *403/678–8819, 877/317–1178* ⊕ *www.canmorecavetours.com* ✉ *From C$135.*

Yamnuska Mountain Adventures

ADVENTURE TOURS | This Canmore-based company provides mountaineering, ice climbing, rock climbing, backcountry skiing, avalanche training and trekking experiences in the Canadian Rockies. There are trips, programs, and courses from beginner to expert level with some of the top mountain guides in Canada. ✉ *50 Lincoln Park, #200, Canmore*

☎ *403/678-4164* ⊕ *yamnuska.com* ✉ *from C$280.*

Bow Valley Provincial Park

102 km (63 miles) west of Calgary

Bow Valley Provincial Park is the gateway park for most visitors to Kananaskis Country. The 32.9-square-km (12.7-square-mile) park was established in 1959 and expanded in 2000. It protects an important region of the Bow Valley at the confluence of the Bow River and the Kananaskis River. The park sits at the north end of Kananaskis Country straddling the Trans-Canada Highway west of the Highway 40 junction and strectes along the Kananaskis River to include Barrier Lake.

The park is dominated by aspen and evergreen forests, but there are a total of three vegetative zones and more than 300 species of plants. Some 60 species of birds nest inside the park and there is a vast amount of other wildlife that can be seen along roads and trails.

There's an information center near Barrier Lake that provides information and free interpretive programs. The park also has several campgrounds, day-use areas, and trails. Hiking and cycling are popular activities. Boating is allowed on Lac Des Arcs and Gap Lake and you can fish in the Bow River, Gap Lake, and Grotto Pond. The Bow River is a world-famous fly fishing river and anglers vie for rainbow, brown, and brook trout.

GETTING HERE AND AROUND

Bow Valley Provincial Park is located just outside the town of Canmore at the arc of the Bow River at its confluence with the Kananaskis River. You'll find the Kananaskis Visitor Information Centre about 7 km (4.3 miles) off Highway 1 on Kananaskis Trail (Hwy. 40), about a 20-minute drive southeast of Canmore. Eleven day-use areas, seven campgrounds, and many spectacular trails run through this beautiful provincial park.

 Sights

SCENIC STOPS

Barrier Lake Day Use Area

OTHER ATTRACTION | Picnic tables, indoor toilets, a boat launch, a visitor center, free Wi-Fi access, and lovely views are the draws at this day-use area in Kananaskis Country. ⊠ *Barrier Lake Visitor Centre, Kananaskis Village.*

Canoe Meadows

NATURE SIGHT | You get great views of the Kananaskis River from this day-use site along Highway 40 and if you're lucky, you can watch kayakers navigating artificial rapids. There are toilets, a picnic shelter, and a water pump. ⊠ *Canoe Meadows Campground, Kananaskis Village.*

TRAILS

Bow Valley Paved Trail

TRAIL | This 4.2-km (2.6-mile) one-way paved trail stretches from the Bow Valley Campground and information center through forest and rolling terrain with good views of meadows along the way. There are short steep hills at either end of the trail making it less accommodating for wheelchairs. *Easy.* ⊠ *Bow Valley Information Centre, Kananaskis Village.*

Flowing Water Interpretive Trail

TRAIL | This 2.0-km (1.2-mile) round-trip trail passes through the montane forest above the Kananaskis River and has nice views of the mountains, the Kananaskis River, and a beaver pond. Interpretive signs describe the water cycle. *Easy.* ⊠ *Willow Rock Campground, Kananaskis Village* ⊹ *Trailhead: Willow Rock Campground.*

Many Springs Interpretive Trail

TRAIL | This 1.3-km (0.8-mile) interpretive trail encircles a wetland that is fed by warm underground springs. There's an observation deck to observe birds and plants in the wetland and interpretive signs that describe the unique environment. *Easy.* ⊠ *Kananaskis Village* ⊹ *Trailhead: Whitefish Day Use Area.*

Montane Interpretive Trail

TRAIL | You'll find the trailhead for this 1.5-km (0.9-mile) interpretive loop trail at the visitor center. It's great for children and has views of forest, meadows, and seasonal wildflowers. *Easy.* ⊠ *Bow Valley Visitor Centre, Kananaskis Village* ⊹ *Trailhead: Visitor Center.*

🏃 Activities

CAMPING

There are six frontcountry campgrounds, one backcountry campground, and five group camping areas in Bow Valley Provincial Park (*www.bowvalley-campgrounds.com*). There are also 11 day-use areas. Most of the campgrounds require advance reservations (*www.*

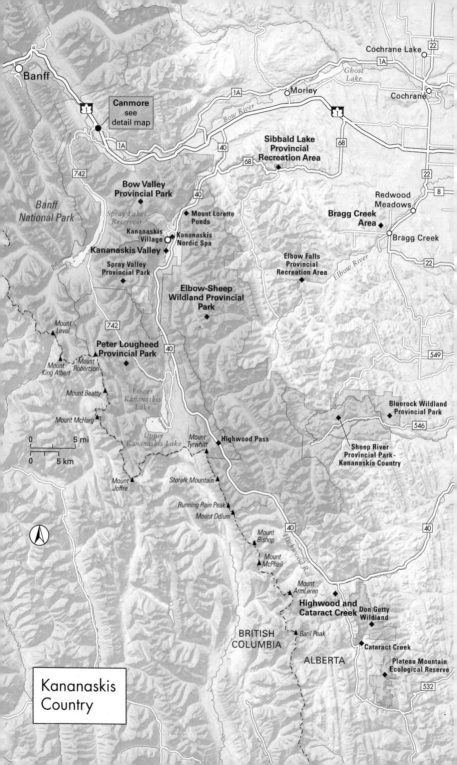

Banff

Cochrane Lake · 22

1A

Ghost Lake

Canmore
see
detail map

1

Morley

Cochrane

Bow River

1A

40

Sibbald Lake
Provincial
Recreation Area

68

22

8

742

Bow Valley
Provincial Park

Banff National Park

Spray Lakes Reservoir

40

Redwood
Meadows

Bragg Creek
Area

· Mount Lorette Ponds

Kananaskis Village

Kananaskis
Nordic Spa

Kananaskis Valley

Bragg Creek

22

Spray Valley
Provincial Park

Elbow-Sheep
Wildland Provincial
Park

Elbow Falls
Provincial
Recreation Area

Elbow River

Mount Leval

742

Peter Lougheed
Provincial Park

40

Mount Robertson

Mount King Albert

Mount Beatty

Lower Kananaskis Lake

549

Bluerock Wildland
Provincial Park

Mount McHarg

546

Upper Kananaskis Lake

0   5 mi

0   5 km

Mount Tyrwhitt

Highwood Pass

Sheep River
Provincial Park -
Kananaskis Country

Mount Joffre

Storelk Mountain

Running Rain Peak

Mount Odlum

40

Highwood R.

Mount Bishop

Mount McPhail

40

Mount ArmLaren

Highwood and
Cataract Creek

Don Getty
Wildland

BRITISH
COLUMBIA

Baril Peak

ALBERTA

Cataract Creek

Plateau Mountain
Ecological Reserve

532

Kananaskis
Country

reserve.albertaparks.ca 877/537–2757). Unserviced sites cost C$31 per night and serviced sites cost C$47 per night.

Bow River Campground. Situated next to the Bow River, this lovely campground has seven walk-in unserviced sites and 59 sites with 30 amp power and water hookups. There are many activities available, including hiking, biking, fishing, and paddling. Each site has a firepit and a picnic table. There are showers, pit toilets, and a water pump at the campground. Firewood is available for purchase. *6.8 km (4.2 mile) south of Canmore off the Three Sisters Parkway.*

Bow Valley Campground. One of the park's largest campgrounds has well treed sites with nice views. There are 42 walk-in tent sites and 131 sites serviced with power and water. This campground is situated along the Bow River and has many amenities including interpretive programs, a concession, a playground, and showers. *30 km (18 miles) east of Canmore just north of Hwy. 1, off the Hwy. 1X.*

Canoe Meadows Campground. This small campground has 10 unserviced walk-in tent sites and is a convenient staging area for kayakers, rafters, and river surfers. There are pit toilets and firepits. *36 km (22 miles) southeast of Canmore. Off Hwy. 40 at about 5.7 km (3 miles).*

Lac Des Arcs Campground. Located on the shores of Lac Des Arcs, a popular spot for windsurfers, this campground has 28 unserviced sites that must be pre-reserved. There are firepits, a playground, pit toilets, a hand launch, a water pump, and a picnic shelter. *14 km (8.7 miles) east of Canmore on Hwy. 1.*

Three Sisters Campground. Beside the Bow River, this campground is popular with canoeists, because it has a hand launch for non-motorized boats. There are 36 unserved walk-in sites and the campground has plenty of trees. The campground has firepits, a water pump, pit toilets, and a picnic shelter. *Located in Deadman's Flats 12 km (7 miles) east of Canmore on Hwy. 1.*

Willow Rock Campground. This campground has 90 unserviced sites and 34 powered sites that are first-come, first served. There is a playground, showers, firepits, picnic shelters, sewage disposal, tap water, and flush toilets. *30 km (18.6 miles) east of Canmore just north of Hwy. 1 and east off Hwy. 1X.*

EDUCATIONAL PROGRAMS
Stop in at the Kananaskis Visitor Information Centre to find out more about the free interpretive programs offered in Bow Valley Provincial Park as well as other parts of Kananaskis Country.

HIKING
There are at least 13 different trails in Bow Valley Provincial Park including several short interpretive ones that are suitable for families with young children. There's also a paved trail that is good for road cycling and several others that are built to accommodate both cyclists and hikers. Stoney Trail can accommodate e-bikes, mountain bikes, hikers, and horses.

Kananaskis Valley

The Kananaskis Valley is the most developed region of Kananaskis Country and Kananaskis Village is the site of most of the services. Highway 40, also known as Kananaskis Trail, is the main road. It follows the Kananaskis River through the valley to Peter Lougheed Provincial Park. Kananaskis Village was developed in anticipation of the 1988 Winter Olympic Games and is one of the many lasting legacies from that event.

GETTING HERE AND AROUND
Kananaskis Village is the main service area in the Kananaskis Valley. It's located 57 km (35 miles) southeast of Canmore and 26 km (16 miles) south of the Trans-Canada Highway (Highway 1). From there, it's 3 km (1.9 miles) west

of Highway 40 (Kananaskis Trail) via Mt. Allan Drive and Centennial Drive.

VISITOR INFORMATION

The wheelchair-accessible Kananaskis Visitor Information Centre can supply maps, brochures, and information about Kananaskis Country. There are also public toilets, sewage disposal, and free Wi-Fi.

CONTACTS Kananaskis Visitor Information Centre. ⊠ *Kananaskis Visitor Information Centre* ☎ *403/678–0760* ⊕ *www.alberta-parks.ca.*

 # Sights

SCENIC STOPS

Kananaskis Nordic Spa

OTHER ATTRACTION | This 50,000-square-foot, Scandinavian-style spa has five outdoor pools, four steam and sauna cabins, an exfoliation room, and eight treatment rooms. Other blissful offerings include a relaxation area with heated hammocks, fireside lounges, and a wellness bistro. Following an age-old tradition, spa-goers cycle through a circuit of hot, cold, and relaxation phases. This adults-only experience takes several hours. There are two sessions daily: 9 am–2:30 pm and 3:30 pm–9 pm. ⊠ *1 Centennial Dr., Kananaskis Village* ☎ *403/591–7711* ⊕ *knordicspa. com* ☒ *C$119 Mon.–Thurs., C$129 Fri.–Sun.*

Kananaskis Village

TOWN | This unincorporated mountain village 90 km (56 miles) southwest of Calgary was built for the 1988 Winter Olympic Games and is the location of the main facilities and services in the Kananaskis region. It was also the hosting site of the 28th G8 summit in 2002. ⊠ *Kananaskis Village, Kananaskis Village ✛ 26 km (16 miles) south of the Trans-Canada Highway (Highway 1), 3 km (1.9 miles) west of Highway 40 (Kananaskis Trail) via Mt. Allan Drive and Centennial Drive.*

Mount Lorette Ponds

BODY OF WATER | Mt. Lorette and Mary Barklay's Mountain reflected in these beautiful ponds—which are looped by a paved, 930-meter (0.6-mile), wheelchair-accessible trail—provide a stunning backdrop for photos at this spot. There are also picnic tables, firepits, pit toilets, and a water pump here. ⊠ *Mount Lorette Ponds, Kananaskis Village ✛ 49 km (30 miles) southwest of Canmore off Kananaskis Trail (Hwy. 40).*

TRAILS

Mount Kidd Lookout Trail

TRAIL | A 7.4-km (4.6-mile) round-trip hike will take you through the forest to a fire lookout with amazing views of Mount Kidd. Be careful if you do this hike in winter as it is in an avalanche area and proper safety measures must be taken. There's a 734-meter (2,408-foot) elevation gain. *Moderate.* ⊠ *Mount Kidd Lookout Trailhead, Kananaskis Village.*

Prairie View Trail

TRAIL | Often called the Barrier Fire Lookout trail, the Prairie View Trail switchbacks uphill on an old forestry road to a spectacular viewpoint looking south over Barrier Lake. From this viewpoint, you can either continue to the Barrier Fire Lookout on the north side of the ridge or descend along Jewel Pass. The Jewel Pass trail goes alongside Jewell Creek and passes Jewell Falls before ending on the shores of Barrier Lake. It's 9.8-km (6.1-miles) round-trip with a 475-meter (1,558-foot) elevation gain to the McConnell Ridge viewpoint and another 1.4-km (0.9-miles) round-trip with an 80-meter (262-foot) elevation gain to the Barrier Fire Lookout. If you add Jewell Pass, it's 14 km (8.7 miles) round-trip. *Moderate.* ⊠ *Prairie View Trailhead, Kananaskis Village ✛ Trailhead: Cross the Barrier Dam, take the right trail fork at the first junction and go left at the second junction.*

The icy blue water of the Kananaskis River snakes its way through the Kananaskis Valley.

Troll Falls

TRAIL | This short, family-friendly trail goes through an aspen forest and leads to a lovely waterfall. It's popular in both summer and winter and can be reached by hiking, mountain biking, snowshoeing, or skiing. It's 1.7 km (1.1 mile) one-way with very little elevation gain. *Easy.* ✉ *Troll Falls Trailhead, Kananaskis Village* ✥ *Trailhead: 3.3 km (2 miles) north of Kananaskis Village on Centennial Dr.*

🍴 Restaurants

Forte

$$ | **ITALIAN** | **FAMILY** | Open for breakfast, lunch, and dinner, the restaurant is known for locally sourced ingredients that are used in their delicious wood-fired pizzas and house-made pasta, creative salads, seafood and chicken dishes, and Alberta beef steaks; there's also an excellent breakfast buffet. The dining area includes a long bar, an open kitchen, and expansive windows with gorgeous mountain views along one side of the restaurant. **Known for:** locally sourced ingredients; wood-fired pizzas; house made pastas. [$] *Average main: C$28* ✉ *Pomeroy Kananaskis Mountain Lodge, 1 Centennial Dr., Kananaskis Village* ☎ *403/591–7711* 🌐 *lodgeatkananaskis.com/forte-restaurant.*

🛏 Hotels

★ **Pomeroy Kananaskis Mountain Lodge**

$$$$ | **RESORT** | **FAMILY** | Many of the large rooms at this lodge have fireplaces, hot tubs, and sitting areas, and although its location is second to none—close to area trails, ski resorts, and golf courses—it's almost a destination unto itself thanks to a large indoor pool and waterpark, hot tubs, tennis courts, a eucalyptus-infused steam room, a large fitness area, and a spa. **Pros:** beautiful mountain setting; hiking, biking, golf, and skiing nearby; concierge, family activities and many amenities. **Cons:** resort can get noisy with many small children; no air-conditioning; 30-minute drive to Canmore. [$] *Rooms from: C$364* ✉ *1 Centennial Dr., Kananaskis Village* ✥ *Hwy. 40, 28 km (17* *miles) south of Hwy. 1* ☎ *403/591–7711, 888/244–8666 toll-free in North America* ⊕ *lodgeatkananaskis.com* ⎮◎⎮ *No Meals* ⇥ *412 rooms.*

 Activities

BIKING

Cycling is a popular activity in Kananaskis Country and whether you have a road bike, a mountain bike, an e-bike, or a fat bike, there are multiple trail options. You can pop in one of the visitor centers to get advice, directions and maps of cycling trails or stop in Kananaskis Outfitters (*See Tours for more information*) in Kananaskis Village. The outfitter rents bikes, offers mountain biking lessons, tours and can provide trail advice.

Ribbon Creek

BIKING | Mountain bikes are allowed on the first 4 km (2½ miles) of the 8.2-km (5-mile) trail to Ribbon Falls. It's a good trail choice for novice mountain bikers that follows a wide winter ski trail and has 140 meters (460 feet) of elevation gain. The trail follows Ribbon Creek. If you want to see the falls, leave the bikes at the 4-km (2½-mile) mark and hike the rest of the way. ⊠ *Ribbon Creek Day Use Area, Kananaskis Village.*

CAMPING

The two closest campgrounds to Kananaskis Village are the privately operated Sundance Lodges and Mount Kidd RV Park.

Mount Kidd RV Park. There are unserviced sites, semi-serviced sites, and fully serviced sites (water, sewer, electrical), but each of the campground's 229 campsites comes with a picnic table and a firepit. Tents, trailers, and RVs can be accommodated year-round. Amenities include a front desk, a café, a camp store, coin showers, toilets, and a camper's lounge/game room. Unserviced sites are C$36.15 per night, power-only sites are C$45.60 per night, power and water are C$47.85 per night, and full-service sites are

C$53.40 per night. The campground also has two tennis courts and paved biking trails nearby. *9 km (5.6 miles) south of Kananaskis Village off Hwy. 40 403/591–7700 www.mountkiddrv.com.*

Sundance Lodges. Canvas teepees, trapper's tents, and unserviced campsites in a forested area along a river are on offer here. You can bring your own camping supplies or rent them for an extra charge. There's a camp store with basic supplies and hot coffee in the morning as well as showers and flush toilets. The campground is open from mid-May to late September. Unserviced campsites rent for C$36 per night plus a C$12 reservation fee. Teepees and trapper's tents range in price from C$79.50 per night to C$105 per night. *Located 22 km (13.6 miles) south of the Trans-Canada Hwy. (Hwy. 1) on Hwy.40 in Kananaskis Country 403-591–7122 www.sundancelodges.com.*

CROSS-COUNTRY SKIING

There are some 200 km (124 miles) of ski trails in Kananaskis Country and the most accessible trails are in the Kananaskis Valley region. The most popular trails are those near Kananaskis Village and the trails near Nakiska. There are a number of beginner and intermediate trails that depart from the Ribbon Creek Day Use Area. The 5-km (3.1-mile) trail along Ribbon Creek is particularly nice for beginners.

GOLF

Kananaskis Country Golf Course

GOLF | One of the premier golf courses in the Canadian Rockies has 36 holes across two layouts: Mt. Kidd and Mt. Lorette. After being damaged by a 2013 flood, the entire course was redone, opening again in 2018. Surrounded by mountains, rivers, creeks, and ponds, the greens have beautiful bent grass greens, more than 120 silica sand bunkers, and six sets of tee boxes. Wildlife sightings are common. ⊠ *1 Lorette Dr., Kananaskis Village* ☎ *877/591–2525 toll-free, 403/591–7070* ⊕ *www.kananaskisgolf. com* ⎘ *C$118 Mon.–Thurs.; C$125*

Fri.–Sun. ⊘ *Closed Oct.–Apr.* 🏌 *Mt. Kidd:*
18 holes, 7136 yards, par 72. Mt. Lorette:
18 holes, 7232 yards, par 72.

HIKING

There are many hiking trails in the Kananaskis Valley ranging from short, easy,
family-friendly hikes like Troll Falls to
more moderate trails like Prairie View and
Mount Kidd Lookout to strenuous full-day
hikes like the Mount Allan Centennial
Trail. Stop in at the information center to
get hiking advice, directions and maps.

HORSEBACK RIDING
Boundary Ranch

HORSEBACK RIDING | A variety of trail rides
on trails with beautiful mountain views
is available at Boundary Ranch. They also
offer multiday pack trips and packages
that include other adventures like dog
carting or dogsledding. There's an on-site
restaurant where you can enjoy lunch.
Group barbecues and other group events
can also be arranged. Many of the rides
go past the ranch's bison paddock,
so you can get a closer look at these
animals. There are pony rides for younger
children.   ✉ *2 Guinn's Rd., Kananaskis*
Village ☎ *403/591-7171, 877/591-7177*
⊕ *boundaryranch.com* 🎫 *from C$65.*

MULTI-SPORT OUTFITTERS

Kananaskis Outfitters (*See Tours for more*
information) rents the gear you need in
Kananaskis. Bike rentals, canoes, stand-up
paddleboards, kayaks, hiking gear, tennis,
and basketball equipment are available to
rent in summer. In winter, you can rent
skis, snowshoes, winter boots, fat bikes,
ice skates, and hockey sticks. They also
provide lessons and guided tours.

SLEDDING

Sledding is a fun winter activity and there's
a free sledding hill right in Kananaskis Village. There's also a tubing park at Nakiska
Ski Area. If you want to try dogsledding,
Snowy Owl Sled Dog Tours (*See Activities*
in the Canmore section for more infor-
mation) offers dogsledding at Boundary
Ranch.

SKIING
Nakiska Ski Area

SKIING & SNOWBOARDING | The site of the
1988 Olympic alpine events, Nakiska is
a 45-minute drive southeast of Banff in
Kananaskis Country and has wide-trail
intermediate skiing and a sophisticated
snow-making and grooming system.
There's also a tube park. **Facilities:** 71
trails; 1,021 acres; 2,412-foot vertical
drop; 6 lifts. ✉ *2 Mt. Allan Dr., Kananaskis*
Village ✛ *Off Hwy. 40* ☎ *403/591-7777*
⊕ *skinakiska.com* 🎫 *Lift Ticket: C$95*
⊘ *Closed mid-Mar.–mid-Nov.*

Peter Lougheed Provincial Park

One of the largest provincial parks in
Alberta, this park protects 304 square kilometers (117 square miles) of mountains,
lakes, valleys, and streams in Kananaskis
Country. The park was dedicated on September 22, 1977 as "Kananaskis Provincial
Park" by Premier Peter Lougheed who
served as the Premier of Alberta from
1971 to 1985. After his retirement, the
park was renamed in 1986. Lougheed
was responsible for the development and
expansion of Kananaskis Country with the
help of a booming oil economy.

This park has many incredible features.
The Upper and Lower Kananaskis Lakes
are two undisputed highlights of the park
and there are many campgrounds and
facilities near these lakes. Highway 40 is
the main road through the park and there
are many excellent hiking trails right
along the roadside.

GETTING HERE AND AROUND

Peter Lougheed Provincial Park is the
southern extension of the Kananaskis Valley. The easiest access is via Highway 40
through the Kananaskis Valley. The park is
about 43 km (27 mi) south of Kananaskis
Village.

VISITOR INFORMATION

There's a free interpretive museum at the park's information center, as well as a theater for interpretive programming and an information counter with trained staff who can provide information about Kananaskis Country. There are also flush toilets and free Wi-Fi.

CONTACTS Peter Lougheed Park Discovery & Information Centre. ✉ *Peter Lougheed Park Discovery & Information Centre* ☎ *403/678–0760* ⊕ *www.albertaparks.ca.*

◉ Sights

SCENIC DRIVES
★ Highwood Pass

SCENIC DRIVE | At 2,227 meters (7,310 ft), this high mountain pass along Highway 40 is the highest paved road pass in Canada. It's a beautiful driving route with stunning mountain scenery and superlative hiking trails and other sites just off the top of the pass. Since the pass is located right at the tree line, this is one of the most accessible high alpine areas in the Rockies. Near the summit, you'll find the Highwood Meadows Trail, a 0.6-km (0.4-mile) accessible interpretive trail that will take you through a fragile alpine meadow. This road over Highwood Pass is closed to motor vehicles from December through mid-June. Early June is a great time for cyclists to enjoy the route without the worry of encountering motor vehicles. Watch for elk, deer, moose, bighorn sheep, grizzly and black bears as you traverse this pass. ✉ *Highwood Pass.*

TRAILS
Arethusa Cirque

TRAIL | Just south of Ptarmigan Cirque, this 5-km (3.1-mile) loop trail actually has more larches than its better-known neighbor. The trail begins by passing through a forested area and then opens up into a wide meadow. There's 274 meters (899 feet) of elevation gain, but it's a relatively easy hike. *Easy.* ✉ *Arethusa Cirque* ⊹ *Trailhead: Off Hwy. 40, 1.3 km (.8 miles) south of Highwood Pass parking lot - just after crossing Arethusa Creek.*

Black Prince Cirque Interpretive Trail

TRAIL | This easy 4.2-km (2.6-mile) interpretive loop trail climbs 90 meters (300 feet) to beautiful Warspite Lake through forested and open areas. The first section of the trail follows an old logging road. Alberta Parks has created a four-page interpretive brochure for this trail, which you can pick up at any of the visitor centers in the park. Numbered posts along the trail correspond to numbers in the booklet. *Easy.* ✉ *Black Prince Day Use Area* ⊹ *Trailhead: Black Prince Day Use Area.*

Blackshale Suspension Bridge

TRAIL | This 1-km (0.6-mile) loop trail leads to a dramatic suspension bridge over Blackshale Creek. This is a section of the High Rockies Trail, which is a part of the Trans-Canada Trail. You can do a longer hike along the trail or just do a short loop and take in the bridge and its wonderful views. The trail is best used from April to October and has an elevation gain of 53 meters (174 feet). Dogs are also able to use this trail if they are kept on a leash. *Easy.* ✉ *Blackshale Suspension Bridge* ⊹ *Trailhead: Black Prince Day Use Area.*

Burstall Pass

TRAIL | Winding through the forest, this 7.4-km (4.6-mile) one-way trail leads to two shallow bodies of water known as the Burstall Lakes. From there, you cross what is known as the Willow Flats, an area with many streams, before climbing through forest and then across a picturesque valley to a *cirque* (an amphitheater-like valley formed by glacial erosion). The views of the remote southern end of Banff National Park at the end of this challenging hike are worth the effort. There's 470 meters (1,550 feet) of elevation gain. *Moderate.* ✉ *Burstall Pass Day Use Area* ⊹ *Trailhead: on Smith-Dorrien Trail, 20 km (12.4 miles) from Kananaskis Lake Rd.*

Elbow Lake

TRAIL | This pretty lake is a good spot for a picnic hike. The 1.4-km (0.9-mile) one-way trail begins at the Elbow Pass Day Use Area and follows a wide road. If you're hiking, keep an eye out for mountain bikers and horses, as both are allowed to use the trail. There is a 120-meter (400-foot) elevation gain. *Easy.* ⊠ *Elbow Pass Day Use Area* ⊹ *Trailhead: Hwy. 40, 13 km (8 miles) south of Kananaskis Lakes Rd.*

High Rockies Trail

TRAIL | One of the premier mountain biking and hiking trails in Kananaskis Country and an important part of the Canada-wide Trans-Canada Trail, this 80-km (50-mile) one-way trail can be cycled or hiked in its entirety or enjoyed in smaller sections. The northern end of the trail begins at the Goat Creek Day Use Area in Spray Valley Provincial Park, 1-km (0.6-mile) from the Banff National Park Boundary. If you want to experience part of the trail, one of the highlights is the Blackshale Suspension Bridge, which is a 1-km (0.6-mile) hike and offers spectacular views and photos. Another nice section, the 6.9-km (4.3-mile) stretch between Spray Lakes Day Use Area and the Buller Pass Trail, has beautiful lake views. At the Driftwood Day Use area, the trail crosses Hwy. 742 (the Smith-Dorrien/Spray Trail) and continues south beyond the Sawmill Day Use area in Peter Lougheed Provincial Park before crossing back across Hwy. 742 at the Pocaterra Dam, which is north of the Peninsula Day Use Area at the north end of Lower Kananaskis Lake. The section of this trail that passes through Peter Lougheed Provincial Park traverses diverse landscapes with incredible views. It's common to see bear, moose, and coyotes along the trail. *Moderate.* ⊠ *Goat Creek Day Use Area, Kananaskis Village* ⊹ *Trailhead: 64 km (40 miles) northwest of Kananaskis Village.*

★ Ptarmigan Cirque

TRAIL | Explore the Highwood Meadows Interpretive Trail before you cross Highway 40 to begin the Ptarmigan Cirque trail. The trail leads to a high alpine meadow with incredible views of the surrounding mountains. This hike is popular with wildflower enthusiasts, especially in early to mid-July when glacier lilies blossom shortly after the snow melts. In late July to early August, more than 80 different species of wildflowers might be seen in the meadows. The hike is also popular in autumn when the larch trees turn golden before dropping their needles. The 4.5-km (2.8-mile) trail has 225 meters (700 feet) of elevation gain. *Moderate.* ⊠ *Highwood Meadows Day Use Area* ⊹ *Trailhead: Highwood Pass, Hwy. 40, 17 km (10.6 miles) south of Kananaskis Lake Rd.*

Rawson Lake

TRAIL | This 3.9-km (2.4-mile) one-way trail leads to a beautiful high alpine lake surrounded by mountain peaks and alpine meadows; it's one of the prettiest spots in Kananaskis Country. The trail goes along Upper Kananaskis Lake and through a pine forest to Rawson Lake. It's a popular hiking trail in summer and a snowshoeing trail in winter. There is 320 meters (1,050 feet) of elevation gain, and because of the high elevation, it's possible to encounter snow on this trail into mid-July. *Moderate.* ⊠ *Upper Lake Day Use Area* ⊹ *Trailhead: Upper Lake Day Use Area.*

🛏 Hotels

William Watson Lodge

$ | APARTMENT | The facility is dedicated to making the great outdoors accessible and affordable for Albertans with physical disabilities, seniors, and their families with 22 barrier-free cabins and an accessible campground. **Pros:** situated by Lower Kananaskis Lake; fully accessible lodge and campground; on-site accessible trails. **Cons:** must book well in

In late January, an international biathlon and dogsled races take place at the Canmore Nordic Centre as part of the Canmore Winter Carnival.

advance; Albertans with disabilities and seniors take priority over non-Albertans; ongoing renovations through late 2022. [$] *Rooms from: C$30* ✉ *William Watson Lodge, Kananaskis Village* ☎ *403/591-7227* 🌐 *www.williamwatsonlodgesociety.com* 🍴 *No Meals* 🛏 *22 cabins.*

Shopping

Boulton Creek Trading Post

GENERAL STORE | This camp store sells basic groceries, camping supplies, fishing tackle, fishing licenses, climbing gear, snacks, souvenirs, and convenience items. There's a small cafe and an ice cream shop. You can rent canoes, kayaks, bicycles, and roller blades to use in the park. ✉ *Boulton Creek Trading Post, Kananaskis Village* ✥ *Kananaskis Lakes Tr, 65 km (40 miles) south of Hwy 1* ☎ *403/591–7544* ⏲ *Closed early Oct.–mid-May.*

Activities

CAMPING

There are six auto-accessible campgrounds in Peter Lougheed Provincial Park containing in total more than 500 sites. There are also five backcountry campgrounds. The campgrounds are operated by Kananaskis Camping Inc. (*www.kananaskiscamping.com 403/591–7226*) and you can find out more information about the campgrounds on the website. Reservations can be made through the Alberta Parks Reservations system (*www.reserve.albertaparks.ca 877/537–2757*). You can make reservations up to 90 days in advance. Unserviced sites typically cost C$31 per night, partially serviced cost C$47 per night and fully serviced sites cost C$55.

Boulton Creek Campground. This campground has 161 sites suitable for RVs, trailers, and tents. There are unserviced sites, partially serviced sites, and fully serviced sites as well as 6 walk-in tent sites. The campground is close to the

Kananaskis Lakes and it has many amenities and activities to enjoy. There are showers, flush toilets, sewage disposal, equipment rentals, tap water, a camp store, hiking trails, and paved bike paths. The campground is open from early May to early October. *50 km (31 miles) south of Hwy. 1 on Hwy. 40. South of Boulton Creek Trading Post.*

Canyon Campground. There are 50 unserviced sites suitable for RVs and tents at this campground north of the Pocaterra Hydroelectric Dam on Lower Kananaskis Lake. There's access to hiking and mountain biking trails and paved bike trails, and there's a playground, a boat launch, tap water, pit toilets, and sewage disposal; the campground is open from late May–late September. *50 km south of Hwy. 1 on Hwy. 40 and south 4 km on Kananaskis Lakes Trail.*

Elkwood Campground. Larger campground with sites for RVs and tents. Hiking and mountain biking trails and paved bike trails are nearby. There's a playground, interpretive programs, tap water, showers, and toilets; the campground is open from mid-May–mid-October. *50 km (31 miles) south of Hwy. 1 on Hwy. 40 and south on Kananaskis Lakes Trail. 1 km (0.6 miles) south of the information center.*

Interlakes Campground. Along the shore of Lower Kananaskis Lake, this pretty campground has 48 well-treed unserviced campsites for RVs and tents. Many of the sites have lake views. Amenities include firepits, a hand launch, toilets, and a water pump. There are also many hiking, mountain biking, and paved trails nearby. The campground is open from mid-May to mid-October. *50 km (31 miles) south of Hwy. 1 on Hwy. 40 and south on Kananaskis Lakes Trail. Between Upper and Lower Kananaskis Lakes.*

Lower Lake Campground. There are 95 well-treed unserviced sites for tents and RVs in this campground. Kananaskis

Lakes, hiking and mountain biking trails, and paved paths are nearby. There are two playgrounds, toilets, firepits, and tap water on-site and the Boulton Creek Trading Post is a short walk away. The campground is open from mid-May to mid-October. *50 km (31 miles) south of Hwy. 1 on Hwy. 40 and south on Kananaskis Lakes Trail. Just Beyond Boulton Creek Campground.*

Mount Sarrail Walk-in Tenting Campground. This campground at the south end of Upper Kananaskis Lake is for tenters only and has 44 walk-in tent sites. Campground amenities are basic with pit toilets, fire pits, and a water pump. The campground is reasonably close to the lake and there are hiking, mountain biking, and paved trails nearby. The campground is open from late June to early September. Drive 50 km (31 miles) south of Hwy. 1 on Hwy. 40 and south on Kananaskis Lakes Trail. *2½ km (1.6 miles) beyond Lower Lake Campground.*

EDUCATIONAL PROGRAMS
Check out the interpretive museum in the Peter Lougheed Park Discovery and Information Centre and get some maps, brochures, and information about educational and interpretive programming. Educational programming is often hosted in the theater inside the building.

FISHING
Upper Kananaskis Lake is popular with anglers. There are some trophy-sized rainbow trout in the lake and there's a boat launch. The day-use area has toilets, firepits, and picnic tables. You can also fish on Lower Kananaskis Lake.

HIKING
Many of the incredible trails in Peter Lougheed Provincial Park are multi-use and can be used by both hikers and mountain bikers. Some trails are also open to equestrian users.

Every season has its own special scenic highlights. Wildflowers are a highlight of hiking in the early summer. In autumn, golden larches dot the landscape. Winter provides an opportunity to see the landscape blanketed in sparking white.

In recent years, larch hiking has become incredibly popular in this mountain park. Some of the best larch hikes in Alberta are found here. Larch trees are deciduous conifers that drop their needles each fall and regrow them in the spring. For a few weeks in late September to early October larches turn golden. It's one of the prettiest seasons to hike in Kananaskis. If you want to experience this phenomenon, get to the trailheads early in the day to beat the crowds. It's also a good idea to use ice cleats and poles if there is any snow or rain on the trails.

In every season, be bear aware when you're hiking in Kananaskis Country. Make lots of noise, carry bear spray and hike with a buddy if you can.

Spray Valley Provincial Park

Located along the Spray River, Spray Valley Provincial Park has nine day-use areas, six campgrounds, a biathlon range, cross-country ski trails, a backcountry lodge, and many hiking trails. Canoeing, kayaking, and fishing are popular activities at the Spray Lakes. The park is open to campers year-round.

GETTING HERE AND AROUND

Bordering the eastern edge of Banff National Park, Spray Valley is about an hour's drive from Canmore off Spray Lakes Road (Hwy. 742). It can also be accessed via Kananaskis Trail (Hwy. 40) if you're traveling from Calgary.

◉ Sights

SCENIC DRIVES

Smith-Dorian Trail

SCENIC DRIVE | The Smith-Dorrien/Spray Trail (Hwy. 742) connects the Town of Canmore with Peter Lougheed Provincial Park and is the only road through Spray Valley Provincial Park. On the Canmore end, it is also known as Spray Lakes Road. Though this 60-kilometer (37-mile) unpaved road is featured on a dangerous roads website, you don't need a special kind of vehicle to traverse it. The road is dusty in summer and there are potholes, but the views are lovely, especially those of Mount Assiniboine, which is the highest peak in the Southern Continental Ranges of the Canadian Rockies. The pyramidal-shaped mountain has sometimes been called the "Matterhorn of the Rockies." The road's highest point is the Smith-Dorrien Pass, at 1,905 meters (6,250 feet) above sea level. ⊠ *Smith-Dorrien road, Kananaskis Village.*

TRAILS

Goat Creek Trail

TRAIL | You'll need to pre-arrange transportation for this 19.3-km (12-mile) hike, but it gives you the unique opportunity to hike or mountain bike from Kananaskis to the Banff townsite. The trail, which begins at the north end of Spray Valley Provincial Park and follows Goat Creek for the first 9 km (5.6 miles) to its confluence with the Spray River, is relatively easy with just 150 meters (500 feet) of elevation gain. From there it follows the Spray River all the way to the grounds of the beautiful Fairmont Banff Springs hotel. *Moderate.* ⊠ *Goat Creek Day Use Area, Kananaskis Village* ✛ *Trailhead: Goat Creek Day Use Area.*

Watridge Lake Trail

TRAIL | This 3.7-km (2.3-mile) trail is used for hiking and mountain biking in summer and cross-country skiing and snowshoeing in winter. The trail follows an old exploration road to a junction. Visitors who wish to see the lake, which is popular with trout anglers, must then follow a short, steep 200-meter (656-foot) trail to the muddy lakeshore. If you continue 900 meters (0.6 mile), you'll come to a lovely spring that gushes out of a wall of rock on Mount Shark. *Moderate.* ✉ *Mount Shark Day Use Area, Banff* ✣ *Trailhead: Mount Shark Day Use Area, behind the information board at the entrance to the main parking lot.*

Hotels

Mount Engadine Lodge
$$$$ | ALL-INCLUSIVE | Located about an hour's drive from Canmore, this backcountry lodge is surrounded by rugged mountain peaks and it's one of the few backcountry lodges you can drive to. **Pros:** delicious meals included; bikes and snowshoes available for guest use; beautiful scenery with hiking trails right outside the door. **Cons:** no TVs; no in-room phones; no cell signal. [$] *Rooms from: C$550* ✉ *1 Mount Shark Rd., Canmore* ☎ *587/807–0570* 🌐 *mountengadine.com* 🍴 *All-Inclusive* 🛏 *15 units.*

Activities

CAMPING

Eau Claire Campground and Spray Lakes West are the park's two front country campgrounds; there are four backcountry campgrounds as well.

Eau Claire Campground. There are 51 unserviced sites suitable for RVs and tents in this campground. Sites are well-spaced and surrounded by pine and spruce trees and cost C$31 per night. From the campground, you can access the Eau Claire Interpretive trail, some unmaintained trails, or fish in the Kananaskis River. The campground is open from May 19–September 6 and is first-come, first-served. Food lockers are available for cyclists. *38 km (23.6 miles) south of Hwy. 1 on Hwy. 40.*

Spray Lakes West. There are 50 unserviced sites in this peaceful campground on the shores of the Spray Lakes Reservoir. Sites, some very close to the lake, are suitable for both RVs and tents. Hiking trails, boating, and fishing are nearby. There are picnic tables, fire pits, and pit toilets. Sites cost C$31 per night. Food lockers, a bike tool maintenance stand, and bike racks are available to cyclists in the overflow camping area near the campground entrance. The campground is open from May 19 to September 19 and all sites are first-come, first-served. *16 km (10 miles) south of Canmore on the Smith Dorrien/Spray Lakes Trail (Hwy. 742).*

CROSS-COUNTRY SKIING

The Mount Shark Trails System was developed for skiers who were interested in racing and training. There are six different loops of maintained trails with a total distance of 42 km (26 miles). There is one short 2-km (1.2-mile) loop classified as easy, one 10-km (6-mile) intermediate loop, and four trails classed as difficult. This area can be closed if there is a scheduled race.

The Ruedi Setz Memorial Biathlon Range is located by the Mount Shark Trails System. The range was built in 1991 and was named after Ruedi Setz, a Nordic athlete and enthusiastic contributor to the development of biathlon and cross-country skiing in Alberta.

The Watridge Lake Trail is another popular cross-country ski trail. This 3.7-km (2.3-mile) trail follows an old exploration road to a junction where visitors wishing to see the lake must descend a short, steep, connector trail to the lakeshore. Use caution when descending the trail, as there might be skiers working their way back up the trail.

Trail and avalanche information can be obtained from albertaparks.ca/kananaskis or by calling the Kananaskis information line (*403/678–0760*).

Visitors are asked to purchase a day or season parking pass from Nordiq Alberta (*www.kananaskisgrooming.ca*) to use the cross-country ski trails in Kananaskis. Revenue from the sales is used to cover the costs of trail grooming and maintenance. It's C$10 for a day pass or C$50 for the season.

Sibbald Lake Provincial Recreation Area

This small recreation area is situated in the foothills west of Calgary in the north of Kananaskis Country. Surrounded by aspen trees, Sibbald Lake was named after Frank Sibbald, a long-time rancher who settled in the area around 1875. The lake is stocked twice a year with rainbow trout and Sibbald Meadows Pond is also stocked.

Opened in 1988, Jumpingpound Demonstration Forest is one of the more interesting areas. Surrounded by a gravel road with signs identifying the different species of trees, it's a popular destination to learn about plant ecosystems, trees, and forests. A portable sawmill, a picnic area, and a wetland can also be explored.

GETTING HERE AND AROUND

The recreation area is about an hour west of Calgary via the Trans-Canada Highway (AB-1 W) and Sibbald Creek Trail (AB-68 S). There is no public transportation so renting a car is a must if you want to explore this area.

Sights

TRAILS

Cox Hill Ridge

TRAIL | This moderate/difficult 13-km (8-mile) hike takes hikers to the top of Cox Hill and features beautiful wildflowers and fantastic panoramic views. This trail is not highly traveled, fairly steep at the start, and you may have the summit

all to yourself—make sure you don't stop at the false summit. By continuing along the trail through a treed section, you will arrive at the true summit. The best time to hike this trail is June through October. *Difficult ⊠ Dawson Day Use Area ⊹ Trailhead: Dawson Day Use Area.*

Ole Buck Loop

TRAIL | This easy to moderate hike is great for families and is accessible in all seasons, although April through November is best. The hike is 3.6 km (2.2 miles) return with an elevation gain of 168 meters (546 feet); some great views of Moose Mountain can be seen to the south. *Easy ⊠ Sibbald Lake Day Use Area ⊹ Trailhead: Sibbald Lake Day Use Area. Follow the Sibbald Reforestation Interpretive Trail for one km (0.6 miles) then take the trail on the left.*

Activities

CAMPING

Sibbald Lake Campground. This large campground is the only one in Spray Lake Provincial Park. It contains 134 large treed, unserviced campsites suitable for RV's or tents. Amenities include water, dry toilets, picnic tables, fire pits, a playground, an amphitheater, and interpretive trails. A fire permit is required and firewood can be purchased on-site. The lake is stocked with rainbow trout and fishing licenses are required. The area around the campground is great for hiking, mountain biking, cross-country skiing, and snowshoeing. Each site is C$31 per night and all sites can be reserved in advance. *53 km (33 miles) east of Canmore, 6 km (3.7 miles) south on Hwy. 40 and then 12 km (7.4 miles) east on Hwy. 68 www. reserve.albertaparks.ca 877/537–2757.*

Elbow-Sheep Wildland Provincial Park

The Elbow River Valley includes Elbow-Sheep Wildland, Don Getty Wildland, Sheep River Provincial Park, and Bluerock Wildland Provincial Park. Elbow Lake is the source of the Elbow River, which was named after the point where it abruptly makes an elbow-like curve as it enters the Bow River. This region also neighbors Peter Lougheed and Spray Valley Provincial Parks and all are connected with trails, roads, and rivers.

During the summer months, this valley is very busy with activities like hiking, backpacking, horseback riding, camping, mountain biking, canoeing, kayaking, fishing, and swimming. Winter activities include snowshoeing, cross-country skiing, snowmobiling, and ice fishing.

A few highlights of this region include McClean Pond, which lies close to the eastern boundary and is stocked with rainbow trout. Moose Mountain can be seen on the north side of the highway and Elbow Falls is a six-meter (20-foot) high waterfall along the Elbow River, west of the hamlet of Bragg Creek. It is the tallest road-accessible waterfall in Kananaskis Country.

GETTING HERE AND AROUND

Best explored in your own car, the Elbow River Valley is 8 km (5 miles) west of the hamlet of Bragg Creek on Highway 66. You know you're entering the area when you pass the Elbow Valley Visitor Centre.

VISITOR INFORMATION

Visitor information, a pay telephone, flush toilets, and free Wi-Fi are available at the Elbow Valley Visitor Information Centre.

CONTACTS Elbow Valley Visitor Information Centre. ⊠ *Elbow Valley Visitor Information Centre* ☎ *403/678–0760* ⊕ *www. albertaparks.ca.*

◉ Sights

TRAILS

Fullerton Loop Trail

TRAIL | This moderate 6.9-km (4.3-mile) heavily trafficked loop provides some great views. Once you're on the loop, go clockwise to enjoy a gradual incline and a slightly steeper descent. Stop frequently on the descent—elevation gain is 239 meters (784 feet)—to notice some of the amazing views. The trail does pass through some alpine farming pastures and cattle may be seen, but the wildflowers can be stunning if you're there at the right time. *Moderate* ⊠ *Allen Bill Day Use Area* ✛ *Trailhead: accessed from across the Allen Bill Day Use Access Rd.*

Little Elbow Interpretive Trail

TRAIL | Interpretive signs on this easy 2.5-km (1.6-mi) trail describe river ecology and mammals of the area. Hikers will walk along a small section of the Little Elbow River just before it empties into the Elbow River. *Easy.* ⊠ *Forgetmenot Pond* ✛ *Trailhead: Forgetmenot Pond.*

Paddy's Flat Interpretive Trail

TRAIL | This 2.2-km (1.4-mile) interpretive trail is an easy hike that passes through a mixed forest of lodgepole pine, white spruce, aspen, and poplar trees. After looping around, the trail takes you downstream along the Elbow River back to the campground. *Easy.* ⊠ *Paddy's Flat Campground* ✛ *Trailhead: Paddy's Flat Campground.*

Sulphur Springs Riverview Loop Trail

TRAIL | This moderate 11.6-km (7.2-mile) hike begins on the north side of Hwy. 66. After hiking up about 150 meters (492 feet), you merge onto the Elbow Valley Trail. After about 1 km (0.6 mile), you will find the sign for the start of the Sulphur Springs Trail. Follow the Sulphur Springs Trail for about 4 km (2½ miles) and enjoy great views of Prairie Mountain and Nihahi Ridge. As the trail descends, the trail merges with the Elbow River Trail and the Sulphur Springs Trail ends and the Riverview Trail begins. The Riverview Trail follows along the Elbow River and provides great views into the gorges of the river. As you follow the river, the trail will take you to Paddy's Flat campground. From the campground, you can either walk the roadway or continue along the Elbow River back to the day-use area. This trail has 416 meters (1365 feet) of elevation gain. *Moderate.* ⊠ *Paddy's Flat Day Use Area* ⊕ *Trailhead: Paddy's Flat Day Use Area.*

 ## Activities

CAMPING

There are five campgrounds in the Elbow River Valley and their close proximity to Calgary and Bragg Creek makes them all popular. You can make reservations (*www.reserve.albertaparks.ca 877/537–2757*) 90 days in advance at McLean Creek, Little Elbow, and Gooseberry, but the other campgrounds are first-come, first served. Unserviced sites cost C$31 per night and power sites cost C$39 per night.

Beaver Flats Campground. This campground is found in Elbow Falls Provincial Recreation Area. There are 49 large, well-treed unserviced sites and six walk-in tenting sites along the Elbow River. There are many nearby trails for hiking, mountain biking and horseback riding, as well as exciting and challenging waters for experienced paddlers. *30 km (18.6 mi) west of Bragg Creek along Hwy. 66.*

Gooseberry Campground. In Gooseberry Provincial Recreation Area, this campground is in an aspen and pine forest near the Elbow River. There are 28 unserviced sites, 51 power sites, and 6 walk-in tent sites. The campground is suitable for both RVs, trailers, and tents; it's open from May to mid-October. *10 km (6.2 miles) west of Bragg Creek along Hwy. 66.*

Little Elbow Campground. This large well-treed campground is located in Little Elbow Provincial Recreation Area. There are over 60 well-spaced sites suitable for RVs or tents, as well as 30 dedicated walk-in tenting sites. All sites are unserviced. The campground is open from mid-May through mid-September. *50 km (31 miles) west of Bragg Creek along Hwy. 66.*

McLean Creek Campground. This large campground has sites for both RVs and tents. There are 74 unserviced sites and 96 power sites. There are also 170 serviced and unserviced sites available for winter camping. *12 km (7½ miles) west of Bragg Creek along Hwy. 66 and 1.3 km (.8 miles) south on McLean Creek Trail.*

Paddy's Flat Campground. This first-come, first-served campground is in Elbow River Provincial Recreation Area. There are 98 well-treed unserviced sites that are suitable for RVs, trailers, and tents. Some of the sites back up to the Elbow River. There are interpretive trails accessible from the campground and other trails nearby. The campground is open from May through mid-September. *20 km (12.4 miles) west of Bragg Creek along Hwy. 66.*

Highwood and Cataract Creek

Stretching from the boundary of Peter Lougheed Provincial Park to the southern border of Kananaskis Country, this region includes the upper reaches of the Highwood River watershed. It's one of the least developed regions in Kananaskis Country and you'll need to be prepared with a survival kit and an understanding of how to camp and hike in the wild if you want to go exploring.

There is a wide range of landscapes in this region from lush spruce and pine forests to grazing lands in the foothills of the Rockies. Interesting features include the Highwood Road Corridor Wildlife Sanctuary, the Plateau Mountain Ecological Reserve, and parts of Don Getty and Elbow-Sheep Wildland Provincial Parks.

In winter, Cataract Creek is a popular snowmobile area as there's an extensive snowmobile trail system in the area.

GETTING HERE AND AROUND

This region can be reached by car from the east via Highway 541 or from the north via Highway 40.

Sights

TRAILS

Picklejar Lakes

TRAIL | The four lakes at the southern end of Elbow-Sheep Wildland Provincial Park are popular with anglers. They can be reached via a 4.2-km (2.6-mile) trail that passes through a forested area before it drops down to the lakes. There is a 450-meter (1,475-foot) elevation gain. *Moderate.* ⊠ *Lantern Creek Day Use Area* ⚹ *Trailhead: Lantern Creek Day Use Area.*

Zephyr Creek Trail

TRAIL | Ancient Indigenous pictographs are a highlight of this 9.4-km (5.8-mile) round-trip hike. The trail follows Painted Creek to the narrows where you can see pictographs left by the Kootenai People some 400 years ago. It's a fairly easy hike with a 195-meter (640-foot) elevation gain, but you do have to wade across the Highwood River. After you cross the river, turn right on an old logging road. The trail will cross Zephyr Creek twice before you reach the pictographs. *Moderate.* ⊠ *Sentinel Day Use Area.*

🛍 Shopping

Highwood House General Store

CONVENIENCE STORE | Located south of Highwood Pass on Highway 40, this site has a gas station and a grocery store that's open Friday to Sunday from May to June; daily from July to September; and Saturday and Sunday, October to April. ⊠ *Highwood House.*

🏃 Activities

HIKING

This region is one of the least developed areas of Kananaskis Country. Only a few trails are signposted. Some hikes will require river crossings and many are not clearly marks.

Bragg Creek Area

30-minute drive west of Calgary.

Just outside Kananaskis at the entrance to the Elbow River Valley, the charming hamlet of Bragg Creek is often called the Gateway to Kananaskis. The tiny community has unique stores and boutiques, a golf course, a provincial park, a provincial recreation area, and about nine different places to eat and drink.

Summer activities include golfing, fishing, hiking, mountain biking, e-biking, trail running, and horseback riding, while winter activities include cross-country skiing, fat biking, and snowshoeing.

West Bragg Creek Day Use Area has 166 km (103 miles) of summer and winter cross-country ski trails that are maintained by volunteers with the Bragg Creek Trails Association. You will find details about the trails and their condition on the organization's website. The rolling terrain is lovely for cross-country skiing and passes through aspen and evergreen forest with many lovely vistas. Creeks, springs, and wetlands add interest for summer hikers. Bragg Creek Day Use

Area in Bragg Creek Provincial Park is very close to the hamlet. It's a great spot to enjoy a picnic.

GETTING HERE AND AROUND

Bragg Creek is about 40 km (25 miles) from the southwest corner of Calgary on Highway 22 or Highway 22X. It's about 91 km (57 miles) southeast of Canmore.

VISITOR INFORMATION

CONTACTS Bragg Creek Trails Association. ✉ *Bragg Creek* 🌐 *braggcreektrails.org.*

🍴 Restaurants

Creekers Bistro

$ | **AMERICAN** | Located in the back corner of a shopping mall, this family-run restaurant has a casual menu, a kids menu, and a pet-friendly patio. Along with burgers and pizza, you'll find steaks, shrimp, salmon, ribs, and a few specialties like bibimbap and bulgogi (the owners immigrated from South Korea). **Known for:** daily specials before 5 pm; good burgers; nice selection of craft beer. [$] *Average main: C$20* ✉ *20 White Ave., Bragg Creek* ☎ *403/949-3361* 🌐 *creekersbistro.ca.*

The Italian Farmhouse

$ | **ITALIAN** | Fresh contemporary Italian cuisine in a farmhouse-style atmosphere is the specialty of this restaurant. The menu has classic Italian appetizers like bruschetta, calamari, and beef carpaccio along with house-made pizzas and pasta, and there are meat dishes like salmon, chicken, veal, and bison short ribs. **Known for:** daily specials; quaint atmosphere; delicious pasta daily specials. [$] *Average main: C$24* ✉ *20 Balsam Ave., Bragg Creek* ☎ *403/949–2750* 🌐 *theitalianfarmhouse.ca.*

🛏 Hotels

Riverside Chateau

$$ | **B&B/INN** | This luxurious 5-room bed and breakfast is located in the hamlet of Bragg Creek and is within walking distance of restaurants, bars, art galleries, shops, and hiking trails. **Pros:** luxurious adults-only accommodations; the only 5-star Canada Select rated accommodation in the area; breakfast included. **Cons:** no self catering/food preparation in kitchen; no pets or children allowed; strictly enforced quiet hours from 11 pm–7 am. [$] *Rooms from: C$289* ✉ *104 White Ave., Bragg Creek* ☎ *403/835–6032* 🌐 *www.riversidechateau.com* 🍽 *Free Breakfast* 🛏 *5 rooms.*

🛍 Shopping

Archer's Antiques

ANTIQUES & COLLECTIBLES | This antique shop has been in business since 1959 and specializes in restored North American furnishings and artifacts from the 1700s to the late 1900s. ✉ *24 White Crescent, Bragg Creek* ☎ *403/949–3655* 🌐 *archersantiques.ca* 🕒 *Closed Mon.–Wed.*

Branded Visuals

ART GALLERIES | This shop sells Canadian Rockies photo art including stunning scenery and wildlife photography by gallery owner Bob Cook. You'll also find novelty gifts like puzzles, coasters, and magnets. ✉ *1 White Ave., Bragg Creek* ☎ *403/949–3000* 🌐 *www.brandedvisuals.com* 🕒 *Closed Mon.–Tues.*

Chapter 7

YOHO
NATIONAL PARK

7

By
Kate Robertson

🏕 Camping
★★★★☆

🛏 Hotels
★★☆☆☆

🤸 Activities
★★☆☆☆

👁 Scenery
★★★★★

🎡 Crowds
★★★☆☆

WELCOME TO YOHO NATIONAL PARK

TOP REASONS TO GO

★ **Amazing scenery:** Yoho is home to some of Canada's most spectacular natural environments, with numerous glaciers and icefields, vertical rock wall features, and 28 peaks over 3,000 meters (9,842 feet) tall.

★ **Accessible points of interest:** Some of the park's highlights, like Canada's second tallest waterfall or stunning glacier-fed lakes, can be seen from your car, or via a very short walk.

★ **Burgess Shale fossils:** Touted as one of the most important fossil discoveries on the planet, Yoho is home to two of the largest known archaeological sites.

★ **Trainspotting:** Established in 1883 as a railway work camp, this is one of North America's steepest and most scenic railway lines with two unique spiral train tunnels and 25 to 30 trains passing daily.

★ **Unique alpine environment:** The sensitive alpine region of Lake O'Hara offers an excellent trail network with extraordinary views of hanging valleys, crystal-blue lakes, and mountain vistas.

1 Field Townsite. The only townsite within the park, Field offers restaurants, accommodation, fuel, shopping, and other facilities like the Yoho Visitor Centre.

2 Kicking Horse Pass. A National Historic Site of Canada, this 1,643-meter (5,390-foot) high mountain pass was constructed across the Continental Divide by the Canadian Pacific Railway in 1884. The Trans-Canada Highway was subsequently built following the same route in 1962.

3 Lake O'Hara. Stunning hanging valleys, vividly blue glacier lakes, and an excellent trail network make this unique region of the park a favorite spot for grizzly bears and one of the world's most coveted alpine destinations. Reservations, usually made well in advance, are required for the 11-km (6.8-mile) bus ride in, as well as for the backcountry camping, and other accommodations, including the Elizabeth Parker Alpine Club hut and Lake O'Hara Lodge.

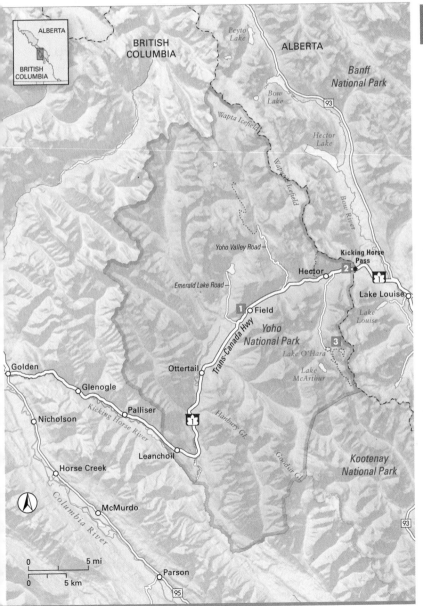

ALBERTA

BRITISH
COLUMBIA

BRITISH
COLUMBIA

ALBERTA

Banff
National Park

Peyto
Lake

Bow
Lake

93

Wapta Icefield

Hector
Lake

Waputik Icefield

Bow River

Yoho Valley Road

Kicking Horse
Pass

Emerald Lake Road

Hector

2

Lake Louise

1 Field

Lake
Louise

Yoho
National Park

Trans-Canada Hwy

3

Lake O'Hara

Golden

Ottertail

Lake
McArthur

Glenogle

Kicking Horse River

Palliser

Hanbury Gl.

Nicholson

Leanchoil

Kootenay
National Park

Goodsir Gl.

Horse Creek

Columbia River

McMurdo

93

0   5 mi

0   5 km

Parson

95

Yoho may be small, but when it comes to what it has to offer, it rates right up there with its larger neighboring Rocky Mountain National Parks. Jagged snow-covered peaks, vertical rock walls, cascading waterfalls, expansive glaciers, shimmering green-blue lakes—Yoho has them all. It's also the home to two icefields, Waputik and Wapta, where the Kicking Horse River, a Canadian Heritage River, originates.

For centuries, Yoho was used by Indigenous nations, primarily Ktunaxa and Shuswap, as a seasonal route to the plains on the eastern side of the Rocky Mountains. The abundance of high peaks (28 within the park reach higher than 3,000 meters [9,843 feet]) made it a difficult and undesirable region for hunting so the Indigenous nations never settled here. The highest peak in the park, South Goodsir Tower, has a summit elevation of 3,562 meters (11,686 feet).

In 1858, James Hector, a geologist traveling with the Palliser Expedition to survey the west and report back to the British government on suitability for settlement and transportation routes, became the first European to encounter Kicking Horse Pass. It's said his horse kicked him in the chest here, hence the name. A little more than 20 years later, Major A.B. Rogers (for whom the Rogers Pass is named), surveyed Kicking Horse Pass and his subsequent report to the Canadian Pacific Railway (CPR) resulted in the railway route being pushed through. The

CPR reached the Kicking Horse Valley by 1884, where it established the town of Field as a railway maintenance depot at the bottom of a steep, treacherous hill. When the railbed was laid here in 1885, the grade was much steeper than usual, resulting in numerous brake failures, derailings, and loss of lives. Subsequently, in 1909, the CPR re-routed the steepest section of the line through the Spiral Tunnels and the highway now follows the original railbed.

In 1886 the CPR opened Mount Stephen House in Field to encourage visitors to the area and as a dining stop for train customers. They then built lodges at several of the natural attractions in the area: Emerald Lake Lodge in 1902, Lake O'Hara in 1913, and Wapta Lodge Bungalow Camp in 1921.

The coming of the railway was a catalyst in the park's formation. In 1886, the Canadian government reserved 27 square km (10 square miles) at the base of Mount Stephen as a dominion park,

Canada's second national park, enlarging it several times before today's park came into being in 1930. The railway route, and later the Trans-Canada Highway, follow the Kicking Horse River through the heart of the park. Mining of zinc, lead, and silver continued until 1952, and remnants of the Monarch and Kicking Horse mines can still be seen today.

The railway also opened the valley to scientists, who eventually learned that the valley bottom was rich with fossils. In 1909, while searching for fossil sites, Dr. Charles Doolittle Walcott, an American paleontologist from the Smithsonian Institute, discovered the Burgess Shale fossils, well-preserved soft-bodied fossils, on the ridge now named the Walcott Quarry. These fossil beds show the active evolution of soft-bodied marine animals from 510 to 520 million years ago, providing scientists with the clearest record of Cambrian marine life.

The extraordinarily beautiful Lake O'Hara-protected alpine region was first explored by Samuel Allen, who first accessed the valley by a hike from Paradise Valley near Lake Louise. It was Allen who provided many of the Stoney Indian names for the peaks surrounding the lake. Named after Lieutenant-Colonel Robert O'Hara, the region is rich in climbing history and renowned mountaineers like J.J. MacArthur, Conrad Kain and Charlie Locke. Female mountaineers have also left their mark, like Mary Vaux (who would eventually marry Dr. Charles Walcott), who in 1900 became the first woman in Canada to reach a peak over 3,000 meters (10,000 feet), when she summited Mount Stephen.

Known today for its archaeological and geological treasures, unique railway history, diverse wildlife, extensive hiking trail network and extraordinary natural landscapes, Yoho National Park continues to be an outdoor enthusiast's dream and a train buff's delight.

Planning

When to Go

Although the highway through Yoho National Park is well maintained year-round, many of the visitor services, including the Visitor Centre, in Yoho National Park are only open from May to early October, which means that these months are the busiest time for travel. The vast majority of visitors arrive in July and August, the warmest weather months. In the spring, the waterfalls are powerful due to the glacial meltwaters and wildflowers tend to peak towards the end of July. In the fall, the park is full of reds and goldens, although there are not as many larch stands as in some of the nearby parks. Due to the high elevations in the park, the mountains are snow-capped all year round, and spring comes late (generally in June). With its location in the far west side of the mountain time zone, summer nights are long and splendid.

However, Yoho is also a prime destination for winter sports enthusiasts looking for stellar backcountry skiing, ice climbing, and snowshoeing activities. When traveling in the winter, be sure to check the road conditions before you go. The only gas station or charging stations are in Field.

Many of the higher altitude hikes can have snow on the trails until late June. Remember that mountain weather can be unpredictable, with possible significant weather shifts from day-to-day, or even within the same day. If you're hiking or on the water, you will need to be prepared with suitable clothing and equipment.

AVERAGE HIGH/LOW TEMPERATURES IN CELSIUS					
Jan.	Feb.	Mar.	Apr.	May	June
-12/-22	-8/-20	-4/-16	2/-13	6/-8	10/-3
July	Aug.	Sept.	Oct.	Nov.	Dec.
14/-2	14/-3	9/-7	0/-11	-9/-16	-14/-23

AVERAGE HIGH/LOW TEMPERATURES IN FAHRENHEIT					
Jan.	Feb.	Mar.	Apr.	May	June
10/-8	18/-4	25/3	36/9	43/18	50/27
July	Aug.	Sept.	Oct.	Nov.	Dec.
57/28	57/27	48/19	32/12	16/3	7/-9

FESTIVALS AND EVENTS

Canada Day. Admission to the national parks is free on July 1, Canada's birthday. Field celebrates July 1 with a parade of the town's fire trucks before the whole town participates in a water fight.

Field Summer Music Festival. An annual music festival in July features a diverse line-up of bands and musicians, activities for the kids, and food, beverage, and local art vendors. *fieldmusicfest.ca.*

Yoho Blow Daze. This winter weekend in February has been held in Field for over 35 years. All about fun, events include human bowling, street bocce, and a snowshoe relay, with a potluck to finish off. *www.facebook.com/YohoBlowDaze/.*

Getting Here and Around

Yoho National Park is in the Canadian Rockies region of British Columbia. It borders Alberta and Banff National Park to the east, and Kootenay National Park to the south. Field, the only townsite in the park, is located 84 km (52 miles) northwest of Banff Townsite.

AIR

The closest international airport is in Calgary, 192 km (119 miles) to the southeast. Vancouver International Airport (YVR) is 748 km (465 miles) southwest.

BUS

There are no public buses that stop in the park.

CAR

Driving is the easiest way to get from the Calgary airport to Yoho, via the Trans-Canada Highway. Car rental agencies can be easily accessed at the airports, or at car-rental agencies in Banff or Lake Louise.

TRAIN

The Rocky Mountaineer luxury passenger train journeys between Vancouver and Banff, passing through Yoho National Park six times a week, three times in each direction. The regular season runs from mid-April to mid-October. There is no train service from Calgary to Yoho.

CONTACTS Rocky Mountaineer.
☎ 877/460–3200 ⊕ *www.rockymountaineer.com.*

Inspiration

Life of the Trail 2: Historic Hikes in Northern Yoho National Park, is part of a series where authors Janice Sanford Beck and Emerson Sanford follow in the footsteps of historic adventurers, like David Thompson, to uncover the stories behind the routes through Yoho National Park and the town of Field.

Yoho in One Day

From the west entrance, start with a visit to the Wapta Falls, the largest waterfall on the Kicking Horse River. The easy 1.9-km (1.2-mile) trail from the parking lot will bring you to the lookout point where you can watch the thundering falls cascade. From there, continue east on the Trans-Canada Highway to Emerald Lake, one of the most admired views in the park. If you have time, rent a canoe to fully experience the bright emerald-green waters and vistas of the surrounding snowcapped mountains. Back on the highway, take the next turn into Field, where you can get information on the park's major attractions at the Yoho Information Centre. As you continue to drive east on the Trans-Canada Highway turn onto the Yoho Valley Road and continue to Takakkaw Falls, Canada's second tallest. Take a picture of the park's iconic red chairs while you're there. Then head back to Field and cross the train tracks into the village center to enjoy a delicious dinner at the Truffle Pigs Bistro.

The Canadian Rockies Trail Guide (ninth edition), by Brian Patton and Bart Robinson, provides descriptions of hikes in the Canadian Rockies, including Yoho National Park, complete with routes and GPS coordinates for trailheads and maps.

The Spiral Tunnels and the Big Hill: A Canadian Railway Adventure, by Graeme Pole, is a must-read for railway enthusiasts. It describes the history of the construction of the Canadian Pacific Railway through the treacherous Kicking Horse Pass and the operation of the Spiral Tunnels are explained through stories, maps, and diagrams.

Park Essentials

ACCESSIBILITY
The Yoho Visitor Centre in Field is wheelchair accessible, as are the viewpoints at Natural Bridge and Spiral Tunnel. Emerald Lake and Takakkaw Falls trails also have a short, paved section that is suitable for wheelchairs.

PARK FEES AND PERMITS
All prices in this chapter are in Canadian dollars, unless otherwise stated. A park entrance pass is C$10 per person or C$20 per vehicle (up to seven people) per day. A day pass for seniors is C$8.40 and children and youth under the age of 18 are free. An annual pass costs C$69.19 per adult, C$59.17 for a senior or C$139.40 per family or group, so if you're staying a week or more in the park, you should go with this option.

Backcountry camping permits cost C$10.02 per person per day, and if on a horse, a grazing permit is C$1.94 per day. A fishing permit is C$9.80 per day. Campgrounds have various prices, and often you will need to pay for a separate fire and dumping permit. Transit to Lake O'Hara is C$14.70 per adult and C$7.30 for a youth (6-17 years).

PARK HOURS
The park is open every day year-round. It is located in the Mountain Time Zone.

CELL PHONE RECEPTION
Cell phone reception is available in Field and within a small radius of the town, otherwise, cell phone reception in the national park is unreliable.

A UNESCO World Heritage Site, the Burgess Shale Fossils were first discovered in 1886 by a Canadian Pacific Railway worker.

Hotels

Accommodations in Yoho are varied, meaning that there's something for every taste and budget, including affordable inns, guesthouses, luxury cabins, and backcountry lodges. Most are located in the Field region. All accommodations can book up during the busy summer months of July and August, so if planning travel during that time, reserve your accommodations well in advance.

Another option, though more remote, are the ACC Huts maintained by the Alpine Club of Canada. These huts are communal, and while foam mattresses and cooking and eating utensils are provided, guests must bring their own sleeping bags and food and you must hike in. The plus side is many of these lodgings are located in beautiful, serene, and remote locations. Yoho's most popular is the Elizabeth Parker Hut, followed by the Scott Duncan and Stanley Mitchell huts and must be reserved in advance; access to the Elizabeth Parker hut is done through a lottery.

Hotel reviews have been shortened. For full information, visit Fodors.com.

Restaurants

There may only be a few dining options within the park, and most of those are near Field, but the choices are always good. Menu offerings range from eclectic fusion dishes and pizza to Canadian Rocky Mountain cuisine, all made with fresh, local ingredients.

Restaurant reviews have been shortened. For full information, visit Fodors. com.

HOTEL AND RESTAURANT PRICES

Hotel prices in the reviews are the lowest cost of a standard double room in high season. Restaurant prices in the reviews are the average cost of a main course at dinner, or if dinner is not served, at lunch.

What It Costs In Canadian Dollars

	$	$$	$$$	$$$$
RESTAURANTS				
	under C$25	C$25–C$30	C$31–C$35	over C$35
HOTELS				
	under C$250	C$250–C$300	C$301–C$350	over C$350

Tours

Burgess Shale Geoscience Foundation
Passionate guides with geoscience degrees lead hikes for this charitable, not-for-profit organization. Group tours are available to the park's two Burgess Shale sites, Walcott Quarry and Mount Stephen Trilobite Beds, both of which are only accessible with a guide. ⊠ 201 Kicking Horse Ave., Field ☎ 250/343–6006, 800/343–3006 toll free ⊕ www.burgess-shale.bc.ca ⊠ C$94.50.

East Kootenay Mountain Guides
Experience rock climbing, mountaineering, scrambling, or ski touring in the park with certified guides. ⊠ Invermere, Invermere ✛ Invermere ☎ 250/341–1212 ⊕ www.ekmountainguides.com ⊠ From C$400.

Sawback Alpine Adventures
This company offers high-end ski touring trips to British Columbia's finest backcountry lodges. ⊠ 234 Grizzly Cr., Canmore ☎ 403/707–9996 ⊕ sawback.com.

Western Canyoning Adventures
Guided adventures explore a multitude of canyons and deep narrow gorges in the park by scrambling, sliding, and rappelling down waterfalls and swimming in natural pools. Canyoning courses are also available. There are options suitable for a range of abilities. ⊠ 1309 Stoney La., Golden ☎ 250/838–5336 ⊕ www.westcanyon.ca ⊠ From C$170.

Visitor Information

The Parks Canada office in Yoho is open from May until mid-October. The center has information brochures, and you can get permits, make backcountry reservations, and get updates on weather, trail, and road conditions. Outside of these months, you can get park information from the person staffing the gatehouse at the park boundary, or direct questions to the Parks Canada National Information Centre (888/773–8888), which is open year-round.

The visitor center shares a building with the Friends of Yoho (an organization that promotes appreciation, understanding, and stewardship of the ecology and culture of Yoho National Park) and there is also a small scale exhibit of a train passing through the Spiral Tunnels as well as some Burgess Shale fossil interpretive panels.

Reservations for backcountry huts in the park can be made through the Alpine Club of Canada.

CONTACTS Alpine Club of Canada. ⊠ Yoho National Park ☎ 403/678–3200 ⊕ www.alpineclubofcanada.ca.**Friends of Yoho National Park Society.** ⊠ Yoho National Park ☎ 250/343–6393 ⊕ www.friendsofyoho.ca.**Yoho National Park.** ⊠ 5764 Trans-Canada Hwy., Field ☎ 250/343–6783 ⊕ www.pc.gc.ca/en/pn-np/bc/yoho.

In the Park

The east park boundary is 192 km (119 miles) northwest of Calgary and 66 km (41 miles) northwest of Banff. The west park boundary is 28 km (17 miles) east of Golden, 275 km (171 miles) north of Cranbrook, and 736 km (457 miles) northeast of Vancouver.

The only amenities within the park are at Field, where you can find limited year-round dining and accommodation. Other backcountry lodges and cabins in the park are seasonal, operating only

A close up of the amazingly detailed Burgess Shale Fossils.

in the summer. Visitors also use nearby Golden, which has full amenities and many accommodations and restaurant options, as a base to explore the Yoho National Park.

 Sights

GEOLOGICAL FORMATIONS

Burgess Shale Fossils

NATURE SIGHT | Recognized as a UNESCO World Heritage Site and part of the larger Canadian Rocky Mountain Parks World Heritage Site, this layer of rock deposits contains amazingly well-preserved fossil specimens that have visible details from the creatures that existed in an underwater ecosystem over 505 million years ago. The Mount Stephen trilobite beds were discovered in 1886 after a railway worker reported finding stone "bugs" in the talus. Paleontologist Charles Walcott from the Smithsonian Institute visited Mt. Field in 1909, where he opened a quarry and started collecting and analyzing specimens. ⊠ *Burgess Shale Fossils, Trans-Canada Hwy., Yoho National Park.*

Natural Bridge

NATURE SIGHT | Spanning the Kicking Horse River, this natural rock formation was created when the hard limestone eroded more quickly than the softer rock causing cracks to widen until the flow of water changed and formed a bridge. A short pathway displays interpretive signage explaining the erosion process as you walk to several lookouts that provide views of the geological formation from different vantage points. ⊠ *Emerald Lake Rd., Yoho National Park.*

HISTORIC SIGHTS

Kicking Horse Pass

HISTORIC SIGHT | This legendary pass, designated a National Historic Site for its importance as a transportation corridor in Western Canada, was punched through the Rocky Mountains in the late 1800s to allow the railway and subsequently, the highway, to pass into British Columbia. At 1,627 meters (2,415 feet), this is the highest point on the entire Trans-Canada Highway and it straddles the Continental Divide and the British Columbia/Alberta border. The pass earned its name thanks to James Hector, the first European to come upon the pass, where it's said his horse kicked him in the chest. From the lookout point, you can look down onto the transportation corridor to the west and view the Spiral Tunnels that were ingeniously engineered to allow trains to go from one elevation to another through the steep Canadian Rockies. ⊠ *Kicking Horse Pass, Trans-Canada Hwy., Yoho National Park* ⊹ *84 km (52 miles) west of Banff Townsite and 73 km (45 miles) east of Golden.*

Spiral Tunnels
VIEWPOINT | FAMILY | The Kicking Horse Pass is one of the steepest terrains in North America for a railway, which posed a real problem for the engineers who were tasked with punching a railway line through it. To solve the problem of numerous runaway trains and crashes, two circular tunnels were driven into the valley walls of Cathedral Mountain and Mt. Ogden to reduce the 4.4% grade to a safer and more normal 2.2%. The viewing platform at Lower Spiral Tunnel lookout is one of the best places to watch passing freight trains (25–30 trains pass through daily) going in and out of the tunnels, and there are several interpretive panels explaining the facts and history of building the railway through the Canadian Rocky Mountains. ⊠ *Spiral Tunnels, Trans-Canada Hwy., Yoho National Park* ⊹ *From the viewpoint 7.4 km (4.6 miles) east of Field on the Trans-Canada Hwy., you can see the Lower Spiral Tunnel in Mt. Ogden. The Upper Spiral Tunnel in Cathedral Mountain can be seen from the pull-off 2.3 km (1.4 miles) up the Yoho Valley Rd.*

Twin Falls Tea House National Historic Site
HISTORIC SIGHT | Accessible only by foot, this historical log chalet provides lodging for guests or food and tea for day guests in the summer months. Built in a clearing across from the Twin Falls Creek in three phases between 1908–1928, the teahouse provides phenomenal views of the double falls (keep your eyes peeled for mountain goats, they are often spotted hanging out above the falls). The 16.4-km (10-mile) mostly forested out-and-back trail will take you three hours to reach the teahouse. Access to the trailhead is from the Takakkaw Falls parking lot. Reservations are required for an overnight stay. Recently, the teahouse was shut down for renovations, and a new operator will be taking it over, so be sure to check the website for updated information on both accommodation and dining options. ⊠ *Marpole Lake, Yoho National Park* ⊕ *www.pc.gc.ca/en/pn-np/ bc/yoho/culture/twin/visit.*

PICNIC AREAS
Faeder Lake Day-Use Area
OTHER ATTRACTION | FAMILY | This picnic site is located right next to the brilliantly colored Faedar Lake. On a stroll along the pathway that goes around the lake, you will have stunning views of the surrounding mountain peaks, and in the summer months, you'll likely see wildflowers. Outhouse toilets are available. Note that the parking area is not suitable for large RVs or trailers and is accessible only by west-bound traffic. ⊠ *Faeder Lake, near Trans-Canada Hwy., Yoho National Park.*

Finn Creek Day-Use Area
OTHER ATTRACTION | FAMILY | On the confluence of where the Porcupine Creek joins the Kicking Horse River, with a wildly scenic backdrop of towering Rocky Mountain peaks, this is a perfect spot for a picnic. There are picnic tables and outhouse toilet facilities. It's accessible by westbound traffic only. ⊠ *Faeder Lake, near Trans-Canada Hwy., Yoho National Park.*

SCENIC DRIVES
Emerald Lake Road
SCENIC DRIVE | This 8.8-km (5.5-mile) scenic road briefly parallels the fast-flowing Kicking Horse River before passing the Natural Bridge and traveling through the forest where it ultimately ends at the bright, deep green Emerald Lake.

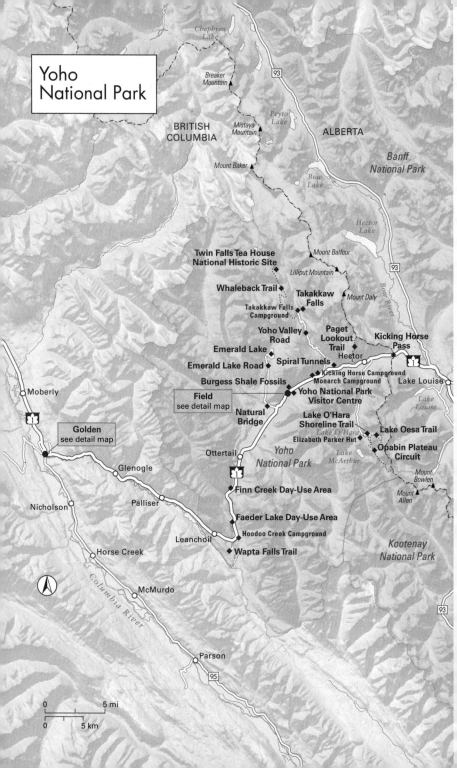

Yoho National Park

Chephren Lake

Breaker Mountain

93

BRITISH COLUMBIA

Mistaya Mountain

Peyto Lake

ALBERTA

Mount Baker

Bow Lake

Banff National Park

Hector Lake

Twin Falls Tea House National Historic Site

Mount Balfour

Lilliput Mountain

Whaleback Trail

Takakkaw Falls

Mount Daly

93

Takakkaw Falls Campground

Yoho Valley Road

Paget Lookout Trail

Kicking Horse Pass

Emerald Lake

Hector

Emerald Lake Road

Spiral Tunnels

Burgess Shale Fossils

Kicking Horse Campground

Monarch Campground

Lake Louise

Field see detail map

Yoho National Park Visitor Centre

Lake Louise

Natural Bridge

Lake O'Hara Shoreline Trail

Lake Oesa Trail

Moberly

Golden see detail map

Lake O'Hara

Elizabeth Parker Hut

Opabin Plateau Circuit

1

Ottertail

Yoho National Park

Lake McArthur

Mount Bowlen

Glenogle

Mount Allen

Finn Creek Day-Use Area

Palliser

Nicholson

Faeder Lake Day-Use Area

Hoodoo Creek Campground

Leanchoil

Kootenay National Park

Horse Creek

Wapta Falls Trail

Columbia River

McMurdo

93

Parson

95

0 ———— 5 mi

0 ———— 5 km

Compared to Lake Louise in Banff National Park, Emerald Lake is most definitely under-visited. The road is open year-round, and the speed limit is slow (50 km/h [30 mph]), allowing you plenty of opportunities to spot wildlife. ⊠ *Emerald Lake Rd., Yoho National Park ✛ Turn off the Trans-Canada Hwy. 3 km (2 miles) west of Field.*

Yoho Valley Road
SCENIC DRIVE | Hands down, this is the most scenic route in the whole park. After initially passing the Monarch and Kicking Horse campgrounds and the Meeting of the Waters viewpoint (where the Kicking Horse and Yoho Rivers meet), the 13.7-km (8.5-mile) road climbs up through a deep valley with impressive views of snow-covered mountain peaks, glaciers, waterfalls, and rivers. The road ends at the parking lot of the spectacular Takakkaw Falls, the second-highest waterfall in Canada. Note that the winding road has a couple of sharp, hairpin switchbacks that can be very difficult for larger RVs to navigate, and the road is open seasonally from late June to mid-October, weather permitting. ⊠ *Yoho Valley Rd., Yoho National Park ✛ Turnoff is 5 km (3 miles) east of Field on the Trans-Canada Hwy.*

SCENIC STOPS
★ Emerald Lake
BODY OF WATER | The vivid green water of Yoho's largest lake is absolutely breathtaking and rivals any other lake found in the Canadian Rocky Mountain parks. It was discovered by European explorer Tom Wilson in 1882, and by 1902, the Canadian Pacific Railway had built the Emerald Lake Lodge wilderness resort for its guests to enjoy the stunning landscape. It's worthwhile to hike the 5.3-km (3.2-mile) mostly flat trail around the lake, where you can see a diversity of plants, including orchids found on the lake's southeast side, and animals like bald eagles, moose, and osprey. There are picnic areas, and Emerald Lake Lodge has

a patio restaurant where you can enjoy lunch or coffee lakeside. There are canoe and rowboat rentals in the summer, and in the winter, Emerald is a good place to cross-country ski or snowshoe. Due to its high altitude, the lake is frozen from about November to July. ⊠ *Emerald Lake Rd., Yoho National Park ✛ 3 km (1.8 miles) west of Field, turn on to the Emerald Lake Rd. and a 9-km (5.6 mile) drive will bring you to the Emerald Lake Parking Lot.*

Takakkaw Falls
WATERFALL | FAMILY |"Takakkaw" means wonderful in Cree, and when you see these falls—Canada's highest at 373 meters (1,224 feet)—there's no question how it got its name. Although an incredible marvel of nature even when viewed from the parking lot, the falls are best experienced at the viewing spot accessed via a short, easy walk, where the roar of the water becomes great and you can feel the water spray your face. On the trail, right before you cross the Yoho River footbridge, take time to sit in Parks Canada's signature red Adirondack chairs. ⊠ *Yoho Valley Rd., Yoho National Park ✛ 15 km (9.3 miles) from the Trans-Canada Hwy. turnoff on Yoho Valley Rd.*

TRAILS
Lake O'Hara Shoreline Trail
TRAIL | This 2.8-km (1.7-mile) trail with minimal ups and downs in elevation takes you close to the shoreline of the vibrant, turquoise-colored Lake O'Hara. You generally follow the shoreline, and at times the trail cuts higher along the mountain and across gullies above the lake. A highlight is the Seven Veils Falls that cascades into the lake. *Easy.* ⊠ *Lake O'Hara, Yoho National Park ✛ Trailhead: at the O'Hara Warden Cabin.*

Lake Oesa Trail
TRAIL | This 6.6-km (4.1-mile) well-signed trail starts along Lake O'Hara, then proceeds past a waterfall and another small turquoise lake before reaching Lake Oesa, which is nestled among the scree slopes

After numerous runaway trains and crashes, the Spiral Tunnels were created to make train travel safer on Cathedral Mountain.

at the bottom of towering snow-covered mountains. Although the trail is above Lake O'Hara, elevation gain is minimal at 240 meters (787 feet) made via a series of switchbacks that pass through some grassy slopes and meadows surrounded by quartzite cliffs. In places, huge slabs of flat rock provide a stable walking surface. *Moderate.* ⊠ *Lake O'Hara, Yoho National Park* ⊹ *Trailhead: shore of Lake O'Hara across from Le Relais.*

Opabin Plateau Circuit

TRAIL | It will take 2–3 hours to hike this 5.9-km (3.7-mile) circuit with an elevation gain of 250 meters (820 feet). You can access it either via the West Opabin or East Opabin arm. The west arm trail takes you up along the shores of Mary Lake and then climbs steeply for approximately 120 meters (394 feet) onto the rolling terrain of the Opabin Plateau, a beautiful hanging valley above Lake O'Hara. From there, the circuit continues into the Opabin Creek Valley and finally arrives at Opabin Lake, where you can see the foot of a glacier in the narrow gap in the peaks at the end

of the lake. *Moderate.* ⊠ *Yoho National Park, Lake O'Hara, Yoho National Park* ⊹ *Trailhead: a sign at the southwest end of Lake O'Hara marks the beginning of the west arm.*

Paget Lookout Trail

TRAIL | Due to severe fires in the early to mid-1900s, several fire lookouts were built in the Rockies, and the Paget Fire Lookout is the oldest in Canada's national parks. This 7-km (4.3-mile) moderately difficult round-trip hike with 520 meters (1,706 feet) of elevation gain, will have you switchbacking through the forest until you almost reach the lookout. Allow plenty of time to take in the amazing views of the Kicking Horse River valley, the Continental Divide, and the surrounding peaks from the strategically placed bench at the lookout which is now a shelter. (Note that Parks Canada also does a guided conservation hike up this trail; find more info at their website). If you're feeling energetic, you can continue on to Paget Peak, but beware that it's steep, with a 446-meter (1,463-foot) elevation gain on the 1.4-km (.8-mile) trail. The trail is also challenging because of several scree-filled and exposed sections, and there can be snow at the summit well into July. If you're a seasoned hiker, however, the views from the top are worth it. *Difficult.* ☒ *Paget Lookout Trail, Yoho National Park* ✛ *Trailhead: 11.5 km (7.1 miles) east of Field, the same trailhead as the Sherbrooke Lake Trail* ⊕ *www.pc.gc.ca/en/pn-np/bc/yoho/activ/ guidee-conservation-guided/paget.*

Wapta Falls Trail

TRAIL | FAMILY | This 4.6-km (3-mile) out-and-back trail has minimal elevation, making it a fun one for the whole family. The trail is a wide, heavily trafficked path through the forest, until you eventually reach the Wapta Falls ("wapta" means "river" in the Sioux language of the Stoney people). The falls are especially forceful and impressive in June and early July, when the run-off is still high. *Easy.* ☒ *Wapta Falls, Yoho National Park* ✛ *Trailhead: 26 km (16 miles) west of Field and 32 km (20 miles) east of Golden, and continue down the gravel road until you can't go any further. Note that the trail is not marked westbound, as left turns are not allowed, so you must continue to the park boundary and turn around to come back and enter from the east.*

Whaleback Trail

TRAIL | This is a 21.3-km (13.2-mile) circuit with 700 meters (2,297 feet) of elevation gain which takes you to Twin Falls backcountry campground. The trail takes you through the Yoho Valley and past Twin Falls and Marpole Lake. There is a seasonal suspension bridge, so check the trail report to ensure it's in operation before you go. Note that reservations for the campground must also be made in advance. *Difficult.* ☒ *Takakkaw Falls, Yoho National Park* ✛ *Trailhead: Takakkaw Falls parking lot.*

VISITOR CENTERS

Yoho National Park Visitor Centre

VISITOR CENTER | The park's only visitor center is located in Field and is only available seasonally (May until mid-October). At the center, you can obtain information brochures, permits, backcountry reservations, and get updates on weather, trail, and road conditions. The visitor center shares a building with the Friends of Yoho (an organization that promotes appreciation, understanding, and stewardship of the ecology and culture of Yoho National Park) and there is also a small-scale exhibit of a train passing through the Spiral Tunnels and Burgess Shale fossil interpretive panels. ☒ *5764 Trans-Canada Hwy., Field* ☏ *250/343–6783* ⊕ *www. pc.gc.ca/en/pn-np/bc/yoho.*

 Hotels

Lake O'Hara Lodge

$$$$ | ALL-INCLUSIVE | The vistas don't get any better than from this 1920s luxury lodge and log cabins, situated on the edge of the turquoise-blue Lake O'Hara. **Pros:** great hiking and skiing options; a beautiful, pristine setting; top-notch gourmet dining. **Cons:** minimum two-night stay; one of the park's most expensive accommodations; remote and hard to get to. ⓢ *Rooms from: C$770* ☒ *Lake O'Hara Lodge, Yoho National Park* ☏ *250/343– 6418* ⊕ *www.lakeohara.com* ¶ *All-Inclusive* ⮑ *23 rooms.*

Field Townsite

83 km (52 miles) northwest of Banff Townsite, 207 km (129 miles) northwest of Calgary, 766 km (476 miles) northeast of Vancouver.

Field was started as a Canadian Pacific Railway town back in the late nineteenth century. Still a crew-change point today, with 25 to 30 trains passing through here daily, the railway remains an important part of the community. Despite being an

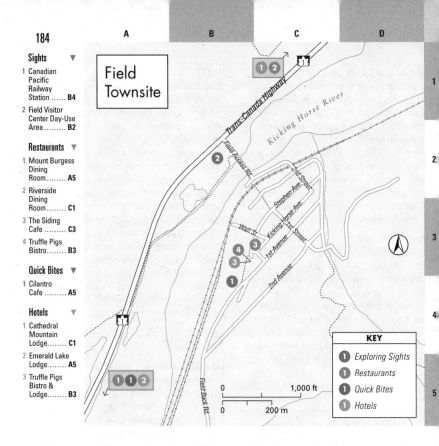

Field Townsite

KEY

1 *Exploring Sights*
1 *Restaurants*
1 *Quick Bites*
1 *Hotels*

---

unincorporated community of only 200 or so permanent residents, most of whom are Parks Canada employees or people who work at the nearby lodges and restaurants, downtown Field has some important tourist amenities: a post office, community center, pottery studio, an inn with a dining room/bar, several guesthouses with extraordinary gardens, and a grab-and-go cafe. Most other park lodges and accommodations, as well as many scenic spots, are close to the village.

◉ Sights

Canadian Pacific Railway Station
TRANSPORTATION | FAMILY | Built in 1953–54, Field's International-style train station is located next to the tracks and is one of the few remaining buildings from this once-major railway complex. While it's no longer in operation and

you can't go inside, it's a great spot to sit a spell and watch for one of the trains that pass through here 25 to 30 times a day. It was added to the Canadian Register of Historic Places in 2006. ⊠ *Stephen Ave., Field.*

Field Visitor Center Day-Use Area
VISITOR CENTER | FAMILY | Immediately adjacent to the Field Visitor Centre parking lot, this day-use area is a popular family-picnic spot in the summer months. On hot days, the small lake is perfect for a refreshing swim. The large parking lot is suitable for RVs, and there are accessible washrooms and a shop that sells T-shirts and other tourist merchandise inside the visitor center. ⊠ *Field Visitor Centre, off of Trans Canada Hwy., .*

🍴 Restaurants

Mount Burgess Dining Room
$$$$ | **CANADIAN** | Part of the Canadian Rocky Mountains Resorts collection, the dining room at Emerald Lake Lodge is famed for its Rocky Mountain cuisine, with roots that go back to the hearty meals prepared by the mountain guides and the fine dining served in the early CPR rail cars. The seasonal menu features selections like free-range elk striploin served with foraged mushroom terrine or seared Skuna Bay salmon for dinner, or breakfast options like a wild boar chorizo breakfast burger; the resort sources its game meat from its own ranch near Calgary. **Known for:** impressive blend of modern dining with elegant, historic surroundings; excellent selection of BC and international wines; game meat raised on their own ranch. [$] *Average main: C$39* ✉ *Emerald Lake Lodge, 1 Emerald Lake Rd., Field* ☎ *800/663–6336* 🌐 *crmr.com/resorts/emerald-lake* 🕒 *No lunch.*

Riverside Dining Room
$$$$ | **CANADIAN** | In a forest on the edge of the Kicking Horse River, Cathedral Mountain Lodge is a romantic setting for dinner. In a small dining room with lots of windows and wood accents, guests can order gourmet dishes made with fresh local ingredients from a menu that's updated a few times a week and includes items like Alberta grass-fed ribeye, Arctic char with Okanagan tomato salsa, or wild mushroom tagliatelle. **Known for:** constantly changing menu; local seasonal ingredients; mountain and river views from window-side tables and outdoor terrace. [$] *Average main: C$43* ✉ *1 Yoho Valley Rd., Field* ☎ *250/343–6442* 🌐 *www.cathedralmountainlodge.com.*

The Siding Cafe
$ | **CAFÉ** | **FAMILY** | Originally constructed in 1915 by the Canadian Pacific Railway, this building has been home to a variety of businesses, including a ham radio spot and a grocery store, and has been operated as a café by the current family since 1991. The café's small menu can be dine-in or ordered to go for a picnic somewhere in the park. **Known for:** half-portions of almost every menu item; scenic backdrop of the surrounding mountains; grab-and-go items. [$] *Average main: C$17* ✉ *318 Stephen Ave., Field* ☎ *250/343–6002* 🌐 *thesidingcafe.ca* 🕒 *No dinner.*

Trainspotting in Field

Once home to a major railway complex, Field is now a crew-change station for the Canadian Pacific Railway trains that pass through here 25 to 30 times a day. In fact, Field was part of CPR's post-war modernization plan, which included converting the cars to diesel and offering passenger service. If you're a train lover, there are plenty of places to sit and watch the trains go by, including at the old train station, right next to the tracks in Field.

★ **Truffle Pigs Bistro**
$$$ | **ECLECTIC** | **FAMILY** | With an eclectic assortment of knick-knacks, most with a "pig" theme, this cute, bright bistro grabs your attention as soon as you walk through the door. Fiercely local, the wine/beer menu is totally BC-centric and dishes use fresh, local ingredients with menu selections ranging from burgers or crispy duck to ethnic fusion dishes like a Moroccan lamb shank. **Known for:** tasty menu items with catchy names (eg. Don't Say Jack About Being Vegan- a grilled vegan jackfruit patty served with a pearl couscous salad); British Columbia beer and wine menu; covered patio with a mountain view. [$] *Average main: C$33* ✉ *100 Center St., Field* ☎ *800/659–4944* 🌐 *www.trufflepigs.com.*

The vivid green water of Yoho's largest lake is absolutely breathtaking.

☕ Coffee and Quick Bites

Cilantro Cafe

$ | **CANADIAN** | On a sunny day, there's no better place to grab a coffee and house-baked cookie or a light lunch than at the newish log cabin next to the bridge at the Emerald Lake Lodge entry houses. The patio with its bright yellow umbrella tables has stunning views of the lake, and the interior is equally stunning with sweeping cathedral ceilings, wood accents, and a grand river-stone fireplace. **Known for:** stunning lake views; Rocky Mountain cuisine; large river stone fireplace. $ *Average main: C$17* ✉ *Emerald Lake Lodge, Emerald Lake Rd., Field* ☎ *800/663–6336* ⊕ *crmr.com/resorts/ emerald-lake* ⊙ *No dinner.*

🛏 Hotels

★ Cathedral Mountain Lodge

$$$ | **RESORT** | Guests here stay in luxury log cabins dotted among the forest, on the edge of the fast-flowing Kicking Horse River. **Pros:** high-end dining menu; beautiful scenery; just a short drive off of the Trans-Canada Hwy., so not too remote. **Cons:** 30-day cancellation policy; limited phone/Wi-Fi reception; only open through summer months. $ *Rooms from: C$303* ✉ *1 Yoho Valley Rd., Field* ☎ *250/343–6442* ⊕ *www.cathedralmoun- tainlodge.com* ⊙ *Closed Nov.–Mid-May* ⧖ *Free Breakfast* ⇄ *31 rooms.*

Emerald Lake Lodge

$$$$ | **RESORT** | Nestled on a 13-acre peninsula, next to the bright jade-colored Emerald Lake, this Canadian Pacific Rail-way hand-hewn timber lodge dates back to 1902, keeping the historical integrity intact with antique tables and furnishings. **Pros:** log cabins with lovely stone fireplac-es; exemplary on-site dining; extraordinary views of the surrounding mountains and Emerald Lake. **Cons:** 15-minute drive to village of Field; no kitchenettes, except in the exclusive suites; no TV, phone, or Wi-Fi, if that's important to you. $ *Rooms from: C$489* ✉ *Emerald Lake Rd., Field* ☎ *403/410–7417, 800/663–6336* ⊕ *crmr.*

com/resorts/emerald-lake 🍴 *No Meals* 🛏 *85 rooms.*

Truffle Pigs Bistro & Lodge

$ | **HOTEL** | **FAMILY** | The only lodge in the village of Field, this small spot has cozy rooms with mini-fridges and in-floor heating, and it's home to the delicious Truffle Pigs Bistro that serves light breakfast and coffee as well as lunch and dinner. **Pros:** affordable rates; outstanding views down the valley; excellent on-site dining. **Cons:** noise from frequent nearby trains; must carry luggage up the stairs to second-story rooms; no air-conditioning. [$] *Rooms from: C$212* ✉ *100 Center St., Field* ☎ *250/343–6303* 🌐 *www.trufflepigs.com* 🍴 *No Meals* 🛏 *12 rooms.*

Activities

BIKING

Yoho National Park has turned more than 80 km (50 miles) of scenic old fire roads into mountain bike trails, some suitable for beginners and others for advanced bikers. Bikes must give way to hikers and horse riders sharing the trail, and always keep an eye out for bears and other wildlife. Note that biking on Lake O'Hara Fire Road is prohibited.

Shorter rides include Tally Ho Trail from Hwy. 1 to Emerald Lake Road (one-way 3 km; 1.9 miles) and Kicking Horse Trail from the Natural Bridge to Otterhead Road (one-way is 6.3 km [3.9 miles]). The longer Amiskwi Trail (one-way 18.8 km/11.7 miles) also starts at the Natural Bridge and goes to Otto Creek. Four road cycling options are also available including the family-friendly Great Divide/Old 1A Hwy. Trail (one-way 3.0 km [1.9 miles]) which goes from the Lake O'Hara parking lot to the Great Divide.

Derailed Sports

BIKING | This shop sells and services all kinds of bicycles, and also sells a wide range of biking accessories and quality gear. They are also a good source for trail maps and directions to bike trails, as well as experts on trail conditions. ✉ *804 Park Dr., Golden* ☎ *250/439–9959* 🌐 *derailedsports.com.*

Higher Ground Sports

BIKING | This company offers bike and accessory rentals, including e-bikes and BMX, as well as cross-country ski and snowshoe rentals. Mountain biking apparel, wetsuits, and ski apparel are also for sale. ✉ *510 9th Ave. N., Golden* ☎ *250/344–7980* 🌐 *highergroundsports.ca* 🎟 *From C$70 for half-day mountain-bike rental.*

BIRD-WATCHING

Birdlife is abundant in Yoho, and more than 224 species of birds have been recorded. Many migratory birds, including bald and golden eagles, harlequin ducks, songbirds, and hawks, can be spotted in the spring, summer, and fall, but some, like chickadees, dippers, and grosbeaks can be seen all year long. Three threatened species are being studied closely by the park, including the bank swallow, the barn swallow, and the Olive-sided flycatcher, which migrates over 8,000 km (4,971 miles) to winter in the Andes.

BOATING AND RAFTING

Visitors can use non-motorized watercraft (any boat, canoe, kayak, raft, stand-up paddleboard, inflatable, or other type or class of vessel that is not motorized) in Yoho as long as they have completed a self-certification permit and dropped it at a visitor center or with a Parks Canada staff member or in a self-certification dropbox (available at some locations). This permit can be found online or at the park's gate, Kicking Horse Campground, Lake O'Hara Bus Station, and the Yoho Visitor Centre. Self-certification stations are available at Emerald Lake, Faedar Lake, Finn Creek, and Field Pond.

TIP→ The only rafting companies are outside the park in the Golden area.

Glacier Raft Company

RAFTING | This company provides a variety of adventures, from easy family floats to heart-thumping whitewater rapids. You can rent one- and two-person inflatable kayaks for a half- or full day. ⊠ 1509a Lafontaine Rd., Yoho National Park ☎ 877/344–7238 ⊕ glacierraft.com ⊠ From C$109 for rafting adventures, C$69 for kayak rentals.

Higher Ground Sports

BOATING | Stand-up paddleboards are available for rent here. They also offer bike and accessory rentals, including e-bikes and BMX, as well as cross-country ski and snowshoe rentals. Mountain-biking apparel, wetsuits, and ski apparel are also for sale. ⊠ 501 9th Ave. N., Yoho National Park ☎ 250/344–7980 ⊕ highergroundsports.ca ⊠ From C$49 for half-day SUP rental.

CAMPING

Parks Canada operates a total of 150 campsites in four frontcountry campgrounds in Yoho National Park, none of which are serviced. Prices for a one-night stay range from C$16.05 to C$28. Campsite firepits within the park have an extra charge of C$8.80 per day (no firepits at Monarch). Each campground has a different opening and closing date, ranging between early May and mid-October. Note that all campgrounds are first-come-first-served, except for Kicking Horse, which has a few reservable campsites, and demand is especially heavy on weekends in July and August and long weekends. For more information, call 877/737-3783 or visit reservation.pc.gc.ca.

Hoodoo Creek Campground. Closer to the park's west boundary, this campground is an excellent basecamp to access numerous local trails, including Wapta Falls, the historic Deer Lodge Cabin, or the famous Hoodoos trail overlooking the campground. Surrounded by a sunny, open meadow with stellar views of Mt. Hunter, there are 30 sites to choose from. None

of the sites are serviced; however, there are firepits and disabled access. No cell service and no reservations available. 23 km (15 miles) west of Field on Trans-Canada Hwy.

Kicking Horse Campground. Just down the road from the village of Field, this centrally located campground is Yoho's largest. There are a total of 88 campsites, including riverside, forested, and open meadow options, with remarkable views of Cathedral Mountain. Two short hiking trails start from the campground. Aside from the campsites, facilities include kitchen shelters, showers, potable water, a sani-dump station, and fire rings and firewood (for a fee). Cell phone coverage is spotty. 2.5 km (1.6 miles) up Yoho Valley Road 5.6 km (3.5 miles) from Field.

Monarch Campground. Close to the Kicking Horse River, these bright, open sites are nestled below the Monarch mine shafts, where it's not unusual to see wildlife on the nearby river flats and the cliffs above. Suitable for tents and small to mid-sized RVs, there's a cooking shelter and a sani-dump station, but no other services. The location allows easy access to the village of Field, and attractions like Takakkaw Falls, Emerald Lake, and the Continental Divide. Note that sites are not reservable, and are available on a first-come-first-serve basis only. Limited cell service. 5.4 km (3.4 miles) east of the village of Field on Trans-Canada Hwy.

Takakkaw Campground. This walk-in-only, 35-site campground offers a sub-alpine wilderness experience with exceptional panoramic views of the roaring Takakkaw Falls. The campground is the gateway to Little Yoho Valley and the main trailhead for Laughing Falls, Twin Falls, Ice Line, Whaleback, and Yoho Glacier Trails. 13.2 km (8.2 miles) north on the Yoho Road, after Trans-Canada Hwy. turnoff.

CANOEING

Canoeing is allowed on the lakes and rivers in Yoho National Park. Although lakes, like Emerald Lake, are lovely and calm, rivers can be fast flowing with waterfalls, chutes, and rapids. A Parks Canada self-certification permit is required before canoeing in the park. You can obtain this permit from any Yoho park gate, Kicking Horse Campground, or the Yoho Visitor Centre in Field. All equipment must be cleaned and dried for more than 48 hours before entering Yoho waters. Canoe rentals are available at Emerald Lake.

Boathouse Trading Co.

CANOEING & ROWING | Canoes are for rent here on the shores of Emerald Lake. ⊠ *Emerald Lake Lodge, Emerald Lake Rd.* ☎ *250/343–6000* ⊕ *www.facebook. com/theboathousetradingco/* ⊠ *C$75 per hour.*

CROSS-COUNTRY SKIING

There are several kilometers of trails in Yoho, including easy access to trails from within the village of Field. The Tally Ho/ Connector trail is track-set by Kicking Horse Cross Country Ski Club and winds for 12 km (7.5 miles) around Mount Burgess from Field to Emerald Lake, where you will find other groomed trails. Once well frozen, trails are also tracked on Emerald Lake. Check out the Parks Canada website for a map that indicates the winter trails found throughout the park.

Higher Ground Sports (*see Boating & Rafting*) has cross-country skis and snowshoes for rent.

EDUCATIONAL PROGRAMS

Evening theater programs are offered at Kicking Horse Campground. You can also get free activity booklets at the visitor center or campground kiosk to participate in a self-guided high-tech treasure hunt into Yoho's past. For more information on these campground programs, check at the visitor center or online at *www.pc.gc. ca/en/pn-np/bc/yoho/activ/interp.*

Mount Stephen Guided Hike

GUIDED TOURS | This guided hike happens two to four times a week, depending on the season. This hike takes you to the trilobite beds that overlook the town of Field, the historical site where railway workers first reported finding "stone bugs" in the 1880s. ⊠ *Field* ⊕ *pc.gc.ca/ en/pn-np/bc/yoho/activ/burgess/stephen* ⊠ *C$55.*

Paget Fire Lookout Conservation Hike

GUIDED TOURS | This guided hike takes place two times a week. Parks Canada guides educate on how species and their habitats are connected, including information on how Parks Canada is protecting species at risk, (like the whitebark pine), and restoring balance in critical habitats, from grizzly bears to fungi. ⊠ *Sherbrooke Lake, Yoho National Park* ⊹ *Meet at Sherbrooke Lake parking lot* ⊕ *pc.gc.ca/en/pn-np/bc/yoho/activ/ guidee-conservation-guided/paget* ⊠ *C$55.*

Walcott Quarry Guided Hike

GUIDED TOURS | Two to six times a week, Parks Canada Heritage Interpreters lead guided hikes to this Burgess Shale fossil quarry that was discovered by Charles Walcott in 1909. You will have hands-on learning about the fossils, the geology that led to their formation, and the flora and fauna of the region, topped off with an amazing view of Emerald Lake from the top. ⊠ *Walcott Quarry, Yoho National Park* ⊕ *pc.gc.ca/en/pn-np/bc/yoho/activ/ burgess/walcott* ⊠ *C$70.*

Xplorer Program and Club Park

SELF-GUIDED TOURS | Parks Canada offers both of these programs year-round. Xplorer Program, for children age 6 to 11, and Club Parka, for pre-schoolers, encourage kids to explore the world around them and the nature and history of the parks. The booklets for these programs are available from a park interpreter or at the Yoho National Park Visitor Centre. ⊠ *Field* ⊠ *Free*

FISHING

Popular fishing options in the park are Emerald Lake, where brook char and rainbow trout are common catches; cutthroat trout fishing at Lake O'Hara; and trout fishing at Wapta Lake. Fly-fishing is popular on Kicking Horse River, but it's permitted only after the confluence with the Yoho River, downstream to the park boundary. A national park fishing permit (available at the visitor center; C$9.80/day or C$34.30 annually) is required for any angling within the park. Children and youth under 16 may fish without a permit if accompanied by a permit holder who is 16 years or older. Yoho National Park has a catch-and-release only policy and there's a ban on felt-soled wading boots.

HIKING

This protected alpine region is comprised of a collection of lakes and valleys linked by a well-marked and maintained trail network, making it a hiker's paradise. Trails range from easy, minimal elevation-gain options like the Lake O'Hara Shoreline Trail (2.8-km [1.7-mile] loop) to strenuous all-day hikes made up of a combination of trails. Trail closures happen regularly to reduce disturbance to wildlife, especially grizzly bears, so check the park's website before you go. Note that access to Lake O'Hara is limited and advanced reservations are required for both the bus ride-in and overnight camping. However, it is possible to hike the 11-km (6.8-mile, one-way) forestry road in for day-use exploration of the area, if you haven't reserved the bus. In the winter, this is also a popular road for snowshoers and cross-country skiers.

Self Propelled Adventures

HIKING & WALKING | This company offers guided hikes into Yoho National Park and to Lake O'Hara. ⊠ *Golden* ☎ *250/344–8597* ⊕ *selfpropelledadventures.ca* ✉ *From C$125 per person or C$175 for a single person.*

HORSEBACK RIDING

Equine use, travel, and transport are allowed in the park, except where prohibited, namely: Emerald Lake area and trails; trails and road to Lake O'Hara; trails of Yoho Valley area and upper section of Yoho Valley Road. For more specific information, refer to the map on the Parks Canada website.

KAYAKING

Kayaking is allowed on the lakes and rivers in Yoho National Park. Rivers can be treacherous and unpredictable, so always ensure that you are well-versed with the terrain. A Parks Canada self-certification permit is required before paddling in the park. You can obtain this permit from any Yoho park gate, Kicking Horse Campground, or the Yoho Visitor Centre in Field. All equipment must be cleaned and dried for more than 48 hours before entering Yoho waters. Equipment can be rented in Golden.

Glacier Raft Company

KAYAKING | This operator rents one- and two-person inflatable kayaks for a half- or full day. ⊠ *1509a Lafontaine Rd., Golden* ☎ *250/344–6521, 877/344–7238 toll-free* ⊕ *glacierraft.com* ✉ *From C$109.*

MULTI-SPORT OUTFITTERS

Higher Ground Sports

LOCAL SPORTS | This shop sells and rents skis, snowboards, snowshoes, and bicycles, and is a good spot to buy camping gear and outdoor clothing. ⊠ *501 9th Ave. N., Golden* ☎ *250/344–7980* ⊕ *highergroundsports.ca/.*

Selkirk Ski & Bike

LOCAL SPORTS | Conveniently located at the base of Kicking Horse Mountain Resort, this shop rents, demos (they are known for their try-before-you-buy program), and sells bikes, accessories, and clothing in the summer months. In the winter, they rent, demo, and sell skis and snowboards, and carry accessories and clothing. They are also known for their expert boot fitting. ✉ *1549 Kicking Horse Trail, Golden* ☎ *250/344–2925* ⊕ *selkirkskiandbike.com.*

SCENIC FLIGHTS
Kicking Horse Aviation
AIR EXCURSIONS | Flying out of the Golden airport, this company offers custom scenic flights in a Cessna 185, a high-winged aircraft with bubble windows allowing for unobstructed views. ✉ *815 Oster Rd., Golden* ☎ *250/939–9082* ⊕ *kickinghorseaviation.com/* 🍽 *$600 per hour.*

SWIMMING
While it's possible to swim in many of the lakes in the park, the two safest and best locations are Emerald Lake and the Field pond, beside the Yoho Visitor Centre. Keep in mind that Yoho's lakes are glacier fed, meaning they are very cold, and a swim would more likely be a quick dip.

What's Nearby

Numerous small towns surround Yoho National Park, including Banff townsite and Lake Louise, but Golden is really the best place to base yourself, as it has all the amenities you'll need while visiting the park.

Golden

713 km (443 miles) northeast of Vancouver, 362 km (225 miles) northwest of Calgary, and 140 km (87 miles) east of the townsite of Banff.

Just 27.6 km (17 miles) from the Yoho National Park west boundary, Golden is a popular base for tourists who want to experience the nearby national parks and all of the splendor and recreational opportunities offered by the three surrounding mountain ranges: the Canadian Rockies, the Selkirks, and the Purcells. Because motorized sports like ATVing, snowmobiling, and boating are not allowed in the national park, Golden has several opportunities for these activities. It's particularly well known for its snowmobiling, fly-fishing and whitewater river rafting on the Kicking Horse River, mountain biking on over 185 km (115 miles) of trails, and of course, the Kicking Horse Mountain Resort.

GETTING HERE AND AROUND
Calgary International Airport (YYC) and Edmonton International Airport (YEG) are the closest international airports to Yoho National Park. Car rentals are available at both airports.

Private transfers via SUV or minibus are available from Calgary International Airport to Golden with Beyond Banff.

CONTACTS Beyond Banff. ✉ *Yoho National Park* ☎ *587/897–1354* ⊕ *www.beyondbanff.com.*

◉ Sights

Confluence Park
STATE/PROVINCIAL PARK | This park is located at the confluence of the Columbia and Kicking Horse Rivers near the Golden airport. The trail meanders along the wetland and forests along the eastern edge of the Columbia River. In the spring, during high waters, parts of the trail may be underwater. ✉ *Fisher Rd., near the Golden Airport, Golden.*

Golden Skybridge
BRIDGE | **FAMILY** | At this newly opened park, a forested trail will take you across a canyon via Canada's two highest suspension bridges (130 meters [426 feet]; 80 meters [263 feet]). There are also viewing platforms where you can marvel over the canyon formation and the surrounding mountain ranges. A play park for kids is included in the fee, but there's an extra charge for the rope challenge course, giant canyon swing, and zipline. ✉ *503 Golden Donald Upper Rd., Golden* ☎ *800/270–1238* ⊕ *www.banffjaspercollect ion.com/attractions/golden-skybridge* 🍽 *C$34.*

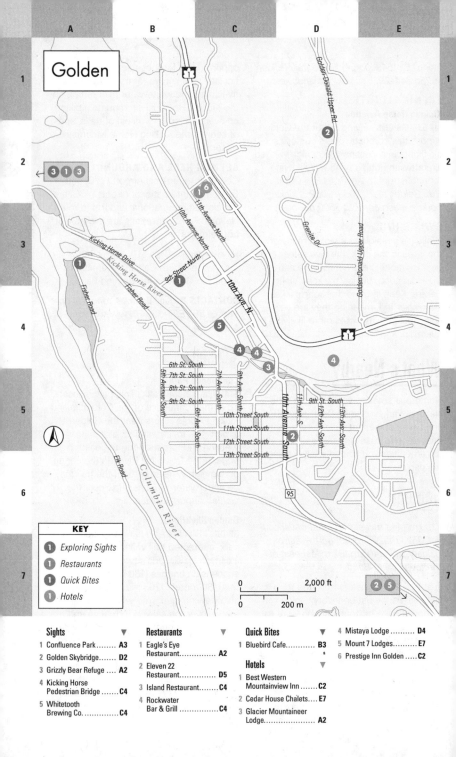

Golden

KEY

- **1** Exploring Sights
- **1** Restaurants
- **1** Quick Bites
- **1** Hotels

0   2,000 ft
0   200 m

Grizzly Bear Refuge

WILDLIFE REFUGE | Boo, an adult grizzly bear, has called this 20-acre forested area in the middle of the Kicking Horse Mountain Resort home since 2002. Although born in the wild, Boo's mother was poached when he was young, leaving him unable to live on his own. At this refuge center, you can see Boo going about his day, take an interpretive tour, or visit an interpretive center that provides more information on grizzlies in the wild. ⌧ *Kicking Horse Mountain Resort, 1500 Kicking Horse Tr., Golden* ☎ *800/258–7669* ⊕ *kickinghorseresort.com/purchase/boo-grizzly-bear* ☞ *C$33.95.*

Kicking Horse Pedestrian Bridge

BRIDGE | Spanning the Kicking Horse River in downtown Golden, at 46 meters (151 feet), this is the longest freestanding timberframe bridge in Canada. Built with a Swiss design from local wood, the bridge reflects the Swiss guide heritage of the city. ⌧ *8th Ave. N., Golden* ☞ *Free.*

Whitetooth Brewing Co.

BREWERY | This brewery crafts award-winning small-batch Belgian-inspired and West Coast-influenced beers. There's no kitchen on-site, but guests are encouraged to order takeout from local restaurants. Indoor tastings are available, and the large outdoor patio has amazing views of the Purcell Mountains. ⌧ *623 8th Ave. N., Golden* ☎ *250/344–2838* ⊕ *www.whitetoothbrewing.com.*

 Restaurants

Eagle's Eye Restaurant

$$$$ | ECLECTIC | A gondola ride to 7,700 feet brings you to this beautiful, mountaintop chalet with floor-to-ceiling windows and soaring cathedral ceilings; the views of the surrounding peaks are unrivaled. Despite being Canada's highest restaurant, the chef uses fresh local ingredients to create elegant dishes like beef tenderloin served with haskap berry (also known as honeyberries)

port sauce and truffle roasted potatoes. **Known for:** highest-altitude restaurant in Canada; panoramic mountain views; gondola-ride access. ⓢ *Average main: C$39* ⌧ *Kicking Horse Ranch, 1500 Kicking Horse Tr., Golden* ☎ *250/439–5425* ⊕ *kickinghorseresort.com/purchase/eagles-eye-restaurant.*

★ Eleven 22 Restaurant

$$ | ECLECTIC | Chef/owner Konan Mar's passion for cultural diversity and his talent for fusing Canadian and Asian cuisine with a distinctly European flair shape this restaurant's regularly changing menu (think pork and kimchi potstickers and stout-braised duck shepherd's pie). Based in one of Golden's oldest houses and decorated with local art, the space is cozy. **Known for:** early-bird 3-course dinner special between 5 and 6 pm; intimate summer outdoor patio with mountain views; original, modern food. ⓢ *Average main: C$27* ⌧ *122 10 Ave. S., Golden* ☎ *250/344–2443* ⊕ *www.eleven22restaurant.com.*

Island Restaurant

$$ | ECLECTIC | You can't miss this beautiful timberframe restaurant located right next to the roaring Kicking Horse River in downtown Golden. They serve Canadian Rocky Mountain cuisine with Asian/European influences. **Known for:** Rocky Mountain cuisine with Asian/European influences; second-story patio overlooking the river; cocktails on the patio. ⓢ *Average main: C$28* ⌧ *101 Gould's Island, 10th Ave, Golden* ☎ *250/344–2400* ⊕ *www.islandrestaurant.ca.*

Rockwater Bar & Grill

$ | ECLECTIC | This is Golden's main music venue, specializing in upscale pub food like burgers, sandwiches, and starters like oyster shooters, ceviche tacos, and Korean fried cauliflower. They have eight rotating beers on tap, all from British Columbia. **Known for:** extensive beer-on-tap selection; live music; multilevel rooftop patio next to the Kicking Horse River. ⓢ *Average main: C$24* ⌧ *429 9th Ave. N., Golden* ☎ *250/344–5951* ⊕ *rockwatergrill.com.*

Coffee and Quick Bites

Bluebird Cafe

$ | **CAFÉ** | This cozy café serves a variety of hot beverages, breakfast, and lunch options. Windows all-round provide light and an airy interior seating, while outside tables provide a sunny alternative during the summer months. **Known for:** excellent bagged lunches; specialty coffees; grab-and-go items. [$] *Average main: C$12* ✉ *802 9th St. N., Golden* ☎ *250/439–0008* 🌐 *bluebirdcafegolden.com* ⏲ *No dinner.*

Hotels

Best Western Mountainview Inn

$ | **HOTEL** | **FAMILY** | Located on the edge of town, just off the Trans-Canada Highway, this hotel features a heated indoor pool, guest laundry, and RV parking spots. **Pros:** bikes available to use; some green space at back of property for dogs; breakfast included. **Cons:** 20-minute walk to town; highway noise. [$] *Rooms from: C$229* ✉ *1024 11th St. N., Golden* ☎ *800/780–7234* 🌐 *www.bestwestern.com* 🍴 *Free Breakfast* 🛏 *71 rooms.*

★ **Cedar House Chalets**

$$ | **APARTMENT** | The private, modern luxury chalets on the 10-acre property feature private hot tubs, wood-burning fireplaces, mountain views, full-size kitchens, and BBQs. **Pros:** central grassy play area for kids; walking trails; on-site restaurant. **Cons:** no in-room phones; only one dining choice on-site; 10-minute drive to town. [$] *Rooms from: C$280* ✉ *735 Hefli Rd., Golden* ☎ *250/290–0001* 🌐 *www.cedarhousechalets.com* 🍴 *No Meals* 🛏 *7 units.*

Glacier Mountaineer Lodge

$ | **HOTEL** | **FAMILY** | In the middle of the Kicking Horse Mountain Resort alpine village, right at the base of the gondola, this accommodation offers a full ski-in-ski-out experience with guest rooms or one-, two-, and three-bedroom condo suites. **Pros:** easy access to the mountain/resort activities; washers and dryers; suites have fireplaces. **Cons:** no swimming pool; limited dining options; 15-minute drive to activities in Golden. [$] *Rooms from: C$159* ✉ *1549 Kicking Horse Tr., Golden* ☎ *877/754–5486* 🌐 *www.kickinghorselodging.com* 🍴 *No Meals* 🛏 *94 units.*

★ **Mistaya Lodge**

$$$$ | **ALL-INCLUSIVE** | Mistaya is a heli-access lodge in the Canadian Rocky Mountains which offers guided alpine hiking trips in the summer and guided ski touring in the winter. **Pros:** amazing mountain and glacier views; alpine hiking and skiing with certified guides; gourmet meals. **Cons:** no bathrooms in the rooms; limited Wi-Fi access; some rooms are on the smaller side. [$] *Rooms from: C$600* ✉ *Golden* ☎ *866/647–8292* 🌐 *mistayalodge.com* 🍴 *All-Inclusive* 🛏 *7 rooms.*

Mount 7 Lodges

$$$ | **HOUSE** | This luxury wilderness custom-built self-catering lodge is nestled on a mountainside just outside of Golden. **Pros:** hot tubs with mountain views; private secluded location; fully equipped kitchens. **Cons:** no in-room phones; no on-site dining; 15-minute drive to activities in Golden. [$] *Rooms from: C$325* ✉ *891 Crandall Rd., Golden* ☎ *250/344–8973* 🌐 *mount7lodges.com* 🍴 *No Meals* 🛏 *4 rooms.*

Prestige Inn Golden

$ | **HOTEL** | **FAMILY** | This property is located on the Trans-Canada Hwy. at the edge of town and features an indoor pool and hot tub, an on-site restaurant and liquor store, as well as a fitness room. **Pros:** kitchenettes; indoor pool and hot tub; handicap-accessible and dog-friendly rooms. **Cons:** 20-minute walk to Golden; limited green space on property; highway noise. [$] *Rooms from: C$220* ✉ *1049 Trans-Canada Hwy., Golden* ☎ *250/344–7990* 🌐 *www.prestigehotelsandresorts.com* 🍴 *No Meals* 🛏 *91 rooms.*

⚡ Activities

BOATING & RAFTING

Glacier Raft Company

RAFTING | This company provides a variety of adventures, from easy family floats to heart-thumping whitewater rapids. You can rent one- and two-person inflatable kayaks for a half- or full day. ⊠ *1509a Lafontaine Rd., Golden* ☎ *877/344–7238* ⊕ *glacierraft.com* ✉ *From C$109.*

FISHING

Due to its location on the Columbia River, there is an abundance of tributaries as well as crystal-clear alpine lakes suitable for spin casting, fly-fishing, and ice fishing in the Golden area. Fish species range from rainbow and cutthroat trout in the lakes to char in the rivers.

Golden Gillie

FISHING | This company offers guided fishing adventures for all abilities. ⊠ *Golden* ☎ *250/344–1217* ⊕ *goldengillie.com* ✉ *From C$200.*

FOUR-WHEELING

Canadian Off Road Adventures

FOUR-WHEELING | Guided ATV off-road adventures into Golden's backcountry mountain ranges are offered here and are suitable for first-timers to experts. ⊠ *Golden* ☎ *250/290–0002* ⊕ *www.canadianoffroadadventures.com* ✉ *From C$219.*

SKIING

Kicking Horse Mountain Resort

SKIING & SNOWBOARDING | FAMILY | The sixth-largest mountain resort in Canada, Kicking Horse has more than 3,486 acres of skiable terrain, with 1,315 meters (4,314 feet) of vertical drop and 120 trails. In the summer there are over 50 km (31 miles) of mountain-biking trails and eight hiking trails, accessible via chairlift and a gondola that ascends 2,345 meters (7,700 feet). The resort also offers several dining, shopping, and accommodation options, and in the summer months you can also visit the grizzly bear refuge, where you can see Boo, the resident grizzly bear in its 29-acre home, or do the Via Ferrata climbing routes. ⊠ *1500 Kicking Horse Tr., Golden* ☎ *250/439–5425* ⊕ *kickinghorseresort.com* ✉ *From C$124.*

SNOWMOBILING

Golden Snowmobile Rentals

SNOW SPORTS | Snowmobile rentals and tours are offered by this company. ⊠ *1416 Goldenview Rd., Golden* ☎ *888/753-3669* ⊕ *goldensnowmobilerentals.com* ✉ *C$300 for rental; from C$399 for tour.*

Chapter 8

KOOTENAY NATIONAL PARK

8

By
Kate Robertson

⛺ Camping	🏨 Hotels	🏃 Activities	👁 Scenery	👥 Crowds
★★★★☆	★☆☆☆☆	★☆☆☆☆	★★★★★	★☆☆☆☆

WELCOME TO KOOTENAY NATIONAL PARK

TOP REASONS TO GO

★ **Radium Hot Springs:** Naturally heated outdoor mineral pools are located in a dramatic red wall canyon just inside the park's southwest entrance.

★ **Extraordinary wildfire burn areas:** Several massive forest fires swept through the park in the past couple of decades leaving residual burn sites that give it a unique gothic-romance feel. The park is using the opportunity to educate visitors on the natural forest regeneration cycle.

★ **Relatively under-visited:** Compared to nearby Banff and Jasper, Kootenay has been slow to be discovered, leaving the park's trails and activities generally less crowded.

★ **Diverse geography, flora, and fauna:** The park ranges from glaciers in the north to a semi-arid region in the southwest, allowing for a diverse range of animal species. The warmer southern region provides an important winter range for wildlife, especially the Rocky Mountain bighorn sheep.

Dominated by several mountain ranges and river valleys, Kootenay National Park encompasses a total of 1,406 square km (543 square miles). Established in 1920 to build a 94-km (58-mile) highway from Banff to the Windermere Valley, the first highway to cross the central Rocky Mountains, the park's long, narrow shape is due to the initial agreement which set aside 8 km (5 miles) of park lands on either side of the road. Highway 93S runs from the Banff National Park boundary (which is also the British Columbia-Alberta border) in the northeast corner straight through the center of the park to Radium Hot Springs in the southwest corner.

1 Continental Divide. The north entrance of the park marks the Continental Divide, the dividing line between the Pacific and Atlantic watersheds. Highway 93 runs south from here through the entire park.

2 Radium Hot Springs. The hot spring pools are located just within the south park boundary. Immediately outside of the park entrance is the village of Radium Hot Springs, where the visitor center for Kootenay National Park is located, as well as Redstreak, the park's largest campground.

3 Vermilion Crossing. This crossing is where the Kootenay Park Lodge, the park's only accommodation and convenience store, is located. It is 63½ km (39 miles) north of the village of Radium Hot Springs, or 42 km (26 miles) south of the Highway 1 Castle Junction turnoff in Banff National Park.

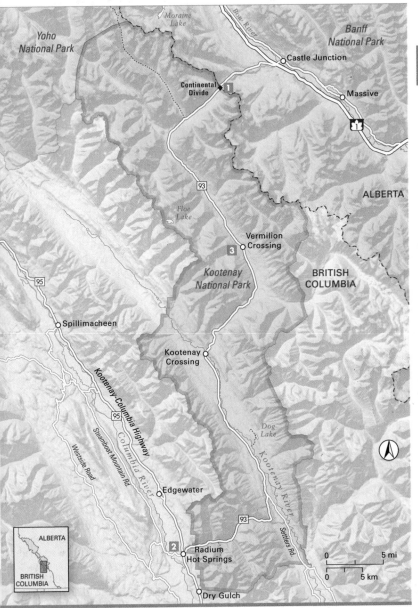

From crystal-blue glacial rivers to steaming hot springs, cacti to interior wet-belt western red cedars and alpine tundra to dense coniferous forests, Kootenay National Park is a place of unique contrasts.

Established in 1920 as part of an agreement to build a 94-km (58-mile) highway in exchange for a strip of land approximately 8 km (5 miles) wide on either side of the road to be used as a park, it was the first national park to be centered around a roadway, rather than a railway. The park's size and shape are a result of this road construction agreement, and consequently, the park cuts through several mountain ranges and river valleys.

Archaeological evidence suggests humans have been traveling through this region of the Rockies for centuries. Pictographs found in the hot springs indicate it was likely the Ktunaxa people who made more use of the area, especially the hot springs. European traders also passed through the area, as well as George Simpson during his circumnavigation of the world in 1841, through what would later be named Simpson Pass. The Palliser Expedition, which was exploring the west for possible settlements and transportation routes, used the region's Vermilion Pass in 1858. In 1905, Rudolph Bruce, an Invermere businessman, persuaded the Canadian government and Canadian Pacific Railway to build a route from the Columbia River Valley to Calgary, so that their products could ship to the eastern markets.

Historically, the park's hot springs have been one of the park's biggest attractions and draw visitors from across the world.

It was an early homesteader who included them in a land claim in the 1880s, but it was Roland Stuart who was successful in acquiring the springs in 1890, initially intending on bottling the spring water. Development of the hot springs began in earnest after a chemical analysis by McGill University confirmed the presence of radium in the water. Stuart found an investor to help expand it, but with the development of the park, the land was expropriated by the federal government in 1922, when development to attract tourists began in earnest. The hot springs were promoted as a therapeutic cure, due to the mild radioactivity. Meanwhile, the town of Radium, just outside the park boundary, was being commercially developed for tourism, and this is where the bulk of the hotels, restaurants, and shops that service the park are located.

Kootenay National Park was also put on the map when in 2012, a team of scientists discovered a site of extraordinary fossil preservation, comparable to the Burgess Shale beds previously found in neighboring Yoho National Park. Active research of these fossil beds continues today.

No discussion of Kootenay National Park is complete without mention of the hauntingly beautiful patches of blackened tree snags that you will see, especially in the north end of the park. In 2003, lightning started one of the largest forest

AVERAGE HIGH/LOW TEMP. IN CELSIUS					
Jan.	Feb.	Mar.	Apr.	May	June
-8/-19	-3/-16	3/-11	9/-6	14/-2	18/1
July	Aug.	Sept.	Oct.	Nov.	Dec.
21/3	21/2	15/-2	7/-6	-3/-12	-9/-18

AVERAGE HIGH/LOW TEMP. IN FAHRENHEIT					
Jan.	Feb.	Mar.	Apr.	May	June
18/-2	27/3.2	37/12	48/21	57/28	64/24
July	Aug.	Sept.	Oct.	Nov.	Dec.
70/37	70/36	59/28	45/21	27/10	16/0

forest fires in British Columbia's history, which burned 17,000 hectares (42,007 acres) of Rocky Mountain forests. Significant forest fires also ravaged the park in 2017 and 2018. Parks Canada is using education to help visitors appreciate and understand that fires are a natural part of a forest's natural cycle, and necessary to regenerate the forest and maintain its flora and fauna biodiversity.

Kootenay National Park is still often used as a scenic route from Alberta to British Columbia to catch views of snowcapped peaks, glaciers, cascading waterfalls, icy-blue rivers, wide valleys, and wildlife galore. More often these days, however, it's becoming a go-to destination for visitors who want to experience the plentiful four-season outdoor activities that the park has to offer in an uncrowded and extremely pristine environment.

Planning

When to Go

Due to the surrounding mountain ranges and its location on the Continental Divide, Kootenay National Park experiences a milder climate than most of the other Canadian Rocky Mountain National parks. However, winters are still long and cold, with temperatures below freezing;

snow is common throughout the park starting in October. When traveling in the winter, be sure to check the road conditions before you go, as although the highways are plowed and maintained, a significant snowstorm can make driving hazardous or even result in temporary road closures. Note that there are no gas stations within the park, nor is there cell service.

Many of the higher altitude hikes can have snow on the trails until late June. Remember that mountain weather can be unpredictable, with possible significant weather shifts from day to day, or even within the same day. If you're hiking or on the water, you will need to be prepared with suitable clothing and equipment.

Campgrounds are open from mid-May through mid-October, but the park's busy season is the summer months, from June through August, and accommodations and campgrounds should be booked well in advance. Kootenay Park Lodge, the only hotel accommodation within the park, is open from mid-May through October, depending on the snowfall. If you're mostly interested in the hot springs experience, fall through spring are the best times, as summer temperatures in the south end of the park can get hot, and it's absolutely magical when the snow is falling on the pools.

FESTIVALS AND EVENTS

Canada Day. Admission to all national parks is free on Canada's birthday, July 1.

Columbia Valley Classics Autumn Show and Shine. Held each year on the third weekend in September in the village of Radium Hot Springs, this event draws in classic car enthusiasts from all over North America. *www.radiumhotsprings.com/about.*

Headbanger Festival. This weekend festival takes place in the fall, to coincide with the local bighorn sheep's annual rut. Aside from the high likelihood of seeing rams compete for the ewes' attention by charging each other with their horns, the event is full of interactive and educational workshops and presentations. *radium-hotsprings.ca/village-living/arts-culture/headbanger-festival.*

Wings Over the Rockies Nature Festival. Every May, the birding festival takes place in the Columbia Wetlands with workshops, field trips, interpretive walks, tours, and hikes. *www.wingsovertherockies.org.*

Getting Here and Around

Kootenay National Park is in the Canadian Rockies region of British Columbia. It borders Alberta and Banff National Park to the east, and Yoho National Park to the south. There are no townsites in the park; however, the village of Radium Hot springs is located at its southwest entrance.

AIR

The closest international airport is Calgary International Airport (YYC), 167 km (104 miles) to the east. Vancouver International Airport (YVR) is 828 km (514 miles) to the southwest of the park. Air connections may be made to Canadian Rockies International Airport (YXC) in Cranbrook, 145 km (90 miles) south of Radium Hot Springs.

CAR

There is no public transportation or train service in or to Kootenay National Park, so you must travel here by car. Vehicle rentals are available at Calgary or Vancouver airports, or at car-rental agencies in Banff, Lake Louise, or Cranbrook. Highway 93 through the park is maintained year-round, although closures occasionally occur due to poor weather conditions. Road conditions can be found at the Drive BC website (*www.drivebc.ca*). Note that there are no gas stations within the park.

Inspiration

Kootenay National Park, by Bob Hahn, is a colorful guide written in collaboration with The Friends of the Kootenay Park (a non-profit charitable society committed to enhancing the park experience for visitors) which provides information about the park's history, flora, and fauna.

Hiking Yoho, Kootenay, Glacier, & Mt. Revelstoke National Parks, by Michelle Gurney and Kathy Howe, details the best hikes in the park, including maps.

Wonderful Life: The Burgess Shale and the Nature of History. Stephen Jay Gould, a Harvard paleontologist, writes about what the Burgess shale teaches us about evolution and the nature of history.

Park Essentials

ACCESSIBILITY

The boardwalk trail around Olive Lake is the only park trail that is wheelchair accessible.

PARK FEES AND PERMITS

All prices in this chapter are in Canadian dollars, unless otherwise stated. A park entrance pass is C$10 per person or C$20 per vehicle (up to seven people) per day. A day pass for seniors is C$8.40 and children and youth under the age of 18 are free. An annual pass costs

Kootenay in One Day

Stop by the Kootenay National Park Visitor Centre in the village of Radium Hot Springs for brochures and maps that set out the park's highlights. Grab some items for a picnic lunch while in the village, then drive to the Olive Lake Day Use Area. Hike the easy ½-km (.3-mile) boardwalk loop around the lake and scan the clear green water for brook trout. Pull into the parking lot at the Kootenay Valley viewpoint and get out to take in the views of the Mitchell and Vermilion valleys. Continue north to the Vermilion Crossing day-use area to have your picnic lunch beside the gushing blue-green waters of the Verendrye Creek. The burn areas from the wildfires over the past decades become significant here, and you start to see a difference in the vegetation with more greenery and wildflowers visible. After lunch trek the easy Paint Pots Trail to see the uniquely colored mineral springs that hold an important history with the Indigenous people. Just down the highway stop at Marble Canyon trail to admire the shapes and colors of the deeply cut canyon as the creek thunders far below. Before you walk back to your vehicle, get a photo in the national parks' signature Big Red Chairs strategically placed with a stunning view down the valley. Now it's time to drive back to the village of Radium for dinner and a rewarding dip in the hot springs.

C$69.19 per adult, C$59.17 for a senior, or C$139.40 per family or group, so if you're staying a week or more in the park, you should go with this option.

Backcountry camping permits cost C$10 per person per day, and if on a horse, a grazing permit is C$1.94 per day. A fishing permit is C$9.80 per day. Campgrounds have various prices, and often you will need to pay for a separate fire and dumping permit.

The entrance fee for the Radium Hot Springs pools is C$10 for an adult, C$8.40 for a senior, and children and youth under the age of 18 are free.

PARK HOURS
The park is open every day year round. It is located in the Mountain Time Zone.

CELL PHONE RECEPTION
Cell service is unavailable in Kootenay National Park. When you enter the park from the south, just past the Radium Hot Springs, you will see a sign notifying you that you will be leaving cell service for the duration of the 94-km (58-mile) drive through the park. However, there are emergency phones available inside the park at various locations, which are clearly marked with highway signage.

Hotels

The only hotel accommodation option in Kootenay is Kootenay Park Lodge located at Vermilion Crossing, in the north-central section of the park. Here you'll find a historical wilderness lodge and log cabins which are only open from May until October. Dining is available in the lodge and some food and snack food options are available in the gift shop and convenience store. The store also sells maps and knowledgeable staff can provide information on the area.

Most visitors to the park stay in Banff, Lake Louise, or the nearby village of Radium Hot Springs, where many accommodation options are available, including luxury suites, hotels, numerous motels, and luxury glamping in off-the-grid yurts. There is also a gravel-road access wilderness resort located just over the park boundary in the southeast corner of the park.

The high season for accommodation is mid-June through mid-September and between Christmas and New Year's and rates will be higher in these periods. For lower rates, plan your travel through the shoulder seasons of spring and fall.

Hotel reviews have been shortened. For full information, visit Fodors.com.

Restaurants

There is only one dining and snack food option within the park itself which can be found at Kootenay Park Lodge. Most visitors to the park dine in the nearby village of Radium Hot Springs, where there are several options, ranging from fine dining to fast-food and food truck options. There is a strong European influence In Radium, especially Austrian, and even though the village has a population of only about 800, you will find two Austrian-style schnitzel restaurants. Many restaurants in Radium don't take reservations, but this is usually not an issue, and any wait times will generally be short. Many of the restaurants also offer take-out menus. As Radium is a vacation spot, casual dress is the norm.

Restaurant reviews have been shortened. For full information, visit Fodors. com.

HOTEL AND RESTAURANT PRICES

Hotel prices in the reviews are the lowest cost of a standard double room in high season. Restaurant prices in the reviews are the average cost of a main course at dinner, or if dinner is not served, at lunch.

What It Costs In Canadian Dollars

	$	$$	$$$	$$$$
RESTAURANTS				
	under C$25	C$25-C$30	C$31-C$35	over C$35
HOTELS				
	under C$250	C$250-C$300	C$301-C$350	over C$350

Tours

Babin Air
Charter a private scenic flight to get a bird's-eye view of the valleys, peaks, and glaciers in the park. Flights leave from Invermere Airport and planes can accommodate up to four passengers. ⊠ *Invermere Airport, Invermere* ☎ *250/342–3565* ⊕ *www.babinair.com* ✉ *From C$200 per person per hour.*

East Kootenay Mountain Guides
This operator offers rock climbing, mountaineering, scrambling, and backcountry ski tours with certified ACGM guides, both in Kootenay National Park and the other nearby mountain ranges in the region. ⊠ *Invermere Airport, Invermere* ☎ *250/341–1212* ⊕ *www.ekmountainguides.com* ✉ *From C$400.*

★ Playwest Mountain Experience
This company offers all-inclusive guided hikes into Kootenay National Park with professionally certified Association of Canadian Mountain Guides (ACMG), luxury transportation, freshly packed lunches, and small group sizes. ⊠ *Invermere, Invermere* ☎ *250/341–7283* ⊕ *playwest.ca/* ✉ *From C$79 person for a half day hike.*

Visitor Information

The Parks Canada visitor information center for Kootenay National Park is in the village of Radium, in the same office building as Tourism Radium. Note that this Parks Canada service is only

The current site of the Burgess Shale fossils in Kootenay wasn't discovered until 2012 at the base of the Stanley Glacier.

available seasonally (from mid-May until mid-October). Here you will be able to find everything you need to know about the park, like information brochures, permits, backcountry reservations, and get updates on weather, trail, and road conditions. Outside of these months, you can get park information from the person staffing the gatehouse at the park boundary, or direct questions to the Parks Canada National Information Centre (*888/773-8888*), which is open year-round.

The Tourism Radium office is open year-round (except Christmas Day, Boxing Day, and New Year's Day), and can provide information on dining options, accommodations, and tour operators, as well as community events and other important information. Both the Kootenay National Park and Tourism Radium have their own websites.

CONTACTS Radium Tourism. ✉ *7556 Main St. East, Radium Hot Springs* ☎ *250/347–9331* ⊕ *www.radiumhotsprings.com.*

In the Park

The north park boundary is 185 km (115 miles) west of Calgary and 41 km (15 miles) west of Banff. The south park boundary is 1½km (1 mile) north of the village of Radium, 145 km (90 miles) north of Cranbrook, and 828 km (515 miles) northeast of Vancouver.

The only amenities within the park are at Vermilion Crossing, which is 31 km (19 miles) from the north boundary and 64 km (40 miles) from the village of Radium. At Vermilion Crossing there is seasonal accommodation available from mid-May until mid-September, as well as a general store and information center. Dinner is available between 5 and 8 pm (during the summer months) at the Kootenay Park Lodge, the only place with meals available in the park.

◉ Sights

GEOLOGICAL FORMATIONS

Burgess Shale Fossils

NATURE SIGHT | A layer of rock deposits containing amazingly well-preserved fossil specimens, Burgess shale formations were first discovered in 1886 by a railway worker in nearby Yoho National Park. Subsequently in 1909, Smithsonian Institute paleontologist Charles Walcott started collecting and analyzing specimens. The current site at the base of the Stanley Glacier in Kootenay was not discovered until 2012 and contains fossils with clearly visible details of the bones and insides of creatures from the underwater ecosystem that existed for a short time after the first explosion of multicellular life on earth over 505 million years ago. The Burgess shale fossils are recognized as a UNESCO World Heritage Site and part of the larger Canadian Rocky Mountain Parks World Heritage Site. ⊠ *Stanley Glacier, Kootenay National Park* 🖼 *Free.*

Paint Pots

NATURE SIGHT | **FAMILY** | The paint pots are a geological formation formed by rich deposits of iron oxide that bubbles up from mineral springs, resulting in liquid with pigments ranging from red to orange to brown. The area is sacred to the Ktunaxa people, who have gathered the ochre liquid to color their clay and paints since ancient times. By the early 1900s, European settlers also started to mine the pigments for manufacturing paints. This mining stopped when the area became a park in 1920, but the paint pots continue to bubble the brightly colored pigments to the surface. ⊠ *Paint Pots, Hwy. 93, Kootenay National Park* 🖼 *Free.*

HISTORIC SIGHTS

Floe Lake Warden Patrol Cabin

HISTORIC SIGHT | Known for its spectacular setting on a glacier-cleared field close to the shores of Floe Lake, this cabin was constructed in 1960 along one of the patrol trails that formed part of the network established by the National Park Warden Service to enforce fish and game regulations and fight forest fires within the park boundaries. The one-story log structure on a lovely rubble stone foundation is a good example of the typical rustic architecture and design. ⊠ *Floe Lake, Kootenay National Park* 🖼 *Free.*

★ Radium Hot Springs

HISTORIC SIGHT | **FAMILY** | The first recorded visit to Radium Hot Springs was by Sir George Simpson, the governor of the Hudson Bay Company. Construction of cement bath pools and a bathhouse happened in 1914, but by 1922 the springs were expropriated and taken over by the park after it was formed in 1920. The subsequent U-shaped aquacourt that you see today was constructed between 1949 and 1951 and is claimed as the first major post-war building project in the western parks. Its construction helped the region gain international recognition as a spa destination and is the reason that the nearby village of Radium was constructed. The healing mineral-rich waters are still the main tourist attraction within the Kootenay National Park. Today there's a cooler swimming pool with a diving board and slides and a large hot pool for soaking. Although popular year-round, the hot springs are a truly magical experience when it's snowing. It's recommended that you bring a water bottle to stay hydrated, and swimsuits and towel rentals are available on-site. ⊠ *5420 Hwy. 93, Radium Hot Sprrings, Kootenay National Park* ✛ *3 km (1.8 miles) northeast of the village of Radium Hot Springs on Hwy. 93* ⊕ *www.hot-springs.ca/radium* 🖼 *C$7.46.*

PICNIC AREAS

Continental Divide Day Use Area

OTHER ATTRACTION | **FAMILY** | This day-use picnic area with accessible picnic tables and restrooms allows for the unique experience of standing on the dividing line between the Pacific and Atlantic watersheds. The trailhead for the

A geological formation, the bubbling iron oxide paint pots have been used since ancient times by the Ktunaxa people to decorate their clay vessels.

Fireweed Loop trails is here, a ½-km (.3-mile) and a 2-km (1.2-mile) loop trail with minimal elevation gain, where you can walk through a quiet forest and read the interpretive signs that tell the story of the region after the 1968 wildfire. ⊠ *Kootenay National Park east entrance, off Hwy. 93, Kootenay National Park* 🎟 *Free.*

Dolly Varden Day Use Area

OTHER ATTRACTION | As the only day-use area in the park with small playground climbing structures, if you have children, you won't want to drive past this rest area. There are also several interpretive signs explaining how Parks Canada is helping wildlife (including bears, wolves, cougars, and ungulates) stay safe with the construction of underpasses and fencing. Read the signs before walking through Dolly Varden underpass (there are nine of them in the park) that the animals use to cross the highway to access important habitat and connect with mates. The site also has picnic tables and toilets. ⊠ *Dolly Varden Day-Use Area, Kootenay National Park* 🎟 *Free.*

Numa Falls Day Use Area

OTHER ATTRACTION | This picnic site is located right next to rushing waterfalls; a very short walk brings you to the bridge that crosses in front of them. There are toilets and an abundance of picnic tables. ⊠ *Numa Falls, Hwy. 93, Kootenay National Park* 🎟 *Free.*

Olive Lake Day Use Area

OTHER ATTRACTION | As the name indicates, the strong green color of this lake is stunning. Immediately next to the parking lot, there are a shelter, picnic tables, and outhouses, with other tables scattered throughout the forest. A hike on the interpretive lakeshore boardwalk trail takes you through the forest around the lake, where you can often see brook trout leisurely swimming in the crystal-clear water. ⊠ *Olive Lake, Kootenay National Park* ✛ *Near Hwy. 93 at the top of Sinclair Pass.*

Vermilion Crossing Day Use Area

OTHER ATTRACTION | Located directly across from the Kootenay Park Lodge, this beautiful picnic area is just off the highway with ample parking, outhouses,

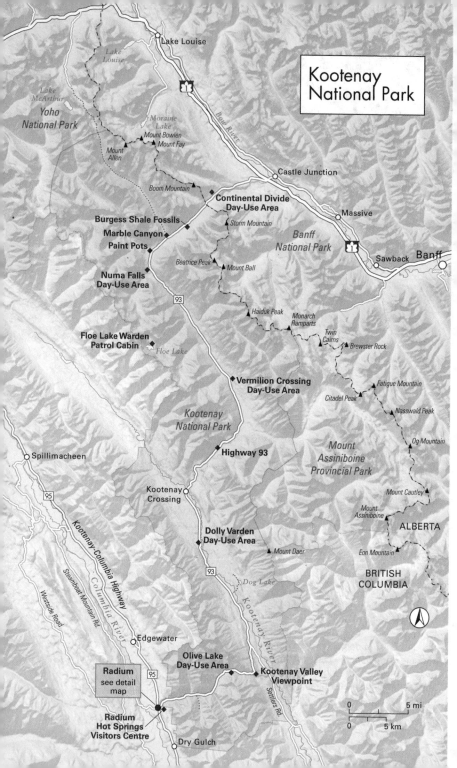

Kootenay National Park

Lake Louise

Lake Louise

Lake McArthur

Yoho National Park

Moraine Lake

Mount Bowlen
Mount Fay

Mount Allen

Boom Mountain

Castle Junction

Massive

Continental Divide Day-Use Area

Storm Mountain

Banff National Park

Sawback

Banff

Burgess Shale Fossils
Marble Canyon
Paint Pots

Beatrice Peak

Mount Ball

Numa Falls Day-Use Area

93

Haiduk Peak

Monarch Ramparts

Twin Cairns

Brewster Rock

Floe Lake Warden Patrol Cabin

Floe Lake

Fatigue Mountain

Citadel Peak

Nasswald Peak

Vermilion Crossing Day-Use Area

Kootenay National Park

Og Mountain

Mount Assiniboine Provincial Park

Spillimacheen

95

Highway 93

Mount Cautley

Kootenay Crossing

Mount Assiniboine

ALBERTA

Kootenay-Columbia Highway

Steamboat Mountain Rd.

Columbia River

Dolly Varden Day-Use Area

Mount Daer

Eon Mountain

BRITISH COLUMBIA

93

Dog Lake

Westside Road

Kootenay River

Edgewater

95

Olive Lake Day-Use Area

Kootenay Valley Viewpoint

Radium
see detail map

Senters Rd.

Radium Hot Springs Visitors Centre

Dry Gulch

0   5 mi

0   5 km

and tables placed along the scenic banks of the fast-flowing Vermilion River. ⊠ *Vermilion Crossing, Kootenay National Park.*

SCENIC DRIVES

Highway 93

SCENIC DRIVE | With only one highway through Kootenay National Park, many travelers choose this route as a scenic option to get from Banff to Windermere Valley. The park's terrain is rugged and natural with amazing views of the mountain ranges and the glacial blue rivers that often run alongside the highway. More so than the neighboring Canadian Rocky Mountain National Parks, wildfires have been significant in Kootenay, and, especially in the northern portion of the park, the large stands of burned trees allow a stark view of the mountain peaks and give a romantic, haunting feel to the terrain. These burn areas quickly grow over with lush greenery and wildflowers, providing an important ecosystem for several species of flora and fauna within the park. ⊠ *Hwy. 93, Kootenay National Park.*

SCENIC STOPS

Kootenay Valley Viewpoint

VIEWPOINT | This viewpoint arguably provides the best vistas in the entire park. Situated as you begin the ascent to Sinclair Pass (from the north), stop at this pull-out for stunning views up and down the Mitchell and Vermilion mountain ranges. ⊠ *Sinclair Pass, Kootenay National Park* ⌂ *Free.*

Marble Canyon

NATURE SIGHT | A definite highlight of Kootenay National Park, Marble Canyon trail starts immediately from the parking lot at the side of Highway 93. The short hike (1.4 km [.87 miles] with minimal elevation) takes you across seven bridges that criss-cross the deeply carved limestone gorge, as the torrential glacial blue waters rush downward far below. At the top of the trail, you can see a small waterfall on the river, right where it drops into the canyon. ⊠ *Marble Canyon, Kootenay National Park* ⌂ *Free.*

Big Red Chairs 👁

Need a place to rest? There are more than 200 red Adirondack chairs found throughout Parks Canada's national parks. Strategically placed in some of the parks' most beautiful spots, there are three in Kootenay National Park: Marble Canyon, Simpson River, and Radium Hot Pools (Juniper Trail). Some of the chairs are easy to find, while others require more effort, but all will provide that "wow" moment and you'll want to have your camera ready.

VISITOR CENTERS

Radium Hot Springs Visitor Centre

VISITOR CENTER | The visitor center is located in the village of Radium Hot Springs just outside the south entrance to the park. Parks Canada and the Tourism Radium office are housed within the same building. Parks Canada can provide you with all the information you need about the park, including camping, hiking, and interpretive programs. Tourism staff provides comprehensive information about restaurants, accommodations, and tour operators in the region. Of note is that the Tourism side is open all year long, while Parks Canada is only staffed during the summer months. ⊠ *7556 Main St. East, Radium Hot Springs, Radium* ☎ *250/347-9505* ⊕ *www.pc.gc.ca/en/pn-np/bc/kootenay.*

🍴 Restaurants

Kootenay Park Lodge Dining Room

$ | **CANADIAN** | The menu here isn't huge, but there's enough variety that there's something to appeal to everybody's palate. Simple, house-cooked meals made from locally sourced ingredients are served by friendly staff. **Known for:** down-home cooking; historical setting;

The historic cabins at Kootenay Park Lodge overlook Vermilion River.

in-house baking, including hamburger buns. $ *Average main: C$19* ✉ *Vermilion Crossing, Kootenay National Park* ☎ *250/434–9648* ⊕ *kootenayparklodge. com* ⊗ *Closed mid-Sept.–Mid-May. No lunch.*

☕ Coffee and Quick Bites

Kootenay Park Lodge General Store
$ | SANDWICHES | The lodge's general store sells fresh coffee, deli sandwiches (on house-made focaccia bread), baked goods and other snacks, as well as park maps, and unique souvenirs during the summer season (from mid-May to mid-September). **Known for:** only store in the park; house-baked goods; park maps and information. $ *Average main: C$10* ✉ *Vermilion Crossing, Kootenay National Park* ☎ *250/434–9648* ⊕ *kootenaypark- lodge.com* ⊗ *Closed mid-Sept.–Mid-May. No dinner.*

🛏 Hotels

Kootenay Park Lodge
$ | HOUSE | The setting for Kootenay Park Lodge is inspirational, perched next to a roaring creek on a forested property with a gorgeous hiking trail that circumnavigates the 2-hectare (5-acre) property with accommodations that include 10 heritage cabins and a newer duplex cabin. **Pros:** amazing scenery; on-site dining; convenient location to access all sights and activities in the park. **Cons:** only open during the summer season (mid-May–mid-Sept.); highway noise; plumbing and electrical need some updates. $ *Rooms from: C$175* ✉ *Vermilion Crossing, Kootenay National Park* ☎ *250/434–9648* ⊕ *www.kootenaypark- lodge.com* ⊗ *Closed mid-Sept.–Mid-May* ⦿ *No Meals* ⇌ *12 cabins.*

Talus Backcountry Lodge
$$$$ | ALL-INCLUSIVE | This is a back-to-the-basics wilderness lodge in the Canadian Rocky Mountains that specializes in first-class guided hiking in the summer and

backcountry skiing in the winter. **Pros:** excellent wilderness experience; knowledgeable guides; all-inclusive, with hearty meals. **Cons:** requires advance planning; must commit to a minimum of 3 nights; no Wi-Fi. [$] *Rooms from: C$425* ✉ *Talus Backcountry Lodge, Kootenay National Park* ☎ *403/609–0482* 🌐 *www.taluslodge.com* 🍴 *All-Inclusive* 🛏 *6 units.*

Activities

BIKING

Kootenay National Park has several good fire roads that make for perfect mountain-biking trails, although many are unmarked. Note that bikers must give way to hikers and horse riders sharing the trail, and always keep an eye out for bears and other wildlife.

Most trails are on the shorter side, under 13 km (8 miles), namely: the Dolly Varden Trail (between Kootenay Crossing and the Crooks Meadow Group Campground) that leads to an abandoned silver mine and the Kitsault River, the East Kootenay Trail from Pitts Creek to Daer Creek with access mid-trail at McLeod Meadows Picnic Area via Dog Lake Trail (note biking is not permitted on the Dog Lake Trail and there is no bridge over Daer Creek), Hector Gorge Trail (south trailhead 1.8 km (1.1 miles) north of Dolly Varden Picnic Area and a north trailhead 2 km (1.2 miles) north of Kootenay Crossing and West Kootenay Trail, which starts at Kootenay Crossing and ends at the northern park boundary.

Bikes and accessories can be rented from Far Out Adventure Hub (*see Multi-Sport Outfitters*) in the village of Radium.

Nipika Mountain Resort

BIKING | Fifty km (31 miles) of biking trails (that serve double duty for cross-country skiing in the winter) provide terrain for a range of abilities, from smooth and flowy for the beginner to technical and expert, with a stunning backdrop of the park's mountain peaks. There is a donation box for contributions to help cover the maintenance of the trails. The resort also offers multiday canoeing trips throughout the summer that are all-inclusive of accommodation, meals, and equipment. ✉ *9200 Settlers Rd., Kootenay National Park* ✣ *14 km (8.7 miles) off Hwy. 93* ☎ *250/342–6516, 877/647–4525 toll free* 🌐 *nipika.com.*

BIRD-WATCHING

Over 180 species of birds have been found in Kootenay National Park. Characteristic high-altitude birds include the white-tailed ptarmigan, water pipit, and rosy finch. Numerous species are found in the shrubby vegetation, especially along the west side of the Vermilion River Valley, where there is the greatest concentration of avalanche slopes.

The Valley View trail, a steep trail from the Redstreak Campground to the village of Radium Hot Springs is one of the best locations to observe birds in the dry Douglas Fir forest, where common species include blue grouse, common nighthawk, northern flicker, and the solitary vireo.

The Columbia Wetlands, one of the largest intact wetlands in North America and a hotspot of biodiversity, is home to over 260 species of birds, including raptors, songbirds, shorebirds, and waterfowl, is just past the park boundary by the village of Radium. Every year in May, the Wings Over the Rockies Bird Festival (*www.wingsovertherockies.org*), takes place here to help guests discover the world of birds and their ecosystems with special guests, workshops, field trips, interpretive walks, tours, and hikes.

BOATING AND RAFTING

Visitors can use non-motorized watercraft (any boat, canoe, kayak, raft, stand-up paddleboard, inflatable, or other type or class of vessel that is not motorized) in Kootenay as long as they have completed a self-certification permit and dropped it at a visitor center or with a Parks Canada

Did You Know?

A hike through Marble Canyon takes you across seven bridges that cross over rushing glacial blue waters.

staff or in a self-certification dropbox (available at some locations). This permit can be found online or at the Kootenay Park Gate, Redstreak Campground, or Kootenay Visitor Centre, when staffed. Equipment can be rented from Far Out Adventure Hub (see *Multi-Sport Outfitters*) in the village of Radium.

CAMPING

Parks Canada operates three scenic frontcountry campsites in Kootenay National Park: Marble Canyon, McLeod Meadows, and Redstreak; Crook's Meadow is available for groups only. Prices for a one-night stay range from C$21.97 for an unserviced site to C$39.04 for a 3-way services site (electricity, water, sewer). Campsite firepits within the park have an extra charge of C$8.80 per day. The only campground with serviced sites is Redstreak Campground, which is just minutes outside of the village of Radium. Redstreak has the longest season, from the beginning of May until mid-October, while the others have varying opening times beginning mid-June and running through sometime in September. Redstreak also offers oTENTik units (a cross between a cabin and a tent that's heated and sleeps up to six people on foam mattresses), with a private picnic table and fire pit (C$122.64 a night). *877/737–3783 reservation.pc.gc.ca.*

Marble Canyon Campground. Closer to the north end of the park, this campground is an excellent base to access park attractions like the Continental Divide; a Burgess Shale fossils guided hike to Stanley Glacier; and the popular Floe Lake, Paint Pots, and Marble Canyon (just across the highway) trails. Surrounded by a lush coniferous forest, the campground is at the confluence of the Vermilion River and the Haffner Creek. Although none of the campsites are serviced, the bathrooms do have running water and flush toilets and there is a sani-dump station. Firepits and firewood are available for a fee. There's no cell service. *C$21.97*

per night 88 km (55 miles) north of the village of Radium on Hwy. 93.

McLeod Meadows Campground. Nestled on the shores of the Kootenay River, with amazing views of the surrounding mountains, this is the perfect place to stay if you want easy access to both the park attractions and the amenities of Radium. The forested campground is next to some open meadows, ideal for wildlife viewing, and in the early summer they are full of wildflowers, including orchids. Campsites are not serviced, but bathrooms have running water and flush toilets and there is a sani-dump station. Firepits and firewood are available for a fee. There's no cell service. *C$21.97 per night 27 km (17 miles) north of the village of Radium on Hwy. 93.*

Redstreak Campground. This large campground is situated on a plateau in a lovely forested area at the very southwestern edge of the park. On the short drive from the campground to the nearby village of Radium, it's not unusual to see bighorn sheep next to the road. There are several hiking trails, including a 2.7-km (1.7-mile) trail to the Radium Hot Spring pools. Aside from the campsites, facilities include 10 oTENTik sites, kitchen shelters, showers, potable water, a sani-dump station, fire rings and firewood (for a fee), playgrounds, and safe food storage bins. Cell phone coverage is available. *Starting at C$28 per night 2½ km (1.6 miles) up Redstreak Rd. from the village of Radium.*

CANOEING AND KAYAKING

Canoeing and kayaking are allowed on the lakes and rivers in Kootenay National Park. You will want to ensure that you are well-versed with the terrain. Rivers can be fast flowing with waterfalls and chutes, as well as branching channels, sweepers, and occasional log jams, and rapids as high as Class IV, which can require long portages. Equipment can be rented from Far Out Adventure Hub (see *Multi-Sport Outfitters*) in the village of

Radium or you can join one of the guided multiday canoe trips offered by Nipika Mountain Resort (*see Biking*).

CROSS-COUNTRY SKIING

There are no groomed cross-country ski trails in the park. Note that not all summer hiking trails are safe for winter travel, so check with the National Parks Canada office for advice on safe options. Avalanche season in the park backcountry extends from November through June. Trails with a known hazard are identified with an avalanche symbol. Nipika Mountain Resort (*see Biking*), just past the park boundary, has groomed cross-country trails.

EDUCATIONAL PROGRAMS

Evening theater programs are offered at Redstreak Campground. At the campground there is also a challenge where you can search for five species at risk and discover why they like the restoration area that Parks Canada is implementing to restore open forest and grassland habitat. To learn more, pick up a booklet at the Kootenay Visitor Centre (in Radium), or at the campground kiosk. Guided hikes are offered in the national park. For more information, check at the visitor center or online (*www.pc.gc.ca/en/pn-np/bc/kootenay/activ/interp*).

Redstreak Campground Theatre

THEMED ENTERTAINMENT | FAMILY | During the summer months, there are nightly educational shows at 8 pm at the theatre at Redstreak Campground. ⊠ *Redstreak Campground, Redstreak Rd., Kootenay National Park* ☎ *877/737-3783* ⊕ *www.pc.gc.ca/en/pn-np/bc/kootenay/activ/camping*.

Stanley Glacier Guided Hike

GUIDED TOURS | Three times a week, Parks Canada Heritage Interpreters lead guided hikes to the recently discovered Burgess Shale fossil site. You will have hands-on learning about the fossils, the geology that lead to their formation, and the flora and fauna of the region, topped off with amazing alpine views. ⊠ *Stanley Glacier, Kootenay National Park* ⊹ *Stanley Glacier trailhead* ⊕ *www.pc.gc.ca/en/pn-np/bc/kootenay/activ/burgess/stanley* ⊠ *C$55*.

Xplorer Program and Club Parka

SELF-GUIDED TOURS | FAMILY | Xplorer Program, for children age 6 to 11, and Club Parka, for pre-schoolers, encourages kids to explore the world around them and the nature and history of the parks. The booklets for these programs are available from a park interpreter or at the Kootenay National Park visitor center. Parks Canada offers both of these programs year-round. Kids receive a prize when they finish their visit or booklet (whatever comes first). ⊠ *Kootenay Park Visitor Centre, Radium* ⊕ *www.pc.gc.ca/en/serapprocher-connect/xplorateurs-xplorers* ⊠ *Free*.

A Virtual Museum Tour 👁

Interested in learning about the origins of the famous Burgess Shale, which is part of the Canadian Rocky Mountain Parks World Heritage Site? The Virtual Museum of Canada has an online exhibit (*burgess-shale.rom.on.ca/en/index.php*) that explores the history and science behind the Burgess Shale, which preserves one of the world's first complex marine ecosystems. An animated tour takes you on a journey through the Cambrian seas that once occupied Kootenay National Park and neighboring Yoho National Park.

FISHING

Some fishing options in the park are to hike into Cobb Lake or Dog Lake, or find a spot on the Kootenay or Vermillion Rivers. A national park fishing permit (C$9.80; available at the visitor center) is required for any angling within the park. Children and youth under 16 may fish without a permit, if accompanied by a permit holder who is 16 years or older. In Kootenay National Park it is catch-and-release only and there is a ban of felt-soled wading boots.

HIKING
Self Propelled Adventures
HIKING & WALKING | This company offers guided hikes into the park. ⊠ *Golden, Golden* ☎ *250/344–8597* ⊕ *www.self-propelledadventures.ca/* ⊠ *From C$125/person; C$175 for single person.*

MULTI-SPORT OUTFITTERS
Columbia Cycle & Ski
SNOW SPORTS | Rent ski or snowboard packages here. They also offer bike rentals. ⊠ *375 Laurier St., Invermere* ☎ *250/342–6164* ⊕ *columbiacycle.ca/* ⊠ *From C$48/day for ski and snowboard packages.*

Far Out Adventure Hub
BIKING | Bicycle and accessory rentals are available for pick-up or delivery. Kayaks, stand-up paddleboards, and canoes are also available. ⊠ *7514 Main St. East, Radium* ☎ *778/527–5047, 844/376–0632 toll-free* ⊕ *www.rentfarout.com* ⊠ *From C$40 per day.*

Inside Edge Boutique & Sports
SNOW SPORTS | This is the place to buy active wear and camping supplies. They also have cross-country ski and snowshoes rentals for the winter. ⊠ *905 7th Ave., Invermere* ☎ *250/342–0402* ⊕ *insideedgeboutiqueandsports.com/.*

What's Nearby

The closest full-service towns to Kootenay National Park are Radium Hot Springs, British Columbia, which is just outside the park's southern boundary, and Banff, Alberta, which is 132 km (82 miles) northeast of the park.

Radium

Known as the gateway to Kootenay National Park, the tiny town (approximately 800 population) of Radium Hot Springs is located just outside the park's southern boundary. As the park has limited services, this is the place to base yourself during your visit as there is a wealth of accommodation and dining options.

Flanked by the Canadian Rocky Mountains to the east and the Columbia Valley and the Purcell Mountains to the west, this is also a four-season tourist destination, and outdoor activities include golfing, skiing, bird-watching, snowmobiling, hiking and biking, snowshoeing, and whitewater rafting.

⊙ Sights

Columbia Valley Wetlands
NATURE SIGHT | Over 180 km (112 miles) in length, the Columbia Valley Wetlands is one of the longest wetland regions in North America. It's also one of the few remaining intact portions of the "Pacific Flyway," a major north-south pathway for migratory birds in America, extending from Alaska to Patagonia. This protected ecosystem provides sanctuary for over 216 animal species, including birds, fish, reptiles, amphibians, and mammals, and more than 250 different migrating bird species. One of the best ways to explore the wetlands is via canoe or kayak. ⊠ *Canal Flats, Radium* ✛ *The Upper Columbia River, between Canal*

Canoeing is a great way to explore the more than 180 km (112 miles) of Columbia Valley Wetlands.

Flats and Golden ⊕ columbiavalley.com/columbia-river-wetlands/.

The Old Coach Trail

TRAIL | For beautiful views of the Columbia Valley Wetlands, a protected ecosystem with over 216 animal species, this 9-km (5.6-mile), mostly flat trail is the answer for both biking and hiking. ⊠ *Main St. West, Radium* ✛ *Access the trailhead 1 km (.6 miles) south of the village of Radium or at the south end of Main St. West right in the village.*

Radium Brewing

BREWERY | This is Radium's newest addition, and first craft brewery. Views of the nearby mountainscape from the large, raised deck, coupled with a cold frothy pint, are the perfect combo. The brewery doesn't serve food, but they encourage guests to bring in their own from the nearby snack shack, pizzeria, and other local eateries. ⊠ *7537 Main St. West, Radium* ⊕ *www.radiumbrewing.ca* ⊗ *Closed Tues.*

Sinclair Canyon Trail and Picnic Area

TRAIL | This lovely trail system follows a 2-km (1.2-mile) loop, crossing Sinclair Creek with two footbridges. Interpretive signs educate users on the environment and history of the area. There are picnic tables by the lower parking lot, and benches along the trail provide good rest stops to enjoy the scenery. ⊠ *Rotary Park, Radium* ✛ *There are three trailheads, one at Rotary Park, one off of Forsters Landing Road across from Revelstoke Avenue and one from the lower parking lot at Sinclair Creek.*

🍴 Restaurants

Conrad's Kitchen & Grill/Don Agave Cantina

$ | MEXICAN | The Prestige Radium Hot Springs Hotel houses both these restaurants, with the added bonus that you can order from either menu in both the cantina-style Don Agave Mexican-theme room with a long bar, or the large, airy Conrad's Kitchen & Grill side which has magnificent mountain views. Conrad's dinner menu features favorites like pizza, pasta, and burgers, while the Don Agave menu is all about Mexican food, from tacos to fajitas. **Known for:** freshly smashed guacamole; tequila drinks and Mexican dishes; weekend brunch. $ *Average main: C$22* ✉ *7493 Main St. West, Radium* ☎ *250/347-2340* ⊕ *www. prestigehotelsandresorts.com* ✆ *Closed Mon. No lunch.*

★ Helna's Stube

$$$ | **AUSTRIAN** | At this authentic Austrian cuisine restaurant, house specialties like schnitzel, rack of lamb, and venison cutlets are served by a welcoming, friendly staff. The decor is reminiscent of an Austrian schnitzel house—cozy, with warm wood accents and walls, plus a feature fireplace for cold winter nights. **Known for:** Austrian schnitzels; patio dining area; signature apple strudel. $ *Average main: C$35* ✉ *7547 Main St. West, Radium* ☎ *250/347-0047* ⊕ *helnas. com* ✆ *No lunch.*

Horsethief Creek Pub & Eatery

$ | **CONTEMPORARY** | This pub offers good eats in a lively atmosphere with indoor and outdoor seating. The extensive menu ranges from crowd-pleasing appetizers like stuffed bacon-wrapped prawns to Asian stir-fries and curries, soups, salads, burgers, and pub classics like Philly cheesesteak. **Known for:** daily menu specials (found on their Facebook page); build-your-own burger; live performance events. $ *Average main: C$21* ✉ *7538 Main St. East, Radium* ☎ *250/347-6400* ⊕ *horsethiefpub.ca/.*

Leo Burrito

$ | **MEXICAN** | With an eclectic assortment of knick-knacks on every brightly painted wall, this fun, fast-food taco place grabs your attention as soon as you walk through the door. Here you can also play a game of mini-golf, indulge your sweet tooth with some house-made gelato, or order a bag of popcorn from the popcorn machine. **Known for:** tacos and burritos; house-made slushy margaritas; fun family atmosphere. $ *Average main: C$13* ✉ *4951 Hwy. 93, Radium* ☎ *778/527-4999* ⊕ *leoburrito.com/.*

Old Salzburg Restaurant

$$ | **AUSTRIAN** | The classic alpine-chalet lodge exterior and interior of this restaurant provide the perfect backdrop to enjoy traditional Austrian dishes like schnitzels and bratwurst. The menu also includes a variety of steak dishes and a BC salmon filet. **Known for:** traditional Austrian cuisine; alpine chalet decor; family-friendly patio dining. $ *Average main: C$30* ✉ *4943 Hwy. 93, Radium* ☎ *250/347-6553* ⊕ *www.oldsalzburgrestaurant.com/* ✆ *No lunch.*

☕ Coffee and Quick Bites

Big Horn Cafe

$ | **CAFÉ** | So much more than a specialty coffee shop, Radium's only café offers a full selection of grab-and-go soup and sandwiches, breakfast burritos, quiche, and baked goods for breakfast and lunch. A bright, spacious room with high, open-duct industrial-style ceilings contrasts nicely with the warmth of the custom-made Douglas fir tabletops, plants throughout, and a wall filled with locally made BC products. **Known for:** grab-and-go breakfast and lunch; scones and cinnamon buns; breakfast special on weekends for C$9.95. $ *Average main: C$10* ✉ *7527 Main St. West, Radium* ☎ *778/527-5005* ⊕ *www.bighorncafe.net* ✆ *Closed December 24, 25, and 31st. No dinner.*

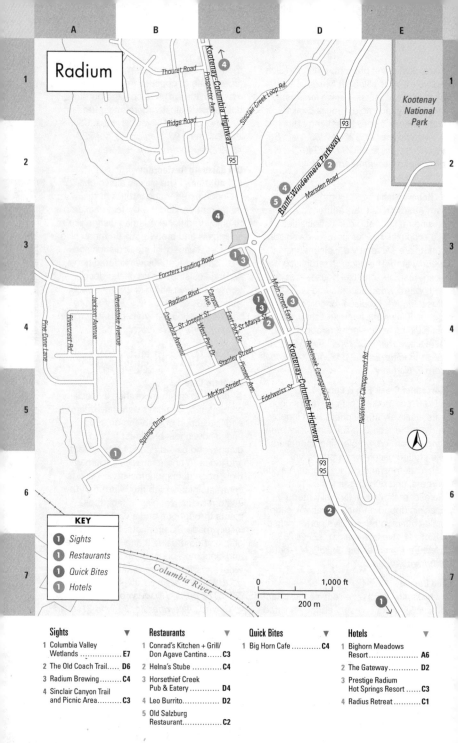

Radium

Kootenay National Park

KEY
- ● *Sights*
- ● *Restaurants*
- ● *Quick Bites*
- ● *Hotels*

Hotels

Bighorn Meadows Resort

$$ | RESORT | FAMILY | These luxury condo/town house vacation rentals are surrounded on three sides by the fairways of the prestigious Springs Golf Course. **Pros:** new, modern suites; 5-minute walk to downtown Radium; amenities, including a swimming pool in the summer and hot tubs in the winter. **Cons:** no restaurants on-site, except for the golf club house in the summer months; no underground parking; smaller guest rooms have very small windows, allowing for limited natural light. ⓢ *Rooms from: C$284* ✉ *10 Bighorn Blvd., Radium* ☎ *250/347–2323, 888/950–3045* ⊕ *www.bighornmeadows.com* ⓘ *No Meals* ⤳ *205 suites.*

The Gateway

$ | MOTEL | FAMILY | Just minutes down the road from the hot springs, this family-friendly motel with a cute alpine-style exterior offers kitchenettes and 1- and 2-bed accommodations. **Pros:** well-tended grounds; delicious free breakfast; good value. **Cons:** highway noise; no kitchens in some of the rooms; limited amenities. ⓢ *Rooms from: C$110* ✉ *4992 Hwy. 93, Radium* ☎ *250/347–9655, 800/838–4238* ⊕ *www.radiumgateway.com/* ⤳ *15 rooms* ⓘ *Free Breakfast.*

Prestige Radium Hot Springs Resort

$ | HOTEL | FAMILY | Now part of the Best Western Premier Collection, this property is conveniently located in downtown Radium, overlooking the Sinclair Canyon, with stunning views across the valley to the Columbia Mountain range. **Pros:** part of the trusted Best Western brand; on-site dining and spa services; indoor swimming pool. **Cons:** kitchen suites are limited; on-site dining is not open for lunch or through the afternoon hours; depending on room location, there can be highway noise. ⓢ *Rooms from: C$204* ✉ *7493 Main St. West, Radium* ☎ *250/347–2300, 800/780–7234* ⊕ *www.prestigehotelsandresorts.com* ⓘ *No Meals* ⤳ *85 rooms.*

Radius Retreat

$ | HOUSE | Offering return-to-nature style retreats, these year-round walk-in yurt rentals are on 1,000 acres of forested mountainside wilderness. **Pros:** each yurt is secluded; beautiful natural setting; environmentally friendly accommodation. **Cons:** you need to bring everything with you, including ice for your food; hike-in means you must be prepared to carry your stuff varying distances to your accommodation; outside of town center. ⓢ *Rooms from: C$172* ✉ *7058 Hwy. 95, Radium* ⊕ *www.radiusretreat.com* ⓘ *No Meals* ☞ *2-night minimum booking* ⤳ *8 suites.*

Activities

SKIING

Panorama Mountain Resort

SKIING & SNOWBOARDING | Only 35 kms (22 miles) south of Kootenay National Park, Panorama is one of Canada's largest ski resorts. It boasts 2,975 acres of terrain, 133 trails, and a vertical drop of 1,300 meters (4,265 feet). With 75% of the runs suitable for beginner and intermediate riders, the resort is perfect for the whole family. ✉ *2000 Panorama Dr., Invermere* ☎ *250/342–6941, 800/663–2929 toll-free* ⊕ *www.panoramaresort.com/* ◫ *From C$128 for day ticket.*

SPAS

Elevation Massage & Spa

SPAS | Located in the Prestige Radium Hot Springs Resort, this full-service spa offers treatments like facials, massage, body exfoliation, lash and brow care, and manicures/pedicures. ⊠ *7493 Main St. West, Radium* ☎ *778/527–5090* ⊕ *elevationmassage.ca/* ⊠ *From C$69 for a 30-minute massage.*

Juniper Heights Healing

SPAS | This spa offers massage and osteopathic therapy, as well as treatments with a European-flair, like lymphatic drainage and cold water bathing therapy. ⊠ *9444 Juniper Heights Rd., Radium* ☎ *780/235–5983* ⊕ *rwosteotherapy.janeapp.com/* ⊠ *From C$89 for a 50-minute massage.*

Chapter 9

JASPER NATIONAL PARK

By
Debbie Olsen

⛺ **Camping**
★★★★★

🛏 **Hotels**
★★★☆☆

🏃 **Activities**
★★★★★

👁 **Scenery**
★★★★★

👥 **Crowds**
★★☆☆☆

WELCOME TO JASPER NATIONAL PARK

TOP REASONS TO GO

★ **Larger than life:** Almost the size of the state of Connecticut, Jasper is the largest of the Canadian Rocky Mountain national parks, the world's second largest Dark Sky Preserve, and one of the world's largest protected mountain ecosystems.

★ **Spectacular scenery:** Jasper's scenery is rugged and mountainous. Within its boundaries are crystal-clear mountain lakes, thundering waterfalls, jagged mountain peaks, and ancient glaciers.

★ **Wonderful wildlife:** The Canadian Rockies provide a diverse habitat for 277 bird species and 69 species of mammals, including deer, elk, moose, sheep, goats, and bears.

★ **Columbia Icefield:** The largest icefield south of Alaska is also the hydrographic apex of North America, with water flowing to three different oceans from one point.

★ **Authentic mountain community:** The town of Jasper makes a great home base for forays into the park. With hotels, restaurants, and shopping, it has all the amenities you need.

Wild and untamed, the 11,228 square km (4,335 square miles) of Jasper National Park encompass rugged mountain terrain, natural hot springs, crystal-clear lakes and rivers, majestic waterfalls, ancient glaciers, and an abundance of wildlife.

1 Jasper Townsite. Shops, restaurants, nightclubs, and the main park information center are here. Just outside town are Lac Beauvert, Lake Annette, and Lake Edith, plus Old Fort Point and Jasper Skytram.

2 Yellowhead Corridor. The 2,859-km (1,777-mile) Trans-Canada Highway 16 (Yellowhead Highway) runs east–west across the nation, including through the foothills and main ranges of the Canadian Rockies. Highlights along the 366-km (227-mile) stretch southwest from Edmonton to Jasper include views of the Jasper Lake sand dunes (km 27) and Miette Hot Springs Road (km 58).

3 Maligne Valley. Highlights of this region include the Athabasca Valley Lookout (km 5.8), Maligne Canyon (km 7), Medicine Lake (km 20.7), and Maligne Lake (km 45), where the paved road ends.

4 Cavell Road. The road is just past the Astoria River bridge (Km 11.7) on Highway 93A, south of Jasper Townsite. Weather permitting, it's generally open from mid-June to mid-October. Highlights include Astoria Valley Viewpoint, Mount Edith Cavell, and Cavell Meadows.

5 Icefields Parkway. Highway 93, which travels 230 km (143 miles) between Jasper Townsite and Lake Louise in Banff National Park, is one of the world's most spectacular drives. Highlights in Jasper National Park include Athabasca Falls (km 31), Sunwapta Falls (km 55), Columbia Icefield (km 103), Sunwapta Pass (km 108), and the Weeping Wall (km 125).

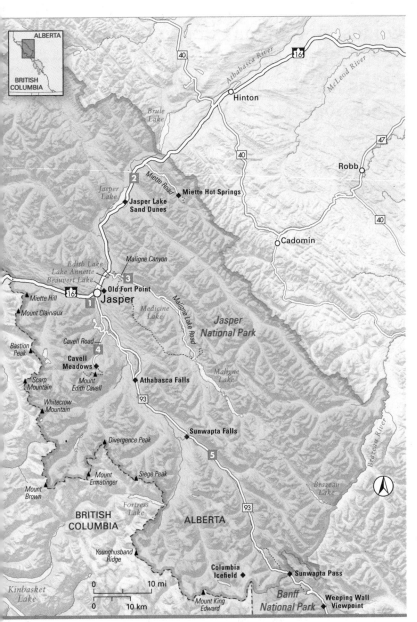

ALBERTA

BRITISH COLUMBIA

Athabasca River

40

16

Hinton

McLeod River

Brule Lake

40

47

Robb

Jasper Lake

2

Miette Road

Miette Hot Springs

Jasper Lake Sand Dunes

40

Cadomin

Edith Lake
Lake Annette
Beauvert Lake

Maligne Canyon

3

16

Old Fort Point

1

Jasper

Miette Hill

Medicine Lake

Maligne Lake Road

Jasper National Park

Mount Clairvaux

Bastion Peak

Cavell Road

4

Cavell Meadows

Maligne Lake

Scarp Mountain

Mount Edith Cavell

Athabasca Falls

Whitecrow Mountain

93

Brazeau River

Divergence Peak

Sunwapta Falls

5

Mount Ermatinger

Siege Peak

Brazeau Lake

Mount Brown

Fortress Lake

BRITISH COLUMBIA

ALBERTA

93

Younghusband Ridge

Kinbasket Lake

0   10 mi

0   10 km

Columbia Icefield

Sunwapta Pass

Mount King Edward

Banff National Park

Weeping Wall Viewpoint

Jagged peaks, crystal-clear lakes, and an astonishing variety of wildlife are just some of the wonders in the largest and wildest of Canada's Rocky Mountain parks. Situated along the eastern slopes of the Alberta Rockies and part of a collective UNESCO World Heritage Site, Jasper is also home to the largest icefield in the Canadian Rockies.

Since time immemorial, a diversity of Indigenous peoples lived on the land that is now known as Jasper National Park. Some groups lived in the area all year, while others passed through seasonally. Jasper National Park is located in Treaty 6 and Treaty 8 as well as the traditional lands of the Beaver, Cree, Ojibway, Secwépemc, Stoney, and Métis. Indigenous peoples protected the land and conserved its resources with the understanding that mankind must live in balance and harmony with the land and the ecosystems which they rely upon.

When the first Europeans arrived in the early 1800s, Indigenous people guided them through the mountains, and also worked as trappers, traders, and interpreters. It wasn't until the 1885 completion of the Canadian Pacific Railway and the creation of Canada's first national park (Banff), however, that interest in the region broadened. It was spurred along by the efforts of several adventurers, including British explorer J. Norman Collie, who first described the Columbia Icefield in 1898 and who traversed the area with his friends and fellow mountaineers, Hugh Stutfield and Herman Woolley—all of them guided by the legendary Banff outfitter, Bill Peyto. More than 30 peaks along the continental divide were named by Collie.

In 1907, the area became protected as Jasper National Forest and Indigenous people were forcibly removed and excluded from this part of their traditional territories. When the National Parks Act passed in 1930, Jasper officially achieved park status. Today, people visit for the same reasons they did in those early years: to see wildly beautiful landscapes, to spot wildlife, to gaze at the stars, and to simply experience nature.

In recent years, Parks Canada has made efforts to reconnect Indigenous Peoples with their traditional territory and to relate the Indigenous history of the land to visitors. In 2012, a dedicated cultural heritage space was created for Indigenous partners within Jasper National Park to use for reconnecting to the land, cultural learning, ceremony, and celebration.

Jasper National Park is unique in the world. The scenery is unparalleled and there are myriad activities that can be enjoyed throughout all four seasons. There are plentiful hotels, restaurants, and shops in the hub town of Jasper,

AVG. HIGH/LOW TEMPS. IN CELSIUS					
Jan.	Feb.	Mar.	Apr.	May	June
-4/-15	3/-11	6/-5	13/-4	19/1	19/6
July	Aug.	Sept.	Oct.	Nov.	Dec.
21/7	21/4	14/2	11/-2	3/-6	-2/-12

AVG. HIGH/LOW TEMPS IN FAHRENHEIT					
Jan.	Feb.	Mar.	Apr.	May	June
24/5	38/12	42/23	55/24	66/34	66/43
July	Aug.	Sept.	Oct.	Nov.	Dec.
70/44	70/40	58/35	52/29	38/21	29/10

and you have everything you need for a spectacular adventure in an unforgettable place.

Planning

When to Go

An old saying in the Canadian Rockies states, "If you don't like the weather, just wait a minute." The weather in Jasper National Park is unpredictable and ever changing, so you need to prepare for all sorts of conditions, especially when hiking. In summer, it can be hot enough for swimming in Lake Edith one day and icy cold the next. Temperatures in winter are usually well below freezing, but occasionally warm air blows in and causes snow and ice to melt. Temporary road closures may occur due to adverse weather conditions.

July and August are the peak travel visitation months—and the best time for hiking and viewing wildflowers. If you are traveling then, book accommodations well in advance, and expect to pay a bit more than at other times of the year.

FESTIVALS AND EVENTS

Canada Day. July 1, Canada's birthday, is celebrated with parades and other day-time events, fireworks at dusk, and free admission to all the country's national parks. ⊕ *www.jaspercanadaday.com*.

Jasper Dark Sky Festival. Held since 2011, when Jasper was declared an official Dark Sky Preserve (the world's second largest), this October event welcomes stargazing adventurers for nine days of outdoor activities, lectures, scientific presentations, photography workshops, food, and family-friendly fun. Science celebrities like astronaut Chris Hadfield often attend. ⊕ *jasperdarksky.travel*.

Jasper Heritage Rodeo. This rodeo that debuted in 1926 is the only one that takes place inside a Canadian national park. On the second weekend in August, cowboys compete in bull riding, bareback riding, barrel racing, and steer wrestling events. An evening dance and a pancake breakfast are also part of the festivities. ⊕ *www.jasperheritagerodeo.com*.

Jasper in January. Jasper's biggest winter celebration takes place during the last half of the month. A street festival, fire-works, wine tasting, live-music shows, and a chili cook-off are among the high-lights. ⊕ *jasperinjanuary.com*.

Jasper Pride. This four-day festival in March is the only gay pride festival in the Canadian Rockies. Activities include movie nights, canyon walks, ski events, music, and food. ⊕ *jasperpride.ca*.

Jasper in One Day

Stop by the **Jasper Information Centre** to get maps of the park and information about any special activities before driving up to **Mount Edith Cavell**. The 1-km (½-mile) trail from the parking lot leads to the base of an imposing cliff where you can see the stunning Angel Glacier. If you are feeling energetic, take the steep 8½-km (5.3-mile) trail that climbs up the valley to **Cavell Meadows**, which is carpeted with wildflowers from mid-July to mid-August. Return to Jasper Townsite for lunch. In the afternoon, make the one-hour drive southeast of the townsite to beautiful **Maligne Lake**, the second-largest glacier-fed lake in the world. Explore the shore, and travel out to **Spirit Island** on a 1½-hour guided boat tour with Maligne Lake Cruise. Return to the townsite for supper, and end your day with a free evening interpretive program at **Whistlers Outdoor Theatre**, at Whistlers Campground.

Parks Day. Celebrating the country's natural wonders, this event takes place on the third Saturday in July. There are activities for the whole family, a fair on the lawn in the middle of town, and free guided hikes to some of Jasper National Park's most interesting spots. ⊕ *www.friendsofjasper.com.*

Getting Here and Around

Jasper National Park is in the Canadian Rockies region of Alberta. It borders Banff National Park to the south, with Jasper Townsite located 287 km (178 miles) northwest of Banff Townsite.

AIR

The closest international airports are in Edmonton, 362 km (225 miles) to the northeast, and Calgary, 480 km (298 miles) to the southeast.

BUS

Brewster Sightseeing Excursions provides transportation between the Calgary and Edmonton airports and Jasper. SunDog Tours operates shuttles between Jasper and Edmonton, Hinton, Edson, Lake Louise, Banff, and Calgary.

CONTACTS Brewster Express. ☎ 800/760–6934 ⊕ *www.explorerockies.com.***SunDog Tours.** ☎ 888/786–3641 ⊕ *www.sundogtours.com.*

CAR

Driving is the easiest way to get from Edmonton or Calgary airport to Jasper. Car-rental agencies do business at both airports and in Jasper.

TRAIN

VIA Rail Canada provides train service three times a week from Edmonton, twice from Vancouver, and five times from Prince Rupert. Rocky Mountaineer offers luxury train journeys between Jasper and Vancouver twice per week. There is no train service from Calgary to Jasper.

CONTACTS Rocky Mountaineer. ☎ 877/460–3200 ⊕ *www.rockymountaineer.com.***VIA Rail Canada.** ☎ 888/842–7245 ⊕ *www.viarail.ca.*

Inspiration

Cougar's Crossing: A Canadian Historical Novel of Pioneer Adventure (second edition), by Lillian Ross, is based on the true-life story of Frank (Cougar) Wright, an early-1900s pioneer, and tells the story of a homesteading family's struggle to tame the Canadian wilderness.

Handbook of the Canadian Rockies, by Ben Gadd, offers a good overview of geology, history, climate, flora, fauna, and hiking trails in the Canadian Rockies, including Jasper National Park.

No Ordinary Woman: The Story of Mary Schaffer Warren, by Janice Sanford Beck, is a fascinating, bestselling biography of Mary Schaffer Warren (1861–1939), who embarked on a series of explorations of the Canadian Rockies at a time when it was considered improper for a woman to do so. She was an artist, photographer, writer, and explorer, and her most famous trips in 1907 and 1908 led to the rediscovery of Maligne Lake in Jasper National Park.

On Mountaintop Rock, by John McLay, provides a glimpse of what Jasper was like in 1954. It's a charming, humorous, young-adult novel that local students read as part of their curriculum.

River of No Return, a 1954 American Western directed by Otto Preminger and starring Robert Mitchum and Marilyn Monroe, was shot on location in Jasper and Banff. Monroe almost drowned when she slipped and fell into the icy waters of the Maligne River in Jasper.

Through Ice and Time, produced by Parks Canada, is the short film that plays at the Columbia Icefield Glacier Discovery Centre and is also available on YouTube.

Park Essentials

ACCESSIBILITY

Miette Hot Springs has wheelchair-accessible restrooms and changing rooms and a ramp descending to the pool with a railing. Several trails, scenic viewpoints, and day-use areas are paved. Whistlers Campground has two paved sites, each with adapted picnic tables and fireboxes. Ask for a key at the kiosk for wheelchair-accessible showers. Other campgrounds have various facilities for people with disabilities.

PARK FEES AND PERMITS

A park entrance pass is C$10 per person or C$20 maximum per vehicle per day. Larger buses and vans pay a group rate. An annual pass costs C$69.19 per adult or C$139.40 per family or group. Children ages 17 and under get into Canadian national parks for free. Park passes can be purchased at the park gates, on the Parks Canada website (*www.pc.gc.ca*) or on the Tourism Jasper website (*www. jasper.travel/parkpass/*).

Backcountry camping permits (C$10.02 per day) can be booked online (*pc.gc.ca/ bookjasperbackcountry*) or by phone (*877/737–3783*). Campfire permits (C$8.80 per day) can be purchased when reserving campgrounds and are not required for public firepits. A permit is required for fishing (C$9.80 per day).

PARK HOURS

The park is open 24/7 year-round. It is in the Mountain Time Zone.

AUTOMOBILE SERVICE STATIONS

AUTO REPAIRS Jasper Tire and Auto. ⊠ *18 Stan Wright Industrial, Jasper* ☎ *780/852–5561.*

GAS STATIONS Esso 7-Eleven. ⊠ *702 Connaught Dr., Jasper* ☎ *780/852–4721* ⊕ *www.esso.ca/en-ca/find-station/ jasper-ab-esso-200302439.***Jasper Petro Canada.** ⊠ *701 Connaught Dr., Jasper* ☎ *780/852–3114* ⊕ *www.petro-canada.ca/en/personal/gas-station-locations/701-connaught-drive-jasper.*

CELL PHONE RECEPTION

Cell phones generally work only in and around the town of Jasper.

EMERGENCIES

For all emergencies dial 911.

CONTACTS Cottage Medical Clinic. ⊠ *300 Miette Ave., Jasper* ☎ *780/852–4885.* **Seton General Hospital.** ⊠ *518 Robson St., Jasper* ☎ *780/852–3344* ⊕ *www. albertahealthservices.ca/findhealth/facility.aspx?id=1000410.*

Hotels

Accommodations in this area include luxury resorts, fine hotels, reasonably priced motels, rustic cabins, hostels, bed-and-breakfast inns, and backcountry lodges. Reserve your accommodations well ahead if traveling here in summer.

Hotel reviews have been shortened. For full information, visit Fodors.com.

Restaurants

Canadian Rocky Mountain cuisine focuses on sustainably grown, regionally sourced ingredients. Look for beef, lamb, venison, elk, bison, chicken, and trout from Alberta, as well as salmon from British Columbia. In addition to places serving local cuisine, Jasper also has Greek, Italian, Japanese, Korean, Mediterranean, Jamaican, and Indian restaurants.

Restaurant reviews have been shortened. For full information, visit Fodors.com.

What It Costs in Canadian Dollars			
$	$$	$$$	$$$$
RESTAURANTS			
under C$25	C$25–C$30	C$31–C$35	over C$35
HOTELS			
under C$250	C$250–C$300	C$301–C$350	over C$350

Tours

Alpine Club of Canada

The Alpine Club offers a variety of scheduled tours and courses like introduction to rock climbing, backcountry skiing, trekking, mountaineering, etc. You can also book backcountry huts through them, but you'll have to book those well in advance. Note that the huts are basic accommodations in high mountain locations that are typically difficult to hike to. ☎ 403/678–3200 ⊕ www.alpineclubof-canada.ca.

Jasper Adventure Centre

Guided hikes, ice walks on the Athabasca Glacier, tours of the Icefields Parkway, canoe and rafting outings, e-bike rentals, and train excursions are among the many adventures this outfitter organizes. ✉ 611 Patricia St., Jasper National Park ☎ 780/852–5595, 800/565–7547 ⊕ www.jasperadventurecentre.com ⛴ From C$69.

Jasper Food Tours

This company offers a variety of guided food outings, including the Downtown Foodie Tour, which visits four local restaurants for tastings. One of the most unique tours involves a hike up a mountain, a backcountry cooking lesson, and a delicious meal with an incredible view. ✉ Jasper ☎ 780/931–3287 ⊕ jasperfood-tours.com ⛴ From C$115.

Jasper Motorcycle Tours

Experience the Canadian Rockies in comfort on a thrilling chauffeured motorcycle tour. A professional driver can carry up to two guests per sidecar-style motorcycle. Rentals of Harley Davidson Heritage Classic and Harley Fatboy motorcycles are also available to licensed drivers. ✉ 610 Patricia St., Jasper ☎ 780/931–6100 ⊕ www.jaspermotorcycletours.com ⛴ From C$175.

Jasper Tour Company

Experience Jasper's wildlife and history from an Indigenous perspective. A Métis guide leads small-group sightseeing and wildlife tours for this company. ✉ Jasper ☎ 780/852–7070 ⊕ www.jaspertourcom-pany.com ⛴ From C$65.

Maligne Adventures

Wildlife-watching excursions, day hikes, river-rafting trips, and a hiker shuttle are among this company's offerings. ✉ 616 Patricia St., Jasper National Park ☎ 780/852–3331, 844/808–7177 ⊕ www.maligneadventures.com ⛴ From C$69.

Remote Helicopters Ltd.

Operating out of the Jasper-Hinton airport, this helicopter tour company is the closest to Jasper National Park and offers several different helicopter tours inside the park and in the area surrounding the park. Customized tours can also be arranged. ✉ *Jasper-Hinton Airport, Hinton ⊕ 19 km southwest of Hinton* ☎ *800/340-1179 toll-free* ⊕ *www. remotehelicopters.com/tours/jasper-hinton/* 🖥 *from C$199.*

Rockies Heli Canada

You can arrange heli-hiking, horseback riding, yoga, camping and snowshoeing adventures with this company whose flights depart from its Icefield Adventure Base, 43 km (27 miles) east of the Icefields Parkway on Highway 11 East in Bighorn Backcountry. ✉ *Rockies Heli Canada* ☎ *403/721–2100, 888/844–3514* ⊕ *www.rockiesheli.com* 🖥 *From C$278.*

Skyline Trail Rides

This company offers horse-assisted hiking on the Skyline Trail, midway along which is the Shovel Pass Lodge—also operated by this company. Book a stay at the lodge, and enjoy comfortable accommodations, delicious meals, and a pack horse to carry your gear. ✉ *Fairmont Jasper Park Lodge, Hwy. 16, Jasper National Park* ☎ *780/852–4215* ⊕ *www. skylinetrail.com* 🖥 *From C$280.*

SunDog Tour Co

Sightseeing and group coach excursions are this Jasper-based tour company's specialty. It also has nature walks, ice walks, wildlife tours, e-bike rentals and more, with some Jasper and Banff offerings conducted in partnership with the Jasper Adventure Centre. Sightseeing tours aboard antique, retractable-roof, "jammer" buses are among this company's newest offerings. ✉ *414 Connaught Dr., Jasper* ☎ *780/852–4056, 888/786–3641* ⊕ *www. sundogtours.com* 🖥 *From C$69.*

Walks and Talks Jasper

Most of this company's nature walks and hiking, snowshoe, icefield, and other tours last about three hours. ✉ *626 Connaught Dr., Jasper National Park* ☎ *780/852–4994, 888/242–3343* ⊕ *www. walksntalks.com* 🖥 *From C$70.*

Visitor Information

You will receive the Jasper Visitor Guide upon entry to the park. This has maps and good general information such as points of interest, safety messages, programs and events, camping information, and fees.

Stop in at the Jasper Information Centre to get the latest information about trail conditions and wildlife advisories. You can also pick up a more detailed Points of Interest map. The Day Hiking Guide contains maps and details about summer hiking. The Backcountry Visitor's Guide provides an overview of backcountry options. Parks Canada also produces guides for mountain biking, wildlife viewing, and other interests.

PARK CONTACT INFORMATION Jasper National Park. ☎ *780/852–6176* ⊕ *www. pc.gc.ca/jasper.***Tourism Jasper.** ✉ *414 Patricia St., Jasper* ☎ *780/852–6236* ⊕ *www.jasper.travel.*

Jasper Townsite

287 km (178 miles) northwest of the Banff Townsite, 413 km (257 miles) northwest of Calgary, 366 km (227 miles) southwest of Edmonton, 80 km (50 miles) southwest of Hinton.

Most visitors to Jasper National Park's administrative and commercial hub arrive from Calgary or Edmonton—both with international airports. Jasper Townsite has a permanent population of about 5,000 people as well as many amenities, including tour operators, hotels, restaurants, pubs, and nightclubs. Here you can also shop for anything from souvenirs to groceries to outdoor-adventure clothing and gear. Several lakes—Beauvert, Annette, Edith, Patricia, and Pyramid—in and around the town are beautiful spots to go for a paddle or just to take in the views. If you're just looking for a really great view, though, hike up to Old Fort Point or ride the Jasper Skytram up Whistlers Mountain.

◉ Sights

PICNIC AREAS

Lake Annette picnic area

OTHER ATTRACTION | FAMILY | Beside Lake Annette, this picnic area has shelters and tables. It's a favorite with families who come to the lake to swim. ⊠ *Near junction of Maligne Lake Rd. and Hwy. 16, Jasper National Park.*

Pyramid Lake Beach

BEACH | Pyramid Lake sits below Pyramid Mountain and is surrounded by gorgeous mountain views. There are picnic tables and fire rings on the beach and there's a large dock with chairs where you can sit and enjoy the views. Farther along the lake is the trail that leads to Pyramid Lake Island. ⊠ *Pyramid Lake Rd., Jasper National Park* ⊹ *6½ km (4 miles) north of townsite.*

SCENIC DRIVES

Pyramid Lake Road

SCENIC DRIVE | The drive from Jasper Townsite to Pyramid Lake is only 7 km (4 miles), but it's a pretty one that passes the equally stunning Patricia Lake (also worth a stop). At Pyramid Lake, you can rent a boat or take the short hike out to Pyramid Island. Be on the lookout for elk, bears, and other wildlife. ⊠ *Pyramid Lake Rd., Jasper.*

SCENIC STOPS

Jasper Planetarium

OBSERVATORY | Located at the Fairmont Jasper Park Lodge, this planetarium has the largest telescope in the Canadian Rockies. In its dome, an astronomy

expert conducts an interactive tour of the dark night sky—a fitting experience given that Jasper is the world's second largest Dark Sky Preserve. ⊠ *1 Old Lodge Rd., Jasper* ☎ *888/786–3641, 780/931–3275* ⊕ *www.jasperplanetarium.ca* ⊠ *From C$29.*

Jasper SkyTram

TRANSPORTATION | FAMILY | The tram whisks you 973 vertical meters (3,191 vertical feet) up the steep flank of Whistlers Mountain to an impressive overlook of the town and the surrounding mountains. The seven-minute ride deposits you above the tree line (be sure to bring warm clothes) at the upper station. From here, a 30- to 45-minute hike leads to the summit, which is 2,464 meters (8,085 feet) above sea level. Several unmarked trails lead through alpine meadows beyond. ⊠ *Whistlers Mountain Rd., Jasper National Park* ⊹ *3 km (2 miles) south of Jasper off Hwy. 93* ☎ *780/852–3093* ⊕ *www.jasperskytram.com* ⊠ *C$55 roundtrip* ⊘ *Closed Nov.–mid-Mar.*

Lac Beauvert

BODY OF WATER | Located beside The Fairmont Jasper Park Lodge, this glacier-fed lake is surrounded by majestic mountains. A scenic 4-km (2.5-mile) hiking trail surrounds the lake, and bicycles, canoes, kayaks, pedal boats, and stand-up paddleboards can be rented at The Boathouse (open during the summer season) on the lake's shore. ⊠ *Lac Beauvert, Jasper National Park.*

Lake Annette

BODY OF WATER | FAMILY | This lake is a favorite sandy beach and swimming area with locals. There is a dock, a playground, a grassy area for throwing a ball or frisbee, and a day-use area with picnic tables, fire rings, and grills. A paved interpretive trail loops around the lakeshore. Dogs are not allowed on the beach, but they are allowed in other areas. ⊠ *Lake Annette Day Use Area, Jasper National Park* ⊹ *From Jasper townsite, travel north on Hwy. 16, turn onto Maligne*

Two Brothers Totem Pole uses wildlife commonly found in Jasper to tell the story of the journey of two brothers to the Rockies.

Lake Rd., take Old Lodge Rd. and Lake Annette Rd. 🚇 *Free.*

Lake Edith

BODY OF WATER | This beautiful turquoise lake is surrounded by mountains. It has a quiet beach and a dock. The glacier-fed water is cold, but on a hot summer day, it's a popular spot to paddle and wade. You can get there by car or bike, or hiking. Dogs are not allowed on the beach area of the lake. ✉ *Lake Edith, Jasper National Park.*

Two Brothers Totem Pole

INDIGENOUS SIGHT | When Jasper National Park was established in 1907, the Indigenous people who had inhabited the land since time immemorial were forced to leave. Soon after that, a totem pole featuring a Raven was created by Haida carvers and erected for park tourists to enjoy. It stood for 94 years until it was removed and returned to the Haida people who live in an archipelago off British Columbia's west coast. In 2011, a new totem pole that had been carved by brothers Gwaii and Jaalen Edenshaw replaced the original one. The new totem pole uses imagery of wildlife commonly found in Jasper to tell the story of two brothers who travel from Haidi Gwaii to the Rockies. One of them stays while the other returns home. The totem pole is meant to suggest a connection between the Haida and the Indigenous Peoples of Jasper National Park. It is also intended to be viewed as a gift between Indigenous nations. ✉ *416 Connaught Dr., Jasper.*

TRAILS

Lake Annette Loop

TRAIL | **FAMILY** | This kid-friendly 2.4-km (1½-mile) loop trail with interpretive signage is paved and mostly level. It takes most people less than two hours to complete. Toilets are at two locations, and there is a shelter halfway around. *Easy.* ✉ *Lake Annette Rd., Jasper National Park* ⊹ *Trailhead: on right side of Lake Annette picnic area's western parking lot. From townsite take Hwy. 16 north to Maligne Lake Rd. east to Old Lodge Rd. and Lake Annette Rd.*

Sights ▼

1 Jasper Information Centre **E6**
2 Jasper Planetarium **G5**
3 Jasper SkyTram.......... **B9**
4 Lac Beauvert........... **G6**
5 Lake Annette **H3**
6 Lake Annette Loop...... **H3**
7 Lake Annette picnic area **H3**
8 Lake Edith............... **H2**
9 Old Fort Point Loop **H7**
10 Pyramid Lake Beach ... **D1**
11 Pyramid Lake Road...... **E4**
12 Tourism Jasper Visitor Information Centre **E6**
13 Two Brothers Totem Pole............... **E6**
14 Valley of the Five Lakes **F9**

Restaurants ▼

1 Alba Restaurant.......... **E7**
2 Evil Dave's Grill........... **E5**
3 Fiddle River **E6**
4 Jasper Brewing Company....... **E7**
5 Jasper Pizza Place **E6**
6 Kumama Bistro & Canteen **F5**
7 ORSO Trattoria **G5**
8 The Pines **E1**
9 The Raven Bistro **E6**
10 Summit Café............. **A9**
11 Syrahs Of Jasper **E6**

Quick Bites ▼

1 Bear's Paw Bakery **E6**
2 Sunhouse Cafe **E6**

Hotels ▼

1 Alpine Village............. **E8**
2 Bear Hill Lodge........... **E5**
3 The Crimson Jasper..... **E6**
4 Fairmont Jasper Park Lodge **G5**
5 Jasper Downtown Hostel **E6**
6 Jasper Inn & Suites **E5**
7 Mount Robson Inn...... **D7**
8 Park Place Inn **E7**
9 Patricia Lake Bungalows **D3**
10 Pine Bungalows **F5**
11 Pyramid Lake Resort **E1**
12 Tekarra Lodge............ **F8**

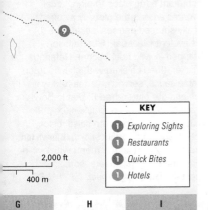

KEY

- ① Exploring Sights
- ① Restaurants
- ① Quick Bites
- ① Hotels

2,000 ft

400 m

Old Fort Point Loop

TRAIL | Shaped by glaciers, Old Fort Point is a bedrock knob that provides an excellent view of Jasper. It will take an hour or two to complete the 3½-km (2.2-mile) loop trail. A wide, easy path that begins behind the information kiosk leads to a very steep section of trail. It's common to see Rocky Mountain bighorn sheep, the provincial mammal of Alberta, from this trail. Along the way you'll pass Jasper National Park's oldest rock, but the real highlight is the view from the top. *Easy.* ✉ *Old Fort Point/Lac Beauvert access road, Jasper* ✣ *Trailhead: 1.6 km (1 mile) east of Jasper Townsite. Follow Hwy. 93A to Old Fort Point/Lac Beauvert access road. Turn left, cross the Athabasca River, and park in lot on right.*

Valley of the Five Lakes

TRAIL | FAMILY | It takes two to three hours to complete this family-friendly 4.2-km (2.3-mile) hike. Five small lakes are the highlight of the trip, which takes you through a lodgepole-pine forest, across the Wabasso Creek wetlands, and through a flowery meadow. Watch for birds, beavers, and other wildlife along the way. Turn this into a moderately difficult hike by continuing another 10 km (6.2 miles) to Old Fort Point. *Easy.* ✉ *Jasper National Park* ✣ *Trailhead: 9 km (5.6 miles) south of Jasper Townsite on Hwy. 93.*

VISITOR CENTERS

Jasper Information Centre

VISITOR CENTER | The 1914 cobblestone-and-timber structure that houses the Jasper Townsite visitor center is a superb example of rustic Canadian architecture. Parks Canada staffers here have information about trails, backcountry hiking, wildlife viewing, and interpretive programs. You can pick up maps, brochures, and other helpful materials as well. Parks Canada also operates an information desk at the Columbia Icefield Glacier Discovery Centre, 103 km (64 miles) south of Jasper Townsite. ✉ *500 Connaught Dr., Jasper National Park* ☎ *780/852–6176* 🌐 *www.pc.gc.ca/eng/pn-np/ab/jasper/visit.aspx* 🎟 *Free.*

Tourism Jasper Visitor Information Centre

VISITOR CENTER | Located in the Heritage Fire Hall, staff at the Tourism Jasper Visitor Information Centre can provide advice about tours, restaurants, and accommodations. The website also contains a vast amount of information about the park and the businesses and amenities within it. ✉ *414 Patricia St., Jasper* ☎ *403/852–6236* 🌐 *www.jasper.travel.*

🍴 Restaurants

Alba Restaurant

$$ | ITALIAN | This second-floor restaurant in downtown Jasper has an open kitchen, a terrace, and plenty of windows with lovely mountain views. The decor isn't fancy, but the food is excellent, featuring crispy calamari, beef carpaccio, baked meatballs, and house-made pasta dishes served alongside beef, salmon, lamb, and duck entrees. **Known for:** solid cocktail, wine, and beer selection; delicious, beautifully presented Italian fare; mountain views from window-side tables and outdoor terrace. [$] *Average main: C$28* ✉ *610 Patricia St., Jasper* ☎ *780/852–4002* 🌐 *albarestaurant.ca.*

Evil Dave's Grill

$ | CANADIAN | A funky atmosphere and an "evil"-inspired menu make this Jasper restaurant a fun place to dine. Local favorites among the globally inspired, locally sourced entrées include the Malevolent Meatloaf (Alberta bison wrapped in wild boar bacon), Nefarious Chicken (fried chicken with chili bourbon maple sauce, served on a toasted waffle), and the gluten-free El Diablo Bowl (marinated free-range chicken, chipotle sauce, jasmine rice, corn salsa, black beans, and corn tortilla sticks). **Known for:** chef's cut specials; fun menu with evil-inspired names; craft beers, sodas, and cocktails. [$] *Average main: C$21* ✉ *86*

Jasper's Dark Sky Preserve 👁

The Royal Astronomical Society in Canada designated Jasper National Park as a Dark Sky Preserve in 2011; a Dark Sky Preserve is an area where light pollution is limited and conditions are ideal for viewing the night sky. Jasper is the world's second-largest Dark Sky Preserve, as well as the world's largest accessible Dark Sky Preserve because there is a town within the limits of the preserve. It might seem odd that there's a town within the preserve's limits, but to achieve this status, the town had to take measures to ensure that light pollution from street lights and other artificial light sources wouldn't interfere with night sky viewing—you won't find any neon signs or upward facing street lamps here. The annual Jasper Dark Sky Festival (every October) has speakers and events that celebrate the night sky.

Connaught Dr., Jasper ☎ *780/852–3323* ⊕ *evildavesgrill.com* ⊙ *Closed Mon. and Tues. No lunch.*

Fiddle River

$$ | **CANADIAN** | This pine-finished, second-floor dining room has great views of the railway station, downtown Jasper, and the mountains. The Canadian seafood, wild game, and Alberta beef dishes are classic and delicious, and daily specials are noted on a chalkboard menu. **Known for:** wine list with noteworthy Canadian options; Alberta game meats; Atlantic Canada halibut and lobster. Ⓢ *Average main: C$30* ⊠ *620 Connaught Dr., Jasper* ☎ *780/852–3032* ⊕ *www. fiddleriverrestaurant.com* ⊙ *No lunch.*

Jasper Brewing Company

$ | **AMERICAN** | The park's only brewery is a fine stop for a beer and a burger, though the menu also features wings, poutine, nachos, fish-and-chips, and other pub fare in addition to well-made salads, steaks, and seafood dishes. Premium hops and natural mountain water go into the six signature beers brewed on site. **Known for:** local brews; great apres-ski (or -hike) spot; sports action on big-screen TVs. Ⓢ *Average main: C$23* ⊠ *624 Connaught Dr., Jasper* ☎ *780/852–4111* ⊕ *www.jasperbrewingco.ca.*

Jasper Pizza Place

$ | **PIZZA** | **FAMILY** | The views are amazing from the newly renovated rooftop patio of this popular downtown Jasper restaurant. Pizza from the wood-fired and traditional pizza ovens is the star attraction here, but you'll also find burgers, pastas, salads, and a broad selection of appetizers. **Known for:** popular local hangout; wood-fired and thick-crust pizza; amazing views from rooftop patio. Ⓢ *Average main:C$24* ⊠ *402 Connaught Dr., Jasper* ☎ *780/852–3225* ⊕ *www.jasperpizza.ca.*

Kumama Bistro & Canteen

$$ | **CAMBODIAN** | With wooden walls and ceilings, this small 28-seat restaurant has a cozy, homey feel. There isn't a lot of selection on the menu, but it's innovative and very well done like the Eggs in Purgatory (two soft poached eggs braised in spiced tomato beef ragu served with baguette) at breakfast or the braised bison pasta or pan-seared B.C. trout at dinner. **Known for:** delicious food, artfully displayed; small but innovative menu; popular for both breakfast and dinner. Ⓢ *Average main: C$27* ⊠ *Pine Bungalows Resort, 2 Cottonwood Creek Rd., Jasper* ☎ *780/852–8847* ⊕ *kumama.ca* ⊙ *Closed mid-Oct.–early Apr.*

Jasper National Park is the world's second largest Dark Sky Preserve.

ORSO Trattoria

$$$$ | ITALIAN | Get a taste of northern Italy while enjoying one of the best views in the Canadian Rockies; on warm evenings, you can dine on the heated patio while enjoying the vistas of Lac Beauvert, Mount Edith Cavell, and Whistlers Mountain. All the pastas are house-made, and the produce is locally sourced. **Known for:** family friendly; dishes that highlight the bounty of Canada; vegetarian and gluten-free options. $ *Average main: C$38* ⌧ *1 Old Lodge Rd., Jasper* ☎ *780/852–6090* ⊕ *www.fairmont.com/jasper/dining/orso-trattoria.*

The Pines

$$$ | CANADIAN | Beautiful views of Pyramid Lake and Pyramid Mountain are complimented by a menu of gourmet comfort food with a Canadian twist. Breakfast options include brioche French Toast with a haskap berry compote and maple syrup, while dinner offers a five-course carnivore tasting menu or a five-course vegetarian tasting menu; you can also order à la carte from the dinner menu. **Known for:** amazing views; delicious food; exceptional service. $ *Average main: C$31* ⌧ *Pyramid Lake Resort, Pyramid Lake Rd., Jasper National Park* ✛ *6 km (3.7 miles) north of Jasper townsite* ☎ *780/852–4900* ⊕ *www.banffjaspercollection.com/dining/the-pines.*

The Raven Bistro

$$$ | MEDITERRANEAN | This intimate dining space combines delicious with nutritious, using regionally sourced seafood, beef, pork, and game to create Mediterranean-fusion fare. Consider the seafood pot, with ingredients simmered in a broth made with tomatoes, coconut, and kaffir lime and served over sweet-potato noodles with Asian vegetables; just save room for the delicious chocolate-pecan tart (surprise … it's vegan and gluten-free!). **Known for:** great place to grab a cocktail; wholesome, inventive dishes; vegan and gluten-free options. $ *Average main: C$31* ⌧ *504 Patricia St., Jasper* ☎ *780/852–5151* ⊕ *theravenbistro.com.*

Summit Café

$ | **CANADIAN** | Near the top of Whistlers Mountain, spectacular views and casual dining are the big draws at this restaurant that is operated by the Jasper Skytram. It's a good spot for breakfast, lunch, or possibly an early dinner—depending on the season—as casual Canadian-style sandwiches, burgers, wraps, soups, and salads are served with beer, wine, coolers and soft drinks. **Known for:** healthy salads; incredible views; breakfast and lunch sandwiches. [$] *Average main: C$19* ✉ *Jasper Skytram, Jasper National Park* ✣ *Whistlers Rd, Jasper* ☎ *780/852–3093* 🌐 *www.jasperskytram.com* 🕒 *Closed Sept.–Mar.*

Syrahs of Jasper

$$$ | **CANADIAN** | At this intimate, 15-table, downtown dining room, chef Jason Munn's menus change regularly but always feature entrees made with fresh Alberta bison, Angus beef, and British Columbian seafood and creative sides like hand-made potato gnocchi or white-cheddar poutine. The restaurant's name is inspired by the Syrah (Shiraz) grape varietal, so you'll find a nice selection of wines (as well as craft beers) to pair with your meal. **Known for:** signature white-chocolate goat-cheese cake; reservations essential; house-made everything. [$] *Average main: C$33* ✉ *606 Patricia St., Jasper* ☎ *780/852–4559* 🌐 *syrahsofjasper.com.*

Coffee and Quick Bites

Bear's Paw Bakery

$ | **BAKERY** | This cozy downtown bakery is a great stop for a breakfast of tasty muffins and other confections or a lunch of sandwiches and wraps. Freshly baked cookies, cakes, and artisanal breads are also available, along with a wide variety of coffees and teas. **Known for:** local hangout with good coffee; white-chocolate and raspberry scones (as recommended by Oprah Winfrey's O magazine); gooey cinnamon rolls. [$] *Average main: C$9* ✉ *4 Pyramid Lake Rd, near Connaught Dr., Jasper* ☎ *780/852–3233* 🌐 *www.bearspawbakery.com* 🕒 *No dinner.*

Sunhouse Cafe

$ | **AUSTRALIAN** | If you want a taste of Australian café culture, this is the place, with six types of coffee, a variety of organic teas, kombucha, and healthy smoothies. The food menu includes breakfast sandwiches and bowls, sausage rolls, apple-cider loaf, and other nibbles. **Known for:** terrace with great views; possibly the best coffee in town; Australian-style café. [$] *Average main: C$14* ✉ *610 Patricia St., Jasper* ☎ *780/852–4742* 🌐 *sunhousejasper.com.*

Hotels

Alpine Village

$$ | **HOTEL** | **FAMILY** | Facing the Athabasca River, this family-owned cabin resort feels like it's miles away from civilization even though the drive to Jasper takes only three minutes. **Pros:** location across from the Athabasca River; well-kept property; kitchen suites. **Cons:** closed in winter; outside town; no in-room phones. [$] *Rooms from: C$250* ✉ *On Hwy. 93A N, 2½ km (1½ miles) southeast of Jasper Townsite, Jasper National Park* ☎ *780/852–3285, 780/852–1955* 🌐 *www.alpinevillagejasper.com* 🛏 *49 rooms* 🍴 *No Meals.*

Bear Hill Lodge

$ | **B&B/INN** | **FAMILY** | The grounds are well kept at this property, where accommodations range from small studio units to larger cabins that sleep up to five people and have fireplaces and kitchenettes. **Pros:** close to restaurants and shops; one of the few properties with cabins that are open in winter; some rooms and cabins are pet-friendly. **Cons:** no accessible rooms; some units do not have kitchens; no a/c. [$] *Rooms from: C$249* ✉ *100 Bonhomme St., Jasper* ☎ *780/852–3209* 🌐 *bearhilllodge.com* 🛏 *45 rooms* 🍴 *Free Breakfast.*

The Crimson Jasper
$$$$ | **HOTEL** | This modern-looking hotel has given Jasper a mild jolt of style: rooms here are well-equipped and contemporary, with splashes of crimson and other rich colors, and on-site amenities include a restaurant and lounge, indoor pool, hot tub, and fitness room. **Pros:** in-room mini-refrigerators and microwaves; one block from downtown; rooms have a/c (rare in Jasper). **Cons:** small elevator; small parking lot, some guests have to park on the street; across from train tracks. [$] *Rooms from: C$359* ✉ *200 Connaught Dr., Jasper* ☎ *780/852–3394, 780/852–3833, 866/606–6700* 🌐 *www.banffjaspercollection.com/hotels/the-crimson* 🛏 *99 rooms* 🍴 *No Meals.*

★ **Fairmont Jasper Park Lodge**
$$$$ | **RESORT** | **FAMILY** | On the shores of magnificent Lac Beauvert, 7 km (4½ miles) northeast of town, this lodge not only blends civilized luxury with rustic Canadian charm, but it also offers plenty of dining options and year-round recreational opportunities. **Pros:** top-notch dining; lots of recreation options; beautiful setting. **Cons:** on-site dining can be pricey; 10-minute drive to townsite; one of the park's most expensive accommodations. [$] *Rooms from: C$739* ✉ *1 Old Lodge Rd., Jasper National Park* ☎ *780/852–3301, 866/441–1414* 🌐 *www.fairmont.com/jasper* 🛏 *546 rooms* 🍴 *No Meals.*

Jasper Downtown Hostel
$ | **MOTEL** | Located in the heart of downtown Jasper, this hostel has dorm rooms with shared facilities as well as private rooms with en suite bathrooms that can accommodate up to five people. **Pros:** central location; economical price; kitchen facilities. **Cons:** institutional-style accommodation; less privacy in dorm rooms; basic amenitites. [$] *Rooms from: C$203* ✉ *400 Patricia St., Jasper* ☎ *780/852–2000* 🌐 *jasperdowntownhostel.ca* 🍴 *No Meals* 🛏 *13 private rooms, 45 dorm beds.*

Jasper Inn & Suites
$$ | **HOTEL** | Located right in Jasper Townsite, this family-owned hotel has many amenities, both on-site and within its 16 different types of rooms—some of which are newly renovated; have kitchenettes, fireplaces, and balconies; and are pet-friendly. **Pros:** great for skiiers (with lockers and a ski shuttle); close to restaurants and shops and away from train noise; indoor swimming pool, sauna, and steam room. **Cons:** there can be noise between some rooms; some rooms need updating; no a/c. [$] *Rooms from: C$279* ✉ *98 Geikie St., Jasper* ☎ *800/661–1933 toll-free, 780/852–4461* 🌐 *jasperinn.com* 🍴 *No Meals* 🛏 *146 rooms.*

Mount Robson Inn
$$ | **HOTEL** | A breakfast room with a hot and cold breakfast buffet is included with your stay at this hotel in downtown Jasper. **Pros:** 2 outdoor hot tubs with changing area; breakfast included; walking distance to downtown. **Cons:** small parking lot; no individual balconies; no elevator. [$] *Rooms from: C$299* ✉ *902 Connaught Dr., Jasper* ☎ *855/552–7737 toll-free* 🌐 *mountrobsoninn.com* 🍴 *Free Breakfast* 🛏 *81 rooms.*

Park Place Inn
$ | **B&B/INN** | This boutique hotel in the heart of Jasper has just 14 rooms, each uniquely decorated with vintage-style furnishings. **Pros:** heritage-style boutique inn; convenient location in town; underground parking. **Cons:** no pool; small property with few amenities; street noise a problem in some rooms. [$] *Rooms from: C$249* ✉ *623 Patricia St., Jasper* ☎ *780/852–9770, 866/852–9770* 🌐 *www.parkplaceinn.com* 🛏 *14 rooms* 🍴 *No Meals.*

Patricia Lake Bungalows
$$$ | **HOTEL** | **FAMILY** | With a setting on the shores of tranquil Patricia Lake, solitude is a highlight at this comfortable property, where well-tended grounds have a playground, a hot tub, fire-pit and barbecue

areas, and a boat dock where you can rent canoes and kayaks. **Pros:** well-tended grounds; good value; quiet location. **Cons:** limited Wi-Fi access; five-minute drive from town; some rooms are dated. $ *Rooms from: C$275* ✉ *Pyramid Lake Rd., Jasper National Park* ☎ *780/852–3560, 888/499–6848* 🌐 *www.patricialakebungalows.com* 🕓 *Closed mid-Oct.–Apr.* 🛏 *50 units* 🍴 *No Meals.*

Pine Bungalows

$$ | **B&B/INN** | **FAMILY** | On the banks of the Athabasca River, where wildlife sightings are common, this property is ideal for families thanks to its rustic cabins with outdoor barbecue grills and picnic tables. **Pros:** kitchen facilities in most cabins; beautiful natural setting; secluded cabins. **Cons:** weak Wi-Fi; no TV to speak of; 15-minute walk to town. $ *Rooms from: C$250* ✉ *2 Cottonwood Creek Rd., approximately 2 km (1 mile) east of Jasper, Jasper* ☎ *780/852–3491* 🌐 *www.pinebungalows.com* 🕓 *Closed mid-Oct.–Apr.* 🛏 *72 cabins* 🍴 *No Meals.*

Pyramid Lake Resort

$$$ | **RESORT** | The boathouse at this lakefront, chalet-style resort rents boats and bikes in summer and skates and snowshoes in winter; a nearby outfitter offers horseback riding or sleigh rides, depending the season. **Pros:** fireplaces in all rooms, kitchenettes in some rooms; beautiful location; on-site equipment rentals. **Cons:** no accessible rooms or bathrooms for people with disabilities; a little ways out of town; no a/c. $ *Rooms from: C$349* ✉ *Pyramid Lake Rd., Jasper National Park* ✣ *6 km (4 miles) north on Pyramid Lake Rd.* ☎ *800/541–9779 toll-free, 780/852–4900* 🌐 *www.banffjaspercollection.com/hotels/pyramid-lake-resort* 🍴 *No Meals* 🛏 *62 rooms.*

Tekarra Lodge

$$ | **B&B/INN** | This 1947 property has standard main-lodge hotel rooms, fireplace- and kitchen-equipped cabins, and some very interesting history: in 1953, when Marilyn Monroe was kicked out of the Jasper Park Lodge for dressing provocatively at dinner, she dined and stayed (in Cabin 37) here instead. **Pros:** some cabins have incredible mountain views; historic cabins that have been nicely updated; on-site restaurant serves breakfast and dinner and offers room service. **Cons:** no TVs or phones and limited Wi-Fi; 15-minute walk to townsite; closed in winter. $ *Rooms from: C$263* ✉ *Hwy. 93 A South, Jasper* ☎ *800/709–1827 toll-free, 780/852–4636* 🌐 *tekarralodge.com* 🕓 *Closed mid-Oct.–mid-May* 🍴 *No Meals* 🛏 *53 units.*

Yellowhead Corridor

366 km (227 miles) from Edmonton to Jasper Townsite.

A portion of the Trans-Canada Highway 16, also known as the Yellowhead Highway, runs southeast from Edmonton to Jasper, and highlights along it include more than just remarkable scenery. The Jasper Lake sand dunes are the only sand dunes in the Canadian Rockies, and the lake is a nice place to cool off in summer. Watch for bighorn sheep on this route and on the road that leads to Miette Hot Springs, the hottest in the Canadian Rockies. The nearby Sulphur Skyline Trail, not to be confused with the Skyline Trail, is renowned for its views.

Sights

SCENIC STOPS

Jasper Lake

BODY OF WATER | Jasper Lake is actually part of the Athabasca River—it's a point where the river broadens—and you can wade far out into its shallow waters and the beach is sandy. The scenery is beautiful, with lovely reflections on the water, and the Jasper Lake Sand Dunes, the Canadian Rockies' only sand dunes, are dunes nearby. ✉ *Jasper Lake, Jasper National Park* ✣ *30 km (19 miles) north of Jasper Townsite on Hwy. 16.*

Did You Know?

Considered a sacred place by the Stoney Nakoda First Nation, Spirit Island can only be reached by canoe, kayak, or boat cruise.

Jasper Lake Sand Dunes

NATURE SIGHT | The only sand dunes in the Canadian Rockies were formed during the last ice age and are constantly being reshaped by wind. They sit along the edge of Jasper Lake, which is not really a lake as it's part of the Athabasca River. The river widens and you can wade out very far on its sandy bottom; it's particularly popular on hot summer days. There's also a large roadside pullout and toilets. ✉ *Jasper Lake Sand Dunes, Jasper National Park.*

Miette Hot Springs

HOT SPRING | The naturally heated mineral waters here originate in three springs and are cooled to 40°C (104°F) to allow bathing in the two pools. At 15°C (59°F), the adjacent pool refreshingly negates all that heat. A short walk leads to the remnants of the original hot-springs facility, where several springs still pour hot sulfurous water into the nearby creek. Day passes and bathing-suit, locker, and towel rentals are available. ✉ *Miette Hot Springs Rd., off Hwy. 16, 58 km (36 miles) northeast of Jasper, Jasper National Park* ☎ *780/866–3939* 🌐 *www.parkscanada.gc.ca/hotsprings* 🎟 *C$7.21.*

TRAILS

Sulphur Skyline Trail

TRAIL | Some of the most beautiful panoramic views in Jasper can be enjoyed on this 8-km (5-mile) trail. From the summit, you can see the Fiddle River Valley, the foothills, the Miette Mountain Range, and the cliffs of Asher Ridge; it's particularly lovely in the autumn. This is a difficult hike with 700 meters (2,297 feet) of elevation gain, and the first 2.2 km (1.4 miles) is a steady climb across an open mountainside to Shuey Pass. Take the right branch when the trail splits and continue up the switchbacks to reach the summit. Along the way, you'll pass a large boulder that is a white quartzite glacial erratic that was moved there during the ice age. Near the top, the trail becomes very rocky and steep. Hiking poles can be helpful going up and coming down the steep sections. A soak in Miette Hot Springs is a great reward after the hike. *Moderate.* ■ **TIP→ Miette Road leading to the trailhead is closed from mid-October to mid-May.** ✉ *Miette Hot Springs, Miette Rd., Jasper National Park* ✣ *Trailhead: 16.6 km (10.3 miles) up Miette Rd. Trailhead is just past the passenger drop off loop for the Miette Hot Springs parking lot.*

🍴 Restaurants

★ Stone Peak

$$$$ | CANADIAN | Just outside the Jasper National Park gates, this gourmet farm-to-table restaurant is a hidden gem with wonderful mountain views. The menu changes often, but the food is always made from locally sourced, seasonal ingredients (try the bison burger) and everything, including the desserts, is prepared fresh on-site; there's also about two dozen beer choices including an extensive locally made craft beer list and a fun cocktail and martini menu. **Known for:** vegetarian, vegan, and gluten-free choices are available; award-winning wine list; excellent views from dining room and patio. [$] *Average main: C$36* ✉ *Overlander Mountain Lodge, Jasper National Park* ✣ *50 km (31 miles) east of Jasper townsite on Yellowhead Hwy.* ☎ *877/866–2330* 🌐 *www.overlander-mountainlodge.com/dining* 🕒 *Closed Jan.*

🛏 Hotels

Overlander Mountain Lodge

$$ | HOTEL | Just outside the western gate of Jasper National Park, this rustic log-hewn lodge has wonderful mountain views, an excellent gourmet restaurant, a lounge, and comfortable rooms. **Pros:** excellent on-site restaurant; lovely mountain views; secluded location. **Cons:** no TV, no phone, no a/c in lodge rooms; 50 km (31 miles) from Jasper townsite; poor cell signal. [$] *Rooms from: C$279*

⊠ *Overlander Mountain Lodge, Jasper National Park* ⊕ *50 km (31 miles) east of Jasper Townsite - just outside the park gates* ☎ *877/866–2330 toll free* ⊕ *www.overlandermountainlodge.com* ⊗ *Closed Jan.* ⦿ *No Meals* ⌑ *40 rooms.*

Maligne Valley

47 km (29 miles) from Jasper Townsite to Maligne Lake.

As you drive through the Maligne Valley, carved by glaciers and situated between two mountain ranges, you'll probably stop the car frequently, either to take in some of the park's most breathtaking scenery from a wayside viewpoint or to hike one of the wonderful trails. You'll definitely want to stop and explore the deep Maligne Canyon, which has fascinating geology and an intrepretive trail with six bridges that take you back and forth across the Maligne River. Although the canyon walk is beautiful in every season, in winter you can also opt for a guided ice walk on the frozen river to view the canyon from the bottom up. About halfway up Maligne Lake Road is the legendary Medicine Lake, which periodically drains into underground caves, disappearing entirely. You'll also pass burned swaths of forest, evidence of the 2015 Excelsior Fire—look at it as a chance to witness the renewing power of fire in a forest ecosystem. The valley is also one of the best spots in the park for seeing wildlife. Watch for bears, moose, elk, and bighorn sheep near—or even on—the road.

 Sights

PICNIC AREAS
Maligne Lake Picnic Area
OTHER ATTRACTION | There are picnic tables, toilets, canoes rentals, and places where you can buy sandwiches and other picnic fixings. ⊠ *Maligne Lake Rd., Jasper* ⊕ *From east end of Jasper Townsite, follow Hwy. 16 east for 3 km (2 miles) to*

right-hand turnoff for *Maligne Lake Rd.; take iron bridge across Athabasca River, go left at the fork, and then travel 48 km (27 miles) to Maligne Lake.*

Sixth Bridge Picnic Area
OTHER ATTRACTION | This picnic area sits beside the Maligne River near where it flows into the Athabasca River. There are no shelters, but it's a favorite with locals because of the scenic location. The Sixth Bridge is part of the Maligne Canyon hike; the hike from the Sixth Bridge to the First Bridge and the trailhead is 3.7 km (2.3 miles) one way. ⊠ *Off Maligne Lake Rd., Jasper National Park* ⊕ *2.2 km (1.3 miles) from Hwy. 16 junction.*

SCENIC DRIVES
★ Maligne Lake Road
SCENIC DRIVE | Scenic Maligne Lake Road was built along the glacier valley that runs between the Maligne and Elizabeth mountain ranges. Along the 44-km (27-mile) drive to Maligne Lake, you'll see spectacular mountain scenery, other blue lakes, and the fast-flowing Maligne River. Highlights along the way also include Maligne Canyon and Medicine Lake. This drive takes you through one of the best places to spot wildlife, especially at dusk and dawn. Look for elk, moose, bighorn sheep, white-tail deer, and grizzly and black bears. ⊠ *Maligne Lake Rd., Jasper* ⊕ *From Jasper Townsite, take the AB-16 (Yellowhead Hwy.) toward Edmonton. After 3 km (2 miles), turn right onto Maligne Lake Rd. It's 44 km (27 miles) to Maligne Lake.*

SCENIC STOPS
Maligne Canyon
NATURE SIGHT | The Maligne River cut 50 meters (165 feet) deep through limestone bedrock to create Maligne Canyon. An interpretive trail winds along the river, switching from side to side over six bridges as the canyon progressively deepens. The 4-km (2½-mile) trail along the canyon can be crowded, especially near the trailhead. Just off the path, you'll find the Maligne Canyon Wilderness

In the fall and winter, Medicine Lake almost completely disappears, garnering it the nickname of "The Disappearing Lake."

Kitchen and a nice gift shop. On a wintertime ice walk, the views from the bottom of the frozen canyon are spectacular.
✉ *Maligne Lake Rd., Jasper National Park* ⊹ *11 km (7 miles) south of Jasper.*

Maligne Lake

BODY OF WATER | The remarkably blue, 22-km-long (14-mile-long) Maligne Lake is one of the world's largest glacier-fed lakes and the largest natural lake in the Canadian Rockies. The lake was well known to Indigenous people who called it "Chaba Imne" (Beaver Lake). The first outsider known to see the lake was Henry MacLeod, a surveyor looking for a possible route for the Canadian Pacific Railway, in 1875. He was on a high mountain and saw the lake from a distance. In 1907, Mary Schäffer, a wealthy Quaker from Philadelphia, led an expedition to the lake following a map drawn by an Indigenous man named Samson Beaver. Schäffer was one of the few female explorers in the Canadian Rockies in the early part of the twentieth century. She wrote about her adventures and her popular book inspired others to travel to the Canadian Rockies. Schäffer returned to survey the lake a few years later for the Geographical Board of Canada. Her work was instrumental in getting the lake included as part of Jasper National Park. Spirit Island is one of the most famous sights in Maligne Lake. The island is 14-km (8.7 mile) up-lake and can be reached by canoe or kayak or on a boat cruise that is offered several times per day. If you choose to paddle to Spirit Island, you may wish to stay in one of the three backcountry campsites along the lake that can only be reached by canoe or kayak. There are many hiking trails near Maligne Lake including Opal Hills Loop and the epic Skyline Trail. Cycling, canoeing, kayaking, and fishing are also popular activities. Cross-country skiing and snowshoeing are favored activities in winter. Wildlife is abundant near the lake. Watch for moose, bears, deer, bighorn sheep, and the rare woodland caribou. At the head of the lake, you'll find three restaurants—Waffle Hut, Lakehouse Café, and The View—that serve everything

Plants and Wildlife in Jasper

In Jasper National Park, it's possible to wander through a field of wildflowers, hike through a thick subalpine forest, stand on a glacier, and revel in the solitude of the fragile alpine zone all in one day. An array of plants occupies the three life zones of montane, alpine, and subalpine. About 1,300 species of plants and 20,000 types of insects and spiders are part of the complex web of life in the Canadian Rockies.

Vast Wilderness

Jasper's vast wilderness is one of the few remaining places with a full range of carnivores, such as grizzly bears, black bears, wolves, coyotes, cougars, and wolverines. There are also large populations of elk, deer, woodland caribou, bighorn sheep, and mountain goats among the more than four dozen species of mammals, many of which are often seen right from the roadsides. Each year hundreds, of animals are killed along Jasper's highways, so it is vital to observe all speed limits and especially to slow down in special animal-sighting speed-zone areas. When hiking, keep your distance from wild animals, and make a lot of noise as a means of avoiding contact with large mammals, especially bears.

---

from waffles to gourmet cuisine. There's also a gift shop where you can buy essentials and souvenirs. ⊠ *Maligne Lake Rd., Jasper National Park* ✛ *44 km (27 miles) southeast of Jasper* ⊕ *www. malignelake.com.*

Medicine Lake

BODY OF WATER | Known as "The Disappearing Lake," Medicine Lake has long been a place of mystery and legend. In summer, it looks like a normal alpine lake, but in the fall and winter, the water almost completely disappears. Indigenous people had legends to explain the phenomenon, but scientists believe it's actually caused by an expansive underground cave system that the lake water is constantly draining through, and in the summer there is enough glacial runoff to maintain water levels. Once the runoff slows, the lake begins to drain and the surface dries up. The underground cave system runs 17 kilometers (11 miles) downstream and resurfaces below Maligne Canyon. It's common to see bald eagles, osprey, bears, moose, and bighorn sheep near this lake. ⊠ *Medicine Lake, Jasper National Park* ✛ *about 20 km (12 miles) southeast of Jasper Townsite.*

Spirit Island

ISLAND | Considered a sacred place by the Stoney Nakoda First Nation, this is one of the most famous scenic spots in the Canadian Rockies, perhaps because an image of the island, taken by Peter Gales, hung in Kodak's Colorama showcase in New York City's Grand Central Terminal in August and September of 1960. Since then, images of Spirit Island have been used in many advertisements and displays including Apple's 2014 campaign to launch their new iPad. Spirit Island lies 14-km (8.7 miles) up-lake and can only be reached by canoe or kayak or on a boat cruise that operates several times per day. For most of the year, Spirit Island isn't really an island; it's connected to the shore except in the early spring when water levels are high. ⊠ *Maligne Lake, Jasper National Park.*

TRAILS

Maligne Canyon

TRAIL | FAMILY | This 4.4-km (2.7-mile), one-way trail east of Jasper Townsite leads to views of the area's famous limestone gorge. Starting at the fifth of six bridges spanning the canyon, the winding trail gains about 100 meters (330 feet) in elevation. There's a waterfall at the head of the canyon. *Easy.* ⊠ *Maligne Lake Rd., Jasper* ✛ *Trailhead: Take Maligne Lake Rd. east to the fifth bridge, 10 km (6 miles) east of Jasper.*

Opal Hills Loop

TRAIL | Near Maligne Lake, this 8.2-km (5.1-mile) hike is very steep and takes from four to six hours to complete. There are excellent views of Maligne Valley, and many opportunities to observe wildlife, including moose and bears. Be sure to make noise as you hike, and keep your distance from the wildlife. During summer, you will spot many wildflowers along the trail. *Difficult.* ⊠ *Maligne Lake Rd., Jasper National Park* ✛ *Trailhead: Take Maligne Lake Rd., cross bridge, and continue 46 km (28½ miles) to the upper parking lot.*

Skyline Trail

TRAIL | The most popular backpacking route in Jasper meanders at or above the tree line for 44 km (27 miles) past some of the park's best scenery. Reservations are essential for backcountry campgrounds along the way. It is the highest trail in Jasper National Park, and weather can be unpredictable at this elevation, so plan accordingly. *Difficult.* ⊠ *Jasper National Park* ✛ *8 km south on the Maligne Lake Rd.* ☎ *780/852–6177.*

🍴 Restaurants

Maligne Canyon Wilderness Kitchen

$$ | **BARBECUE** | As it's right beside the Maligne Canyon trailhead, this restaurant is a convenient stop before or after a hike. There's a nice cocktail and craft beer menu, and you can relax on the patio around one of the gas-fire tables before or after dinner. **Known for:** apres-hike cocktails or a beer; smoke-house meats and classic sides; good-value "wilderness" platter. $ *Average main: C$25* ⊠ *Maligne Lake Rd., Jasper National Park* ✛ *Located at the trailhead*

for Maligne Canyon ☎ 866/606–6700 ⊕ www.banffjaspercollection.com/dining/ maligne-canyon-wilderness-kitchen.

The View

$$ | **CANADIAN** | This aptly named restaurant has an enormous glass-enclosed patio overlooking Maligne Lake, the largest lake in Jasper National Park. Locally sourced gourmet cuisine like the Alberta beef burger or the soy-marinated bison short ribs complement the breathtaking views; save room for the Banoffee tart. **Known for:** craft beer, craft cocktails, and Canadian wine; one of the best patio views in Canada; locally sourced gourmet Canadian flavors. $ *Average main: C$27* ⊠ *Maligne Lake Rd., Jasper National Park* ☎ *888/900–6272* ⊕ *www.banffjaspercollection.com/dining/the-view/* ⊗ *Closed early Oct.–late June.*

☕ Coffee and Quick Bites

Lake House Café

$$ | **AMERICAN** | This cafeteria-style café located just off Maligne Lake is a great spot to get a picnic to go or to relax and eat in. The regionally sourced menu has a wide variety of sandwiches, salads, soup, chili, hot dogs, and three different kinds of poutine, a Canadian indulgence made with potato wedges, cheese curds, and gravy. **Known for:** regionally sourced menu to go or to eat in; casual food including sandwiches, salads and three kinds of poutine; convenient location just off Maligne Lake. $ *Average main: C$18* ⊠ *Maligne Lake Boathouse, Maligne Lake Rd., Jasper National Park* ☎ *888/900–6272* ⊕ *www.banffjaspercollection.com/attractions/maligne-lake-cruise/dining/* ⊗ *Closed Oct.–May. No dinner.*

Waffle Hut

$ | **AMERICAN** | This is the place to start your day with a sweet or savory treat or to reward yourself after a day of hiking or paddling near Maligne Lake. You'll find everything from classic cinnamon sugar

Named after a British WWII nurse, Mount Edith Cavell is the Jasper area's highest mountain.

waffles to smoked salmon waffles, and there's a good coffee and tea menu. **Known for:** ice cream creations; delicious sweet and savory waffles; waffle on a stick. $ *Average main: C$11* ✉ *Maligne Lake Boat House, Maligne Lake Rd., Jasper National Park* ☎ *888/900–6272* ⊕ *www.banffjaspercollection.com/ attractions/maligne-lake-cruise/dining/* ⊙ *Closed Oct.–May. No dinner.*

Cavell Road

26.4 km (16.4 miles) southwest of Jasper Townsite.

The start of the road to the Mount Edith Cavell parking area is just past the Astoria River Bridge on Highway 93A. Highlights along the 14-km (8.6-mile) route, which is generally open from mid-May to mid-October, include the Astoria Valley Viewpoint, Mount Edith Cavell itself, Angel Glacier, and Cavelle Meadows. From the parking area, the Path of the Glacier Trail is a short hike to a beautiful viewpoint of

the mountains and the glacier. The hike to Cavell Meadows is much more difficult, but in July and August it has views of late-blooming wildflowers. You'll also find the trailhead for the Tonquin Valley multiday backpacking trek in this region of the park. (Note: tight switchbacks make this road unsuitable for trailers.)

⊙ Sights

SCENIC STOPS

Angel Glacier

NATURE SIGHT | Stretching along the north face of Mount Edith Cavell, this glacier was named because it looks like an angel with wings. The best views of the glacier can be seen on the Cavell Meadows Hike. ✉ *Angel Glacier, Jasper National Park.*

Astoria Valley Viewpoint

VIEWPOINT | This pull-off along Cavell Road offers views of the Astoria Valley and the glaciers at its head. ✉ *Cavell Rd., Jasper National Park.*

★ Mount Edith Cavell

MOUNTAIN | The Jasper area's highest mountain stands 3,363 meters (11,033 feet) tall. Showing its permanently snow-clad north face to the town, the peak was named for a World War I British nurse who stayed in Belgium to treat wounded Allied soldiers after Brussels fell to the Germans and was subsequently executed for helping prisoners of war escape. The mountain is arguably the most spectacular site in the park reachable by car. From Highway 93A, a narrow, winding 14½-km (9-mile) road (often closed mid-October to late June) leads to a parking lot at the mountain's base. Trailers aren't permitted on this road, but they can be left at a separate parking lot near the junction with 93A. Several scenic lookouts along the route offer access to trails leading up the Tonquin Valley, one of the premier backpacking areas. ⊠ *Off Hwy. 93A, Jasper National Park* ✛ *27 km (17 miles) south of Jasper.*

TRAILS

★ Cavell Meadows Loop

TRAIL | This moderately steep 8-km (5-mile) trail will take four to six hours. Into early summer the upper section is still covered in snow and not recommended, but from mid-July to mid-August you can enjoy the carpet of wildflowers. There's also an excellent view of the Angel Glacier. *Moderate.* ⊠ *Cavell Rd., Jasper National Park* ✛ *Trailhead: Take Cavell Rd. west 15 km (9.3 miles) to the parking lot at west end.*

★ Path of the Glacier Trail

TRAIL | FAMILY | This must-do 1.6-km (1-mile) trail only takes about an hour. The kid-friendly path, paved at the start, runs across a rocky landscape once covered in glacial ice. Eventually you come to a viewpoint overlooking Cavell Pond, which is fed by Cavell Glacier. Small icebergs often float in the water. The view across the valley takes in Angel Glacier, resting her wings between Mount Edith Cavell and Sorrow Peak. *Easy.* ⊠ *Cavell Rd.,*

Jasper National Park ✛ *Trailhead: at parking lot at west end of Cavell Rd.*

Tonquin Valley

TRAIL | Near Mount Edith Cavell, Tonquin Valley is a classic Canadian backpacking area. Its high mountain lakes bounded by steep rocky peaks known as the Ramparts, attract many hikers in summer and fall. *Difficult.* ⊠ *Tonquin Valley.*

🛏 Hotels

Tonquin-Amethyst Lake Lodge

$$$$ | ALL-INCLUSIVE | The lodge, operated by Tonquin Valley Adventures, is located on Amethyst Lake, surrounded by an abundance of wildlife, excellent hiking, and fantastic backcountry fishing. **Pros:** meals included; stunning location with amazing scenery; boat available for guest use. **Cons:** pit toilets; no electricity or running water in cabins; only reachable on foot, skis, or horseback. Ⓢ *Rooms from: C$500* ⊠ *Tonquin Valley, Jasper National Park* ☎ *780/852–1188* ⊕ *tonquinadventures.com* ⊘ *Closed Oct.–mid-Feb. and mid-Apr.– June* ⦿ *All-Inclusive* ⇆ *6 cabins.*

Tonquin Valley Backcountry Lodge

$$$$ | ALL-INCLUSIVE | Located on the shores of Amethyst Lake in the Tonquin Valley, this backcountry lodge has a central dining area where delicious house-cooked meals are served family-style—gluten-free meals can be arranged in advance—and accommodations are in private cabins that range in size from housing two to six people, but there is a central shower facility. **Pros:** boat and canoe available for guest use; beautiful scenery and wildlife viewing; breakfast, lunch, dinner, and snacks included. **Cons:** pit toilets; no Wi-Fi or cell signal; no electricity. Ⓢ *Rooms from: C$650* ⊠ *Tonquin Valley, Jasper National Park* ☎ *780/852–3909* ⊕ *www.tonquinvalley. com* ⊘ *Closed mid-Mar.–mid-July and mid-Sept.–mid-Feb.* ⦿ *All-Inclusive* ⇆ *6 cabins.*

Icefields Parkway

230 km (143 miles) south from Jasper Townsite to village of Lake Louise in Banff National Park.

Scenic drives skirt the base of glaciers, stunning lakes, and exceptional wildlife-viewing areas. In Jasper National Park, the 230-km (143-mile) Icefields Parkway (Highway 93) that connects Jasper with Banff provides access to the largest ice field in the North American Rockies and takes you to the very edge of treeless alpine tundra.

◉ Sights

PICNIC AREAS
Athabasca Day Use Site

OTHER ATTRACTION | This large area has a shelter and is ideal for family reunions because it can be reserved ahead for a fee of C$50. It has beautiful views of the river and mountains. ⊠ *Athabasca Day Use Site, Jasper National Park* ✛ *15 km (9 miles) from Jasper Townsite on Hwy. 16* ☎ *780/852–6176* ⊕ *www.pc.gc.ca/ jasper.*

SCENIC STOPS
Athabasca Falls

WATERFALL | At 23 meters (75 feet), these falls are not the highest in the Canadian Rockies, but they are the most powerful. The Athabasca River carries more water than any other in the Rocky Mountains, and all of it is funneled over this cascade and into a narrow gorge, creating a powerful surge. The falls are especially dramatic in late spring and early summer when the river is at its highest. Trails and overlooks provide good viewpoints. Do not climb past the guard rails: the rocks and vegetation are very slippery, and people have died trying to get a photo of themselves standing closer to the falls. ⊠ *Athabasca Falls, Jasper National Park* ✛ *31 km (19 miles) south of Jasper Townsite, 199 km (113 miles) north of Lake Louise.*

★ **Athabasca Glacier**

NATURE SIGHT | The glacier is a 7-km (4½-mile) tongue of ice flowing from the immense Columbia Icefield almost to the Icefields Parkway. A century ago, the ice flowed over the current location of the highway; signposts depict the gradual retreat of the ice since that time. Several other glaciers are visible from here; they all originate from the Columbia Icefield, a giant alpine lake of ice covering 325 square km (125 square miles). Its edge is visible from the highway. You can hike up to the toe of the glacier, but venturing farther without a trained guide is extremely dangerous because of hidden crevasses. **Athabasca Glacier Ice Walks** (*800/565–7547, www.icewalks.com*) conducts three-, five-, and six-hour guided walks costing from C$115. Reserve a space at the Columbia Icefield Glacier Discovery Centre or through **Jasper Adventure Centre** (*780/852–5595 or 800/565–7547, www. jasperadventurecentre.com*) in Jasper. You can also visit the **Glacier Skywalk,** a glass-floored lookout with incredible views. Tickets for this are also available at the Discovery Centre, as well as on line. ⊠ *Columbia Icefield Glacier Discovery Centre, Jasper National Park* ✛ *103 km (64 miles) south of Jasper Townsite, 127 km (79 miles) north of Lake Louise.*

Columbia Icefield Glacier Discovery Centre

VISITOR CENTER | Opposite the Athabasca Glacier, this facility houses interpretive exhibits, a gift shop, and cafeteria- and buffet-style dining facilities. It's also the place to book glacier treks or skywalk visits. The summer midday rush between 11 and 3 can be intense. The 32 rooms at the Glacier View Inn, on the center's second floor, are available from early May to mid-October. ⊠ *Columbia Icefield Glacier Discovery Centre, Jasper National Park* ✛ *103 km (64 miles) south of Jasper Townsite, 127 km (79 miles) north of Lake Louise* ☎ *877/423–7433* ⊕ *www. explorerockies.com* 🎫 *Free.*

Jackpine
Mountain

Mount Bess

Whiteshield
Mountain

Mount Phillips

Mumm Peak

Lynx Mountain

Jasper
National Park

Mount
Machray

Mount McCord

Razorback
Mountain

Caledonia Mountain

ALBERTA

O'Beirne
Mountain

Moose
Lake

Fraser River

16

5

Valemount

BRITISH
COLUMBIA

Miette Hill

Mount Clairvaux

Vista Peak

Bastion Peak

Tonquin
Valley

Angel
Glacier

Scarp Mountain

Whitecrow
Mountain

Kinbasket
Lake

N. Thompson River

5

Mount
Brown

Kinbasket
Lake

Jasper
National Park

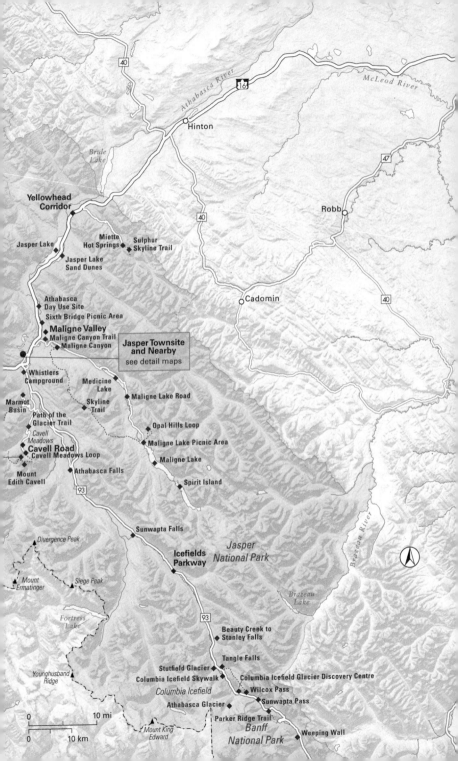

Columbia Icefield Skywalk

VIEWPOINT | This fully accessible, cliff-edge walkway leads to a glass-floor observation platform 280 meters (918 feet) above the Sunwapta Valley. From this vantage point, you'll get a bird's-eye view of the surrounding ice-capped mountain peaks and deep glacier-carved valleys of the Canadian Rockies. A five-minute shuttle from the Columbia Icefield Glacier Discovery Centre delivers you to the walkway. ■**TIP→ It's faster and less costly to book your Skywalk tickets in advance online.** ✉ *Columbia Icefield Glacier Discovery Centre, Jasper National Park* ✛ *103 km (64 miles) south of Jasper Townsite, 127 km (79 miles) north of Lake Louise* ☎ *866/506–0515, 403/762–6700* ⊕ *www.banffjaspercollection.com/ attractions/columbia-icefield-skywalk* 💳 *C$32.*

Stutfield Glacier

SCENIC DRIVE | This stunning glacier stretches down 914 meters (3,000 feet) of cliff face, forming a set of double icefalls visible from a roadside viewpoint. ✉ *Stutfield Glacier, Jasper National Park* ✛ *95 km (57 miles) south of Jasper Townsite, 135 km (86 miles) north of Lake Louise.*

Sunwapta Falls

WATERFALL | "Sunwapta" is the indigenous Stoney word for "turbulent river." There are two sets of falls at this site, but most people just see the Upper Falls, which are a short walk from the parking area. Though smaller than the Athabasca Falls to the north, they have a drop of about 18½ meters (60 feet) and are prettiest in the late spring when the spring melt is at its peak. The second set of falls is just a 3.2-km (2-mile) hike from the first set. ✉ *Sunwapta Falls Parking lot, Jasper National Park* ✛ *1 km (½ mile) west of Sunwapta Falls Rocky Mountain Lodge; 57 km (33 miles) south of Jasper Townsite, 173 km (110 miles) north of Lake Louise.*

Sunwapta Pass

SCENIC DRIVE | The Sunwapta Pass marks the boundary between Banff and Jasper National Parks about 108 km (67 miles) southeast of the town of Jasper and 122 km (76 miles) northwest of the Parkway's junction with the Trans-Canada Highway near Lake Louise. The pass is the second highest point on the Icefields Parkway. You'll know you're there when you see the sign marking the boundary between the two parks. ✉ *Sunwapta Pass, Jasper National Park.*

Tangle Falls

WATERFALL | This beautiful 48-meter (157 foot) tall multi-tiered waterfall lies right off the Icefields Parkway, but it's easy to miss. Look for a small roadside pullout north of the Glacier Skywalk. The waterfalls are across from the parking area. ✉ *Tangle Falls, Jasper National Park.*

Weeping Wall

WATERFALL | Located about 126 km (78 miles) southeast of Jasper on the Icefields Parkway, the Weeping Wall is a series of cascading waterfalls partway up the western base of Circus Mountain. This is truly a mountain that cries; its main waterfall is even called Teardrop. The best view of the wall is from the roadside pullout. Watch for ice climbers in winter. ✉ *Weeping Wall viewpoint, Jasper National Park* ✛ *126 km (78 miles) southeast of Jasper on the Icefields Pkwy.*

TRAILS

Beauty Creek to Stanley Falls

TRAIL | This short and relatively easy hike features a narrow canyon with eight waterfalls—the largest of which is Stanley Falls. The trailhead is not well marked. Look for a highway pullout 2 km south of Beauty Creek Hostel where two large culverts divert water under the highway. The return hike is about 3.9 km (2.4 miles) and has an elevation gain of about 139 meters (456 feet). The views are fantastic, but there are no safety barriers. Be careful to stay back from the canyon

The Weeping Wall is a series of cascading waterfalls at the western base of Circus Mountain which makes it look like it's crying.

edge and keep a tight hold on children, so they do not fall in. *Easy.* ✉ *Beauty Creek, Jasper National Park* ✣ *Trailhead: 86.3 km (53.6 miles) southeast of Jasper Townsite on the Icefields Pkwy. (Hwy. 93).*

Parker Ridge Trail

TRAIL | This short but steep 2½-km (1½-mile) trail takes you above the tree line. At the top of Parker Ridge, there's an excellent view of the Saskatchewan Glacier, where the Saskatchewan River begins. Snowbanks can persist into early summer, but by late July carpets of wildflowers cover the trail. Stay on the path to keep erosion to a minimum. *Moderate.* ✉ *Parker Ridge Trailhead, Jasper National Park* ✣ *Trailhead: 9 km (5½ miles) south of Columbia Icefield Glacier Discovery Centre.*

Wilcox Pass

TRAIL | Excellent views of the Athabasca Glacier are the highlight of this strenuous, 8-km (5-mile) hike near the Columbia Icefield Glacier Discovery Centre. This pass was originally used by explorers and First Nations people and is fairly steep. Keep an eye out for wildflowers and bighorn sheep. Be sure to dress in warm layers, because this pass can be snowy until late July. *Difficult.* ✉ *Wilcox Creek Campground, Jasper National Park* ✣ *Trailhead: off Wilcox Creek Campground entrance road, 3.1 km (2 miles) south of Columbia Icefield Glacier Discovery Centre.*

🛏 Hotels

Becker's Chalets

$ | **HOTEL** | Accommodations at this rustic, family-run, log-cabin resort—in a picturesque forest along the shores of the Athabasca River—range from inexpensive motel-style rooms to multiroom chalets that can sleep six to eight people and have fireplaces and fully equipped kitchens. **Pros:** on-site restaurant; secluded setting; cute log cabins. **Cons:** trains pass behind the property; 5-km (3-mile) drive into town; small bathrooms. [$] *Rooms from: C$210* ✉ *Icefields Pkwy. (Hwy. 93), Jasper National Park* ☎ *780/852–3779*

🌐 *www.beckerschalets.com* 🕓 *Closed mid-Oct.–May* 🛏 *118 rooms* 🍴 *No Meals.*

Glacier View Lodge

$$$$ | **HOTEL** | Breathtaking views of Athabasca Glacier and the towering peaks that surround it are the highlight of this hotel on the top floor of the Columbia Icefield Glacier Discovery Centre. **Pros:** special, all-inclusive experiences include guided tours and gourmet meals; in one of Jasper's most iconic spots with incredible views; recently renovated and luxurious. **Cons:** Columbia Icefields Discovery Centre gets very busy during the day; far from other services; restaurant and cafeteria are pricey. [$] *Rooms from: C$399* ✉ *Icefields Pkwy. (Hwy. 93), Jasper National Park* ✣ *104 km (65 miles) south of Jasper Townsite, 128 km (80 miles) north of Lake Louise* ☎ *888/770–6914* 🌐 *www.banffjaspercollection.com/hotels/glacier-view-lodge* 🕓 *Close mid-Oct.–mid-May* 🍴 *No Meals* 🛏 *32 rooms.*

🎟 Performing Arts

Whistlers Outdoor Theatre

READINGS/LECTURES | Interpretive programs are offered daily during the summer months at the theater at Whistlers Campground. Programs are appropriate for both children and adults, and a schedule of seminars and activities is available at the information center. Parks Canada interpreters use theater, singing, dancing, and storytelling to help visitors young and old learn more about the flora and fauna in the park. The theater is wheelchair accessible and has designated wheelchair seating. ✉ *Whistlers Campground, Hwy. 93, Jasper National Park* 🌐 *www.pc.gc.ca/en/pn-np/ab/jasper/activ/passez-stay/camping/whistlers* 🎫 *Free.*

Activities

BIKING

The Bench Bike Shop

BIKING | Rent mountain bikes and comfort bikes in summer and fat bikes in winter at this shop. The shop also offers bike repairs, tune ups, and cleaning, as well as bikes to purchase; the shop is an authorized Kona and Bomback Bikes dealer. ✉ *606 Patricia St., Jasper* ☎ *780/852–7768* 🌐 *www.thebenchbikeshop.com* 🎫 *from C$25.*

Jasper Adventure Centre/Sundog Tour Co.

BIKING | Rent premium Pedago brand e-bikes from this small shop in downtown Jasper. ✉ *611 Patricia St., Jasper* ☎ *780/852–4056* 🌐 *pedegoelectricbikes.ca/dealers/pedego-rentals-jasper/* 🎫 *from C$25.*

Journey Bike Guides Inc.

BIKING | Enjoy guided mountain bike tours and hassle-free bike rentals with this company. Tours can be customized to your ability and interest. Rentals can be dropped off and picked up at your hotel or campsite. ✉ *Jasper* ☎ *780/852–7738* 🌐 *journeybikeguides.com* 🎫 *from C$20.*

BIRD-WATCHING

An astonishing 277 species of birds make their home in the Canadian Rockies. The golden eagle migration, which occurs in spring and fall, is the park's biggest birding event. During migration period, you might see more than 200 eagles in one day at the east end of the park (Pocahontas area). At other times of year, the best place to observe birds is at Cottonwood Slough, along Pyramid Lake Road. This is a good place to spot Barrow's goldeneye, warblers, snipes, soras and hummingbirds, and red-necked grebe.

BOATING AND RAFTING

Boating in rowboats and canoes is allowed on most ponds and lakes. Boats with electric motors without on-board generators are allowed on most road-accessible lakes, but the use of gas-powered motors is restricted. It's wise to ask park staff about restrictions before launching your boat.

The rafting season runs from May through September. Children as young as six years of age can participate on some of the float trips. The Athabasca River has Class II white-water rapids; the Sunwapta and Fraser rivers have Class III rapids.

Boat House

BOATING | You can rent a kayak, paddle boat, canoe, bicycle and other equipment here. ⊠ 1 Old Lodge Rd., Jasper National Park ☎ 780/852–3301 ⊕ www.fairmont. com/jasper ⊠ From C$45.

Jasper Raft Tours

RAFTING | Take a half-day float trip on the Athabasca with Jasper Raft Tours. ⊠ 611 Patricia St, Jasper ☎ 780/852–2665, 888/553–5628 ⊕ www.jasperrafttours. com ⊠ From C$77.

Jasper's Whitewater Rafting Ltd.

RAFTING | This well-regarded outfit conducts half-day and shorter trips on the Athabasca and Sunwapta rivers. ⊠ 618 Connaught Dr., Jasper ☎ 780/852–7238, 800/557–7238 ⊕ www.whitewaterrafting-jasper.com ⊠ From C$74.

Maligne Lake Cruise

BOAT TOURS | This outfit's tours include a 90-minute interpretive cruise to Spirit Island, one of the most beautiful spots in the Canadian Rockies. The company also offers canoe rentals at Maligne Lake on a first-come, first-served basis, and it operates a restaurant at the lake's historic chalet. ⊠ Maligne Lake Cruise, Jasper National Park ☎ 866/606–6700 ⊕ www.malignelake.com ⊠ From C$69 ☞ Arrange tours/rentals at Maligne Lake tour building.

Maligne Rafting Adventures

WHITE-WATER RAFTING | This operator conducts rafting tours on the Athabasca, Sunwapta, and Fraser rivers. Day trips are available on Class II, III, and IV rapids. ⊠ 616 Patricia St., Jasper ☎ 780/852–3370, 844/808-7177 toll-free ⊕ www. raftjasper.com ⊠ From C$99.

Pyramid Lake Boat House

BOATING | Rent canoes, rowboats, kayaks, and paddleboats at the Pyramid Lake Resort. Bicycles and ice skates are also available to rent, depending on the season. ⊠ Pyramid Lake Resort, Pyramid Lake Rd., Jasper National Park ⊹ 5 km (3 miles) north of Jasper Townsite ☎ 866/606–6700 ⊕ www.banffjaspercol-lection.com/hotels/pyramid-lake-resort/ activities ⊠ From C$20.

Rocky Mountain River Guides

BOATING | The guides conduct trips for rafters of all experience levels. ⊠ 626 Connaught Dr., Jasper ☎ 780/852–3777 ⊕ www.rmriverguides.com ⊠ From C$74.

Wild Current Outfitters

CANOEING & ROWING | Guided canoe trips and canoe rentals are the specialty of this company, which also offers canoe camping and custom group adventures. ⊠ 611 Patricia St., Jasper ☎ 780/931–3662 ⊕ www.wildcurrentoutfitters.ca/ canoe ⊠ From C$55.

CAMPING

Parks Canada operates campgrounds in Jasper National Park that have a total of 1,772 available frontcountry sites during the peak season; there is winter camping at Wapiti Campground. Hook-up sites are available at Whistlers and Wapiti campgrounds only, so reserve a site in advance if you are traveling during the peak summer season. In addition to standard camping sites, Parks Canada operates oTENTiks. These accommodations are a cross between a cabin and a tent and sleep up to six people on foam mattresses. Call 780/852–6176 or 877/737–3783 or go online at *www.pccamping.ca* for reservations.

Columbia Icefield Campground. This rustic tent campground is near a creek and has great views of the Columbia Icefield. *Hwy. 93, 106 km (66 miles) south of Jasper Townsite.*

Honeymoon Lake Campground. Just down the road from Sunwapta Falls, this rustic campground has 35 sites on the shores of Honeymoon Lake, making it a good spot to bring a canoe and enjoy a peaceful paddle. *Hwy. 93, 35 km (22 miles) south of Jasper Townsite.*

Jonas Creek Campground. This small, primitive campground is in a quiet spot along a creek off the Icefields Parkway. Sites are first-come, first served. *Just off Icefields Pkwy., 75 km (47 miles) south of Jasper Townsite.*

Wabasso Campground. Families flock to this campground because of its playground and many amenities. *Hwy. 93A, 16 km (10 miles) south of Jasper Townsite.*

Wapiti Campground. Close to Jasper, this campground is near a number of good hiking trails. A portion of Wapiti remains open during the winter. *Hwy. 93, 5 km (3 miles) south of Jasper Townsite.*

Whistlers Campground. This campground is the largest and has the most amenities and the greatest variety of camping options. It's the number-one choice for families because of the on-site interpretive programs at Whistlers Outdoor Theatre. *Hwy. 93, 3 km (2 miles) south of Jasper Townsite.*

DIVING
Jasper Dive Adventures
DIVING & SNORKELING | During World War II, a top-secret British mission known as Project Habbakuk took place in Jasper National Park. The goal was to produce an unsinkable aircraft carrier from pykrete, a mixture of wood pulp and ice. When the project was canceled, the unfinished ship was sunk in Patricia Lake. This company offers guided diving tours of the remains. It also rents equipment and conducts scuba certification courses. ✉ *Patricia Lake, Jasper* ☎ *780/852–3560, 780/931-2277* ⊕ *www.jasperdiveadventures.com* ⬛ *From C$50.*

EDUCATIONAL PROGRAMS
Friends of Jasper National Park
OTHER ATTRACTION | FAMILY | This group's excellent summer offerings include a junior naturalist program, birding tours, hiking tours, and historical walks. At the information center shop, you can borrow a Friends hiking kit with binoculars, maps, and first-aid and other materials. ✉ *Jasper Information Centre, 500 Connaught Dr., Jasper National Park* ☎ *780/852–4767* ⊕ *www.friendsofjasper.com* ⬛ *Free.*

Parks Canada Interpretive Programs
OTHER ATTRACTION | FAMILY | Park interpretive activities include campground singalongs, wildlife presentations, Indigenous programs, and guided hikes. Many events take place at Whistlers Outdoor Theatre at the Whistlers Campground. ✉ *Whistlers Campground, Whistlers Rd., Jasper* ☎ *780/852–6176* ⊕ *www.pc.gc.ca/eng/pn-np/ab/jasper/activ.aspx* ⬛ *Free.*

FISHING
Currie's Guiding
FISHING | This outfitter offers guided half- and full-day fishing trips as well as boat rentals. It can also arrange backcountry-camping excursions ✉ *404 Connaught Dr., Jasper* ☎ *780/852–5650* ⊕ *www.curriesguiding.com* ⬛ *From C$240.*

On-Line Sport & Tackle
FISHING | Stop in to arrange a guided fishing trip or a fly-fishing lesson. You can also buy tackle or rent boats and fishing gear here. ✉ *600 Patricia St., Jasper* ☎ *780/852–3630, 888/652–3630 toll-free* ⊕ *www.fishonlinejasper.com* ⬛ *From C$249 for half-day trip.*

GOLF

★ Fairmont Jasper Park Lodge

GOLF | Stanley Thompson designed the championship green at this upscale resort and it has consistently been ranked as one of the best places to golf in Canada. Don't be surprised if you see bears and other wildlife on the course. Packages that include accommodations and golfing can be found on the website. ⊠ *1 Lodge Rd., Jasper National Park* ☎ *780/852–6090* ⊕ *www.fairmont.com/jasper* ⌨ *C$225* ⅃. *18 holes, 6663 yards, par 71.*

HIKING

Long before Jasper was established as a national park, a vast network of trails provided an essential passageway for wildlife, First Nations people, explorers, and fur traders. Nearly 1,000 km (621 miles) of hiking trails in Jasper provide an opportunity to truly experience wilderness, and hardcore backpackers will find multiday loops of more than 160 km (100 miles). The trails at Mount Edith Cavell and Maligne Canyon should not be missed.

A few of these trails are restricted to pedestrians, but hikers, mountain bikers, and equestrian users may share most of them. Several paved trails are suitable for wheelchairs and strollers, while others are rugged backcountry trails designed for backpacking trips. Bathrooms can be found along the most popular day-use trails. You might see elk, bighorn sheep, moose, bears, and mountain goats along the way. It is never a good idea to surprise a large animal such as an elk or bear, so make plenty of noise as you go along, avoid hiking alone, stick to designated trails, and carry bear spray and know how to use it.

Jasper's backcountry is some of the wildest and most pristine of any mountain park in the world. Check at the visitor center for information about the hundreds of hiking and mountain-biking trails and the overnight camping quotas on the Skyline and Tonquin Valley trails.

Canadian Skyline Adventures

HIKING & WALKING | Hire an experienced guide to take you to the most scenic places in Jasper National Park, including the world-famous Skyline Trail. Guides can also take you on an epic back-country hiking trip. ⊠ *Hwy. 16, Jasper* ☎ *780/883–0465* ⊕ *www.canadianskylineadventures.com* ⌨ *From C$55.*

Jasper Hikes and Tours

HIKING & WALKING | This outfitter offers guided hikes, rock climbing excursions, wildlife tours, and Maligne Canyon ice walks. ⊠ *Box 2474, Jasper* ☎ *780/931–4453* ⊕ *jasperhikesandtours.ca* ⌨ *From C$70.*

HORSEBACK RIDING

Several outfitters offer one-hour, half-day, full-day, and multiday guided trips within the park. Participants must be at least age six to join a riding trip, but pony rides are available for younger children. It's wise to make your reservations well ahead during July and August and for multiday journeys. Contact the Cottonwood Corral Association (780/852–3121) about horse boarding.

Jasper Riding Stables and Outfitters

HORSEBACK RIDING | These stables offer rides and full-day excursions into the hills overlooking Jasper; there are also carriage rides and winter sleigh rides. ⊠ *Pyramid Resort, Pyramid Lake Rd., Jasper National Park* ☎ *780/852–6476* ⊕ *www.jasperstables.com* ⌨ *From C$57.*

Tonquin Valley Adventures

HORSEBACK RIDING | Guided multiday horseback and hiking trips into the Tonquin Valley are the specialty of this company, which also operates the valley's Amethyst Lake Lodge. In summer, there's a cook on-site; all meals are included in the guided trips. There is also a cabin that can be rented by hikers and skiers who wish to cook their own meals. Bring your fishing gear—there are boats at the cabin and a lake with wild rainbow trout. ⊠ *Portal Creek Trailhead, Jasper* ✛ *Portal Creek Trailhead: Take the*

Icefields Pkwy. toward Banff, and turn right immediately after the park gate, onto Hwy. 93A. Continue along 93A for 2.4 km (1.5 miles), and turn right onto Marmot Rd. The trailhead is on your left at km 12 of the road. ☎ 780/852–1188 ⊕ www.tonquinadventures.com ⊠ From C$1275 for 3-day, 2-night horse trip including meals.

Tonquin Valley Backcountry Lodge

HORSEBACK RIDING | The lodge offers guided multiday horseback trips in the Tonquin Valley that include accommodations and all meals. It also provides accommodations and meals for hikers and skiers on self-guided trips. ⊠ Portal Creek Trailhead, Jasper ✢ Portal Creek Trailhead: Take the Icefields Pkwy. toward Banff, and turn right immediately after the park gate, onto Hwy. 93A. Continue along 93A for 2.4 km (1.5 miles), and turn right onto Marmot Road. The trailhead is on your left at km 12 of the road. ☎ 780/852–3909 ⊕ www.tonquinvalley.com ⊠ From C$2500 for a 5-day package including meals.

MULTISPORT OUTFITTERS

Gravity Gear

LOCAL SPORTS | Gear for ice climbing, backcountry skiing, and mountaineering can be rented or purchased at this company, whose staffers can also recommend certified guides for each of these activities. ⊠ 618 Patricia St., Jasper National Park ☎ 780/852–3155, 888/852–3155 ⊕ www.gravitygearjasper.com ⊠ From C$10.

Jasper Source for Sports

LOCAL SPORTS | Here you can rent bikes, fishing and camping supplies, and ski and snowboard equipment. ⊠ 406 Patricia St., Jasper ☎ 780/852–3654 ⊕ www.jaspersports.com ⊠ from C$40.

ROCK CLIMBING

Rockaboo Mountain Adventures

ADVENTURE TOURS | You can arrange guided rock-climbing, skiing, ice-climbing, and mountaineering experiences through this company. One of its most unique offerings is a hike on the Athabasca Glacier

with an experienced guide. ⊠ 610 Patricia St., Jasper ☎ 780/820–0092 ⊕ rockaboo.ca ⊠ From C$125.

SKIING

Downhill skiers will enjoy Marmot Basin, a 20-minute drive from Jasper Townsite. In addition, Jasper has more than 50 km (31 miles) of groomed cross-country ski trails, as well as plenty of natural trails. Current cross-country ski information is available at the park visitor center. Other popular winter activities include snowshoeing, fat-bike riding, ice climbing, ice walks, skating, and wildlife-watching. Rent gear and arrange guides at area ski and/or multisport shops.

Marmot Basin

SKIING & SNOWBOARDING | At 1,698 meters (5,570 feet), Marmot Basin has the highest base elevation of any Canadian ski area. The resort includes a mix of downhill skiing terrain, and the slopes are a little less crowded than those around Banff, especially on weekdays. There are three day lodges, two of which are at mid-mountain. Shuttles between Marmot Basin and the Jasper Townsite run every day of the season. Discounted lift tickets are available during the Jasper in January winter festival. **Facilities:** 86 trails; 1,675 acres; 2,612-meter drop; 7 lifts. ⊠ 1 Marmot Rd., off Hwy. 93A, Jasper National Park ☎ 780/852–3816, 866/952–3816 ⊕ www.skimarmot.com ⊠ Lift ticket: C$105.

Mildred Lake

ICE SKATING | **FAMILY** | There are groomed cross-country-ski and snowshoe trails in the area around the Fairmont Jasper Park Lodge, which also maintains a skating rink and an oval skating trail on nearby Mildred Lake. ⊠ 1 Old Lodge Rd., off Maligne Lake Rd., Jasper.

Pyramid Lake

ICE SKATING | At this pretty lake, you can ski or snowshoe along groomed cross-country trails, or you can go ice skating or take a sleigh ride. ⊠ Pyramid

At 1,698 meters (5,570 feet), Marmot Basin has the highest base elevation of any Canadian ski area.

Lake Rd., Jasper National Park ✛ 6½ km (4 miles) north of Jasper Townsite, off Hwy. 16A 🎟 Free.

Totem Ski Shop

SKIING & SNOWBOARDING | Come here for winter (and summer) sports equipment and clothing. ✉ *408 Connaught Dr., Jasper National Park* ☎ *780/852–3078* ⊕ *www.totemskishop.com.*

SWIMMING

Hot summer days are meant for wading and swimming, and Jasper has some lovely lakes that are great for cooling off. Lake Annette is the park's most popular swimming and beach destination because it has the most amenities as well as beautiful turquoise water, a long sandy beach, a paved trail, a playground, and picnic shelters. Lake Edith is close to Lake Annette and it also has a sandy beach and clear water. Jasper Lake is another good place to cool off on a hot day as it has a sandy bottom and shallow water that's ideal for wading. All three lakes are surrounded by stunning mountain scenery.

Jasper Aquatic Center

SWIMMING | FAMILY | This recreation facility has a three-story-high, indoor waterslide; a 25-meter (82-foot) swimming pool; a kiddie pool, a steam room, and a hot tub. Towel and suit rentals are available. The center closes for two weeks in the fall. ✉ *305 Bonhomme St., Jasper* ☎ *780/852–3663* ⊕ *www.jasper-alberta.com/2249/fitness-aquatic-centre* 🎟 *C$8.50.*

What's Nearby

Mount Robson Provincial Park and Hamber Provincial Park are adjacent to Jasper National Park and all three parks are included in the Canadian Rocky Mountain Parks UNESCO World Heritage Site. These three parks contain remarkable mountain scenery and abundant wildlife, and each is unique and worth visiting—if you have time. Alberta's largest mountain wilderness area, Willmore Wilderness area, also borders Jasper National Park. It's rugged and remote and those who visit get a taste of what the Canadian Rockies were like for early explorers.

The Town of Hinton lies just outside the eastern entrance of Jasper National Park, about an hour's drive from the Jasper townsite. Hotels are less costly in Hinton than they are in the national park and if you are on a budget and plan to visit attractions near the eastern entrance, a stay in Hinton could be a good option.

Mount Robson Provincial Park

The second oldest park in the British Columbia parks system gets its name from the highest mountain in the Canadian Rockies, which sits at the park's western entrance. At 3,954 meters (12,972 feet), Mount Robson towers above all other peaks near it.

Texqakalit Indigenous people named the mountain "Yexyexéscen" (pronounced Yuh-hai-has-kun), which means "mountain of the spiral road;" the name refers to the grooved lines on the mountain's face. Also known as "Cloud Cap Mountain," it's unclear as to how the peak came to be known as Mount Robson, but many believe it was named after a North West Company and Hudson's Bay Company hunter and trapper with a camp near the mountain.

Established in 1913, the park protects 225,285 hectares (556,691 acres) of land surrounding its namesake mountain including the headwaters of the Fraser River, one of the most productive salmon fisheries in the world. Interestingly, it was designated a provincial park in the same year that William W. Foster, Albert H. McCarthy, and Conrad Kain (an Austrian mountain guide) became the first to reach its summit.

The Yellowhead Highway (Hwy. 16) roughly runs down the middle of the park and many sights of interest can be seen from the road—including the awe-inspiring south face of Mount Robson.

The famed Berg Lake Trail is a highlight of the park. This world-renowned backcountry hiking trail features some of the best scenery in the Rockies including the Valley of a Thousand Falls, stunning Berg Lake, and the massive glaciers that feed into the lake.

Mount Robson Provincial Park offers both vehicle-accessible front country camping and remote backcountry camping. It became part of the Canadian Rocky Mountain Parks UNESCO World Heritage Site in 1990.

◉ Sights

SCENIC STOPS

Moose Marsh and Moose Lake
BODY OF WATER | Keep an eye out for wildlife, especially moose, when you come to Moose Marsh and Moose Lake. A variety of waterfowl are found here and there's a good chance to spot moose, especially at dawn or dusk. This 11.7-km (7.3-mile) long lake is the only lake along the course of the Fraser River. The Fraser flows into the lake on its east end and exits the lake on its western side. Moose Marsh is on the east end of the lake and the Yellowhead Highway runs along its north shore. If you have a BC fishing license, you can fish for wild rainbow trout. ✉ *Moose Lake, Mount Robson Provincial Park ✛ 61.5 km (38.2 miles) west of Jasper townsite on Hwy. 16.*

Portal Lake Rest Area
BODY OF WATER | Just west of the Yellowhead Pass is lovely Portal Lake. A short loop trail around the lake offers the opportunity to walk on the continental divide. There's a lovely picnic area—despite its location next to a major highway. You'll also find toilets and interpretive signs. If you have a British Columbia fishing license, you can fish for rainbow trout in the lake. ✉ *Portal Lake Rest Area, Mount Robson Provincial Park ✛ 26 km (16 miles) west of Jasper townsite on Hwy. 16.*

Yellowhead Lake and Yellowhead Mountain

NATURE SIGHT | This long narrow lake was named for the nearby pass. It's 5.6 km (3.5 miles) long and sits at the foot of Yellowhead Mountain, a stunning 2,458-meter (8,060-foot) peak. The mountain has four officially named summits: Bingley Peak, Leather Peak, Lucerne Peak, and Tête Roche. ✉ *Yellowhead Lake, Mount Robson Provincial Park ✛ 3.7 km (2.3 miles) west of Yellowhead Pass.*

Yellowhead Pass National Historic Site of Canada

HISTORIC SIGHT | Yellowhead Pass is the lowest pass over the Continental Divide at 1,066 meters (3,500 feet). The low elevation made the pass the preferred route of travel for Indigenous people, fur traders, explorers and railways. As you drive west from Jasper on the Yellowhead Highway (Hwy. 16), you'll see a roadside pullout 9 km (5.6 mi) west of Jasper with a small plaque commemorating this historic travel corridor. The name "Yellowhead" was the nickname of a fair-haired Métis-Iroquois-freeman named Pierre Bostonais or "Tête Jaune" who was active in this area in the early 1800s. ✉ *Yellowhead Pass National Historic Site of Canada, Mount Robson Provincial Park ✛ Roadside pullout, 9 km (5.6 mi) west of Jasper on Hwy. 16 in Alberta ⊕ www. pc.gc.ca/en/lhn-nhs/ab/yellowhead.*

TRAILS

Berg Lake Trail

TRAIL | With picturesque views of flowing waterfalls, mountains, and glaciers, the Berg Lake Trail has become a legendary backpacking destination. This moderately difficult 21-km (13-mile) one-way hike is one of the most popular overnight trails in the Canadian Rockies. Turquoise-blue Berg Lake gets its name from the fact that it's dotted with mini icebergs—even in the middle of summer. The lake sits at the base of the north face of Mount Robson and glaciers on the mountain regularly calve off into the water. This well-maintained trail takes hikers to some of the best scenery in the Canadian Rockies. The first 4.5 km (2.8 miles) are relatively easy hiking along the Robson River and then through dense forest before arriving at glacier-fed Kinney Lake. After crossing a steel bridge at the end of Kinney Lake, it's just 2.8 km (1.7 miles) to the Kinney Lake campground. Beyond the Kinney Lake campground, the trail splits and gives the option of hiking through Kinney Lake Flats or continuing through the forest. At that point, the trail merges together again and begins climbing steeply to the Valley of a Thousand Falls where it provides views of four spectacular waterfalls. The trail then crosses the Robson River on a suspension bridge and arrives at Whitehorn campground at the 11-km (6.8-mile) mark. Once the trail gets above the valley, you will start getting glimpses of the Emperor Face of Mount Robson. The Emperor Campground lies about 3 km (1.9 miles) from the shores of Berg Lake. Marmot Campground and Berg Lake Campground sit right on the shores of the lake. Several popular day hikes depart from the Berg Lake Campground and there are two more campgrounds just past the lake, Rearguard and Robson Pass. The Berg Lake Trail is one of the most popular backpacking trails in the Canadian Rockies and campsites should be booked well in advance, especially during the peak summer months. All hikers must check in at the Mount Robson Visitor Centre before setting out on the trail. In 2021, the portion of the trail past Kinney Lake was closed due to flood damage. If you can't get a backcountry camping reservation on the Berg Lake Trail, you could opt to fly into Berg Lake and hike down the trail as a day hike. It would be very difficult to hike the trail in both directions in a single day. *Difficult.* ✉ *Berg Lake Trailhead, Mount Robson Provincial Park ✛ Trailhead: 2 km (1.2 miles) north of Mount Robson Visitor Centre ☎ 519/826–6850, 800/689–9025 toll-free, 778/371–0607 International reservations ⊕ www.discovercamping.*

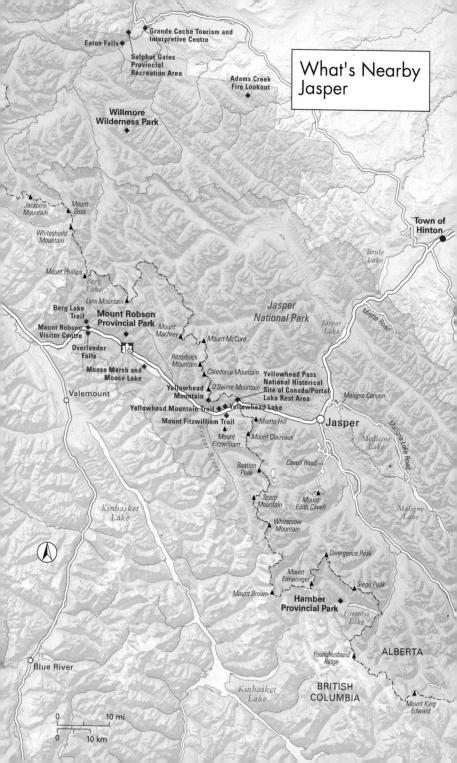

What's Nearby
Jasper

Grande Cache Tourism and
Interpretive Centre

Eaton Falls

Sulphur Gates
Provincial
Recreation Area

Adams Creek
Fire Lookout

Willmore
Wilderness Park

Town of
Hinton

Jackpine
Mountain

Mount
Bess

Whiteshield
Mountain

Brule
Lake

Mount Phillips

Berg
Lake

Jasper
National Park

Jasper
Lake

Miette Road

Lynx Mountain

Berg Lake
Trail

Mount Robson
Provincial Park

Mount Robson
Visitor Centre

16

Overlander
Falls

Moose Marsh and
Moose Lake

Valemount

Mount
Machray

Mount McCord

Razorback
Mountain

Caledonia Mountain

O'Beirne Mountain

Yellowhead
Mountain

Yellowhead Mountain Trail

Mount Fitzwilliam Trail

Yellowhead Lake

Yellowhead Pass
National Historical
Site of Canada/Portal
Lake Rest Area

Maligne Canyon

Jasper

Miette Hill

Mount Clairvaux

Mount
Fitzwilliam

Fraser River

Cavell Road

Medicine
Lake

Bastion
Peak

Scarp
Mountain

Mount
Edith Cavell

Maligne Lake Road

Whitecrow
Mountain

Kinbasket
Lake

Maligne
Lake

Divergence Peak

Mount
Ermatinger

Siege Peak

Mount Brown

Hamber
Provincial Park

Fortress
Lake

ALBERTA

Blue River

Younghusband
Ridge

BRITISH
COLUMBIA

Kinbasket
Lake

Mount King
Edward

0   10 mi

0   10 km

ca 🛏 Campsite reservation fee C$6 (plus tax) per campsite/tent pad, per night, to a maximum of C$18 (plus tax) ⊘ Closed mid-Oct.–mid-May.

Mount Fitzwilliam Trail

TRAIL | When you mention backpacking in Mount Robson Provincial Park, most people automatically think of the world-famous Berg Lake Trail, but it isn't the only backpacking trail in the park. The Mount Fitzwilliam Trail, also known as Fitzwilliam Basin Trail, is another backpacking option in the park that is practically unknown. While the Berg Lake Trail is well-constructed and maintained and fully booked months in advance, the Mount Fitzwilliam is "user maintained" and backpackers can self-register at the trailhead. There are two campgrounds along the 14-km (8.7-mile) trail, one with six tent pads about halfway up at Rockingham Creek and another with two tent pads at the end of the trail. The first half of the trail to Rockingham Creek is a well-constructed trail, but the second half is a far rougher track with roots and rocks. For that reason, some people choose to stay overnight at the first campground and hike to the end of the trail on a day hike. The total elevation gain for this hike is 950 meters (3,120 feet). Mount Fitzwilliam, an imposing 2,901-meter (9,518-foot) peak, was named in 1863 by Dr. Walter Butler Cheadle in honor of his traveling companion William Wentworth Fitzwilliam the Viscount Milton. The pair were likely the first tourists in this region and wrote a book entitled *The North-West Passage by Land* documenting their adventures. *Moderate.* ✉ *Mount Robson, Mount Robson Provincial Park* ⊹ *Trailhead: 7 km (4.3 miles) west of Yellowhead Pass.*

Overlander Falls

WATERFALL | Beautiful Overlander Falls was named for the Overlanders Expedition of 1862. The Overlanders were a group of about 150 settlers (including one woman) who traveled from Fort Garry (now Winnipeg, Manitoba) to the interior of British Columbia for the Cariboo Gold Rush. Just west of Overlander Falls, the group split, with half continuing on to the gold rush and half abandoning the dream of gold and returning down the river to Fort Kamloops. There are two ways to get to the falls, one short and one long. The short route to the falls, 0.6 km (0.4 miles) round-trip, begins at a highway pullout about 2 km (1.2 miles) east of Mount Robson Visitor Centre. The longer trail, 4.5 km (2.8 miles), begins at Robson Meadows Campground. *Moderate.* ✉ *Overlander Falls, Mount Robson Provincial Park* ⊹ *Trailhead: 2 km (1.2 miles) east of the Mount Robson Visitor Centre.*

Yellowhead Mountain Trail

TRAIL | This trail leads to the base of Yellowhead Mountain and up to flower-filled meadows and views of the continental divide. You'll reach the first viewpoint at about the 1-km (0.6-mile) mark on the trail. You can return at that point or continue another 3 km (1.9 miles) up a steep trail on the side of the mountain to reach a meadow and more panoramic views. The elevation gain to the second viewpoint is 720 meters (2,060 feet). *Moderate.* ✉ *Yellowhead Lake, Mount Robson Provincial Park* ⊹ *Trailhead is across the rail line at Yellowhead Lake.*

VISITOR CENTERS

Mount Robson Visitor Centre

VISITOR CENTER | Located at the park's main entrance, this visitor center is the place to go for information, trail reports, informative brochures, detailed trail descriptions, and maps. You can watch informative natural history slide shows and participate in the evening interpretive program. It is open daily from mid-May to mid-October. There are bathrooms and a gift shop on site. ✉ *Mount Robson Visitor Centre, Mount Robson Provincial Park* ⊹ *at the park's western entrance along Hwy. 16* ☎ *250/566–4038* ⊕ *www.facebook.com/ MountRobsonVisitorInformationCentre/.*

Overlander Falls was named after a group of settlers that came to the area in 1862 for the Cariboo Gold Rush; today it's a great place to hike.

☕ Coffee and Quick Bites

Cafe Mount Robson

$ | **CAFÉ** | This café is a great place to enjoy coffee, tea, or ice cream, grab-and-go breakfasts, fine chocolates, or baked goods before or after a hike. There's also a variety of hot and cold sandwiches, pizza, hamburgers, stew, burgers, fries, and poutine. **Known for:** good coffee; house-made pizza; liquor-licensed restaurant. [$] *Average main: C$12* ✉ *18344 Yellowhead Hwy., Mount Robson Provincial Park* ✣ *Beside the Mount Robson Visitor Centre* ☎ *888/814–1600 toll-free, 250/566–4332* 🌐 *www.cafemtrobson.com* ⏲ *Closed mid-Oct.–mid-Apr. No dinner.*

🛏 Hotels

Mount Robson Lodge & Robson Shadows Campground

$ | **B&B/INN** | This rustic hideaway with great views of Mount Robson is family-owned and-operated and sits just outside the west entrance to Mount Robson Provincial Park. **Pros:** on-site rafting trips; great location just outside the park; cabins with kitchenettes. **Cons:** no TV, no a/c, no cell signal, no Wi-Fi; rustic resort; some units affected by highway traffic noise. [$] *Rooms from: C$189* ✉ *Mount Robson Lodge, Mount Robson Provincial Park* ✣ *5 km (3 miles) west of Mount Robson Provincial Park on Hwy. 16* ☎ *250/566–4821, 888/566–4821 toll-free* 🌐 *www.mountrobsonlodge.com* ⏲ *Closed mid-Oct.–mid-May* 🍴 *No Meals* 🛏 *18 cabins.*

Mount Robson Mountain River Lodge

$ | **B&B/INN** | Just outside the west entrance to the park, this lovely riverside B&B lodge has four guestrooms, each with a private bathroom. **Pros:** breakfast included; comfortable rooms; lovely location near a river. **Cons:** remote location; no pool or hot tub; rustic surrounds. [$] *Rooms from: C$189* ✉ *Mount Robson Mountain River Lodge, Mount Robson Provincial Park* ✣ *4 km (2.5 miles) west of the Mount Robson Visitor Centre at the corner of Swift Current Creek Rd.*

and Hwy. 16 ☎ 888/566–9899 toll-free, 250/566–9899 ⊕ mtrobson.com ⊘ Closed mid-Oct.–mid-May ⏀ Free Breakfast ⇥ 4 rooms, 2 cabins.

🏃 Activities

CAMPING
BC Parks operates the campgrounds in Mount Robson Provincial Park; the sites are closed from mid-September to mid-May. Call 800/689–9025 or go online at www.discovercamping.ca/bccweb for reservations.

Robson River Campground. By the Robson River, this small campground is within walking distance of the Mount Robson Visitor Centre. There are 18 standard campsites and 22 campsites with electric hookups. C$28 Next to the Mount Robson Visitor Centre www.discover-camping.ca.

Robson Meadows Campground. This 125-site campground is near the Fraser River and has beautiful treed sites; there are flush toilets and showers, but no hookups. There's also an outdoor theater where they hold evening interpretive programs in the summer. The campground is within walking distance of the Visitor Centre. C$28 Across the highway from the Mount Robson Visitor Centre www.discovercamping.ca.

Lucerne Campground. On the east end of the park, this well-treed campground by Yellowhead Lake has wonderful mountain views. Some of the 36 sites also have lake views, but there's no running water or flush toilets. C$22 Yellowhead Lake www.discovercamping.ca.

HELICOPTER TOURS
Robson HeliMagic
AIR EXCURSIONS | If the hike to Berg Lake seems too daunting, this helicopter tour operator can fly you and your gear there. This company has an exclusive license with Mount Robson Provincial Park to access the Berg Lake Trail. They drop off and pick up guests on Mondays and Fridays. They also offer a variety of helicopter tours in and around Mount Robson. Some people choose to fly into Berg Lake and then hike out on the downward trail themselves as a day hike. ✉ 3010 Selwyn Rd., Valemount, Mount Robson Provincial Park ☎ 877/454–4700 toll free ⊕ www.robsonhelimagic.com ⛨ from C$265 ⊘ Closed mid-Oct.–mid-May.

Hamber Provincial Park

Surrounded on three sides by Jasper National Park, Hamber Provincial Park is 240 square km (93 square miles) of remote mountain wilderness with no roads and very few facilities. The park sits on the Continental Divide in British Columbia.

Established in 1941 and named in honor of Eric W. Hamber, the Lieutenant Governor of British Columbia at that time, it was British Columbia's largest provincial park when it was created at more than 10,000 square km (3,861 square miles) in size. In the early 1960s, the provincial government decreased the size of the park by approximately 98 percent due to pressure from the logging industry, hydroelectric projects, and the rerouting of the Trans-Canada Highway. In 1990, Hamber Provincial Park, Mount Robson Provincial Park, and Mount Assiniboine Provincial Parks were added to the Canadian Rocky Mountain Parks UNESCO World Heritage Site.

Most people who visit this park arrive via helicopter or floatplane, but a few brave souls hike in along a 24-km (15-mile) trail from the Sunwapta Falls parking lot in Jasper National Park. The hike requires crossing the Athabasca and Chaba rivers, which can be both challenging and dangerous. While it is possible to carefully and cautiously wade across the Chaba River, hikers should bring an inflatable kayak or a pack raft to cross the Athabasca River. Those who hike into this remote backcountry wilderness area should be prepared to be self-sufficient and take precautions to avoid bear encounters. The park is prime grizzly and black bear country. A rustic campground at the east end of Fortress Lake has bear poles for hanging food and scented items.

Lovely Fortress Lake is the highlight of the park. The 11-km (6.8-mile) long lake is prized by anglers for trophy brook trout fishing. Chisel Peak, Fortress Mountain, and other imposing peaks surround the lake as well as alpine meadows and spruce forests. There is a fly-in fishing lodge on the lake's south shore.

Hotels

Fortress Lake Fly Fishing Retreat
$$$$ | ALL-INCLUSIVE | This solar-powered wilderness retreat brings luxury to the remote backcountry with six individual guest cabins, a lounge and dining yurt, a kitchen yurt, flush toilets, hot showers, and a wood-fired cedar hot tub. **Pros:** outstanding views; excellent fishing; delicious meals with wine or beer included. **Cons:** limited baggage allowed for helicopter flight; unpredictable weather; strict cancellation policies. [$] *Rooms from: C$1350* ✣ *Fly-in access from Cline River Alberta to Hamber Provincial Park* ☎ *403/899–8815* 🌐 *www.fortresslake.com* ⏲ *Closed mid-Oct.–early June* 🍴 *All-Inclusive* 🛏 *6 cabins.*

Willmore Wilderness Park

At 4,597 square km (1,775 square miles), this park is a place of untouched mountain peaks, glaciers, forests, lakes, rivers, and pristine wilderness. Alberta's largest mountain wilderness area is bordered on the south by Jasper National Park and on the west by the province of British Columbia. Kakwa Wildland Park lies at the north end of the Willmore Wilderness Park. Kakwa Falls, at 30 meters (98 feet), is the tallest waterfall in Alberta. Kakwa-Willmore Interprovincial Park includes Willmore Wilderness Park and Kakwa Wildland Park in Alberta and Kakwa Provincial Park in British Columbia. The interprovincial park was created in recognition of the fact that the three parks share similar terrain and cross-border visitation is a frequent occurrence.

There are three main access points into Willmore Wilderness Park: Sulphur Gates Provincial Recreation Area, Rock Lake Provincial Park, and Big Berland Provincial Recreation Area. Of these, Sulphur Gates is the easiest and most often used access point. The Town of Grande Cache is about 12 km (7.5 miles) from the Sulphur Gates access. In the town, you will find restaurants, hotels, shops, gas stations, and a very helpful tourism and interpretive center that can provide maps and information about Willmore Wilderness Park, Sulphur Gates Provincial Recreation Area, and other area attractions.

There are no roads or bridges and motorized vehicles aren't allowed inside the wilderness park. Though there are some 750 km (466 miles) of trails, they are not well maintained and they are shared with pack horses. It's easy to get lost in the park without a good map and a GPS. There are also no formal campgrounds and no cell signals. Visitors should bring survival gear, and be prepared to be self-sufficient and be bear aware.

Those who venture into this park discover real mountain wilderness that is home to bighorn sheep, mountain goats, woodland caribou, elk, moose, grizzly bears, black bears, cougars, wolves, wolverine, and many other species.

Sights

SCENIC STOPS

Sulphur Gates Provincial Recreation Area
NATURE SIGHT | The place where the Sulphur River meets the Smoky River was formerly known as Hell's Gate. Lookout platforms at this site offer beautiful

views. There is a 15-site campground, two equestrian campgrounds with corrals, and two equestrian day-use sites. This site is the main access to Willmore Wilderness Park. ⊠ *Sulphur Gates Provincial Recreation Area* ✛ *5 km (3 miles) north and 7 km (4 miles) west of Grande Cache off Hwy. 40.*

TRAILS
Adams Creek Fire Lookout
TRAIL | The steep 36.7-km (22.8-mile) round-trip hike to Adams Creek Fire Lookout from the Big Berland River staging area makes a nice overnight expedition in Willmore Wilderness Park. The trail has 1,369 meters (4,491 feet) of elevation gain. *Difficult.* ⊠ *Big Berland River Staging Area* ✛ *Trailhead: at Big Berland River Staging Area.*

Eaton Falls
TRAIL | This half-day hike gives you a taste of the Willmore Wilderness. It's a 6-km (3.7-mile) round-trip hike from the Sulphur Gates parking lot to beautiful Eaton Falls. With 120 meters (394 feet) of elevation gain, the hike is relatively easy and one of the few day-trip options in the Willmore Wilderness. There's a viewpoint part way along the trail that is worth stopping for. *Moderate.* ⊠ *Sulphur Gates Provincial Recreation Area* ✛ *Trailhead: at the Sulphur Gates Parking lot.*

VISITOR CENTERS
Grande Cache Tourism and Interpretive Centre
VISITOR CENTER | The knowledgeable and friendly staff at this site, 13 km (8 miles) northeast of Sulphur Gates, can assist with travel information for the region. Explore the free on-site museum to see casts of dinosaur tracks found in the area as well as fossils, archaeological artifacts, profiles of early settlers, and tools used by early pioneers. You'll also find displays about the plants, animals, and birds found in the Willmore Wilderness

Park. The gift shop and art gallery sell the works of locals artists and writers. Outside are some historical buildings that are fun to explore. ⊠ *9701 AB-40, Grande Cache* ☎ *780/827–3300* ⊕ *mdgreenview. ab.ca/tourism/grande-cache-tourism-centre/* ⊙ *Closed Sun. Sept.–June.*

🏃 Activities

CAMPING
Inside Willmore Wilderness Park, there are no official campgrounds or campsites, but there are unserviced campsites at Sulphur Gates Campground and Big Berland Campground and there is a fee to use them.

There are also three historic backcountry cabins in Willmore Wilderness that are available for public use: Summit Cabin, Sulphur Cabin, and Sheep Creek Cabin. You'll find their locations on a park map. It's expected that those who use these facilities leave them clean and pack out any garbage. There are also a number of patrol cabins used by conservation officers when they visit Willmore Wilderness Park. These cabins are locked and are off-limits to the general public.

If you're going to camp, it's a good idea to use sites that have been previously used whenever possible, so you minimize your impact on the environment. Campers can help to keep this wilderness pristine by practicing "leave no trace" principles and packing out everything they bring in—including human waste when outhouses aren't available. Food, garbage, and scented items (e.g. deodorant) should be hung high in a tree at least 100 meters (328 feet) away from your tent—never *in* your tent. Your cooking area should also be at least 100 meters (328 feet) from your sleeping area.

HORSEBACK RIDING
High Country Vacations

HORSEBACK RIDING | This professional and award-winning outfitter takes guests on multiday horse pack trips into the Willmore Wilderness from the Sulphur Gates staging area. Guests enjoy guided rides through pristine wilderness, tent camping, and delicious home-cooked meals. ☒ *Box 818, Grande Cache, Grande Cache* ☎ *780/827–3246, 780/827–4799* ⊕ *horsebacktherockies.com/* ☚ *from C$400 per person per day all-inclusive.*

WHITE WATER RAFTING
Wild Blue Yonder Rafting

RAFTING | This company can take you rafting on one of the steepest rivers run commercially in Canada as well as through the stunning scenery of Sulphur Gates Canyon. Trips are available for beginners to advanced rafters. ☒ *11113 Hoppe Ave., Grande Cache* ☎ *780/666–9718, 877/945–3786* ⊕ *www.wildblueyonder.ca* ☚ *from C$72.*

Town of Hinton

The Town of Hinton lies 78 km (48 miles) southwest of the Town of Jasper on Hwy. 16. It's 30 km (18 miles) from the east entrance to Jasper National Park. With a population of about 10,000 people, the town has shops, restaurants, hotels, campgrounds and gas stations. Hotel prices tend to be quite a bit lower in Hinton than they are inside the park because it's a little farther away from most of the park's main attractions.

 Sights

Beaver Boardwalk

TRAIL | This unique wooden boardwalk winds through wetlands and a beaver pond and is said to be the longest freshwater boardwalk in the world. Along its 3-km (1.9-mile) length you'll find interpretive signage, benches, and two observation towers. The boardwalk is part of a longer trail system that winds through natural areas in the town. ☒ *Hinton* ⊕ *www.hinton.ca/852/Beaver-Boardwalk.*

Activities

Alternative Adventures Zipline

ZIP LINING | Ever dreamt of soaring through the air like a superhero? Here you can run down a ramp and soar headfirst (just like a superhero) on a 366-meter (1200-foot) zipline. The ride will drop nearly 46 meters (150 feet) before you come back to earth. Single and tandem rides are on offer and there are no weight or age restrictions. ☒ *Alternative Adventures Zipline* ✛ *10 minutes west of the town of Hinton* ☎ *780/817–9696* ⊕ *www.alternativeadventures.ca* ☚ *from C$59.*

Chapter 10

EDMONTON

By
Jeff Gailus

👁 Sights   🍴 Restaurants   🛏 Hotels   🛍 Shopping   🍸 Nightlife

★★★★★   ★★★★★   ★★★★★   ★★★★★   ★★★★★

WELCOME TO EDMONTON

TOP REASONS TO GO

★ **Shop 'til you drop:** Explore North America's largest mall and several hip, shop-filled neighborhoods.

★ **Festival City:** Edmonton hosts more family-friendly festivals than any other Canadian city.

★ **Urban nature:** With the largest urban park in Canada and a nearby national park, you can have the best of both worlds in this urban oasis.

★ **Cultural Capital:** Calgary may be Alberta's economic engine but Edmonton is the province's cultural heart and soul.

★ **Indigenous experience:** Greater Edmonton has the second-largest urban Indigenous population in Canada.

1 Downtown. Government and office buildings mingle with Edmonton's cultural hotspots.

2 124 Street. The area around 124 Street is home to many of the city's fine art galleries, great restaurants, and the 124 Grand Market.

3 Strathcona. Funky and bohemian, Whyte Avenue is one of Canada's best shopping and entertainment districts.

4 West Edmonton. Home to the West Edmonton Mall, North America's biggest mall, this is also where you'll find the Edmonton Valley Zoo and Fort Edmonton.

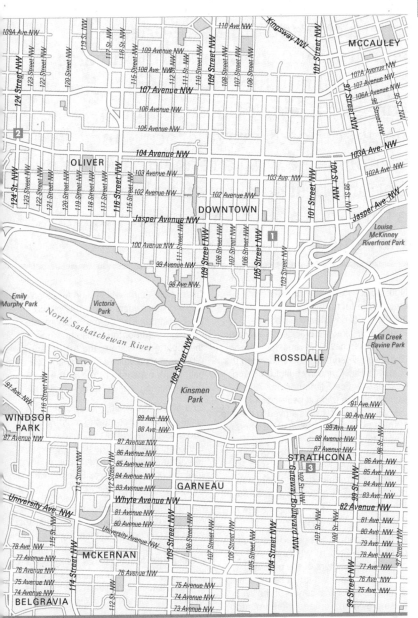

Bisected by the North Saskatchewan River and the miles of green parks that flank it, Canada's Festival City enjoys a perfect blend of nature-oriented activities and the vibrant and diverse culture of city life. The Downtown core and a few of the surrounding neighborhoods provide locals and visitors alike with a range of fine dining options, best-in-class microbrews, and a thriving theater and performing arts movement.

Numerous First Nations lived in the area before fur traders arrived in the late 1700s. The Cree called the place the Beaver Hills, and the Blackfoot knew the North Saskatchewan River as *Omaka-ty* (Big River). Everything changed when the Hudson's Bay Company built Edmonton House, later Fort Edmonton, in 1796 to facilitate the trade in beaver pelts to Europe. Pioneer farmers arrived in the late 19th century, and the town of Edmonton was established shortly thereafter. The first major oil discovery in Alberta gushed from the ground near Leduc in 1947, not far from where the Edmonton airport is now located. This turned Edmonton into the "oil capital of Canada," and oil has been king in Alberta ever since.

Today, Edmonton has ceded the title of oil capital to Calgary, where the corporate headquarters of the oil industry are now located, but it has become the cultural and political center of the Wild Rose province. Home to the Edmonton Oilers NHL team, which won five Stanley Cups in seven years in the 1980s, and the Edmonton Elks (formerly Eskimos) CFL team, Edmonton is also home to the Alberta Legislature; the Art Gallery of Alberta, the province's premier concert hall; the Winspear Centre; and the biggest shopping mall in North America.

One of Edmonton's biggest claims to fame is playing host to the most music and arts festivals in all of Canada. From the world's second-largest Fringe Festival to western Canada's biggest anime festival, Edmonton hosts multiple festivals every month of the year.

And the North Saskatchewan River River runs through it all. If you ask Edmontonians what the best aspect of their city is, it's not the mall or the festivals, it's the biggest urban park in North America, which fills the river valley with natural amenities, wildlife, and a reminder of the landscape that gave birth to this fine city in the first place.

Planning

When to Go

Summer (June through August) is the best time to visit Edmonton. Days are long, sunny, and warm, the nights short and cool. This is also when most of the city's festivals take place and the streets come alive with energy and activity. It's also the busiest time of the year, so if you're planning on a summer visit, plan and book well in advance.

September and early October are other good options; the weather will be cooler but still pleasant and sunny, the fall leaves add a welcome tinge of color, and your fellow tourists will be fewer and farther between. It's also the beginning of Northern Lights season, which can be seen about 90 days of the year in Edmonton, mostly in the winter months. Winters are cold but sunny, and there are opportunities for skating and cross-country skiing.

FESTIVALS AND EVENTS

Ice on Whyte. In late January in the heart of Old Strathcona, sculptors from all over the world descend on Edmonton's McIntyre Park to transform 93,000 pounds of ice into a frozen art gallery. Budding craftspeople can try their hand at the art of carving ice, and the Ice Bar serves delicious food and locally crafted beer and spirits. It's western Canada's premier winter carnival. *www.iceonwhyte.ca.*

Edmonton Folk Music Festival. Perhaps Edmonton's greatest festival, and definitely one of Canada's best music festivals, dozens of musicians—from pop superstars to obscure folkies—descend upon Edmonton for four days in early August. Performances occur on six stages on the banks of the North Saskatchewan River; get tickets early because it always sells out. *www.edmontonfolk-fest.org.*

Edmonton International Fringe Theatre Festival. North America's oldest and largest fringe festival has been surprising, delighting, and shocking audiences for 40 years every August. Located in the hip and artsy neighborhood of Old Strathcona, more than 100,000 tickets are sold for more than 200 shows that will blow your mind. *www.fringetheatre.ca.*

Getting Here and Around

The gateway to northern Alberta is Edmonton. This city is home to Edmonton International Airport (YEG), Canada's fifth-busiest airport and it has an extensive transit and light-rail train system that covers the city. Taxis are readily available, as is the ride-sharing service, Uber. If you'd rather stay above ground, numerous neighborhoods, including Downtown, are extremely walkable.

AIR

Edmonton International Airport (YEG) is located 16 miles south of Downtown on Highway 2 near the town of Leduc. Canada's fifth-busiest airport serves approximately 9 million passengers a year and offers direct flights to and from major cities in Canada, the US, Mexico, Europe, and Central and South America. Major airlines include Air Canada, Alaska, Condor, Flair, Iceland Air, KLM, Swoop, United, and WestJet.

AIRPORT Edmonton International Airport. (*YEG*) ✉ *1000 Airport Rd., Edmonton* ☎ *780/890–8382* ⊕ *flyeia.com.*

AIRPORT TRANSFERS

Several taxi and limousine services serve the airport, with a flat rate of C$55 (C$66 for limos) to Downtown. Route 747 is the Edmonton Transit system's direct service between the Edmonton International Airport and Century Park Transit Centre. The transit center is at the south end of the Capital Line LRT, which goes to and from the University of Alberta and Downtown.

Service runs 7 days a week from 4:10 am–12:30 am; it's C$5 one way.

CONTACTS Edmonton International Airport Service. ✉ *Edmonton* ☎ *780/442–5311* ⊕ *www.edmonton.ca/ets.***Greater Edmonton Taxi Service Inc..** ✉ *Edmonton* ☎ *780/442–4444 24-7 Taxi Line* ⊕ *ed-mtaxi.com.*

CAR

Edmonton is the gateway to northern Alberta. Highway 2 runs north-south from Edmonton to Calgary and points south. Highway 16 runs east-west, from the border with Saskatchewan, through Edmonton and west to Jasper National Park. Highway 63 heads northeast to Fort McMurray, home of the Alberta oil sands, while Highway 43 heads northwest to Grande Prairie and into northeast BC.

Within Edmonton, many sites are localized in specific walkable neighborhoods that can be accessed by public transit, but a car is handy to access attractions farther afield. Street parking is available in most neighborhoods, and the first 30 minutes are free. If you're staying longer than that, you are required to pay via an EPark machine located on the sidewalk.

PUBLIC TRANSPORTATION

Edmonton Transit System (ETS) runs a comprehensive transit and light-rail train system throughout the city. Both the Capital (blue) Line and the Metro Line run between the University of Alberta and the hospital, near Old Strathcona, and Downtown. Adult fares are C$3.50, or you can purchase a book of 10 tickets for C$27.75. Download the third-party Transit app to easily plan routes from place to place.

CONTACTS Edmonton Transit System. ✉ *Edmonton* ☎ *780/442–5311* ⊕ *www.edmonton.ca/edmonton-transit-system-ets.*

TAXI

There are several taxi services in Edmonton, as well as Uber. Taxi rates are between C$2–3 per kilometer, depending on the distance.

CONTACTS Co-op Taxi Line. ✉ *Edmonton* ☎ *780/425–2525* ⊕ *co-optaxi.com/.***Greater Edmonton Taxi Service Inc.** ✉ *Edmonton* ☎ *780/442–4444 24-7 Taxi Line* ⊕ *ed-mtaxi.com.*

Restaurants

The culinary scene has exploded in Edmonton in recent years and there are plenty of options ranging from upscale fine dining to hip new pubs and cafés that serve creative food in casual yet sophisticated settings. Many of the better eateries and bars are concentrated in and around Old Strathcona and the downtown core.

Restaurant reviews have been shortened. For full information, visit Fodors.com.

Hotels

Edmonton offers a range of lodging options, dominated by relatively cheap generic chains throughout, especially in the suburbs. Most of the swankier hotels are concentrated Downtown, and Old Strathcona offers a couple of unique and reasonably priced boutique hotels.

Hotel reviews have been shortened. For full information, visit Fodors.com.

What It Costs in Canadian Dollars			
$	$$	$$$	$$$$
RESTAURANTS			
under C$16	C$16–C$22	C$23–C$30	over C$30
HOTELS			
under C$125	C$125–C$175	C$176–C$225	over C$225

Tours

Quest for the Golden Key

Download the Quest for the Golden Key app and follow the self-guided tour along Edmonton's 10-km (6-mile) Commonwealth Walkway, which travels through the North Saskatchewan River Valley from the Funicular to the Groat Bridge. Along the way, you'll visit the Indigenous Art Park, John Walter Museum, and Alberta Legislature, among other stops, and learn about local nature and history. ✉ *10007 100th St. NW, Edmonton* ✛ *Starting point for self-guided tour* ⊕ *www.edmontoncommonwealthwalkway.com.*

River Valley Adventure Co.

This is a one-stop-shop for recreational equipment rental and year-round adventure tours. Their specialty is Segway tours of the River Valley or other parts of town, but they also offer stand-up paddleboard, bicycle, and snowshoe tours. Equipment rentals are available and they also offer picnic lunches. ✉ *9735 Grierson Hill NW, Edmonton* ☎ *780/995–7347* ⊕ *www.rivervalleyadventure.com* ⊗ *Closed Tues.–Wed.*

Visitor Information

Edmonton no longer has a brick and mortar visitor center, but there are numerous online sources of visitor information. One of the best is www.exploreedmonton.com.

Downtown

Downtown Edmonton has a long history starting in 1830 when Hudson's Bay Company built the fifth iteration of Fort Edmonton on the north bank of the North Saskatchewan River. The town grew to the east of the fort, with the commercial hub centered on Jasper Avenue and 97th Street. Over the last century, the city's business district has expanded out in every direction, creating the vibrant Downtown that visitors and locals enjoy today. With a unique medley of office towers and government buildings, hotels and restaurants, theaters and libraries, plazas and arenas, Edmonton's Downtown can keep you busy for at least a day or three.

GETTING HERE AND AROUND

Most people drive into Downtown, though parking can be tricky, or you can ride the High Level Bridge Streetcar over from Old Strathcona. A funicular can take you down (or up) from the river valley parks and trails. Once Downtown, many of the attractions are centralized enough that walking is a fun and active way of seeing the sights. Taxis are plentiful or you can dial up an Uber for longer distances. There are no rental bikes or scooters handy, but you can rent a Vespa from District Moto during the summer months.

CONTACTS District Moto. ✉ *10309 107th St., Edmonton* ☎ *780/752–2014* ⊕ *www.districtmoto.ca.*

TIMING

Like most downtowns, Edmonton's city center suffers rush hour traffic in the early morning and late afternoon. If you want to avoid it, plan on heading into Downtown before 7 am or after 9 am, and make sure you leave before 3 pm or after 6 pm.

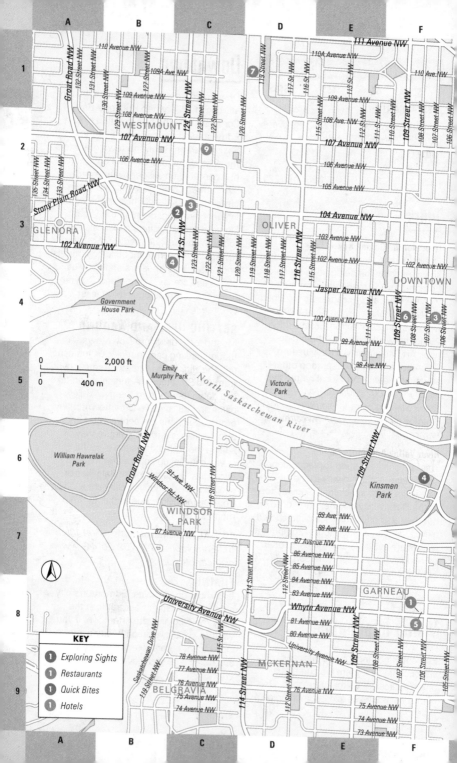

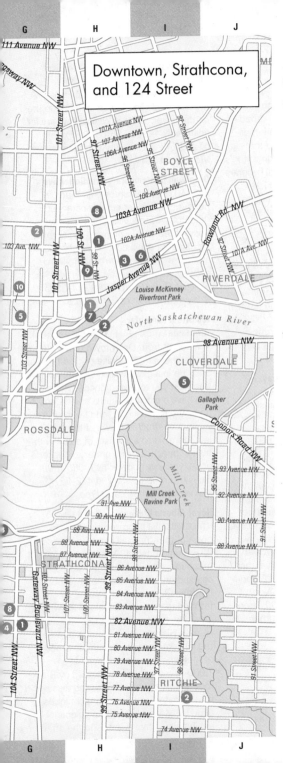

Downtown, Strathcona, and 124 Street

👁 Sights

Art Gallery of Alberta (AGA)

ART MUSEUM | Located across from City Hall, this exquisite building is wrapped with silver ribbons to reflect the importance of the Northern Lights and the North Saskatchewan River to Edmonton's identity and culture. With several galleries spread across three floors, AGA has welcomed exhibits of some of the greats including Degas, the Dutch masters, and an Andy Warhol retrospective. The in-house collection primarily focuses on Canadian abstract painting and sculpture since the 1950s, and BMO World of Creativity on the main floor provides an interactive experience for families to immerse themselves in art. Don't miss the great city views from the rooftop patio. ☒ *2 Sir Winston Churchill Square, Downtown* ☎ *780/422–6223* ⊕ *www.youraga.ca* ☒ *C$14* ⏱ *Closed Mon. and Tues.*

Edmonton Commonwealth Walkway

TRAIL | Starting at the Funicular, the walkway travels for 10 km (6 miles) through the North Saskatchewan River Valley ending at the Groat Bridge. Along the way, the path passes popular city landmarks like the Indigenous Art Park and the John Walter Museum. For an interactive experience, there's a downloadable app (available on the website) that helps you embark on the Quest for the Golden Key along the walkway. There are five storylines (Indigenous, history, family, river, and winter) to follow, and an icon appears on the app's virtual map when you get close to a clue. ☒ *Edmonton* ✛ *walkway starts along the North Saskatchewan River near the 100 Street Funicular* ⊕ *www.edmontoncommonwealthwalkway.com.*

Muttart Conservatory

GARDEN | **FAMILY** | Located across the North Saskatchewan River from Downtown, one of Edmonton's best-known landmarks consists of three city-operated greenhouses and public gardens, as well as four feature pyramids for the display of plant species found across three biomes, as well as a seasonal display. A fifth minor skylight pyramid lights up the central foyer. ■**TIP**➜ **Wednesdays are for adults only.** ☒ *9626 96A St., Edmonton* ☎ *780/442–5311* ⊕ *www.muttartconservatory.ca* ☒ *C$14.95.*

Ociciwan Contemporary Arts Collective

ART GALLERY | Edmonton's first Indigenous-run center for contemporary art is definitely worth a visit. The Collective hosts three or four projects a year that focus on art exhibition, research, public art, and awareness surrounding Indigenous contemporary art. ☒ *10124 96th St. NW, Downtown* ☎ *780/244–5505* ⊕ *www.ociciwan.ca* ⏱ *Closed Sun.–Tues.*

100 Street Funicular

TRANSPORTATION | **FAMILY** | A fun and funky way to get from Downtown to the North Saskatchewan River Valley, this 48-second ride in a glass-walled elevator will transport you to a promenade where you can have a picnic or read a book. Carry on to the Frederick G. Todd Lookout if you want unobstructed views of the river valley. There's also a cool set of stairs with built-in benches if you prefer to descend under your own power. ☒ *10065 100th St. NW, Edmonton* ☎ *780/442–5311* ⊕ *www.edmonton.ca* ☒ *Free.*

Royal Alberta Museum

OTHER MUSEUM | Located two blocks north of the Churchill Light Rail Transit (LTR) station, this 400,000-square-foot museum is the largest in western Canada and one of Canada's top museums. It offers 13 curatorial programs ranging from quaternary paleontology to western Canadian history. The highlight here is the Human History Hall, which celebrates the innovation, culture, and resilience of Indigenous people. Marvel at a 1,600-year-old roasting pit used by Blackfoot people to cook feasts, and discover the intricate floral beading techniques used by Métis people. This poignant exhibit also bears witness to the often

The exterior of the Art Gallery of Alberta is wrapped with silver ribbons to reflect the importance of the Northern Lights and the North Saskatchewan River to the city.

difficult narratives resulting from the First Nations' contact with European settlers. ✉ *9810 103A Ave., Downtown* ☎ *825/468–6000* 🌐 *www.royalalbertamuseum.ca* 🎫 *C$21* 🕒 *Closed Mon.–Tues.*

Stanley A. Milner Public Library
LIBRARY | This recently renovated award-winning library is the second-most visited place in Edmonton, in part because of its new multi-story simulation wall in the lobby; made up of 278 screens, it's North America's biggest digital exhibit. Other innovations include a 10,000-square-foot makerspace area with 3D printing facilities, recording studios, robotics, and fabrication tools, and the Gamerspace that includes the latest gaming consoles as well as retro video games. Pîyêsîw wâskâhikan (Thunderbird House) is a dedicated Indigenous gathering space that includes an independent HVAC system, making it the first public space in the city to support unrestricted smudging. ✉ *7 Sir Winston Churchill Square, Downtown* ☎ *780/496–7070* 🌐 *www.epl.ca.*

🍴 Restaurants

Cask & Barrel
$$ | **MODERN CANADIAN** | It's hard to say whether the Cask & Barrel is a pub or a restaurant, but it's definitely the best of both worlds. This cozy and comfortable place serves upscale food and a wonderful selection of beer, wine, and scotch. Just make sure you say hello to Susan, the owner, when you get there. **Known for:** generous happy hour specials; home away from home vibe; friendly staff and service. [$] *Average main: C$20* ✉ *10041 104th St., Downtown* ☎ *780/498–1224* 🌐 *www.thecaskandbarrel.ca* 🕒 *Closed Sun.–Mon. No lunch.*

District Cafe and Bakery
$ | **CAFÉ** | Every town has at least one outstanding breakfast and lunch place, and in Downtown Edmonton, the District is it. Excellent limitless coffee and fresh baked goods, and a world-class breakfast sandwich make this a great breakfast stop. **Known for:** bright, sunny eatery; large outdoor patio; friendly staff and

service. $ *Average main: C$15* ✉ *10011
109th St., Downtown* ☎ *780/705-7788*
🌐 *www.districtcafe.ca* ☾ *No dinner.*

★ Uccellino

$$$$ | **MODERN ITALIAN** | One of the best
restaurants in town, Uccellino's prepares
traditional Italian fare with a modern flair
like buckwheat pappardelle and ricotta
and mascarpone filled ravioli, but try the
Chef's Tasting Menu to get the most out
of your visit. An innovative cocktail list
and an excellent wine list only enhance
the dining experience. **Known for:** popular
place, reservations recommended; excellent Italian cuisine; modern, comfy ambience. $ *Average main: C$40* ✉ *10349
Jasper Ave., Downtown* ☎ *780/426-0346*
🌐 *www.corso32group.com/uccellino/*
☾ *Closed Mon.–Tues. No lunch.*

☕ Coffee and Quick Bites

The Nook Cafe

$ | **CAFÉ** | Edmonton's first certified
Tatawaw public space based on the Cree
philosophy "Welcome there is room", the
Nook is a warm and friendly café in the
Quarters area of Downtown. **Known for:**
very chill atmosphere; delicious cinnamon
buns; a variety of classic grilled cheese
sammys. $ *Average main: C$10* ✉ *10153
97th St. NW, Downtown* ☎ *780/761-6665*
🌐 *www.nookyeg.com* ☾ *No dinner.*

🛏 Hotels

Fairmont Hotel Macdonald

$$$$ | **HOTEL** | Perched on the rim of the
North Saskatchewan River Valley on the
edge of downtown, the historic Fairmont
Hotel Macdonald offers timeless luxury in a
convenient location with stellar views. **Pros:**
modern luxury in a 19th-century chateau;
lovely pool and gym; outstanding service.
Cons: parking is pricey; downtown noise
noticeable in some rooms; river views cost
extra. $ *Rooms from: C$330* ✉ *10065
100th St. NW, Downtown* ☎ *780/429-6481*
🌐 *www.fairmont.com/macdonald-edmon-
ton* ⧉ *No Meals* ⮂ *198 rooms.*

North Saskatchewan River Valley ◉

When Edmontonians mention what
they like most about their city, it's
rarely West Edmonton Mall or the
hip theatre scene; it's usually the
urban park system, particularly
the Ribbon of Green parks along
the 48-km (30-mile) stretch of river
that runs through the city's heart.
At 22 times the size of New York
City's Central Park, this is Canada's
largest urban park, and with 20
major parks, there's a lot to explore
in both winter and summer.

JW Marriott Edmonton ICE District

$$$$ | **HOTEL** | Located in the heart of
Downtown, the JW Marriott offers large
well-appointed rooms, two restaurants,
two bars, and a spacious health club
with a pool, steam baths, and whirl-
pool—if you're looking for modern luxury
in Edmonton, this is the place. **Pros:**;
convenient Downtown location; excellent
bar and restaurant on-site. **Cons:** when it's
busy service can be slow; luxury prices;
parking not included in price. $ *Rooms
from: C$400* ✉ *10344 102nd St., Down-
town* ☎ *780/784-7950* 🌐 *www.marriott.
com* ⧉ *No Meals* ⮂ *346 rooms.*

Matrix Hotel

$$ | **HOTEL** | The Matrix is a chic, modern
boutique hotel in the heart of Downtown
between the government and business
districts. **Pros:** excellent value; great loca-
tion; full breakfast included. **Cons:** parking
available but not included; some rooms
a little noisy; small bathrooms. $ *Rooms
from: C$155* ✉ *10640 100th Ave.,
Downtown* ☎ *780/429-2861* 🌐 *www.
matrixedmonton.com* ⧉ *Free Breakfast*
⮂ *184 rooms.*

There are some pretty big dinosaur skeletons at the Royal Albert Museum.

 Nightlife

Alchemy

COCKTAIL LOUNGES | You'll have to search for Alchemy, on the fifth floor of the JW Marriott, because it's hidden behind a faux-bookcase door. This intimate cocktail bar has a large patio, upscale bar bites, and delicious cocktails. Ask for the "Dealer's Choice" for something really special. ⊠ *JW Marriott Edmonton, 10344 102nd St. NW, Downtown* ☎ *780/704–7950* ⊕ *www.alchemybar.ca* ⏱ *Closed Sun.–Wed.*

Red Star Pub

PUBS | A coffee shop during the day, a pub in the evening, and a music lounge on weekend nights, the Red Star Pub is a unique Downtown Edmonton institution. Perfect for a date night or a late afternoon/early evening get together with friends, the Red Star offers a comfortable pub-like ambience, a creative menu of restaurant food, and an impressive selection of bottled and draught beer and spirits. No matter the time of day or night, you will find a good time waiting at the Red Star. ⊠ *10534 Jasper Ave., Downtown* ☎ *780/428–0825* ⊕ *www.redstarpub.com* ⏱ *Closed Sun.–Mon.*

The Starlite Room

LIVE MUSIC | Booking managers hosted the likes of Nirvana and Green Day before they were household names, and recent acts include Afroman, Hollerado, Royal Tusk, and Reuben and the Dark. This is one of the best places in Canada to catch both established acts and rising stars in a variety of genres. ⊠ *10030 102nd St., Edmonton* ☎ *780/428–1099* ⊕ *starliteroom.ca.*

Performing Arts

The Citadel Theatre

THEATER | Edmonton's foremost theatrical institution, The Citadel is one of the largest not-for-profit theaters in North America. It houses three stages: a cabaret-style black box theater, an auditorium/cinema, and the Tucker Amphitheatre, which allows the resident theater company to put on bold and distinctive productions year-round. ⊠ *9828 101 A Ave., Downtown* ☎ *780/425–1820* ⊕ *www.citadeltheatre.com* 🎟 *tickets start at C$25.*

Winspear Centre

CONCERTS | The concert hall is the home of the Edmonton Symphony Orchestra and a premier concert venue. With 1,716 seats and crystal-clear sound, it's the perfect venue for your favorite act or an ESO performance. Under the direction of Alexander Prior, the ESO plays classic classical music as well as pop-cultural tributes to the music of *Star Wars, Star Trek,* and *Harry Potter.* ⊠ *4 Sir Winston Churchill Square, Downtown* ☎ *780/428–1414* ⊕ *www.winspearcentre.com* 🎟 *tickets start at C$25.*

👜 Shopping

Edmonton Downtown Farmers Market

MARKET | This year-round market is known for a friendly, open atmosphere and farm-fresh produce, locally raised meats, fresh-baked bread, and a variety of sweet treats. You'll also find handcrafted jewelry, local art, one-of-a-kind clothing, and fresh-cut flowers. ⊠ *10305 97th St., Downtown* ⊕ *www.yegdtmarket.com* ⊙ *Closed Mon.–Fri.*

Manulife Place

MALL | If you're looking for some new duds and want to wear a piece of Edmonton history, stop by Manulife Place and visit Henry Singer. Named for the man who established his first men's fashion shop in Edmonton in 1938 with only $300 in his pocket, this venerable chain is a Canadian institution. Henry Singer sells many fine brands and also offers made-to-measure tailored clothing. Manulife Place also houses many other luxury shops, including Blu's and Nightowl Lingerie. ⊠ *10180 101st St. NW, Downtown* ⊕ *www.manulifeplace.com* ⊙ *Closed Sun.*

Strathcona

Built on the remnants of the old town of Strathcona, high-rise apartments mix with historic homes and walk-ups in this hip and walkable entertainment district. Many of the city's theater venues and festivals are based here, including North America's largest Fringe Festival. Whyte Avenue is lined with some of the city's best bars, restaurants, and shops. The adjacent neighborhoods of Garneau and Ritchie offer similar experiences.

👁 Sights

Indigenous Art Park

PUBLIC ART | The name of the park is ᐄᓃᐤ (ÎNÎW), pronounced (EE-NU), a Cree word meaning "I am of the Earth." The name River Lot 11 acknowledges the historic home of Métis landowner Joseph McDonald. Located in Queen Elizabeth Park, this exhibit includes six artworks by Canadian Indigenous artists, all of which were conceptualized to tell the story of ancestral lands of the Indigenous peoples whose descendants entered into Treaty with the British Crown. ⊠ *Queen Elizabeth Park, 10380 Queen Elizabeth Park Rd., Strathcona* ☎ *780/424–2787* ⊕ *publicart.edmontonarts.ca/IAP/.*

John Walter Museum

HISTORY MUSEUM | FAMILY | Located in Kinsmen Park, this living history museum showcases the life of John Walter, a Scotsman who immigrated to Canada in 1870 to build boats for the Hudson's Bay Company. Walter built one of the city's first permanent residences and the community of Walterdale formed around his property. Today, you can watch crafters at work and visit buildings as they would have looked between 1870-1942. You can also explore Kinsmen Park and its numerous walking and biking trails. ⊠ *9180 Walterdale Hill, Strathcona* ⊕ *www.facebook.com/johnwaltermuseum* 🎟 *Free.*

🍴 Restaurants

Ampersand 27

$$$ | MODERN CANADIAN | Named for the now defunct 27th letter of the alphabet, this Whyte Avenue restaurant is a local favorite. The creative menu is varied and contains lots of vegetarian and vegan options that even meat lovers will enjoy. **Known for:** delicious food; creative cocktails; attentive service. $ *Average main: C$25* ⊠ *10612 82nd Ave., Strathcona* ☎ *780/757–2727* ⊕ *www.ampersand27. com* ⊗ *Closed Mon.*

★ Biera

$$$ | MODERN EUROPEAN | Owner Greg Zeschuk, a former physician and video game developer, aspired to create a unique combination of top-shelf microbrewery and gourmet restaurant, and he succeeded in spades. Located in the Ritchie Market along with Transcend Coffee and the Acme Meat Market, Biera serves light, well-balanced lagers and European-inspired small plates made with the freshest ingredients. **Known for:** outstanding microbrews; great wine selection; creative menu. $ *Average main: C$25* ⊠ *9570 76th Ave. NW, Strathcona* ☎ *587/525–8589* ⊕ *www.biera.ca* ⊗ *Closed Mon.*

The Next Act

$$ | MODERN CANADIAN | The theme of this upscale pub is "come in good, leave better", and a meal here will only improve your day. Award-winning burgers, the best Caesar in town, and an outstanding weekend brunch are just three of the reasons to visit the Next Act Pub. **Known for:** excellent service; movie-themed ambience; award-winning burgers. $ *Average main: C$17* ⊠ *8224 104th St. NW, Strathcona* ☎ *780/433–9345* ⊕ *www. nextactpub.com.*

☕ Coffee and Quick Bites

Block 1912 Cafe

$ | CAFÉ | A locals' favorite, Block 1912 Cafe has the same ambience as the infamous coffee shop, Central Perk, in the TV show *Friends*, which makes it a great place to hang out with friends or work on your laptop. There's even a nook where you can read a book and munch on cakes and pastries as well as tasty sandwiches, soups, and salads. **Known for:** best desserts in town; comfy couches; wine and cocktails too. $ *Average main: C$5* ⊠ *10361 Whyte Ave. NW, Strathcona* ☎ *780/433–6575* ⊕ *www.block1912.com* ⊗ *Closed Sun.–Mon.*

🛏 Hotels

Metterra Hotel on Whyte

$ | HOTEL | One of two boutique hotels on the legendary Whyte Avenue, the Mettera offers affordable luxury in a great location. **Pros:** eclectic collection of art on the walls; a la carte executive breakfast included; right on the hippest street in town. **Cons:** Downtown too far to walk; Whyte Avenue can be noisy on weekend nights; parking lot is two blocks away (though there is a valet service). $ *Rooms from: C$120* ⊠ *10454 82nd Ave., Strathcona* ☎ *780/465–8150* ⊕ *www.metterra.com* ⦿ *Free Breakfast* ⇨ *98 rooms.*

Varscona Hotel on Whyte

$ | HOTEL | Like its sister hotel (Metterra Hotel on Whyte) down the street, the Varscona provides excellent service, value, and comfort for its guests. **Pros:** close to the University of Alberta; on-site parking for C$15/day; great restaurant off the lobby. **Cons:** not particularly close to Downtown; weekend nights can be noisy. $ *Rooms from: C$125* ⊠ *8208 106th St., Strathcona* ☎ *780/434–6111* ⊕ *www.varscona.com* ⦿ *Free Breakfast* ⇨ *89 rooms.*

Nightlife

Beercade

THEMED ENTERTAINMENT | What do you get when you pair craft beer with an arcade? Beercade! Rub elbows with the university crowd, quaff craft beer, and work your way through arcade games old and new. There's also billiards, air hockey, and foosball. If you're looking for a quiet place for good conversation, this is not it, but if you want to blow off some steam and have some fun for a couple of hours, this is a good option. ✉ *10544 82nd Ave., Strathcona* ☎ *780/699–2383* 🌐 *www.beercade.ca* 🕒 *Closed Mon.*

Performing Arts

Varscona Theatre

THEATER | In an old abandoned fire hall nestled off Whyte Avenue, five different companies put on rousing theater all year-round. Expect twisted comedies thick with wit and riveting dramas replete with characters that serve up unforgettable experiences. Try to see *Die Nasty,* an improvised soap opera that has been running for 30 years. ✉ *10329 83rd Ave., Strathcona* ☎ *780/433–3399* 🌐 *www.varsconatheatre.com.*

Shopping

Old Strathcona Farmers' Market

MARKET | Edmonton's original indoor farmers' market has been selling locally grown and produced goods since 1983. Locals flock to the market every Saturday to pick up seasonal fruits and veggies, honey, locally raised beef, and wild game meat, cheese, and other goods. It's also a great place to people watch. ✉ *10310 83rd Ave. NW, Strathcona* ☎ *780/439–1844* 🌐 *www.osfm.ca* 🕒 *Closed Sun.–Fri.*

The Quiltbag

OTHER SPECIALTY STORE | "QUILTBAG" is a fun-to-say variation of the LGBTQ2S+ acronym, and in this case refers to a unique retail shop that carries queer and trans wares. You'll find an eclectic collection of custom and curated accessories like pins, pronoun buttons, patches, stickers; art by local artists; small gifts; and trans gear including chest binders and compression underwear. ✉ *10516 Whyte Ave., Strathcona* ☎ *780/784–5265* 🌐 *www.thequiltbag.gay* 🕒 *Closed Mon.*

124 Street

The 124 Street Corridor is the latest hip-strip to offer a wide range of eateries, boutique shops, and arts and entertainment. Of particular note are a trio of French-style restaurants and bakeries and a half-dozen of Edmonton's finest art galleries within easy walking distance of each other.

Restaurants

Blue Plate Diner

$$ | **DINER** | This recently relocated hip diner serves comfort food and a host of vegan and vegetarian dishes. It's also the only place in town where you can order Eggs Benedict for supper. **Known for:** creative riffs on classic diner favorites; outstanding Ace coffee; weekend brunch. [$] *Average main: C$17* ✉ *12323 Stony Plain Rd.* ☎ *780/429–0740* 🌐 *www.blueplatediner.ca* 🕒 *Closed Mon.–Tues.*

Brasserie Bardot

$$$ | **MODERN FRENCH** | If you're in the mood for a taste of Europe, take a trip to this pub-style bistro for French-inspired cuisine. Situated in a remodeled building from the 1920s, this restaurant serves modern riffs on classic French dishes like pan-seared foie gras on a brioche slider bun and bouillabaise or steak frites. **Known for:** French cuisine; exemplary service; Bridgette Bardot theme. [$] *Average main: C$30* ✉ *10109 125th St. NW* ☎ *780/757–8702* 🌐 *www.brasseriebardot.com* 🕒 *Closed Sun.–Mon.*

The Local Omnivore

$ | **BARBECUE** | The Local Omnivore's simple mantra is "Good Hot Food" and they deliver by making their own brisket, which they use for burgers, pirate spiced fries, and poutine. Although meat is the main ingredient here, they also have plant-based wieners, patties, and gravy, so most menu items can be made vegetarian. **Known for:** quick and friendly service; house-smoked meats; breakfast poutine. [$] *Average main: C$15* ✉ *10933 120th St., Downtown* ☎ *780/660–1051* 🌐 *www.thelocalomnivore.com.*

RGE RD

$$$$ | **MODERN CANADIAN** | RGE RD serves authentic prairie cooking from wood-fired ovens. Chef Blair Lebsack's focus on sourcing fresh local ingredients according to best practices and sustainability means the food served is the best it can be. **Known for:** slow-food vibe; creative vegan and vegetarian options; Canadian craft beer and wine list. [$] *Average main: C$40* ✉ *10643 123rd St.* ☎ *780/447–4577* 🌐 *www.rgerd.ca* 🕒 *Closed Sun.–Mon. No lunch.*

☕ Coffee and Quick Bites

Credo 124

$ | **CAFÉ** | One of three Credo locations in Edmonton, this elegant café serves seriously good coffee and house-made granola bars, brownies, and outstanding cookies. **Known for:** beautifully crafted lattes; modern, chill vibe; limited parking. [$] *Average main: C$5* ✉ *10350 124th St.* ☎ *780/761–3744* 🌐 *www.credocoffee.ca* 🕒 *No dinner.*

🛍 Shopping

Bearclaw Gallery

ART GALLERIES | The gallery specializes in Canadian First Nations, Métis, and Inuit art, including paintings, stone sculptures, wood carvings, clay works, jewelry, craft, and gifts. Various exhibits are hosted throughout the year with artists in attendance on opening day. ✉ *10403 124th St.* ☎ *780/482–1204* 🌐 *www.bearclawgallery.com* 🕒 *Closed Sun.*

Bugera Matheson

ART GALLERIES | Bugera Matheson has been providing a refreshing perspective on Edmonton's vibrant art scene since 1992, while also featuring some of the best of contemporary artworks from artists across Canada. ✉ *10345 124th St.* ☎ *780/482–2854* 🌐 *www.bugeramathesongallery.com* 🕒 *Closed Sun.–Mon.*

Daisy Chain Book Co.

BOOKS | Brandi recently turned her mobile bookshop into a brick-and-mortar store that sells new and gently used books. Peruse the shelves for the latest bestsellers and age-old classics and join one of three in-house book clubs. ✉ *12525 102nd Ave.* ☎ *825/512–1342* 🌐 *www.daisychainbook.co.*

124 Grand Market

MARKET | The market, which runs June through September, has been providing Edmontonians and visitors with local produce, food products, and arts and crafts for more than a decade. On Sunday, you'll find it at 102 Avenue and 124 Street; on Thursday it's located at 108 Avenue and 124 Street. ✉ *102nd Ave. and 124th St.* 🌐 *124grandmarket.com* 🕒 *Closed Oct.–May.*

Scott Gallery

ART GALLERIES | Founded in 1986, the Scott Gallery features contemporary Canadian fine art by more than 30 emerging, mid-career, and established Canadian artists. ✉ *10411 124th St.* ☎ *780/488–3619* 🌐 *www.scottgallery.com* 🕒 *Closed Sun. and Mon.*

West Edmonton

Home to the more than 3.5-million-square-foot West Edmonton Mall, this area is about 20 minutes west of Downtown Edmonton. It's also where you'll find the Edmonton Valley Zoo and Fort Edmonton.

Set on 64 hectares (158 acres), Fort Edmonton Park is a great place to visit to learn about late-19th-century life on the frontier.

◉ Sights

Edmonton Valley Zoo

ZOO | FAMILY | The zoo has seen some renovations and new exhibits over the last decade and is a wonderful place to take the family. The new Nature's Wild Backyard exhibit, built to participate in the international Red Panda Species Survival Plan, holds up to four breeding pairs of these endangered species and allows visitors to get up close to these adorable Himalayan carnivores. You can also meet Lucy, an Asian elephant that is the zoo's longest resident, and more than 300 other animals. ⊠ *13315 Buena Vista Rd. NW* ☎ *780/442–5311* ⊕ *www. edmonton.ca* ⊠ *C$10.95* ⛵ *Reservations recommended.*

Fort Edmonton Footbridge

BRIDGE | This pedestrian bridge, also the city's first suspension bridge, crosses the North Saskatchewan River just below Fort Edmonton connecting the city's extensive trail system on the river's north and south sides. It's a lovely walk and great for views of the river and the city. ⊠ *Fort Edmonton Footbridge.*

Fort Edmonton Park

MUSEUM VILLAGE | FAMILY | Nestled on 64 hectares (158 acres) of wooded parkland in the River Valley, Fort Edmonton Park is an important destination for visitors who want to experience a late-19th-century life on the frontier. New for 2021 is a world-class multi-sensory exhibition of the history, culture, and perspectives of First Nations and Métis people in the Greater Edmonton region. There's also midway, an old theater, and wagon and pony rides. ⊠ *7000 143rd St. NW* ⊕ *www.fortedmontonpark.ca* ⊠ *C$26* ⊗ *Closed fall and winter.*

Galaxyland

AMUSEMENT PARK/CARNIVAL | FAMILY | With more than 27 exhilarating rides and play areas for all ages, including four distinctive roller coasters, the Swing of the Century, and The Flying Galleon, the largest of its kind in North America. For the younger folk, there is a Galaxy Kids Playpark, a carousel, and half-dozen mellower entertainments. ✉ *West Edmonton Mall, 8882 170th St. NW* ☎ *780/444–5321* 🌐 *www.wem.ca* 🎫 *C$30.*

Marine Life

AQUARIUM | **FAMILY** | Marine Life is a great way to get up close and personal with some of the ocean's more charismatic sea creatures. Enjoy an encounter with an African penguin while learning about its habits and then head underground to the Sea Live Caverns, where only a pane of glass separates you from over 100 species, including sharks and sea turtles. ✉ *West Edmonton Mall, 8882 170th St. NW* ☎ *780/444–5300* 🌐 *www.wem.ca* 🎫 *C$10.*

West Edmonton Mall

STORE/MALL | At more than 3.5 million square feet, West Edmonton Mall is a neighborhood unto itself. As North America's most comprehensive retail and entertainment complex, you could spend an entire week here and never get bored. Fantasyland Hotel is located on-site so there's a place to stay while you spend two or more days exploring all this mall has to offer. There's North America's biggest indoor water park (World Water Park) and amusement park (Galaxyland), the Marine Life aquarium, more than 100 restaurants and pubs, and 800 retail shops. There's also an IMAX theater, a bingo parlor, a bowling alley, a casino, mini-golf, and Jubliations live dinner theater for those who are spending the night and want some classic evening entertainment. The two-level, 48-block-long mall is oriented east-west with a main boulevard down the center, which takes about 20 minutes to walk. There's a food court at each end, one near Galaxyland to the east and one near the Fantasyland Hotel, World Waterpark, and Marine Life to the west. BRBN St., which runs north from near the center of the first floor, is where you'll find a collection of the finer dining establishments. If it's your first time, it's worth visiting guest services to get a map and a quick orientation. The staff can also point you in the right direction if you're looking for something in particular. The main office is located north of the Ice Palace hockey rink and beside Dolorama. There's also a kiosk south of Professor Wem's Adventure mini-golf, near the Marine Life aquarium. ✉ *8882 170th St. NW* ☎ *780/444–5321* 🌐 *www.wem.ca.*

World Water Park

WATER PARK | **FAMILY** | With 20 slides, including one called the Sky Screamer, where sliders approach 37 mph, this is the world's largest indoor waterpark and about as fun a way to spend an afternoon there is. There's also a wave pool and a zipline, and plenty of milder slides and pools and fountains for the tykes, too. Admission includes free use of life jackets and swim diapers. ✉ *West Edmonton Mall, 8882 170th St. NW* ☎ *780/444–5300* 🌐 *www.wem.ca* 🎫 *C$54.*

🍴 Restaurants

Earls Kitchen + Bar

$$$ | **MODERN CANADIAN** | With a casual, upscale ambience and a tried-and-true menu, Earls is always a good choice for dinner or drinks. Steaks, pasta, salads, seafood, and Thai options provide something for everyone. **Known for:** fun, friendly service; generous happy hour; vegan and vegetarian options. [$] *Average main: C$30* ✉ *West Edmonton Mall, 8882 170th St. NW, Drumheller* ☎ *780/481–8279* 🌐 *www.earls.ca.*

MR MIKES

$$$ | **STEAKHOUSE** | This good ol' Canadian steakhouse chain always gets top marks from its regular customers. There's two options: a family-friendly restaurant with a laidback vibe and the more adult urbanLODGE that serves the same great steaks in a more festive atmosphere. **Known for:** warm, friendly service; comfy, casual atmosphere; steaks any way you like them. [$] *Average main: C$30* ✉ *West Edmonton Mall, 8882 170th St. NW* ☎ *780/930–1135* 🌐 *www.mrmikes.ca.*

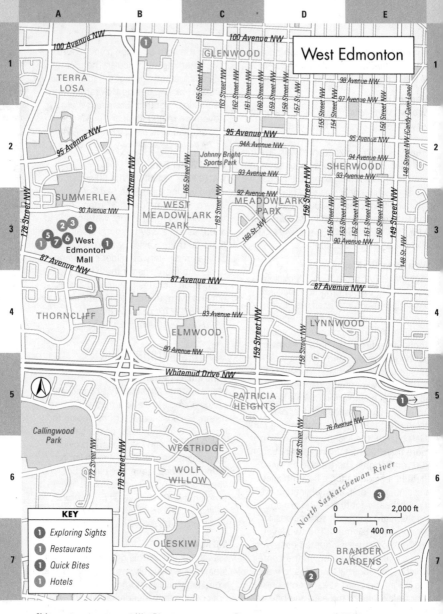

West Edmonton

Sights ▼

1 Edmonton Valley Zoo.... **E5**
2 Fort Edmonton Footbridge **D7**
3 Fort Edmonton Park **E6**
4 Galaxyland.............. **A3**
5 Marine Life **A3**
6 West Edmonton Mall...................... **A3**
7 World Water Park **A3**

Restaurants ▼

1 Earls Kitchen + Bar..... **B1**
2 MR MIKES.............. **A3**
3 Old Spaghetti Factory **A3**

Quick Bites ▼

1 Ayco Bakery............. **B3**

Hotels ▼

1 Fantasyland Hotel **A3**

KEY

① Exploring Sights
① Restaurants
① Quick Bites
① Hotels

Old Spaghetti Factory
$$ | **ITALIAN** | **FAMILY** | A go-to Canadian staple, especially for families with kids, the Old Spaghetti Factory offers a large and varied menu with an emphasis on pasta dishes. Whatever main you order, you also get soup or salad, ice cream for dessert, and coffee or tea. **Known for:** lots of pasta options; outstanding service every time; great value. [$] *Average main: C$20* ✉ *West Edmonton Mall, 8882 170th St. NW* ☎ *780/444–2181* 🌐 *www.oldspaghettifactory.ca.*

Coffee and Quick Bites

Ayco Bakery
$ | **CAFÉ** | This five-star bakery serves wonderful coffee and tasty pastries and donuts. Try the honey-glazed or the chocolate zucchini cake; for a savory treat, you can't go wrong with the spinach feta pastry. **Known for:** exceptional value; friendly staff; great service. [$] *Average main: C$5* ✉ *West Edmonton Mall, 8882 170th St. NW* ☎ *780/966–7900* 🌐 *www.wem.ca/directory/stores/ayco-bakery.*

Hotels

Fantasyland Hotel
$$$ | **HOTEL** | The only hotel in West Edmonton Mall, Fantasyland provides the option of classic hotel rooms or unique theme rooms that provide that extra flair to your stay. **Pros:** kids love the themed family rooms; easy access to water and amusement parks; convenient location to explore the mall. **Cons:** can be a pretty busy place; distant from Downtown and Old Strathcona; bathrooms in some rooms are a bit dated. [$] *Rooms from: C$210* ✉ *West Edmonton Mall, 17700 87th Ave. NW* ☎ *800/737–3783* 🌐 *www.flh.ca* 🍴 *No Meals* 🛏 *355 rooms.*

Nightlife

Jubilations Dinner Theatre
CABARET | **FAMILY** | It's not often you find dinner theater in a shopping mall, and this one is a winner. Diner-watchers usually use superlatives like "magical" or "amazing" to describe their experiences. The prime rib is delicious and the three-act comedies will leave you smiling until the next morning. ✉ *West Edmonton Mall, 8882 170th St. NW* ☎ *780/484–2424* 🌐 *jubilations.ca.*

Shopping

With more than 800 shops spread over a space the size of a small town, West Edmonton Mall allows shoppers to fill almost any desire. Need a prom or wedding dress? There are no less than seven stores to visit. Jewelry? Sixteen shops, including Birks, Tiffany & Co., and Swarovski. How about a new suit? There's Hugo Boss and Harry Rosen and six other options. There are 11 retailers selling shoes, from Aldo to SJP by Sarah Jessica Parker. And this is only the tip of a very large shopping iceberg.

Day Trip from Edmonton

Just 30 miles from Downtown Edmonton is Elk Island National Park, one of western Canada's most unique national parks.

Sights

Elk Island National Park
NATIONAL PARK | Established in 1906 to protect elk in their southern boreal plains habitat, Elk Island has helped recover many species from the brink of extinction, including beavers, bison, and trumpeter swans. It's now home to the densest population of ungulates in Canada, including several hundred elk, plains bison, and wood bison. Beavers, once virtually eliminated from the area,

now dominate the ponds and wetlands, where you'll find large beaver dens the size of studio apartments. The park is open 24 hours a day, seven days a week all year, and makes a perfect day trip or a multiday backcountry option. Hiking and biking are great ways to experience the park; in winter, cross-country skiing and pond skating are the preferred way to enjoy the colder weather. ⊠ *Elks Island National Park* ☎ *888/773–8888* ⊕ *www. pc.gc.ca/en/pn-np/ab/elkisland* 🎫 *C$8.*

Activities

BIKING AND HIKING

With more than 160 km (99 miles) of maintained pathways across 20 major parks, the River Valley is the perfect place for walkers, joggers, and cyclists to get some exercise and spend some time away from the hustle and bustle of the city. Use the Trailforks app to find the trails that are right for you.

River Valley Adventure Co.

BIKING | This company rents mountain bikes and electric bikes. Rates range from C$13 an hour to C$50 a day. ⊠ *Louise McKinney Park, 9735 Grierson Hill NW, Edmonton* ☎ *780/995–7347* ⊕ *www.rivervalleyadventure.com.*

CANOEING AND KAYAKING

With a 48-km (30-mile) stretch of the North Saskatchewan River running through it, Edmonton is a paddler's dream. There are dozens of put-ins along the river, which runs steadily through the city. Canoes, kayaks, and stand-up paddleboards can be rented from Totem Outdoor Outfitters.

Totem Outdoor Outfitters

SPORTING GOODS | This sporting goods store has you covered with a wide selection of outdoor rental gear, including skates, cross-country skis, snowshoes, canoes, and SUP boards. ⊠ *7430 99th St., Edmonton* ☎ *780/432–1223* ⊕ *www. totemoutfitters.ca.*

WINTER SPORTS

Edmonton's long cold winters mean plenty of snow, making the River Valley parks a great place to snowshoe and cross-country ski. The Edmonton Nordic Club grooms trails in Capilano, Goldstick, and Gold Bar parks, where night skiing and warming huts are also available.

There are four skating rinks in the River Valley, and the best one is at William Hawrelak Park, where you can glide across 1.5 hectares (3.7 acres) of ice for hours on end.

Cross-country skis, snowshoes, and skates can be rented from Totem Outdoor Outfitters (*see Canoeing and Kayaking*).

Edmonton Nordic

SNOW SPORTS | Goldbar and Goldstick parks feature 10 km (6 miles) of interconnected, lighted ski trails that range from easy to difficult. They offer lessons, but you need your own equipment. ⊠ *Edmonton* ⊕ *www.edmontonnordic.ca.*

WATERTON LAKES NATIONAL PARK

11

By
Debbie Olsen

⛺ Camping	🛏 Hotels	🤸 Activities	👁 Scenery	👥 Crowds
★★★★★	★★★☆☆	★★★★★	★★★★☆	★★☆☆☆

WELCOME TO
WATERTON LAKES NATIONAL PARK

TOP REASONS TO GO

★ **Dramatic scenery:** Rugged mountains weave their way along the Continental Divide in an awe-inspiring scene that includes glaciers, lakes, rivers, and streams.

★ **World-class hiking:** Hundreds of miles of trails of all levels of difficulty lace the park, from flat and easy half-hour strolls to steep, strenuous all-day hikes.

★ **Float along the border:** A boat tour across beautiful Waterton Lake crosses the US/Canadian border and provides incredible scenery along the way.

★ **View native wildlife:** This is one of the few places in North America where all native carnivores, including grizzlies, black bears, coyotes, and wolves, still survive.

★ **Fewer crowds, more solitude:** Tucked away in the southwest corner of Alberta, this park is less crowded than many of the other parks in the Canadian Rockies, but no less beautiful.

1 Waterton Lakes National Park. This park is tucked away in the southwest corner of the province of Alberta. The closest international airport is in Calgary, 271 km (168 miles) north of Waterton. There are two towns less than an hour's drive from the park. Cardston is 55 km (34 miles) east and slightly north of Waterton, and Pincher Creek is 56 km (35 miles) north of Waterton. To the south of this 526-square-km (203-square-mile) park is the U.S. border and Glacier National Park in Montana. To the north and east are rolling foothills and prairies. To the west is the Continental Divide, which marks the Alberta/British Columbia border.

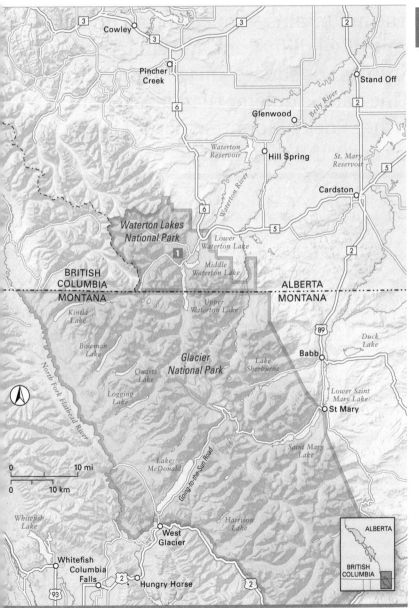

Waterton Lakes National Park represents the meeting of two worlds—the flatlands of the prairie and the abrupt upthrust of the mountains—squeezing an unusual mix of wildlife, flora, and climate zones into its 505 square km (200 square miles). The park is quieter than most of the other Rocky Mountain parks, but it's just as beautiful and diverse.

In 1932, Waterton Lakes National Park in Canada and Glacier National Park in the United States became the Waterton-Glacier International Peace Park, the first park of its kind in the world. The designation was intended as an expression of peace and goodwill between the two nations as well as a statement about the international nature of wilderness and the cooperation required between nations to protect it. The Waterton-Glacier International Peace Park is a UNESCO World Heritage Site.

In September 2017, the Kenow Wildfire burned 19,303 hectares (47,698 acres) of parkland, greatly affecting park infrastructure, including more than 80% of its hiking trail network. Through the efforts of brave firefighters, the townsite was virtually untouched. In 2018, the Boundary Wildfire burned the Boundary Creek Valley region in Glacier National Park and blazed across the U.S.–Canada border into Waterton Lakes National Park. Wildfires play an important role in a forest ecosystem, though, and the park is already recovering. Check the website to learn the status of trails before heading out.

Planning

When to Go

Of the 400,000 annual visitors to Waterton, most come between July and mid-September, when the streams are flowing, wildlife is roaming, and naturalist programs are fully underway. Canada's Victoria Day in late May marks the beginning of the season in Waterton. Spring and fall are quieter.

FESTIVALS AND EVENTS

Canada Day. Special activities for families such as treasure hunts and evening theater programs are held to celebrate Canada's birthday on July 1st.

Parks Day. Special activities and programming is offered on the third Saturday in July to celebrate Parks Day.

Waterton Wildflower Festival. Wildflower walks, horseback rides, hikes, watercolor workshops, photography classes, and family events help visitors and locals celebrate the annual blooming of Waterton's bountiful wildflowers in mid-summer.

WATERTON AVERAGE HIGH/LOW TEMPERATURES IN CELSIUS					
Jan.	Feb.	Mar.	Apr.	May	June
0/-11	1/-10	6/-6	10/-2	15/3	19/6
July	Aug.	Sept.	Oct.	Nov.	Dec.
23/8	22/7	17/3	12/1	3/-6	1/-9

WATERTON AVERAGE HIGH/LOW TEMPERATURES IN FAHRENHEIT					
Jan.	Feb.	Mar.	Apr.	May	June
32/12	34/14	42/22	50/29	59/37	66/43
July	Aug.	Sept.	Oct.	Nov.	Dec.
73/46	72/44	63/38	53/33	38/22	33/15

Waterton Wildlife Weekend. Wildlife viewing is at its best in Waterton during the fall. The weekend's events include viewing on foot, on horseback, and by boat. There are also photography, drawing, and sketching courses.

Winterfest. This winter festival happens in mid-February. Past activities included hot chocolate, bonfires, skating, horse-drawn carriage rides, and art workshops for children and youth.

Getting Here and Around

Visitors coming from Glacier National Park typically reach Waterton via the seasonal Chief Mountain Highway border crossing, 108 km (67 miles) northwest of East Glacier Park Village. It's also possible to access the park from the U.S. via the border crossing at Carway, which is open year-round.

AIR

The nearest airport to Waterton Lakes is Calgary International Airport (YYC). It's 271 km (168 miles) by car.

CAR

To access Waterton from the US by car, take the Chief Mountain Highway (Highway 17) in summer or U.S. 89 to Alberta Highway 2 through Cardston and then west via Highway 5 any time of the year. From the international airport in

Calgary, drive south on Highway 2 to Fort MacLeod, then southwest on Highway 3 to Pincher Creek and south on Highway 6 to Waterton. Repeated freezing and thawing can cause roads—either gravel or paved—to deteriorate, so drive slowly. In summer, road reconstruction is part of the park experience as crews take advantage of the few warm months to complete projects. At any time of the year, anticipate that rocks and wildlife may be just around the bend. Scenic pull-outs are frequent along roads inside the park and near it. Most development, services, and gas stations are located in the Waterton townsite or in the towns near the park.

Inspiration

Charles Waterton, 1782–1865: Traveller and Conservationist, by Julia Blackburn, provides insight on Charles Waterton, the eccentric British naturalist and explorer who was one of the first conservationists of the modern age. The Waterton Lakes were named in his honor by Lieutenant Thomas Blakiston, a member of the Palliser Expedition.

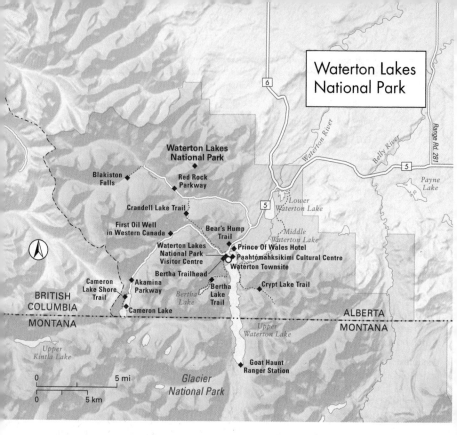

Park Essentials

ACCESSIBILITY

All visitor centers are wheelchair accessible, and most of the campgrounds and picnic areas are paved, with extended-length picnic tables and accessible restrooms. The Linnet Lake Trail, Waterton Townsite Trail, Cameron Lake day-use area, and the International Peace Park Pavilion are also wheelchair accessible.

PARK FEES AND PERMITS

A day pass to the park is C$7.90 for an individual or C$16 per seven people per vehicle.

Backcountry camping permits are required, with reservations available up to 90 days ahead at the visitor reception center. The fee is C$10.02 per person per night. A nonrefundable reservation fee of C$11.96 is also charged.

PARK HOURS

The park is open year-round, but many roads and facilities close from October through May. The park is on Mountain time zone.

CELL PHONE RECEPTION

Cell coverage is improving, but, in mountainous terrain, poor reception is common. Service is best in the Waterton Townsite in Waterton Lakes National Park.

Hotels

Lodgings in the parks tend to be rustic and simple, though there are a few grand lodges. Some modern accommodations have pools, hot tubs, boat rentals, guided excursions, and fine dining. The supply of rooms within both parks is limited, but the prices are relatively reasonable. It's best to reserve well in advance, especially for July and August.

Hotel reviews have been shortened. For full information, visit Fodors.com.

Restaurants

Steak houses serving certified Angus beef are typical of the region; in recent years, resort communities have diversified their menus to include bison, venison, elk, moose, trout, and gluten-free and vegetarian options. Small cafés offer hearty, inexpensive meals and perhaps the chance to chat with locals. Attire everywhere is casual.

Restaurant reviews have been shortened. For full information, visit Fodors. com.

What It Costs in Canadian Dollars			
$	$$	$$$	$$$$
RESTAURANTS			
under C$15	C$15–C$20	C$21–C$25	over C$25
HOTELS			
under C$150	C$150–C$200	C$201–C$250	over C$250

Tours

Dark Sky Guides
A Night Sky Discovery Tour is the most popular offering from this tour company. Hike to a viewing spot, and learn about the legends associated with constellations from a knowledgeable guide. See stars close up with powerful telescopes. The company also conducts twilight wildlife walks and starry skies strolls. ✉ *Box 56, Waterton Lakes National Park* ⊕ *darkskyguides.ca* ✉ *From C$20 per person.*

Visitor Information

CONTACTS Waterton Lakes Chamber of Commerce. ✉ *Waterton Lakes National Park* ⊕ *www.mywaterton.ca.* **Waterton Lakes National Park.** ✉ *Waterton Townsite* ☎ *403/859–5133, 403/859–2224 year-round* ⊕ *www.pc.gc.ca/waterton.*

In the Park

The quaint alpine town of Waterton lies just off the shore of Upper Waterton Lake, and the historic Prince of Wales Hotel sits high on a hill overlooking it all.

◉ Sights

HISTORIC SIGHTS
First Oil Well in Western Canada
HISTORIC SIGHT | Alberta is known worldwide for its oil and gas production, and the first oil well in western Canada was established in 1902 in what is now the park. Stop at this National Historic Site to explore the wellheads, drilling equipment, and remains of the Oil City boomtown. ✉ *Waterton Lakes National Park* ✛ *Watch for sign 7.7 km (4.8 miles) up the Akamina Pkwy.* ☎ ✉ *Free.*

Paahtómahksikimi Cultural Centre
OTHER ATTRACTION | The Blackfoot consider the area around the Waterton Lakes to be sacred. Paahtómahksikimi is the Blackfoot name for Waterton Lake. It means "inner sacred lake." The Paahtómahksikimi Cultural Centre helps visitors connect with the Spirit of Waterton and learn about Blackfoot culture. You can participate in various activities and programs and purchase authentic handcrafted

You can rent a canoe, rowboat, kayak, and fishing gear at Cameron Lake.

artisan products in the on-site craft store. ✉ *117 Waterton Ave., Waterton Townsite* ⊕ *www.facebook.com/pculturalcentre.*

Prince of Wales Hotel

HISTORIC SIGHT | Named for the prince who later became King Edward VIII, this hotel was constructed between 1926 and 1927 and was designated a National Historic Site in 1995. Take in the magnificent view from the ridge outside the hotel, or pop inside to enjoy the vista from the comfort of the expansive lobby, where afternoon tea is served. ✉ *Off Hwy. 5, Waterton Lakes National Park* ☎ *848/868–7474, 403/236–3400* ⊕ *www. glacierparkcollection.com/lodging/ prince-of-wales-hotel* 🎟 *Free* ☉ *Closed late-Sept.–mid-May.*

SCENIC DRIVES

Akamina Parkway

SCENIC DRIVE | Take this winding, 16-km (10-mile) road up to Cameron Lake, but drive slowly and watch for wildlife: it's common to see bears along the way. At the lake you will find a relatively flat, paved, 1.6-km (1-mile) trail that hugs the western shore and makes a nice walk. Bring your binoculars. Grizzly bears are often spotted on the lower slopes of the mountains at the far end of the lake. ✉ *Cameron Lake, Waterton Lakes National Park.*

Red Rock Parkway

SCENIC DRIVE | The 15-km (9-mile) route takes you from the prairie up the Blakiston Valley to Red Rock Canyon, where water has cut through the earth, exposing red sedimentary rock. It's common to see bears just off the road, especially in autumn, when the berries are ripe. ✉ *Red Rock Canyon, Waterton Lakes National Park.*

SCENIC STOPS

Cameron Lake

BODY OF WATER | The jewel of Waterton, Cameron Lake sits in a land of glacially carved *cirques* (steep-walled basins). In summer, hundreds of varieties of alpine wildflowers fill the area, including 22 kinds of wild orchids. Canoes, rowboats, kayaks, and fishing gear can be rented here. ✉ *Akamina Pkwy., Waterton Lakes*

National Park ✤ 13 km (8 miles) south-west of Waterton Townsite.

Goat Haunt Ranger Station

OTHER ATTRACTION | Reached only by foot trail, private boat, or tour boat from Waterton Townsite, this spot on the U.S. end of Waterton Lake is the stomping ground for mountain goats, moose, grizzlies, and black bears. It's also the official border crossing for the U.S. side of Waterton Lake. In recent years, the crossing has not been staffed by U.S. Customs personnel, and, consequently, tour boats do not allow passengers to disembark at Goat Haunt as they once did. If you want to explore the trails on this end of the lake, you will need to hike or paddle in on your own. Check-in before arrival by using the CBP ROAM app. Visitors to this area must carry their passports and proof of ROAM trip approval. The hikes on the U.S. side of the lake were unaffected by the wildfires of recent years. ⊠ *Waterton Lakes National Park ✤ Southern end of Waterton Lake* ☎ *403/859–2362* ⊕ *www.watertoncruise. com* ⊠ *Tour boat C$51.*

Waterton Townsite

TOWN | In roughly the park's geographic center, this low-key townsite swells with tourists in summer, and restaurants and shops open to serve them. In winter only a few motels are open, and services are limited. ⊠ *Waterton, Waterton Townsite.*

TRAILS

Bear's Hump Trail

TRAIL | This steep, 2.8-km (1.4-mile) trail climbs to an overlook with a great view of Upper Waterton Lake and the townsite. *Moderate.* ⊠ *Bear's hump trailhead, Waterton Lakes National Park ✤ Trailhead: across from Prince of Wales access road. Behind site of old visitor information center.*

Bertha Lake Trail

TRAIL | This 11.4-km (7.1-mile) round-trip trail leads from Waterton Townsite through a Douglas fir forest to a beautiful overlook of Upper Waterton Lake, and on to Lower Bertha Falls. From there, a steeper climb takes you past Upper Bertha Falls to Bertha Lake. In June, the wildflowers along the trail are stunning. *Moderate.* ⊠ *Bertha Lake Trailhead, Waterton Lakes National Park ✤ Trailhead: at parking lot off Evergreen Ave., west of Townsite Campground.*

Blakiston Falls

TRAIL | A 2-km (1.2-mile) round-trip hike will take you from Red Rock Canyon to Blakiston Falls. Several viewpoints overlook the falls. *Easy* ⊠ *Blakiston Falls Trailhead, Waterton Lakes National Park ✤ Trailhead: at Red Rock Canyon lower parking lot. Cross the bridge over Red Rock Creek, then turn left across the bridge over Bauerman Creek, and turn right to follow the trail.*

Cameron Lake Shore Trail

TRAIL | **FAMILY** | Relatively flat and paved, this 1.6-km (1-mile) one-way trail offers a peaceful hike. Look for wildflowers along the shoreline and grizzlies on the lower slopes of the mountains at the far end of the lake. *Easy.* ⊠ *Cameron Lake Shoreline Trailhead, Waterton Lakes National Park ✤ Trailhead: at lakeshore in front of parking lot, 13 km (8 miles) southwest of Waterton Townsite.*

Crandell Lake Trail

TRAIL | This 2½-km (1½-mile) trail winds through fragrant pine forest, ending at a popular mountain lake. *Easy.* ⊠ *Crandell Lake Trailhead, Waterton Lakes National Park ✤ Trailhead: about halfway up Akamina Pkwy.*

★ Crypt Lake Trail

TRAIL | Awe-inspiring and strenuous, this 17.2-km (11-mile) round-trip trail is one of the most stunning hikes in the Canadian Rockies. Conquering the trail involves taking a boat taxi across Waterton Lake, climbing 700 meters (2,300 feet), crawling through a tunnel nearly 30 meters (100 feet) long, and scrambling across a sheer rock face. The reward, and well worth it: views of a 183-meter (600-foot) cascading waterfall and the turquoise waters of Crypt Lake. This hike was completely untouched by the wildfires of recent years. *Difficult.* ✉ *Crypt Lake Trailhead, Waterton Lakes National Park* ✣ *Trailhead: at Crypt Landing, accessed by ferry from Waterton Townsite.*

VISITOR CENTERS

Waterton Lakes National Park Visitor Centre

VISITOR CENTER | The brand-new visitor center is in downtown Waterton. The original Waterton Information Centre was destroyed by the Kenow Wildfire in 2017. Stop in to pick up brochures, maps, and books. You can also pick up the booklet for the free Xplorer Program for kids between ages 6 and 11. Park interpreters are on hand to answer questions and give directions. ✉ *404 Cameron Falls Dr., Waterton Lakes National Park* ☎ *403/859–5133.*

🍴 Restaurants

Lakeside Chophouse

$$$$ | **STEAKHOUSE** | Grab a window seat or a spot on the patio to enjoy the spectacular view from Waterton's only lakefront restaurant. This is the place in the park for a steak dinner—locally produced Alberta beef plays a starring role on the globally inspired menu. **Known for:** all-day service; great steaks; lakefront views. [$] *Average main: C$29* ✉ *Bayshore Inn, 111 Waterton Ave., Waterton Townsite* ☎ *888/527–9555, 403/859–2211* 🌐 *www.bayshoreinn.com* ⏲ *Closed early Oct.–mid May.*

★ Red Rock Trattoria

$$$ | **ITALIAN** | There's a large window with lovely mountain views at this intimate Italian restaurant on a quiet side street in the Waterton Townsite. The menu changes regularly, but classic starters like caprese salad and calamari are always popular, and you can't go wrong with pasta for the main course—it's all made from scratch, with sauces that are prepared à la minute. **Known for:** intimate dining; house-made Italian food; local ingredients. [$] *Average main: C$22* ✉ *107 Wind Flower Ave., Waterton Townsite* ☎ *403/859–2004* 🌐 *www.redrockcafe.ca.*

Royal Stewart Dining Room

$$$$ | **CANADIAN** | Enjoy continental-Canadian cuisine before a dazzling view of Waterton Lake in the dining room of this century-old, hilltop chalet high above the Waterton Valley, where there's a fine selection of wines to pair with your meal. To sample locally cured meets and artisanal cheeses, start with the charcuterie board, then select from main courses that include grilled bangers and mash, pan-seared trout, and Alberta Angus beef. **Known for:** British high tea; best view in town; local ingredients. [$] *Average main: C$29* ✉ *Prince of Wales Hotel, off Hwy. 5, outside Waterton Townsite, Waterton Lakes National Park* ☎ *844/868–7474 toll-free, 403/236–3400* 🌐 *www.glacierparkcollection.com/lodging/prince-of-wales-hotel/dining-shopping* ⏲ *Closed Oct.–May.*

Thirsty Bear Kitchen & Bar

$$ | **AMERICAN** | Waterton's only gastropub is the place for live music most weekends and casual eats anytime. The nachos here are the best in town, and there's a wide selection of burgers, sandwiches, and wraps—all served with salad or fries. **Known for:** fun atmosphere with big-screen TVs, pool tables, and foosball; live music and a dance floor; great casual dining. [$] *Average main: C$20* ✉ *111 Waterton Ave., Waterton Townsite* ☎ *403/859–2211 Ext. 309* 🌐 *www.thirstybearwaterton.com* ⏲ *Closed mid-Oct.–mid-May.*

Wieners of Waterton

$ | **HOT DOG** | **FAMILY** | If there is such a thing as a gourmet hot dog, then this is the place to find it. The buns here are baked fresh daily, and the all-beef wieners and smokies are sourced locally with one exception: the genuine Nathan's dogs are shipped from New York City.

Did You Know?

The 17.2-km (11-mile) round-trip Crypt Lake Trail is one of the most stunning hikes in the Canadian Rockies.

Known for: fun menu; gourmet hot dogs; interesting toppings. $ *Average main: C$9* ✉ *301 Wind Flower Ave., Waterton Townsite* ☎ *403/859–0007* ⊕ *www.wienersofwaterton.com* ⊘ *Closed Nov.– Mar.*

☕ Coffee and Quick Bites

Waffleton

$ | AMERICAN | Next door to Weiners, this spot specializes in Belgium Liège waffles, made with yeast dough and pearl sugar that caramelizes on the surface; it also has some of the best coffee in town. These indulgent treats are served with whipped cream and juicy berries or smothered in Nutella and sliced bananas. Known for: great coffee; delicious Leige-style waffles; savory waffle combinations. $ *Average main: C$8* ✉ *301 Wind Flower Ave., Waterton Townsite* ⊕ *www.facebook.com/waffleton/* ⊘ *Closed weekdays Nov.–Mar.*

Windflower Ave. Corner Coffee

$ | CAFÉ | This little coffee shop is attached to the Waterton Lakes Opera House and is a great spot to grab a nibble and re-caffeinate. Excellent breakfast sandwiches, bagels, and hearty lunch sandwiches can be picked up before heading out on a hike. Known for: serves Rocky Mountain-roasted Kicking Horse coffee; tasty made-to-order breakfast sandwiches; great to go options perfect to take on a hike. $ *Average main: C$9* ✉ *309 Wind Flower Ave., Waterton Townsite* ☎ *403/331–8194* ⊕ *www.facebook.com/windfloweravecornercoffee/* ⊘ *Closed late Sept.–early-May. No dinner.*

Hotels

Bayshore Inn

$$$$ | HOTEL | Right in town and on the shores of Waterton Lake, this inn has a lot going for it: lovely views, the only on-site spa in Waterton, multiple dining options, and easy access to many services. Pros: great townsite location; only lakefront accommodation in Waterton;

plenty of on-site amenities. Cons: can sometimes hear noise between rooms; rustic motor inn; older-style hotel. $ *Rooms from: C$269* ✉ *111 Waterton Ave., Waterton Townsite* ☎ *888/527–9555, 403/859–2211* ⊕ *www.bayshore-inn.com* ⊘ *Closed mid-Oct.–Apr.* ⇆ *70 rooms* ⦿ *No Meals.*

Bear Mountain Motel

$ | HOTEL | This classic, 1960s motel offers a variety of affordable accommodations that have painted cinder-block walls, wood-beam ceilings, and small bathrooms with shower stalls. Pros: family-run motel right in townsite; most affordable accommodation in Waterton; clean, comfortable, and very basic. Cons: no in-room coffee or tea (available in main office); closed in winter; noise can be an issue with the old cinder-block construction. $ *Rooms from: C$149* ✉ *208 Mount View Rd, Waterton Townsite* ☎ *403/859–2366* ⊕ *bearmountainmotel.com* ⊘ *Closed Oct.–Apr.* ⇆ *36 rooms* ⦿ *No Meals.*

Northland Lodge

$$$$ | B&B/INN | This historic lodge was once the handsome residence of Great Northern Railway (GNR) tycoon Louis W. Hill, and its large balconies offered excellent views; it's rumored that Hill kept his mistress here. Pros: nice views from the deck; historic B&B; breakfast included. Cons: no a/c; no TV; some rooms do not have private baths. $ *Rooms from: C$255* ✉ *408 Evergreen Ave., Waterton Townsite* ☎ *403/859–2353 Canada phone number, 801/809–9380 U.S. phone number* ⊕ *www.northlandlodge.ca* ⊘ *Closed early Oct.–mid-May* ⦿ *Free Breakfast* ⇆ *9 rooms.*

★ Prince of Wales Hotel

$$$$ | HOTEL | A high steeple crowns this iconic, 1920s hotel, which is fantastically ornamented with eaves, balconies, and turrets; is perched between two lakes with a high-mountain backdrop; and has a lobby where two-story windows capture the views. Pros: spectacular valley

and townsite views; historic property; bellmen wear kilts. **Cons:** no TVs; no a/c; very rustic rooms. $ *Rooms from: C$259* ✉ *Prince of Wales Hotel, Waterton Lakes National Park* ✛ *Old Hwy. 5. Turn left at marked access road at top of hill just before village* ☎ *844/868–7474, 403/859–2231* ⊕ *www.glacierparkcollection.com/lodging/prince-of-wales-hotel* ☉ *Closed late Sept.–mid-May* ⇥ *86 rooms* ⦿| *No Meals.*

Waterton Glacier Suites

$$$$ | **HOTEL** | In the heart of the townsite, this all-suite property is within walking distance of restaurants, shopping, and the dock on beautiful Waterton Lake. **Pros:** convenient location; modern suites with mini-refrigerators and a/c; open year-round. **Cons:** no on-site breakfast; pullout sofas uncomfortable; no views. $ *Rooms from: C$319* ✉ *107 Wild Flower Ave, Waterton Townsite* ☎ *403/859–2004, 866/621–3330* ⊕ *www.watertonsuites.com* ⇥ *26 rooms* ⦿| *No Meals.*

Waterton Lakes Lodge

$$$$ | **HOTEL** | **FAMILY** | This hotel in the heart of the townsite has the only indoor swimming pool in Waterton, along with a hot tub, a games room, an extensive fitness center, and a restaurant. **Pros:** swimming pool, hot tub, restaurant, and fitness center; some kitchens and kitchenettes; some suites can accommodate up to six people. **Cons:** older property; some rooms are small; dated decor. $ *Rooms from: C$269* ✉ *101 Clematis Ave, Waterton Lakes National Park* ☎ *888/985–6343, 403/859–2150, 403/859–2229* ⊕ *www.watertonlakeslodge.com* ⇥ *80 rooms* ⦿| *No Meals.*

🏃 Activities

BIKING

Blakiston and Company

BIKING | Rent electric bikes, canoes, kayaks, and stand-up paddleboards through this company. ✉ *102 Mountain*

Rd., Waterton Townsite ☎ *800/456–0772* ⊕ *www.blakistonandcompany.com* ☉ *Closed mid-Oct.–mid-June* ⇥ *from C$20.*

Pat's Waterton

BIKING | **FAMILY** | Choose from surrey, mountain, and e-bikes or motorized scooters at Pat's, which also rents tennis rackets, strollers, coolers, life jackets, hiking poles, bear spray, and binoculars. ✉ *224 Mt. View Rd., Waterton Townsite* ☎ *403/859–2266* ⊕ *www.patswaterton.com* ⇥ *From C$15* ☉ *Closed mid-Oct.–mid-Apr.*

BOATING

Cameron Lake Boat Rentals

BOATING | Rent canoes, kayaks, rowboats, pedal boats, and stand-up paddleboards right at the docks on Cameron Lake. You can also buy tackle and rent fishing rods. ✉ *Cameron Lake, Waterton Lakes National Park* ✛ *At the boat docks at Cameron Lake, 16 km (10 miles) southwest of the townsite* ☎ *403/627–6443* ⊕ *www.cameronlakeboatrentals.com* ⇥ *from C$30.*

Waterton Inter-Nation Shoreline Cruise Co.

BOATING | This company's two-hour round-trip boat tour along Upper Waterton Lake from Waterton Townsite to Goat Haunt Ranger Station is one of the most popular activities in Waterton. The narrated tour passes scenic bays, sheer cliffs, and snow-clad peaks. This company also offers a shuttle service for the Crypt Lake and Vimy Peak hikes. ✉ *101 Waterton Ave., Waterton Lakes National Park* ✛ *Waterton Townsite Marina, northwest corner of Waterton Lake near Bayshore Inn* ☎ *403/859–2362, 403/859–2362* ⊕ *www.watertoncruise.com* ⇥ *C$55* ☉ *Closed early Oct.–mid-June.*

CAMPING

Parks Canada operates a handful of campgrounds (though one of them, the Crandell, was destroyed by the 2017 wildfire) that range from fully serviced to unserviced sites. There are also some backcountry campsites. Visitors can prebook campsites for a fee of C$11 online or C$13.50 by phone. The reservation service is available at *www.reservation.parkscanada.gc.ca* or by phone at *877/737–3783*.

Crandell Campground. Along the Red Rock Parkway a short hike from Crandell Lake, this campground is surrounded by montane forest. It was heavily damaged by the 2017 wildfire. Check the website to see if the campground has reopened before driving there. *On Red Rock Pkwy., 2 km (1.2 miles) before Crandell Lake 403/859–5133.*

Waterton Townsite Campground. Though the campground is busy and windy, sites here are grassy and flat with access to kitchen shelters and have views down the lake into the U.S. part of the Peace Park. *Waterton and Vimy Aves. 877/737–3783.*

EDUCATIONAL PROGRAMS

Park interpreters lead a variety of free interpretive hikes during the summer months from early July to early September. Guests on the hikes can learn about species at risk, the effects of fire in the park, Waterton's historic past, and other topics. Check the schedule and register in advance at the Waterton Lakes National Park Visitor Centre. Children can also participate in the Parks Canada Xplorers program by picking up a booklet filled with fun educational activities that help guide them in their discovery of the park. There are booklets for younger children who cannot read and for older children who can. At the end of the visit, children ·can return with their booklets to the visitor center to receive an official collectible souvenir recognizing them as Parks Canada Xplorers. Each park in Canada has its own unique Xplorers souvenir.

GOLF

Waterton Lakes Golf Course

GOLF | One of Canada's oldest golf courses, the first nine holes of this course were designed by William Thomson and opened for play in 1922. Stanley Thompson, one of the most renowned Canadian golf course architects, advised on the expansion of the course to 18 holes. The Thompson-designed course was opened for play in 1935. There's a· pro shop with club rentals and sales and a clubhouse with a restaurant. It can be windy, but this 18-hole, par 69 course has outstanding views from nearly every green and tee off box. ⊠ *215 Mountain View Rd., Waterton Lakes National Park* ☎ *403/859–2114* ⊕ *www.lakelandgolf-management.com* ⊠ *C$55* ⊙ *Closed mid-Oct.–mid-May.*

HIKING

There are 225 km (191 miles) of trails in Waterton Lakes that range in difficulty from short strolls to strenuous treks. Some trails connect with the trail systems in Montana's Glacier National Park and British Columbia's Akamina-Kishinina Provincial Park. The wildflowers in June are particularly stunning along most trails. In 2017, the Kenow Wildfire damaged more than 80% of the trails in Waterton Lakes National Park. The Crypt Lake trail and the hikes on the U.S. side of the lake that depart from the Goat Haunt Ranger Station were unaffected by the fire. Trails in other parts of the park received varying amounts of damage. Consult the park website for the latest trail reports. *Hiking Glacier and Waterton National Parks*, by Erik Molvar, has detailed information including pictures and GPS-compatible maps for 60 of the best hiking trails in both parks.

HORSEBACK RIDING

Alpine Stables

HORSEBACK RIDING | At these family-owned stables you can arrange hour-long trail rides and full-day guided excursions within the park, as well as multiday pack trips through the Rockies and foothills. They are open May through September. ⊠ *1 Marquis Rd., Waterton Lakes National Park* ☎ *403/859–2462, 403/653–2449*

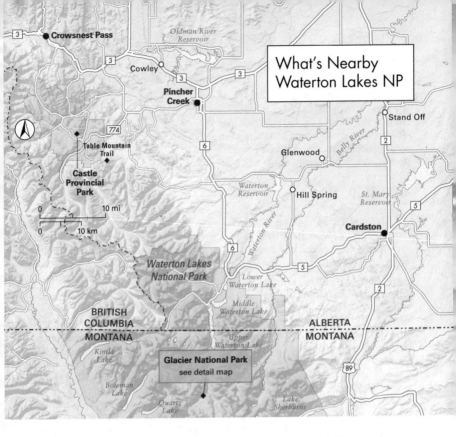

Map labels:
- Crowsnest Pass
- Oldman River Reservoir
- Cowley
- Pincher Creek
- Stand Off
- Table Mountain Trail
- Glenwood
- Castle Provincial Park
- Waterton Reservoir
- Hill Spring
- St. Mary Reservoir
- Cardston
- Waterton Lakes National Park
- Lower Waterton Lake
- Middle Waterton Lake
- BRITISH COLUMBIA
- MONTANA
- ALBERTA
- MONTANA
- Kintla Lake
- Upper Waterton Lake
- Glacier National Park
  see detail map
- Bowman Lake
- Quartz Lake
- Lake Sherburne
- Waterton River
- Belly River

What's Nearby
Waterton Lakes NP

⊕ www.alpinestables.com ✉ From C$45
☾ Closed Oct.–Apr.

What's Nearby

Nature knows no boundaries. The Waterton-Glacier International Peace Park straddles the border between the United States and Canada. The edge of Glacier National Park in Montana is only 44 km (27 miles) southeast of Waterton Lakes National Park. While Glacier National Park is not part of the Canadian Rockies, it is part of the Rockies and part of the Crown of the Continent region. There is much to see in Glacier National Park and it's worth a side-trip if you're visiting Waterton.

There are two ways to get to Glacier National Park—through Chief Mountain Customs or through the Carway border

crossing. Chief Mountain Customs is open seasonally, but Carway is open year-round. If you go through Carway, you'll drive through the Town of Cardston, which is 40 km (25 miles) northeast of Waterton. It's a quaint little town that is home to a unique carriage museum, a historic temple of the Church of Jesus Christ of Latter-day Saints, and good live theater in summer.

Pincher Creek lies 44 km (25 miles) north of Waterton. This small town has some less costly accommodation options if you don't mind staying outside the park. It's also close to Lac Beauvert Provincial Park and Castle Provincial Parks, which are two pretty parks near Waterton that are also worth exploring. About 91 km (56 miles) southeast of Waterton, Castle Mountain Ski Resort is Alberta's second-largest ski area and it's famed for cat skiing.

The Crowsnest Pass Region of Alberta is a hidden gem in the Canadian Rockies, 108 km (67 miles) southeast of Waterton. The scenery is captivating and there are a wide variety of attractions. There's much to see and it's well worth a side trip.

Cardston

55 km (34 miles) northeast of Waterton Lakes National Park and 24½km (15 miles) north of the Montana border.

Cardston is a quaint town with a population of about 3,600 people. The town was established in 1887 by members of The Church of Jesus Christ of Latter-day Saints (LDS) who traveled from Utah in covered wagons—one of the century's last wagon migrations. They were led by Charles Ora Card, the man for whom the town is named. The land on which Cardston was founded was originally inhabited by the Niitsitapi (Blackfoot) people of Kainai, but it was not considered part of Blackfoot Territory by the Government of Canada in the Treaty 7 agreement of 1877. As a result, Cardston sits right next to the Kainai reservation. The population of the town is still predominantly LDS and as a result, it is a dry town. Alcohol is not served in restaurants and there isn't a liquor store in town. Cardston has some unique attractions and can make an interesting stop on the way to visit Glacier National Park in Montana.

GETTING HERE AND AROUND
Cardston is 44 km (27 miles) southeast of Waterton by car on AB-5 East.

 Sights

Cardston Alberta Temple
HISTORIC SIGHT | This Designated National Historic Site of Canada was constructed from 1913–1923 by members of The Church of Jesus Christ of Latter-day

Saints. It was the eighth temple constructed by the church. The monumental granite structure is built on a hill with large landscaped grounds and views of Chief Mountain in the distance. It was designed by American architects, Hyrum Pope and Harold Burton, in the Prairie School style of Frank Lloyd Wright. The building's interlocking geometric shapes form a pyramidal shape, evocative of Pre-Columbian architecture. Only members of the church are allowed inside the temple, but there is a visitor's center that can be explored and anyone is welcome to walk around the grounds. ✉ *348 3rd St. W., Cardston* ☎ *403/653–3552* ⊕ *churchofjesuschristtemples.org/cardston-alberta-temple.*

Carriage House Theatre
PERFORMANCE VENUE | **FAMILY** | This 300-seat air-conditioned theater has been hosting live theater performances since 1989. Productions run regularly throughout July and August with a variety of family-friendly shows on offer. There are also some winter community theater productions. ✉ *353 Main St., Cardston* ☎ *403/653–1000* ⊕ *www.carriagehousetheatre.com* 🎟 *C$32* 🕐 *Closed Sun.*

★ Remington Carriage Museum
HISTORY MUSEUM | This unique museum houses the largest collection of horse-drawn vehicles in North America with over 330 carriages, buggies, wagons and sleighs. The nucleus of the collection, some 48 carriages, was donated by Don Remington, a local Cardston resident who restored and collected horse-drawn vehicles. Carriage rides are offered during the summer months for an extra charge. ✉ *623 Main St., Cardston* ☎ *403/653–5139, 403/653–5141 carriage rides* ⊕ *remingtoncarriagemuseum.ca* 🎟 *C$15; C$7 carriage rides.*

Coffee and Quick Bites

What's Pop'n Pop Shop
$ | **HOT DOG** | This local hangout sells specialty fizzy drinks; guests choose their favorite soda and add flavored syrups. Hot dogs, cookies, ice cream, frozen yogurt, milkshakes, ice cream floats, and seasoned popcorn are also on the menu. **Known for:** good ice cream and frozen yogurt; great selection of flavors and mixes; fun non-alcoholic drinks. [$] *Average main: C$5* ✉ *355 1st St. E, Cardston* 🌐 *www.facebook.com/Whatspopn.popshop/* ⏲ *Closed Sun.*

Hotels

South Country Inn
$ | **HOTEL** | Rooms at this inn come in a variety of different configurations and there are accessible and pet-friendly rooms. **Pros:** indoor swimming pool and hot tub; centrally located; reasonably priced. **Cons:** needs an update; older property; no coffee and tea makers in rooms. [$] *Rooms from: C$115* ✉ *404 Main St., Cardston* ☎ *403/653–8000* 🌐 *southcountryinn.com* 🍴 *No Meals* 🛏 *44 rooms.*

Activities

CAMPING

Lee Creek Campground. Situated near beautiful Lee Creek close to sports fields, the outdoor public swimming pool, and the Remington Carriage Museum, this campground is great for groups, families, and individuals. All sites have firepits and picnic tables. There are 33 fully serviced RV sites (power/water/sewer), 10 partially serviced sites (power/water), and many unserviced and group tenting sites. The campground has free Wi-Fi, washrooms, showers, and coin laundry facilities. Though alcohol is not sold in Cardston, campground guests are welcome to bring their own to consume at their own site. ☎ *877/471–2267* 🌐 *sites.google.com/view/leecreekcampground; from C$24; mid-Sept.–mid-May.*

Castle Provincial Park

Castle Provincial Park and Castle Wildland Provincial Park encompass more than 1,050 square km (405 square miles) of wildly beautiful terrain northwest of Waterton Lakes National Park. This part of the Canadian Rockies was officially designated as a provincial park in 2017 to protect the Crown of the Continent ecosystem and the wildlife that lives there. The park gets its name from the South Castle River which flows through it. It's a place of rugged mountains, foothills, meadows, and thick forests. Visitor amenities include hiking trails, campgrounds, and the second largest ski resort in Alberta.

GETTING HERE AND AROUND

Castle Provincial Park is 78 km (48 miles) southwest of Waterton Lakes National Park by car.

Sights

TRAILS

Table Mountain Trail
TRAIL | The view from the top of Table Mountain is one of the prettiest scenes in the Canadian Rockies. The hike is 10 km (6.2 miles) round-trip and takes about four hours in total. It's a moderately difficult trail with a 700-meter (2,296 feet) elevation gain and a lot of scrambling near the top, but the views are well worth the effort. The trail begins in Castle Provincial Park and ends in Castle Wildlands Provincial Park. You'll find the trailhead at Beaver Mines Lake Campground. *Difficult* ✉ *Beaver Mines Lake Campground, Castle Provincial Park* ✥ *Trailhead: Beaver Mines Lake Campground.*

Coffee and Quick Bites

Miner's Mercantile and Bakery

$ | **SANDWICHES** | At the edge of Castle Provincial Park, this place has a funky deli and bakery with hot and cold sandwiches, breakfast sandwiches, and an impressive coffee and tea menu. The store also sells ice cream and fresh baked goods and you can pick up food, liquor, camping, and fishing supplies in the mercantile. [$] *Average main: C$12* ✉ *602 1st Ave. (Hwy. 774), Beaver Mines, Castle Provincial Park* ☎ *403/627–4878* 🌐 *www.minersmercantile.ca.*

Hotels

Castle Ski Lodge

$$ | **HOTEL** | This small resort-operated hotel is right on the mountain. **Pros:** many amenities; on-mountain hotel rooms; economical. **Cons:** older hotel; hostel rooms have shared bathroom facilities; pets are not allowed. [$] *Rooms from: C$169* ✉ *Castle Mountain Resort, Hwy. 774, Castle Provincial Park* ☎ *403/627–5121* 🌐 *www.staycastle.ca* 🍴 *No Meals* 🛏 *10 rooms, 14 hostel beds.*

Activities

CAMPING

A wide variety of camping options are available in these provincial parks. There are four regular campgrounds at Beaver Mines Lake, Castle Falls, Castle River Bridge, and Lynx Creek. Only Lynx Creek is first-come, first-served, the others require advance reservations. There are two comfort camping options in Castle Provincial Park: rustic cabins at Beaver Mines Lake and cabins with electricity at Castle River Bridge. You can reserve campgrounds and comfort cabins online (*Reserve.AlbertaParks.ca*) or by calling 877/537–2757. Individual campsites can be booked up to 90 days in advance. Comfort camping can be reserved up to 180 days in advance. There are several designated camping areas in the park where you can camp for free, but a permit is required. Backcountry camping is allowed without a permit in Castle Wildland Provincial Park.

SKIING

Castle Mountain Resort

SKIING & SNOWBOARDING | Often called the "best kept secret in the Canadian Rockies," this gem of a ski resort is home to one of North America's only resort-based cat skiing operations. It was founded in 1966 and has grown into the second-largest ski resort in the Alberta. Known for its laid-back vibe, this resort has more than 94 runs across two mountains serviced by six lifts. It's also home to some of the longest, continuous fall line runs in North America. There's a ski lodge offering equipment rentals and lessons as well as food and drinks. ✉ *Castle Mountain Resort, Hwy. 774* ☎ *403/627–5101, 888/754–8667* 🌐 *www.skicastle.ca* 🎟 *$99* 🕒 *Closed early Apr.–early Dec.*

Syncline Cross-Country Ski Area

SKIING & SNOWBOARDING | More than 20 km (12 miles) of packed and tracked cross-country ski trails can be found in this area between the South Castle and West Castle rivers. The trails lead through rolling landscapes of forests and meadows. A nonprofit volunteer group known as the Syncline Castle Trails Association (SCaT) helps maintain these trails. Alberta Parks maintains and plows the parking areas. You can hike or bike the trails in summer and snowshoe, ski, or fat bike in winter. ✉ *Syncline North Day Use Area* 🌐 *synclinecastletrails.org.*

SWIMMING

Castle Falls

SWIMMING | If you like wild swimming holes, you'll love this spot. The turquoise blue water and the waterfall make it a popular place to cool off on a hot summer day. There are several places along the river where people swim. Use your judgment though—if the river is flowing too quickly, just sit on the rocks and soak your feet in the cool water. ✉ *Castle Falls*

Day Use Area ✚ 20 km (12 miles) west of Pincher Creek on Hwy. 507, 16 km (10 miles) south on Hwy. 774 and 6 km (4 miles) west on an access road ⊕ www. albertaparks.ca/parks/south/castle-pp/ information-facilities/day-use/castle-falls.

Glacier National Park, United States

The massive peaks of the Continental Divide in northwest Montana are the backbone of Glacier National Park and its sister park in Canada, Waterton Lakes, which together make up the International Peace Park. From their slopes, melting snow and alpine glaciers yield the headwaters of rivers that flow west to the Pacific Ocean, north to the Arctic Ocean, and southeast to the Atlantic Ocean via the Gulf of Mexico. Coniferous forests, thickly vegetated stream bottoms, and green-carpeted meadows provide homes and sustenance for all kinds of wildlife.

The western side of the park is closest to the airport in the city of Kalispell and has the most amenities. Highlights include the bustling village of West Glacier, Apgar Village, Lake McDonald, and the tiny community of Polebridge. West Glacier Village is just over 2 miles from the Apgar Visitor Center.

The Going-to-the-Sun Road, one of the nation's most beautiful drives, connects Lake McDonald on the western side of Glacier with St. Mary Lake on the east. Turnoffs provide views of the high country and glacier-carved valleys. Consider making the ride in one of the vintage red buses operated by Glacier National Park Lodges (844/868–7474). Drivers double as guides, and they can roll back the tops of the vehicles for better views. Logan Pass, elevation 2,026 meters (6,646 feet), sits at the Continental Divide, the highest point on the Going-to-the-Sun Road.

The park's eastern end has historical and cultural significance to the Blackfeet Nation, and much of this region is on tribal lands. East Glacier Park Village is the hub with shops, restaurants, and hotels. Two Medicine Lake, St. Mary Lake, and Swiftcurrent Lake are scenic highlights of this area. The eastern end of the Going-to-the-Sun Road is near the tiny community of St. Mary on the western border of the Blackfeet Indian Reservation.

GETTING HERE AND AROUND
The nearest airport to Glacier is Glacier Park International Airport (*FCA; 406/257–5994 wiflyglacier.com*) in Kalispell (25 miles). Five major airlines fly into the airport and service the national park and the Flathead Valley region.

The park operates a free hop-on, hop-off shuttle along the Going-to-the-Sun Road from July through early September. The shuttle runs from Apgar to St. Mary Visitor Center; park visitor centers have departure information.

Montana's Amtrak stations are all on the Empire Builder route that connects Glacier National Park with Chicago and Portland/Seattle. The main stops near the park are at East Glacier Park Village, West Glacier, Essex, and Whitefish. From the stations, you can rent a car.

AIRPORT Glacier Park International Airport.
✉ *4170 Hwy. 2 E, Kalispell* ☎ *406/257–5994* ⊕ *iflyglacier.com.*

◉ Sights

HISTORIC SIGHTS
Apgar
TOWN | FAMILY | On the southwest end of Lake McDonald, this tiny village has a few stores, an ice-cream shop, motels, ranger buildings, a campground, and a historic schoolhouse. A store called the Montana House is open year-round, but except for the weekend-only visitor center, no other services remain open from November to mid-May. Across

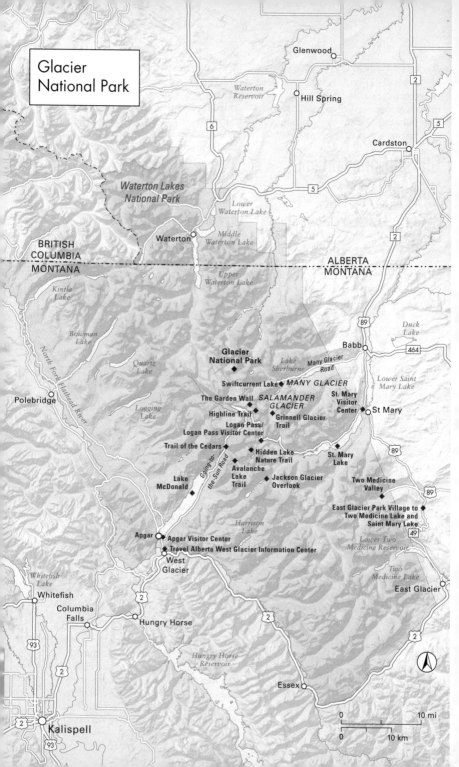

Glacier National Park

Glenwood

Hill Spring

Cardston

Waterton Reservoir

6

5

5

2

Waterton Lakes National Park

2

Lower Waterton Lake

Waterton

Middle Waterton Lake

BRITISH COLUMBIA

ALBERTA

MONTANA

MONTANA

Upper Waterton Lake

Kintla Lake

Bowman Lake

North Fork Flathead River

89

Duck Lake

Babb

464

Quartz Lake

Glacier National Park

Lake Sherburne

Many Glacier Road

Lower Saint Mary Lake

Swiftcurrent Lake ◆ *MANY GLACIER*

Polebridge

Logging Lake

The Garden Wall ◆

SALAMANDER GLACIER

St. Mary Visitor Center ◆

St Mary

Highline Trail ◆

Grinnell Glacier Trail

Logan Pass/ Logan Pass Visitor Center ◆

Trail of the Cedars ◆

Hidden Lake Nature Trail ◆

St. Mary Lake ◆

89

Going-to-the-Sun Road

Avalanche Lake Trail ◆

Lake McDonald ◆

Jackson Glacier Overlook ◆

Two Medicine Valley ◆

East Glacier Park Village to Two Medicine Lake and Saint Mary Lake ◆

89

Harrison Lake

Apgar ◆ Apgar Visitor Center ◆ Travel Alberta West Glacier Information Center ◆

West Glacier

Lower Two Medicine Reservoir

49

Whitefish Lake

Whitefish

Two Medicine Lake

East Glacier

Columbia Falls

93

Hungry Horse

2

2

Hungry Horse Reservoir

2

Essex

Kalispell

93

0   10 mi

0   10 km

the street from the visitor center, **Apgar Discovery Cabin** is filled with animal posters, kids' activities, and maps. ⊠ *Apgar village, Glacier National Park* ✛ *2 miles north of west entrance* ☎ *406/888–7939.*

SCENIC DRIVES

East Glacier Park Village to Two Medicine Lake and Saint Mary Lake

SCENIC DRIVE | You'll see the striking contrast of prairies and mountains as you travel northwest from East Glacier Park Village to Two Medicine Lake on MT-49. Once you turn onto Two Medicine Road, you'll be heading straight toward snowcapped peaks and lovely Two Medicine Lake. From there, head back out to MT-49 and then to US-89 North to make your way to the town of St. Mary and then onto the Going-to-the-Sun Road to reach St. Mary Lake, the park's second largest. The entire route is 49 miles one-way. End the drive with an additional stop at Swiftcurrent Lake, and you'll cover about 75 miles total. ⊠ *East Glacier Village, Glacier National Park.*

SCENIC STOPS

The Garden Wall

NATURE SIGHT | An abrupt and jagged wall of rock juts above the road and is visible for about 10 miles as it follows Logan Creek from just past Avalanche Creek Campground to Logan Pass. ⊠ *Garden Wall, Going-to-the-Sun Rd, Glacier National Park* ✛ *Going-to-the-Sun Rd., 24–34 miles northeast of West Glacier.*

Jackson Glacier Overlook

VIEWPOINT | On the eastern side of the Continental Divide, you come into view of Jackson Glacier looming in a rocky pass across the upper St. Mary River valley. If it isn't covered with snow, you'll see sharp peaks of ice. The glacier is shrinking and may disappear in another 100 years. ⊠ *Jackson Glacier Overlook, Glacier National Park* ✛ *5 miles east of Logan Pass.*

Lake McDonald

BODY OF WATER | This beautiful, 10-mile-long lake, the parks' largest, is accessible year-round from Going-to-the-Sun Road. Cruise to the middle for a view of the surrounding glacier-clad mountains. You can fish and horseback ride at either end, and in winter, snowshoe and cross-country ski. ⊠ *Glacier National Park* ✛ *2 miles north of west entrance.*

Logan Pass

SCENIC DRIVE | At 6,646 feet, this is the park's highest point accessible by motor vehicle. Crowded in July and August, it offers unparalleled views of both sides of the Continental Divide. Mountain goats, bighorn sheep, and grizzly bears frequent the area. The Logan Pass Visitor Center is just east of the pass. ⊠ *Logan Pass, Glacier National Park* ✛ *34 miles east of West Glacier, 18 miles west of St. Mary.*

St. Mary Lake

BODY OF WATER | When the breezes calm, the park's second-largest lake mirrors the snowcapped granite peaks that line the St. Mary Valley. To get a good look at the beautiful scenery, follow the Sun Point Nature Trail (closed for renovation in 2016) along the lake's shore. The hike is 1 mile each way. ⊠ *St. Mary Lake, Glacier National Park* ✛ *1 mile west of St. Mary.*

Swiftcurrent Lake

BODY OF WATER | The Many Glacier Hotel is perched on the shores of Swiftcurrent Lake. The views here are some of the park's prettiest, taking in the mountains that rise more than 3,000 feet immediately west of the lake. Scenic boat tours ply the waters and transport hikers to trails that lead to other lakes and glaciers in the park's Many Glacier region. ⊠ *Swiftcurrent Lake.*

Two Medicine Valley

NATURE SIGHT | Rugged, often windy, and always beautiful, the valley is a remote 9-mile drive from Highway 49 and is surrounded by some of the park's most stark, rocky peaks. Near the valley's lake

On the eastern side of the Continental Divide, the Jackson Glacier is visible in a rocky pass across the St. Mary River valley.

you can rent a canoe, take a narrated boat tour, camp, and hike. Bears frequent the area. The road is closed from late October through late May. ✉ *Glacier National Park ✛ Two Medicine entrance, 9 miles east of Hwy. 49* ☎ *406/888–7800, 406/257–2426 boat tours.*

TRAILS

Avalanche Lake Trail

TRAIL | From Avalanche Creek Campground, take this 3-mile trail leading to mountain-ringed Avalanche Lake. The walk is only moderately difficult (it ascends 730 feet), making this one of the park's most accessible backcountry lakes. Crowds fill the parking area and trail during July and August and on sunny weekends in May and June. *Moderate.* ✉ *Avalanche Creek Campground, Glacier National Park ✛ Trailhead: across from Avalanche Creek Campground, 15 miles north of Apgar on Going-to-the-Sun Rd.*

Grinnell Glacier Trail

TRAIL | In 1926, one giant ice mass broke apart to create the Salamander and Grinnell glaciers, which have been shrinking

ever since. The 5½-mile trail to Grinnell Glacier, the park's most accessible, is marked by several spectacular viewpoints. You start at Swiftcurrent Lake's picnic area, climb a moraine to Lake Josephine, then climb to the Grinnell Glacier overlook. Halfway up, turn around to see the prairie land to the northeast. You can cut about 2 miles (each way) off the hike by taking scenic boat rides across Swiftcurrent Lake and Lake Josephine. From July to mid-September, a ranger-led hike departs from the Many Glacier Hotel boat dock on most mornings at 8:30. *Difficult.* ✉ *Swift Current Lake picnic area, Glacier National Park ✛ Trailheads: Swiftcurrent Lake picnic area or Lake Josephine boat dock.*

Hidden Lake Nature Trail

TRAIL | Hidden Lake Overlook is an easy, 1½-mile hike from the Logan Pass Visitor Center. Along the way, you'll pass through beautiful alpine meadows known as the Hanging Gardens. Enjoy incredible views of Hidden Lake, Bearhat Mountain, Mt. Cannon, Fusillade Mountain,

Gunsight Mountain, and Sperry Glacier. It's common to see mountain goats near the overlook. If you want a challenge, continue hiking all the way down to the edge of the lake—a moderate 5.4-mile round-trip hike. *Easy to moderate.* ⊠ *Logan Pass Visitor Center, Glacier National Park* ✛ *Trailhead: behind Logan Pass Visitor Center.*

★ **Highline Trail**

TRAIL | From the Logan Pass parking lot, hike north along the Garden Wall and just below the craggy Continental Divide. Wildflowers dominate the 7.6 miles to Granite Park Chalet, a National Historic Landmark, where hikers with reservations can overnight. Return to Logan Pass along the same trail or hike down 4½ miles (a 2,500-foot descent) on the Loop Trail. *Moderate.* ⊠ *Logan Pass Visitor Center, Glacier National Park* ✛ *Trailhead: at Logan Pass Visitor Center.*

Trail of the Cedars

TRAIL | **FAMILY** | This ½-mile boardwalk loop through an ancient cedar and hemlock forest is a favorite of families with small children and people with disabilities (it's wheelchair accessible). Interpretive signs describe the habitat and natural history. *Easy.* ⊠ *Trail of Cedars, Glacier National Park* ✛ *Trailhead: across from Avalanche Creek Campground, 15 miles north of Apgar on Going-to-the-Sun Rd.*

VISITOR CENTERS

Apgar Visitor Center

VISITOR CENTER | **FAMILY** | This is a great first stop if you're entering the park from the west. Here you can get all kinds of information, including maps, permits, books, and the *Junior Ranger* newspaper, and you can check out displays that will help you plan your tour of the park. There is a variety of ranger-led programs including free snowshoe walks in winter. Snowshoes can be rented for $2 at the visitor center. ⊠ *Glacier National Park* ✛ *2 miles north of West Glacier in Apgar Village* ☎ *406/888–7800.*

Logan Pass Visitor Center

VISITOR CENTER | Built of stone, this center stands sturdy against the severe weather that forces it to close in winter. When it's open, rangers give 10-minute talks on the alpine environment and offer a variety of activities including guided hikes. You can get advice from them and buy books and maps. ⊠ *Going-to-the-Sun Rd., Glacier National Park* ✛ *34 miles east of West Glacier, 18 miles west of St. Mary* ☎ *406/888–7800.*

St. Mary Visitor Center

VISITOR CENTER | Glacier's largest visitor complex has a huge relief map of the park's peaks and valleys and screens a 15-minute orientation video. Exhibits help visitors understand the park from the perspective of its original inhabitants—the Blackfeet, Salish, Kootenai, and Pend d'Orielle peoples. Rangers conduct evening presentations in summer, and the auditorium hosts Native America Speaks programs. The center also has books and maps for sale, backcountry camping permits, and large viewing windows facing the 10-mile-long St. Mary Lake. ⊠ *Going-to-the-Sun Rd., off U.S. 89, Glacier National Park* ☎ *406/732–7750.*

Travel Alberta West Glacier Information Center

VISITOR CENTER | Plan your visit to the Canadian side of the International Peace Park with the help of travel experts at this visitor center in West Glacier. You'll find maps, pamphlets, displays, and bathroom facilities here. ⊠ *125 Going-to-the-Sun Rd., West Glacier* ☎ *406/888–5743* ⊙ *Closed Mid-Sept.–mid-May.*

🍴 Restaurants

Jammer Joe's Grill & Pizzeria

$$ | **AMERICAN** | Across the parking lot from Lake McDonald Lodge, Jammer Joe's Grill & Pizzeria was named after the historic red jammer buses that have been used for park tours since 1936. The restaurant

Glacier in One Day

It's hard to beat the **Going-to-the-Sun Road** for a one-day trip in Glacier National Park. This itinerary takes you from west to east—if you're starting from St. Mary, take the tour backward. First, however, call the Glacier Park Boat Company (406/257–2426) to make a reservation for a boat tour on **St. Mary Lake** in the east or **Lake McDonald**, in the west, depending on your trip's end point. Then drive up Going-to-the-Sun Road to **Avalanche Creek Campground** for a 30-minute stroll along the fragrant **Trail of the Cedars.** Afterward, continue driving up—you can see views of waterfalls and wildlife to the left and an awe-inspiring, precipitous drop to the right. At the summit, **Logan Pass**, your arduous climb is rewarded with a gorgeous view of immense peaks, sometimes complemented by the sight of a mountain goat. Stop in at the **Logan Pass Visitor Center,** then take the 1½-mile **Hidden Lake Nature Trail** up to prime wildlife-viewing spots. Have a picnic at the overlook above Hidden Lake. In the afternoon, continue driving east over the mountains. Stop at the **Jackson Glacier Overlook** to view one of the park's largest glaciers. Continue down; eventually the forest thins, the vistas grow broader, and a gradual transition to the high plains begins. When you reach **Rising Sun Campground**, take the one-hour St. Mary Lake boat tour to St. Mary Falls. The Going-to-the-Sun Road is generally closed from mid-September to mid-June.

serves an all-you-can-eat lunch buffet, pizzas, soups, burgers, and sandwiches in a casual atmosphere. **Known for:** good pizza; lunch buffet; great place to pick up sandwiches for a picnic. $ *Average main: $15* ⊠ *Lake McDonald Lodge, Glacier National Park* ✛ *10 miles north of Apgar on Going-to-the-Sun Rd.* ☎ *303/265–7010 outside the U.S., 855/733–4522 in the U.S.* ⊕ *www.glaciernationalparklodges. com* ⊘ *Closed mid-Sept.–mid-May.*

Lucke's Lounge

$$ | AMERICAN | The all-day bar menu at Lucke's Lounge features bison burgers, sandwiches, salads, and appetizers alongside yet another great lake view. They also serve a nice selection of Montana micro-brews, wines, and craft cocktails. **Known for:** Montana microbrews; great view; casual dining. $ *Average main: $15* ⊠ *Lake McDonald Lodge, Glacier National Park* ✛ *10 miles north of Apgar on the Going-to-the-Sun Rd.* ☎ *855/733–4522 in the U.S.,* *303/265–7010 outside the U.S.* ⊕ *www. glaciernationalparklodges.com* ⊘ *Closed mid-Sept.–mid-May.*

Russell's Fireside Dining Room

$$$ | AMERICAN | Take in a great view of Lake McDonald while enjoying standards such as pasta, steak, wild game, and salmon; delicious salads; or local favorites like the huckleberry elk burger or the Montana rainbow trout. Many ingredients are locally sourced, and there is a nice selection of cocktails, wine, and craft beer. **Known for:** breakfast and (on request) box lunches; incredible views of Lake McDonald; hearty regional fare. $ *Average main: $17* ⊠ *Lake McDonald Lodge, Glacier National Park* ✛ *10 miles north of Apgar on the Going-to-the-Sun Rd.* ☎ *855/733–452 in the U.S.,* *303/265–7010 outside the U.S.* ⊕ *www. glaciernationalparklodges.com* ⊘ *Closed mid-Sept.–mid-May. No lunch.*

Hotels

★ Lake McDonald Lodge

$$ | **HOTEL** | On the shores of Lake McDonald, near Apgar and West Glacier, this historic lodge—where public spaces feature massive timbers, stone fireplaces, and animal trophies—is an ideal base for exploring the park's western side. **Pros:** close to Apgar, West Glacier, and Going-to-the-Sun Road; lakeside setting; historic property. **Cons:** small bathrooms; no TV (except in suites) and limited Wi-Fi; rustic. [$] *Rooms from: $200* ✉ *Lake McDonald, Going-to-the-Sun Rd., Glacier National Park* ☎ *855/733–4522, 406/888–5431* 🌐 *www.glaciernationalparklodges.com* 🕒 *Closed mid-Sept.–mid-May* 🛏 *80 units* 🍴 *No Meals.*

Many Glacier Hotel

$$$ | **HOTEL** | On Swiftcurrent Lake in the park's northeastern section, this is the most isolated of the grand hotels, and—especially if you are able to book a lake-view balcony room—among the most scenic. **Pros:** good hiking trails nearby; stunning views from lodge; secluded. **Cons:** the road leading to the lodge is very rough; no TV, limited Internet; rustic rooms. [$] *Rooms from: $207* ✉ *Many Glacier Hotel, Glacier National Park* ✣ *12 miles west of Babb on Many Glacier Rd* ☎ *855/733–4522, 406/732–4411* 🌐 *www.glaciernationalparklodges.com* 🕒 *Closed mid-Sept.–mid-June* 🛏 *214 rooms* 🍴 *No Meals.*

Village Inn

$$ | **HOTEL** | Listen to waves gently lap the shores of beautiful Lake McDonald at this motel, which is on the National Register of Historic Places and was fully renovated in recent years, so all its rooms have Wi-Fi, new beds, and furnishings that fit with the historic style. **Pros:** kitchenettes in some rooms; great views; convenient Apgar village location. **Cons:** no in-room phones; no a/c; rustic motel. [$] *Rooms from: $165* ✉ *Village Inn, Glacier National Park* ☎ *855/733–4522* 🌐 *www.glaciernationalparklodges.com* 🕒 *Closed Oct.–late May* 🛏 *36 rooms* 🍴 *No Meals.*

Activities

BIKING

Cyclists in Glacier must stay on roads or bike routes and are not permitted on hiking trails or in the backcountry. The one-lane, unpaved Inside North Fork Road from Apgar to Polebridge is well suited to mountain bikers. Two Medicine Road is an intermediate paved route, with a mild grade at the beginning, becoming steeper as you approach Two Medicine Campground. Much of the western half of Going-to-the-Sun Road is closed to bikes from 11 am to 4 pm. Other restrictions apply during peak traffic periods and road construction. Many cyclists enjoy the Going-to-the-Sun Road prior to its opening to vehicular traffic in mid-June. You cannot cycle all the way over the pass in early June, but you can cycle as far as the road is plowed and ride back down without encountering much traffic besides a few snowplows and construction vehicles. You can find thrilling off-road trails just outside the park in Whitefish, which is the closest place to rent bikes.

Glacier Cyclery

BIKING | Daily and weekly bike rentals of touring, road, and mountain bikes for all ages and skill levels are available here. The shop also sells bikes, equipment, and attire, and does repairs. Information about local trails is available on its website and in the store. ✉ *326 2nd St E, Whitefish* ☎ *406/862–6446* 🌐 *www.glaciercyclery.com* 🎟 *From $30.*

Great Northern Cycle & Ski

BIKING | You can rent road and mountain bikes from this outfitter, which also services and repairs bikes and sells cycling and skiing attire and gear. ✉ *328 Central Ave, Whitefish* ☎ *406/862–5321* 🌐 *www.gncycleski.com* 🎟 *From $75.*

BOATING AND RAFTING

Glacier has many stunning lakes and rivers, and boating is a popular park activity. Many rafting companies provide adventures along the border of the park on the Middle and North Forks of the Flathead River. The Middle Fork has some excellent white water, while the North Fork has both slow- and fast-moving sections. If you bring your own raft or kayak—watercraft such as Sea-Doos or Jet Skis are not allowed in the park—stop at the Hungry Horse Ranger Station in the Flathead National Forest near West Glacier to obtain a permit. Consider starting at Ousel Creek and floating to West Glacier on the Middle Fork of the Flathead River.

Glacier Park Boat Company

BOATING | This company conducts 45- to 90-minute tours of five lakes. A Lake McDonald cruise takes you from the dock at Lake McDonald Lodge to the middle of the lake for an unparalleled view of the Continental Divide's Garden Wall. The Many Glacier tours on Swiftcurrent Lake and Lake Josephine depart from Many Glacier Hotel and provide views of the Continental Divide. Two Medicine Lake cruises leave from the dock near the ranger station and lead to several trails. St. Mary Lake cruises leave from the launch near the Rising Sun Campground and head to Red Eagle Mountain and other spots. You can also rent small watercraft at Apgar, Lake McDonald, Two Medicine, and Many Glacier. ✉ *Lake McDonald Lodge* ☎ *406/257–2426* ⊕ *www.glacierparkboats.com* ☎ *Tours from $22.25, rentals from $15* ⊘ *Closed mid-Sept.–mid-May.*

CAMPING

There are several major campgrounds in Glacier National Park, and excellent backcountry sites for backpackers. Reservations for St. Mary campground are available through the National Park Reservation Service (*877/444–6777 or 518/885–3639*). Reservations may be made up to five months in advance. *www.recreation. gov/camping/gateways/2725.*

Apgar Campground. This popular and large campground on the southern shore of Lake McDonald in the park's western reaches has many activities and services. *Apgar Rd. 406/888–7800.*

Avalanche Creek Campground. This peaceful campground on Going-to-the-Sun Road is shaded by huge red cedars and bordered by Avalanche Creek. *15.7 miles from west entrance on Going-to-the-Sun Rd. 406/888–7800.*

Kintla Lake Campground. Beautiful and remote, this is a trout fisherman's dream. *14 miles north of Polebridge Ranger Station on Inside North Fork Rd.*

Many Glacier Campground. One of the most beautiful spots in the park is also a favorite for bears. *Next to Swiftcurrent Motor Inn on Many Glacier Rd.*

Sprague Creek Campground. This sometimes noisy roadside campground for tents, RVs, and truck campers (no towed units) offers spectacular views of the lake and sunsets, and there's fishing from shore. *Going-to-the-Sun Rd., 1 mile south of Lake McDonald Lodge. 406/888–7800.*

St. Mary Campground. This large, grassy spot alongside the lake and stream has mountain views and cool breezes. *Roughly 1 mile from St. Mary entrance to Going-to-the-Sun Rd. 406/888–7800.*

EDUCATIONAL PROGRAMS

Ranger-led Activities

OTHER ATTRACTION | **FAMILY** | Free ranger-led programs, most of them held daily from July to early September, include guided hikes, group walks, evening talks, historical tours, gaze-at-the-stars parties, and naturalist discussions. For the Native America Speaks program, tribal members share their history and culture through stories, poetry, music, and dance. In winter, guided, two-hour snowshoe treks take place in the Apgar area. Among the activities for children is the **Junior Ranger Program,** for which children between ages 6 and 12 complete fun educational tasks to become Junior Rangers. ✉ *Apgar Village Visitor Center* ☎ *406/888–7800* ⊕ *www.nps.gov/glac/planyourvisit/ranger-led-activities.htm* 🖃 *Free.*

FISHING

Within Glacier there's an almost unlimited range of fishing possibilities, with catch-and-release encouraged. You can fish in most waters of the park, but the best fishing is generally in the least accessible spots. A license is not required inside the park, but you must stop by a park office to pick up a copy of the regulations. The season runs from the third Saturday in May through November. Several companies offer guided fishing trips.

■ TIP→ **Fishing on both the North Fork and the Middle Fork of the Flathead River requires a Montana conservation license ($10), an invasive species pass ($7.50), and a Montana fishing license ($42.50 for two consecutive days or $103.50 for a season).**

They are available at most convenience stores, sports shops, and from the Montana Department of Fish, Wildlife, and Parks (*406/752–5501, www.fwp.mt.gov*).

HIKING

With more than 730 miles of marked trails, Glacier is a hiker's paradise. Trail maps are available at all visitor centers and entrance stations. Before hiking, ask about trail closures due to bear or mountain lion activity. Never hike alone. For backcountry hiking, pick up a permit from park headquarters or the Apgar Backcountry Permit Center (☎ *406/888–7939*) near Glacier's west entrance.

Glacier Guides

HIKING & WALKING | The exclusive backpacking guide service in Glacier National Park can arrange guided full- or multiday hikes. All are customized to match the skill level of the hikers, and they include stops to identify plants, animals, and habitats. ✉ *11970 US 2 E, West Glacier* ☎ *406/387–5555, 800/521–7238* ⊕ *www.glacierguides.com* 🖃 *From $58.*

HORSEBACK RIDING

Horses are permitted on many trails within the parks; check for seasonal exceptions. Horseback riding is prohibited on paved roads. You can pick up a brochure with suggested routes and lists of outfitters from any visitor center or entrance station. The Sperry Chalet Trail to the view of Sperry Glacier above Lake McDonald is a tough 7-mile climb.

Swan Mountain Outfitters - Glacier Division

HORSEBACK RIDING | The only outfitter that offers horseback riding inside the park, Swan begins its treks at Apgar, Lake McDonald, Many Glacier, and West Glacier. Trips for beginning to advanced riders cover both flat and mountainous terrain. Fishing can also be included, and this operator also offers one- or multiday llama pack trips. Riders must be seven or older and weigh less than 250 pounds. Reservations are essential. ✉ *Lake McDonald Lodge, Glacier National Park* ⊹ *Lake McDonald Corral is located across from Lake McDonald Lodge, just east of Going-to-the-Sun Road* ☎ *877/888–5557 central reservations, 406/387–4405 Apgar Corral* ⊕ *www.swanmountainglacier.com* 🖃 *From $55.*

MULTISPORT OUTFITTERS

Glacier Guides and Montana Raft Company

WHITE-WATER RAFTING | Take a raft trip through the Wild-and-Scenic–designated white water of the Middle Fork of the Flathead and combine it with a hike, horseback ride, or barbecue. Other offerings include guided hikes and bike rides, fly-fishing trips, and multiday

adventures. The company also offers bike (including e-bike) rentals and fly-fishing lessons. ✉ *11970 US 2 E, Glacier National Park* ✥ *1 mile west of West Glacier* ☎ *406/387–5555, 800/521–7238* 🌐 *www.glacierguides.com* 🎟 *From $69.*

Glacier Raft Company and Outdoor Center
WHITE-WATER RAFTING | In addition to running fishing trips, family float rides, saddle-and-paddle adventures, kayak trips, and high-adrenaline white-water adventure rafting excursions, this outfitter will set you up with camping, backpacking, and fishing gear. There's also a full-service fly-fishing shop and outdoor store. You can stay in one of 13 log cabins or a glacier-view home. ✉ *12400 U.S 2 E, West Glacier* ☎ *406/888–5454, 800/235–6781* 🌐 *www.glacierraftco.com* 🎟 *From $65.*

SKIING AND SNOWSHOEING

Cross-country skiing and snowshoeing are increasingly popular in the park. Glacier distributes a free pamphlet titled *Ski Trails of Glacier National Park,* with 16 noted trails. You can start at Lake McDonald Lodge and ski cross-country up Going-to-the-Sun Road. The 2½-mile Apgar Natural Trail is popular with snowshoers. No restaurants are open in winter in Glacier, but you can pop into Montana House (🌐 *montanahouse.info*) for hot cider, coffee, cookies, and a little shopping. The park website (🌐 *home.nps.gov/applications/glac/ski/xcski.htm*) has ski trail maps.

Izaak Walton Inn
SKIING & SNOWBOARDING | Just outside the southern edge of the park, this inn has more than 30 miles of groomed cross-country ski trails on its property. It offers equipment rentals and lessons, as well as guided ski and snowshoe tours inside the park. Inn guests can ski for free, but others must purchase a ski pass. The inn is one of the few places in the area that is both open in winter and accessible by Amtrak train, which saves you the worry of driving on icy mountain roads. ✉ *290 Izaak Walton Inn Rd, Essex* ✥ *Off U.S. 2* ☎ *406/888–5700* 🌐 *www.izaakwaltoninn.com/activities/winter-activities* 🎟 *From $15.*

Pincher Creek

The Town of Pincher Creek lies at the eastern edge of the Canadian Rockies halfway between Waterton Lakes National Park and Crowsnest Pass. It is 56 km (35 miles) north of the national park and hotel prices are often less costly than they are inside the national park. The town is also conveniently located for accessing both Castle Provincial Park and Beauvais Lake Provincial Park. Pincher Creek was established in 1878 as a North-West Mounted Police post and farm. It is named after the creek that flows through the area and the creek received its name when a pair of pincers used to trim horses' hooves was found along its banks.

GETTING HERE AND AROUND

Pincher Creek lies 44 km (25 miles) north of Waterton by car.

🍴 Restaurants

Soo Sushi
$$ | **SUSHI** | This restaurant serves Japanese classics like sushi, sashimi, noodles, and tempura along with Korean favorites like beef bulgogi and bibimbap. They also have some stir fry options on the menu. **Known for:** Pincher Creek Roll; broad selection of menu options; lunch boxes. [$] *Average main: C$19* ✉ *1303 Veterans St., Pincher Creek* ☎ *403/627-5557* 🌐 *www.facebook.com/SooSushi/* 🕒 *Closed Mon.*

☕ Coffee and Quick Bites

Harvest Coffee House
$ | **CAFÉ** | Everything is local, fresh and made from scratch at this coffee shop in downtown Pincher Creek. Soups are

made fresh daily and sandwiches are prepared to order. **Known for:** yummy baked goods; good coffee; delicious breakfast sandwiches. [$] *Average main: C$12* ✉ *766 Main St., Pincher Creek* ☎ *403/904–4000* 🌐 *www.harvestcoffee.ca.*

🛏 Hotels

Heritage Inn Hotel & Convention Centre
$ | **HOTEL** | This is an older property, but the rooms are comfortable and reasonably priced and there are plenty of amenities both in the room and in the hotel. **Pros:** rooms have microwaves, mini-fridges, and free local calling; indoor pool and hot tub; on-site restaurant and lounge with room service. **Cons:** not easy to reach the hotel by phone; some rooms are renovated and some need updating; some rooms do not have elevator access. [$] *Rooms from: C$120* ✉ *919 Waterton Ave., Pincher Creek* ☎ *888/888–4374 toll-free reservations, 403/627–5000* 🌐 *heritageinn.net/locations/pincher-creek-ab/home* 🍴 *No Meals* 🛏 *70 rooms.*

Ramada by Wyndham Pincher Creek
$$$ | **HOTEL** | **FAMILY** | Located off Highway 6, this hotel has an indoor pool with a waterslide and a hot tub, a fitness center, and a free hot and cold continental breakfast. **Pros:** kitchenettes in some rooms; free breakfast; indoor swimming pool, hot tub, waterslide. **Cons:** weak Wi-Fi signal; no on-site restaurant; more costly than some other local options. [$] *Rooms from: C$219* ✉ *132 Table Mountain St., Pincher Creek* ☎ *403/627–3777* 🌐 *www.wyndhamhotels.com* 🍴 *Free Breakfast* 🛏 *78 rooms.*

Crowsnest Pass

The term "hidden gem" is used a little too often in travel writing, but if any place deserves the accolade, this is it. Crowsnest Pass is home to incredible scenery, remarkable history, and wonderful attractions.

The Municipality of Crowsnest Pass, known locally as "The Pass," is the result of an amalgamation of five separate Rocky Mountain communities. On January 1, 1979, the Village of Bellevue, the Town of Blairmore, the Town of Coleman, the Village of Frank, and Improvement District No. 5, which included the Hamlet of Hillcrest, combined to become collectively known as Crowsnest Pass. The municipality takes its name from the low mountain pass of the same name that sits at the Continental Divide marking the border between Alberta and British Columbia.

These towns owe their existence to coal mining and the first mine opened here in 1900. The mines attracted an ethnically diverse group of workers and at one time each community was so separate that they did not mix. The unification of the communities was done with the intention to provide greater municipal services and housing for the region.

The history of Crowsnest Pass is fascinating and there are several interesting historical sites to explore in the area. Many of these sites are related to mining tragedies including Frank Slide Interpretive Centre and a cemetery and park that tells the story of the Hillcrest Mine Disaster. The area was also a center for "rumrunning" during prohibition; from 1916–1923, rumrunners illegally brought liquor across the B.C. and Montana borders. In the 1930s, Blairmore became the first community in Canada to elect a communist town council and school board.

Today, Crowsnest Pass is a popular Canadian Rockies vacation spot...for those in the know. There are many wonderful attractions, great scenery, and outdoor adventures to enjoy in this region.

GETTING HERE AND AROUND

The Crowsnest Pass region of the Canadian Rockies is 113 km (70 miles) southwest of the Waterton townsite by car.

◉ Sights

HISTORIC SITES

Alberta Provincial Police Barracks

HISTORY MUSEUM | This unique museum is housed in the original Alberta Provincial Police (APP) barracks building. The APP was created during prohibition (1916–1924) to deal with "rumrunners" who were illegally importing alcohol from the United States and British Columbia. The museum tells the story of this police force, a murder, and the trial of the only woman who was ever executed in Alberta. ✉ 7809 18th Ave., Coleman ☎ 403/562–8858 ⊕ www.appbarracks.com ☜ C$10 ⊘ Closed Sept.–mid-May.

Bellevue Underground Mine

HISTORIC SIGHT | Don a miner's helmet and lamp and go 1,000 feet into a mine on a guided tour with heritage interpreters. Discover the mine's inner workings and feel like you've stepped back in time. ■TIP➔ **All tours must be pre-booked online in advance.** ✉ 2531 213th St., Crowsnest Pass ☎ 403/564–4700 ⊕ www.bellevuemine.com ☜ C$25 ⊘ Closed early Sept.–early-May.

★ Frank Slide Interpretive Centre

HISTORY MUSEUM | Overlooking the devastation of one of Canada's deadliest rock slides, the Frank Slide Interpretive Centre tells the tale of the night Turtle Mountain crumbled and 110-million metric tons of limestone crushed the town below. You can wander through interpretive displays and listen to the stories of survivors. Outside the museum is an overlook and an interpretive hiking trail that winds through the rubble. ✉ Frank Slide Interpretive Centre ⊹ 1.5 km (1 mile) off Hwy. 3 ☎ 403/562–7388 ⊕ frankslide.ca ☜ C$15 ⊘ Closed Mon. early Sept.–mid-May.

Hillcrest Mine and Cemetery

HISTORIC SIGHT | The worst coal mining disaster in Canada happened on June 19, 1914 in the community of Hillcrest. A pocket of methane gas ignited and set off a coal dust explosion that killed 189 miners. Most of the victims were buried in a mass grave and a memorial was later erected in the cemetery. There are interpretive signs and you can go on a self-guided tour of the cemetery. ✉ 200 4th Ave., Crowsnest Pass.

Leitch Collieries Provincial Historic Site

HISTORIC SIGHT | Interpretive panels, walking paths, and listening posts provide insight into the demise of the only fully Canadian-owned and operated coal mine in this region of Alberta. From mid-June to Labor Day, interpretive staff at this site lead tours through the ruins of the coal processing plant and the coke ovens. The sight is self-guided in the fall and winter and toilets are closed. ✉ Leitch Colleries, Crowsnest Pass ⊹ Off Highway 3 ☎ 403/562–7388 ⊕ leitchcollieries.ca ☜ by donation.

SCENIC STOPS

The Burmis Tree

NATURE SIGHT | One of the most photographed trees in Alberta sits near the eastern edge of the Crowsnest Pass. The Burmis Tree is a limber pine that lived for about 700 years before it died in the 1970s. Limber pines have one of the longest life spans of any tree in Alberta and are known for their ability to thrive in harsh conditions. In 1998, high winds toppled the dead tree over, but the community shored it up with rods and brackets to keep it standing. It's considered an important landmark and a symbol of home for residents of the Crowsnest Pass. ✉ The Burmis Tree.

Lundbreck Falls

WATERFALL | These 12-meter (39-foot) falls on the Crowsnest River are stunning in every season. You can watch them from the observation platforms above the falls or walk down into the limestone gorge to see them up close. ✉ *Lundbreck Falls* ✥ *South of Hwy. 3, off Range Road 24B* 🌐 *www.albertaparks.ca.*

TRAILS

Star Creek Falls Loop Trail

TRAIL | This family-friendly 1.9-km (1.2-mile) loop trail leads to a 10-meter (30-foot) waterfall. There's 86 meters (282 feet) of elevation gain on the trail and it's best used from June through October. In winter, you can hike up the creek with ice cleats and poles for a unique icewalk experience. ✉ *Star Creek Falls Trailhead.*

Turtle Mountain Trail

TRAIL | This 7.4-km (4.6-mile) round-trip hike follows along the ridge of Turtle Mountain to the false and true summits. It's a steep and challenging trail, but the views of Frank Slide and the Crowsnest Valley are worth it. Scrambling is required to reach the second peak known as the south peak. This hike has 936 meters (3071 feet) of elevation gain and hiking poles are recommended. ✉ *Turtle Mountain Trailhead* ✥ *Trailhead: Park along 15th Ave in Blairmore, then follow the dirt alley east to the trailhead.*

🍴 Restaurants

Encounters Wine Bar and Small Plate Kitchen

$$ | **AMERICAN** | This wine bar has a small but well-chosen wine list, but the real focus is the food. A broad selection of small plates are on the menu including items like goat cheese-stuffed dates, potato latkes, and warm shrimp dip, while entrees range from prime rib and chicken cordon bleu to Moroccan lamb tagine. **Known for:** great tapas menu; delicious food and good service; bacon-wrapped goat cheese-stuffed dates. [$] *Average main: C$18* ✉ *7655 17th Ave., Colman* ☎ *403/563–5299* 🌐 *www.encounterswinebar.com* ⏲ *Closed Mon.–Tues. No lunch.*

Rum Runner Restaurant and Pub

$$ | **AMERICAN** | This saloon-style pub restaurant is themed around the Prohibition era when rumrunners frequented the Crowsnest Pass. The open kitchen prepares Canadian and European-style pub food like burgers (a half-pound each), pizza, fish-and-chips, appetizers, and salads. **Known for:** lively atmosphere; huge half-pound burgers; great pub food. [$] *Average main: C$18* ✉ *7902 20th Ave., Coleman* ☎ *403/562–7552* 🌐 *www.facebook.com/rum.runner.5/.*

🛏 Hotels

Country Encounters B&B

$ | **B&B/INN** | There are four individually decorated rooms with en suites in the original building and five suites in a newer building all located in the national historic district of Coleman. **Pros:** great location near historical sites; delicious breakfast and cookies included; excellent on-site restaurant. **Cons:** original building is a little quirky; no a/c; older B&B rooms don't have TVs. [$] *Rooms from: C$109* ✉ *7701 17th Ave., Coleman* ☎ *403/563–5299* 🌐 *www.countryencounters.com* 🍽 *Free Breakfast* 🔑 *9 rooms.*

The Kanata Inns Blairmore

$$ | **HOTEL** | A variety of different rooms are available in this hotel from standard queen rooms to two-story family suites, jacuzzi rooms, and business suites with fully equipped kitchenettes. **Pros:** smart TVs; breakfast included; microwaves and fridges in rooms. **Cons:** out of the way; local businesses and restaurants close early; no pool. [$] *Rooms from: C$160* ✉ *11217 21st Ave., Blairmore*

☎ *403/562–8851, 888/700–2264 toll-free* 🌐 *kanatainns.com/locations/hotel-in-blairmore-ab* 🍴 *Free Breakfast* 🛏 *50 rooms.*

York Creek B&B

$ | **B&B/INN** | One of the newest B&B properties in The Pass, most of the six guest bedrooms have remote control king-size beds that can be adjusted to suit individual comfort levels. **Pros:** small-pet friendly and wheelchair accessible; delicious breakfast included; suite with full kitchen and private entrance. **Cons:** indoor footwear required; no TV in some rooms; better suited for couples than families. [$] *Rooms from: C$140* ✉ *1213 85th St., Coleman* ☎ *403/563–3333* 🌐 *www.yorkcreekbb.ca* 🍴 *Free Breakfast* 🛏 *6 rooms.*

Activities

CAMPING

A wide range of camping options are available in the Crowsnest Pass region. In addition to Alberta Parks and Recreation campgrounds (*C$28; 877/537–2757; reserve.albertaparks.ca*), there are community-operated and privately operated campgrounds and RV parks. If you're camping on unserviced Crown land, you'll need to buy a Public Land Camping Pass that can be purchased online (albertarelm.com) or anywhere that sells hunting and fishing licenses.

Chinook Provincial Recreation Area. This campground has 92 well-treed sites with easy access to Chinook Lake. Canoe, kayak, swim in the lake, hike, or mountain bike on the trails in summer. There are groomed cross-country ski trails to enjoy in winter. *8 km (5 miles) west of Coleman off Hwy. 3.*

Lundbreck Falls Provincial Recreation Area. This scenic campground is near beautiful Lundbreck Falls. It has 29 sites with power, 17 unserviced sites, and 10 walk-in tent sites. Campers can walk to the falls and fish for rainbow and cutthroat trout. *Closed Oct.–Mid-May; 5 km (15.5 miles) northwest of Pincher Creek off Hwy. 3.*

CYCLING

An enthusiastic cycling community and great trails make the Crowsnest Pass a special region to explore on two wheels. The 23-km (14 mile) Crowsnest Community Trail connects all the small communities of the Municipality of Crowsnest Pass. The trail is a combination of asphalt, gravel, and natural trail surfaces and is shared by cyclists and walkers. The United Riders of Crowsnest (UROC) was formed to create trails and promote mountain biking in the beautiful Crowsnest Pass. Visit the website (*www.uroc.ca*) for maps and information about local trails and a list of local cycling races and events.

Pass Powderkeg (*see Skiing*) is another great place for mountain biking. The resort has a wide range of trails from beginner to expert, single-track and cross-country as well as a Jay Hoots-designed bike park. You have to get to the top on your own steam as no services or uphill transport are provided.

Sweet Riders

BICYCLE TOURS | This company specializes in cycling tours and cycling clinics in the Crowsnest Pass for all levels of mountain bikers. Mountain bike in summer and fat bike in winter on area trails with a certified cycling coach. They also operate an Airbnb accommodation. ✉ *Blairmore* ☎ *403/563–7809* 🌐 *sweetriders.com* 🎟 *from C$65.*

HIKING

Fantastic Rocky Mountain scenery and a wide variety of trails ranging from short, easy strolls to steep scrambles make

Crowsnest Pass a top hiking destination. Whether you're just passing through and you want to stretch your legs on a short day hike or you have a weekend to go peak bagging, you'll find trails to suit your needs.

Uplift Adventures

GUIDED TOURS | Arrange interpretive tours, guided day hiking, and backpacking trips in Crowsnest Pass and Waterton with this local company in summer. Snowshoeing and icewalks are offered in winter as well a variety of outdoor courses. A mountain mysteries clue solving adventure is also on offer. ⊠ *Coleman* ☎ *403/583-5884* ⊕ *upliftadventures.ca* 🎫 *from C$39.*

SKIING

Pass Powder Keg

SKIING & SNOWBOARDING | Opened in 1938, this not-for-profit ski hill is great fun for the whole family and a real bargain for beginners as bunny hill access is free. With top-to-bottom lighting, it's possible to enjoy night skiing during the long dark winters. The mountain has 27 runs, two T-bars, a terrain park, and a mid-mountain day lodge that offers ski rentals and lessons. ⊠ *12402 18th Ave., Blairmore* ☎ *403/562–8334* ⊕ *www.passpowderkeg.com* 🎫 *C$49.99.*

Index

Photo Credits

Front Cover: Michael Wheatley/Agefotostock [Description: Red canoes, Emerald Lake, Yoho National park, British Columbia, Canada.].
Back cover, from left to right: nurserowan/iStockphoto, Rafa Irusta/Shutterstock, Marina Poushkina/Shutterstock. **Spine:** Angelito de Jesus/Shutterstock. **Interior, from left to right:** Parks Canada / Ryan Bray (1). Travel Alberta (2-3). **Chapter 1: Experience the Canadian Rockies:** Jewhyte/Dreamstime (6-7). Engel Ching/Shutterstock (8-9). argenel (9). Banff Gondola by Pursuit (9). Tourism Jasper (10). Noel Hendrickson (10). Moraine Lake Lodge (10). Jareya Nualthong (10). MotherPixels/Swissclick_photography (11). Destination BC/Kari Medig (12). Parks Canada/Zoya Lynch (12). Calgary Stampede (12). Tourism Jasper (12). Edb316/Dreamstime (13). Andy Best (13). Fallsview/Dreamstime (13). Destination Canada (13). Jason Patrick Ross/Shutterstock. (14). Parks Canada/Ryan Creary (14). Glacier Raft Company (14). Edwin Christopher/Shutterstock (14). Tourism Canmore Kananaskis (15). Wayne Lynch/Parks Canada (18). Dan King (18). Dan King (18). Eva Hawker/Shutterstock (18). Erica L. Wainer (18). Roger Bravo (19). BostonGal (19). Debbie Bowles (19). Darklich14/Wikimedia Commons (19). kavram/Shutterstock (19). Karsten Heuer (20). Mumemories/Shutterstock (20). Courtesy of Zac Bolan (20). Skoki Lodge (21). Norbert von Niman (21). Brewster/Parks Canada (22). Timothy Yue/Shutterstock (23). Jeff Whyte/Dreamstime (24). travellife18/Shutterstock (25). **Chapter 3: Great Itineraries:** i viewfinder/Shutterstock (45). **Chapter 4: Banff National Park:** Sean Xu/Shutterstock (57). Adam Hinchliffe/Shutterstock (67). Nickjene/Dreamstime (70). Bgsmith/Dreamstime (79). i viewfinder/Shutterstock (87). Lukaszkkk/Dreamstime (94). **Chapter 5: Calgary:** MJ_Prototype/iStock (101). Jeff Whyte/Shutterstock (104). Jewhyte/Dreamstime (105). Jewhyte/Dreamstime (105). Jewhyte/Dreamstime. (106). Jeff Whyte/Shutterstock (113). Mbruxelle/Dreamstime (117). EB Adventure Photography/Shutterstock (119). Kit Leong/Shutterstock. (125). **Chapter 6: Canmore and Kananaskis Country:** Martin Capek/Shutterstock (133). Timon Schneider/iStockphoto (139). Marc Bruxelle/iStock Editorial (144). Kaedeenari/Dreamstime (148). Zeljkokcanmore/Dreamstime (150). kavram/Shutterstock (155). Zeljkokcanmore/Dreamstime (160). **Chapter 7: Yoho National Park:** Marcin Szymczak/Shutterstock (169). Jaahnlieb/Dreamstime.com (176). Gavin Howard/Shutterstock (178). Tatsuo Nakamura/Shutterstock (182). Francesco Riccardo Iacomino/Dreamstime (186). **Chapter 8: Kootenay National Park:** Wildnerdpix/Shutterstock (197). NorthStarPhotos/Shutterstock (205). Albertoloyo/Dreamstime.com (207). James_Gabbert/iStock (210). Andreas Prott/Shutterstock (212). freidensonsphoto/Shutterstock (216). **Chapter 9: Jasper National Park:** Ingalin/Dreamstime (221). Ahmed Syed/Shutterstock (231). Mumemories/Shutterstock (236). i viewfinder/Shutterstock (240-241). Don Mammoser/Shutterstock (244). Elena_Suvorova/Shutterstock (247). Alex JW Robinson/Shutterstock (253). Beatrice Payette (259). Menno Schaefer/Shutterstock (264). **Chapter 10: Edmonton:** Jeff Whyte/Shutterstock (269). Jeff Whyte/Shutterstock (279). Nick Fox/Shutterstock (281). 2009fotofriends/Shutterstock (286). **Chapter 11: Waterton Lakes National Park:** BGSmith/Shutterstock (291). Scott Prokop/Shutterstock (298). christopher babcock/Shutterstock (301). Stephen Moehle/Shutterstock (312). Kerrick James (318). **About Our Writers:** All photos are courtesy of the writers.

*Every effort has been made to trace the copyright holders, and we apologize in advance for any accidental errors. We would be happy to apply the corrections in the following edition of this publication.

Notes

Notes

Fodor's CANADIAN ROCKIES

Publisher: Stephen Horowitz, *General Manager*

Editorial: Douglas Stallings, *Editorial Director;* Jill Fergus, Amanda Sadlowski, Caroline Trefler, *Senior Editors;* Kayla Becker, Alexis Kelly, *Editors;* Angelique Kennedy-Chavannes, *Assistant Editor*

Design: Tina Malaney, *Director of Design and Production;* Jessica Gonzalez, *Graphic Designer,* Sophia Almendral, *Production Intern*

Production: Jennifer DePrima, *Editorial Production Manager;* Elyse Rozelle, *Senior Production Editor;* Monica White, *Production Editor*

Maps: Rebecca Baer, *Senior Map Editor;* Mark Stroud (Moon Street Cartography), *Cartographer*

Photography: Viviane Teles, *Senior Photo Editor;* Namrata Aggarwal, Payal Gupta, Ashok Kumar, *Photo Editors;* Rebecca Rimmer, *Photo Production Associate;* Eddie Aldrete, *Photo Production Intern*

Business and Operations: Chuck Hoover, *Chief Marketing Officer;* Robert Ames, *Group General Manager;* Devin Duckworth, *Director of Print Publishing*

Public Relations and Marketing: Joe Ewaskiw, *Senior Director of Communications and Public Relations*

Fodors.com: Jeremy Tarr, *Editorial Director;* Rachael Levitt, *Managing Editor*

Technology: Jon Atkinson, *Director of Technology;* Rudresh Teotia, *Lead Developer;* Jacob Ashpis, *Content Operations Manager*

Writers: Jeff Gailus, Debbie Olsen, Kelsey Olsen, Kate Robertson

Editor: Alexis Kelly

Production Editor: Elyse Rozelle

1st Edition

ISBN 978-1-64097-482-1

ISSN 2771-1765

All details in this book are based on information supplied to us at press time. Always confirm information when it matters, especially if you're making a detour to visit a specific place. Fodor's expressly disclaims any liability, loss, or risk, personal or otherwise, that is incurred as a consequence of the use of any of the contents of this book.

SPECIAL SALES
This book is available at special discounts for bulk purchases for sales promotions or premiums. For more information, e-mail SpecialMarkets@fodors.com.

PRINTED IN CANADA

10 9 8 7 6 5 4 3 2

About Our Writers

Originally from Alberta, Canada, **Jeff Gailus** writes about natural history and environmental politics from his home in Missoula, Montana. He publishes regularly in *The Guardian* and *Alberta Views* magazine, and his first book, *The Grizzly Manifesto,* was a finalist for the Alberta Readers' Choice Award. When he's not sitting at his computer, he's out on local lakes and in the mountains. He wrote the Calgary and Edmonton chapters.

Debbie Olsen is an award-winning Métis writer and a national bestselling author based in Alberta, Canada. Passionate about the Canadian Rockies, Debbie has hiked countless trails and has summited at least five Rocky Mountain peaks. She has contributed to many publications including 13 Fodor's guidebooks. Follow Debbie's adventures on her popular travel blog, Wander Woman Travel Magazine (*www.wandwerwoman.ca*), and on social media at @wwtravelmag. Debbie wrote the Travel Smart, Banff National Park, Jasper National Park, Waterton Lakes National Park, and Canmore and Kananaskis Country chapters.

Kelsey Olsen is an Alberta-based Métis writer and an avid hiker who has explored many trails in the Canadian Rockies and has summited several mountains. She loves art, running, fine food, and exploring new places. Follow her on Instagram at @kelseyrolsen. She wrote the Experience chapter and updated the Great Itineraries chapter.

Kate Robertson is an award-winning writer currently living in the Kootenay Mountains of British Columbia, Canada, who specializes in travel, food, wellness, and outdoor adventures. Her freelance work appears in major publications like *Lonely Planet, Canadian Traveller, Matador Network, Shape, Zagat Stories,* and others. When Kate's not hiking, biking, or playing in the snow, she's dreaming up her next epic adventure. You can follow her adventures at her website (katerobertson.ca) or her Instagram (@kate.flysolo101) or Twitter (@kateflyingsolo) accounts. She wrote the Yoho National Park and Kootenay National Park chapters.